The Catholic Biblical Quarterly
Monograph Series
37

_____

Dear Virginia,
May the Lord's Covenant of Peace happen in our general lifetime long before the amnesty on this book. Thanks for your interest & support.
Fr. Paul

EDITORIAL BOARD

Mark S. Smith, Chairperson

Lawrence E. Boadt, C.S.P.	*Richard J. Clifford, S.J.*
John J. Collins	*Frederick W. Danker*
Robert A. Di Vito	*Daniel J. Harrington, S.J.*
Ralph W. Klein	*Léo Laberge, O.M.I.*
Bruce J. Malina	*Pheme Perkins*
Eugene C. Ulrich	*Ronald D. Witherup, S.S.*

The Disarmament of God

Ezekiel 38–39 in
Its Mythic Context

BY

Paul E. Fitzpatrick, S.M.

The Catholic Biblical Quarterly
Monograph Series
37

© 2004 The Catholic Biblical Association of America,
Washington, DC 20064

All rights reserved. No part of this book may be reproduced in any
form or by any means without permission in writing from
the Catholic Biblical Association of America.

Produced in the United States of America

Library of Congress Cataloging-in-Publication Data

Fitzpatrick, Paul E., 1946-
　　The disarmament of God : Ezekiel 38-39 in its mythic context / by Paul
E. Fitzpatrick.
　　　p. cm. — (Catholic Biblical quarterly. Monograph series ; 37)
　　Includes bibliographical references and index.
　　ISBN 0-915170-36-1 (alk. paper)
　　1. Bible. O.T. Ezekiel XXXVIII-XXXIX—Criticism, interpretation, etc.
2. Myth in the Bible. 3. Bible. O.T. Ezekiel—Criticism, interpretation, etc.
I. Title. II. Series.

BS1545.52.F58 2004
224'.4068—dc22
　　　　　　　　　　　　　　　　　　2004005524

לבורא

אשר ממשיך לברא

Contents

Abbreviations • *ix*

Preface • *xv*

1. A Review of the Critical Study of Ezekiel 38–39 in the Context of Its Placement in the Book • *1*
   First Phase: From the Beginnings of Modern Biblical Scholarship to 1900 • *2*
   Second Phase: From 1900 to 1950 • *9*
   Third Phase: From 1950 to the Present • *23*
   The Present Project • *46*

2. The Significance of Myth in Itself and in Ezekiel • *49*

3. Textual Links between the Gog Pericope and Other Sections of Ezekiel • *74*

4. Ezekiel 38–39, Cosmogony Completed, A Covenant of Peace Fulfilled • *82*

5. Mythic Elements in Ezekiel 1–37 and 40–48 • *113*
   Ezekiel 1:4–28 • *113*
   Ezekiel 8–11 • *125*
   Ezekiel 26:1–28:19, 29:1–32:32 • *133*
   Ezekiel 34:1–31, 37:1–28 • *165*
   Ezekiel 40–48 • *181*

6. SUMMARY AND CONCLUSIONS • *193*

BIBLIOGRAPHY • *199*

INDEX • *227*

Abbreviations

AASF	Annales Academiae Scientiarum Fennicae
AB	Anchor Bible
ABD	D. N. Freedman et al. (eds.), *Anchor Bible Dictionary*
AfO	*Archiv für Orientforschung*
AnBib	Analecta Biblica
ANEP	J. B. Pritchard (ed.), *The Ancient Near East in Pictures*
ANET	J. B. Pritchard (ed.), *Ancient Near Eastern Texts*
AnOr	Analecta orientalia
Anton	*Antonianum*
AOAT	Alter Orient und Altes Testament
AOBib	Altorientalische Bibliothek
ARAB	D. D. Luckenbill (ed.), *Ancient Records of Assyria and Babylonia*
ATD	Das Alte Testament deutsch
BAR	*Biblical Archaeology Review*
BASOR	*Bulletin of the American Schools of Oriental Research*
BDB	Brown, Francis, S. R. Driver and Charles A. Briggs, *A Hebrew and English Lexicon of the Old Testament*
BETL	Bibliotheca Ephemeridum theologicarum Lovaniensium
BHS	*Biblia Hebraica Stuttgartensia*
BHT	Beiträge zur historischen theologie

Bib	*Biblica*
BibLeb	*Bibel und Leben*
BibOr	Biblica et Orientalia
BJRL	*Bulletin of the John Rylands University Library*
BKAT	Biblischer Kommentar. Altes Testament
BO	*Bibliotheca Orientalis*
BRA	Beiträge zur Religionsgeschichte des Altertums
BSOAS	*Bulletin of the School of Oriental and African Studies*
BTB	*Biblical Theology Bulletin*
BWAT	Beiträge zur Wissenschaft vom Alten Testament
BWANT	Beiträge zur Wissenschaft vom Alten und Neuen Testament
BZAW	Beihefte zur Zeitschrift fur die alttestamentliche Wissenschaft,
BZ	*Biblische Zeitschrift*
CBQ	*Catholic Biblical Quarterly*
CBQMS	Catholic Biblical Quarterly Monograph Series
CBSC	The Cambridge Bible for Schools and Colleges
CMHE	F. M. Cross. 1973. *Canaanite Myth and Hebrew Epic.* Cambridge, MA.
ConBOT	Coniectanea biblica, Old Testament
CQR	*Church Quarterly Review*
CTH	*Catalogue des textes hittites*
DMOA	Documenta et Monumenta Orientis Antiqui
ed.	edition and edited by
EHS	Einleitung in die Heilige Schrift
EI	*Eretz Israel*
EncRel	*Encyclopedia of Religion*
enl.	enlarged
ErFor	Erträge der Forschung
ÉTR	*Études théologiques et religieuses*
FAT	Forschungen zum Alten Testament
FB	Forschung zur Bibel
FRLANT	Forschungen zur Religion und Literatur des Alten und Neuen Testaments
GTJ	*Grace Theological Journal*
HALAT	*Hebräisches und aramäisches Lexikon zum Alten Testament*

Abbreviations · xi

HAR	*Hebrew Annual Review*
HAT	Handbuch zum Alten Testament
HCBC	J. L. Mays (ed.), *Harper Collins Bible Commentary*
HDR	Harvard Dissertation in Religion
HKAT	Handkommentar zum Alten Testament.
HO	Handbuch der Orientalistik
HSAT	Die Heilige Schrift des Alten Testamentes
HSM	Harvard Semitic Monographs
HSS	Harvard Semitic Studies
HTR	*Harvard Theological Review*
ICC	International Critical Commentary
IDBSup	*Interpreter's Dictionary of the Bible Supplementary Volume*
IEJ	*Israel Exploration Journal*
Int	*Interpretation*
ISBE	International Standard Bible Encyclopedia
JANES	*Journal of the Ancient Near Eastern Society of Columbia University*
JBL	*Journal of Biblical Literature*
JCS	*Journal of Cuneiform Studies*
JEnc	*The Jewish Encyclopedia*
JETS	*Journal of the Evangelical Theological Society*
JNES	*Journal of Near Eastern Studies*
JNSL	*Journal of Northwest Semitic Languages*
JPS	Jewish Publication Society
JR	*Journal of Religion*
JRAS	*Journal of the Royal Asiatic Society*
JSJSup	Journal for the Study of Judaism Supplements
JSOT	*Journal for the Study of the Old Testament*
JSOTSup	Journal for the Study of the Old Testament Supplement Series
JSS	*Journal of Semitic Studies*
KAT	Kommentar zum Alten Testament
KD	*Kerygma und Dogma*
KEHAT	Kurzgefasstes exegetisches Handbuch zum Alten Testament
KHC	Kurzer Hand-Commentar zum Alten Testament
LBS	The Library of Biblical Studies

LXX	Septuagint
MT	Masoretic Text
MVAG	Mitteilungen der vorderasiatischen-ägyptischen Gesellschaft
NCBC	New Century Bible Commentary
NF	Neue Folge
NRSV	New Revised Standard Version
Ns	Nuova serie
NT	New Testament
OBO	Orbis biblicus et orientalis
Or	*Orientalia*
OT	Old Testament
OTG	Old Testament Guides
OTL	Old Testament Library
OTM	Old Testament Message
OTS	Oudtestamentische studien
PEF	*Palestine Exploration Fund*
RANE	Records of the Ancient Near East
RB	*Revue Biblique*
RES	*Répertoire d'épigraphie sémitique*
rev.	revised
RGG	*Religion in Geschichte und Gegenwart*
RHPR	*Revue d'histoire et de philosophie religieuses*
RSP	*Ras Shamra Parallels*
SANE	Sources from the ancient Near East
SEÅ	*Svensk Exegetisk Årsbok*
SBB	Stuttgarter biblische Beiträge
SBLDS	Society of Biblical Literature Dissertation Series
SBLMS	Society of Biblical Literature Monograph Series
SBLSCS	Society of Biblical Literature: Septuagint and Cognate Studies
SBS	Stuttgarter Bibelstudien
SBT	Studies in Biblical Theology
SKKAT	Stuttgarter kleiner Kommentar, Altes Testament
SS	Studi semitici
ST	*Studia theologica*
suppl.	supplement
TDOT	G. J. Botterweck et al. (eds.), *Theological Dictionary of the Old Testament*

THAT	E. Jenin and C. Westermann, eds., *Theologisches Handwörterbuch zum Alten Testament*
trans.	translated by
TRu	*Theologische Rundschau*
TS	*Theological Studies*
TWAT	G. J. Botterweck et al. (eds.), *Theologisches Wörterbuch zum Alten Testament*
TZ	*Theologische Zeitschrift*
UBL	Ugaritisch-Biblische Literatur
UF	*Ugarit-Forschungen*
USQR	*Union Seminary Quarterly Review*
UUÅ	*Uppsala universitets Årsskrift*
VAB	Vorderasiatische bibliothek
VT	*Vetus Testamentum*
VTSup	Vetus Testamentum Supplements
WF	Wege der Forschung
WMANT	Wissenschaftliche Monographien zum Alten und Neuen Testament
WUNT	Wissenschaftliche Untersuchungen zum Neuen Testament
WZ	*Wissenschaftliche Zeitschrift*
YJS	Yale Judaica Series
YOS	Yale Oriental Series
ZA	*Zeitschrift für Assyriologie*
ZAH	*Zeitschrift für Althebräistik*
ZAW	*Zeitschrift für die alttestamentliche Wissenschaft*
ZDMG	Zeitschrift der deutschen morganländischen Gesellschaft

Preface

The current work comes out of a long-standing interest in the use of mythic language in the Bible. Of all the prophetic writings around the exilic period, Ezekiel makes the boldest use of mythic language and concepts in the construction of the final form of the text. I have been fortunate enough to work on Ezekiel and on the comparative material in the course of my licentiate doctoral studies, and wanted to extend the discussion through a new look at the sources in Ezekiel's final form in order to join the conversation from the prism of my own research.

In discussions of Ezekiel, the placement and function of chapters 38–39 in the final form have long been a point of contention among scholars. Why would the final form interrupt the flow of the restoration sequence of the book with this cosmic battle, pitting every potential enemy of Israel known to them at the time against the God of Israel? Without it, at first glance, the text would move majestically from the restoration of the monarchy to the restoration of the land and the people to the restoration of the Temple, all through the beneficent will of Yhwh. What could be a more fitting consolation and promise to God's people, now, with Jerusalem, their capital, and the Temple, their center point where earth meets heaven, taken from them?

The placement of these chapters has been a puzzlement to biblical scholars from mid-nineteenth century on. We will review that discussion in the first chapter. Initially when I encountered them, they were a puzzlement for myself as well. My own study over the last six years kept leading me back to the religious myths of the people of the ancient Near East, particularly their creation myths, as the venue which would ultimately allow a view of the final form from a vantage point that includes chapters 38–39 as an integral part of this majestic finale. Through a discussion of my research on myth in chapter two I seek to set out the mythic frame of reference of the people of the ancient Near East, as they sought to articulate their beliefs about the creation of the world, not only what for them were its origins but also what for them were its final goal and point of completion.

The undeniable witness of the text is, of course, ever important. In chapter three I review the textual links between chapters 38–39and the rest of the book, to establish from the text a basis for further study of the Gog-Magog account as integral to the work from the perspective of mythic themes. These thematic links are numerous, as we shall see.

For something which was considered by many a misfit in its placement, one must ask why the Gog-Magog account held a meaning which inspired its mention in the religious literature of generations to follow. We begin the fourth chapter with a review of the extensive reference to Gog and Magog in literature after Ezekiel, suggesting that its impact on the religious imagination of people was not minimal. Before exploring the presence of mythic themes in the book, I unpack, as described in chapters 38–39, the non- mythic and mythic dimensions of the Combat Myth, a constituent element of the cosmogonic myth and the mythic pattern in these chapters. If indeed this was Cosmogony brought to completion in the new "after-the-exile" Israelite creation myth, what were the non-mythic and mythic meanings and back-drop in the Gog-Magog account? This occupies the major portion of the discussion in chapter four.

The mythic elements present throughout Ezekiel also merited further study to see the extent to which the final form was influenced by the religious myths of the region, and to determine, if present, the mythic key to the understanding of the placement of chapters 38–39 in the final form of the book. This I undertook in chapter five. I found the study revelatory from the outset for the meaning of the text. It was brought to a climax in the study of chapters 34 and 37 where the promised covenant of peace, in its mythic context, necessitates and gives particular intentionality to the decisive battle of chapters 38–39 which, again as part of a mythic pattern, must take place before the restoration of the Temple.

The discoveries of my research led me to a conclusion which seemed clear. The Book of Ezekiel, in its final form, offered hope after 587, that the sovereign God of Israel would accomplish his purposes, bringing creation to a marvelous completion. All this, with the tragic and devastating events of the exile integrated into the plan when Yhwh, in the Gog-Magog account, unilaterally and irrevocably destroyed his arms, fulfilling the mythic pattern in the covenant of peace, that the events of 597/587 might never happen again.

In gratitude I wish to thank those who helped me to bring this work to completion. Before all others I am grateful to Fr. Richard J. Clifford, S.J., for suggesting this topic, for the enthusiastic and scholarly presentation in his classes and seminars which engaged me with the possibilities it held, and for his helpful support and suggestions in bringing this project to conclusion. I must also thank Fr. Charles Conroy, M.S. C. whose helpful corrections trained me in a thoroughness in scholarly research which will stand me in good stead in the years ahead and who introduced me to a wealth of European scholarship in my research. I want to thank Fr. Lawrence Boadt, C.S.P., for his scholarship on Ezekiel which was foundational in pointing out the need for this area of research in Ezekiel Studies, and also for his generous gift of time one summer which was helpful both academically and in terms of morale. I owe an incalculable debt of gratitude to Mr. Stephen Kuehler, the Research Librarian at EDS-Weston Jesuit Library. Without his generous gift of time in using the research tools of the library and e-mailing the results to me in Rome, I would not have been able to make such rapid progress. Last but not least, I wish to thank Bro. Stephen Glodek, S.M. who approved time for these studies and supported me throughout them. To each, and to those unmentioned, I am in grateful debt.

Paul E. Fitzpatrick, S.M.
Bl. John XXIII National Seminary
Weston, MA 02493
January 22, 2003

CHAPTER 1

A Review of the Critical Study of Ezekiel 38–39 in the Context of Its Placement in the Book

The modern biblical criticism of Ezekiel falls rather naturally into three periods. The first covers its origins in the first half of the nineteenth century and extends to the beginning of the twentieth century. During this period, with a few exceptions, there is agreement that the book is an exilic work written by Ezekiel. Words like insertion and interruption were not used to refer to the Gog pericope. Several authors noted a future orientation in the pericope but mythic elements, as such, were not discussed.

The second time frame encompasses approximately the period from 1900 through 1950 when the pendulum swings completely away from the positions taken during the first phase. Characteristic of this interval is a critical study of the text which, in some cases, denies all but a small percentage of the book to the prophet Ezekiel. The majority of exegetes in this period see the Gog pericope as separate thematically from what precedes and follows it.

The last period of critical study of Ezekiel brings us from 1950 to the present day. In this phase the pendulum initially begins again to swing back toward the center, attributing a basic core of the text to the prophet, but around the mid-point of the period the discussion takes two directions. In one group, the vast majority, the conclusions of the second phase, 1900 to 1950, begin to reassert themselves again, present-

1

ing a work with several layers of redaction composed over a period of several hundred years, with very little overall connection or coherence of the parts to the whole. Those in the second group, looking at the work in its final form, see it, for the most part, as a unified literary work. Concerning the relationship of chapters 38–39 with the overall book, all but a few see chapters 38–39 as an abrupt, discordant insertion or they pursue the study of the redactional history of the text without considering the question of the book as a cohesive literary work.

The focus of this work and the lens for the review of scholarship is the extent to which chapters 38–39 display thematic cohesiveness in the book's final form. Some recent scholarly works on Ezekiel will not be discussed either because they deal with a particular aspect or section of the book which does not lead to a discussion of the placement of chapters 38–39 in the final form or because their treatment is of a more popular vein, broader in its scope and coverage of the issues.

First Phase: From the Beginnings of Modern Biblical Scholarship to 1900

Modern biblical criticism of the OT began in the mid-seventeenth century, yet challenges by a broad spectrum of biblical scholars to commonly held beliefs about Ezekiel traditionally held in the scholarly community did not surface until the beginning of the twentieth century. The review begins however with the first notable exception. Leopold Zunz challenges the dating of the book in his *Die gottesdienstlichen Vorträge der Juden, historisch entwickelt* (1832). He notes that the vision of the Throne Chariot had more in common with Daniel than with other exilic authors.[1] In 1873 he develops his thought at greater length concluding the book must come from the Second

---

[1] He finds it significant that Jeremiah makes no mention of Ezekiel though Jeremiah had contact with the exilic community. He is critical that Ezekiel would be able, only 14 years after the Temple's destruction, to go into such detail about its reconstruction. He considered the imagery in the Gog Pericope much more suitable to the period of the Second Temple than the First Temple. Consequently he concludes that he would give a dating similar to his dating of Job and Zacharia, somewhere between 440 and 400 B.C.E. Leopold Zunz, *Die gottesdienstlichen Vorträge der Juden, historisch entwickelt* (Berlin: A. Asher, 1832) 158.

Temple period.² A mainstay of his thesis is disbelief that Ezekiel could produce such a detailed building plan of the Temple only fourteen years after its destruction. His argument is weakened, however, by the fact that the Second Temple was not a realization of Ezekiel's detailed description. With other exegetes of the period, he considers the book a unified literary work, and the Gog pericope an integral part of that cohesiveness.

Georg Heinrich Ewald published his commentary on Ezekiel in 1841 at the age of thirty-eight. Here he contends that the book developed gradually with several strata, yet, in his judgment, the book as a whole owes its final form to the prophet Ezekiel.³ Ewald sees chapters 38–39 as integral to the third part of the book where the eternal hope of Israel is portrayed. He divides this third part into three sections: chapters 33–36, chapters 37–39, and chapters 40–48.⁴ Ewald also discusses the interrelation of chapters 38–39 with 37 where he ascribes the victory to the strength of the newly raised up dry bones from chapter 37. These bones are a symbol of the true community of Israel, purified of its sins, mobilizing against and triumphing over the terrible forces of Gog's army.⁵ For Ewald, chapters 38–39 showed this newly re-constituted community to be as unassailable now as it had been vulnerable in the earlier portions of the book. The victory over Gog was, for him, a constituent part of the message that went before it, integral to the thematic cohesiveness of Ezekiel's final redaction, as Ewald saw it. A flaw which

---

² He notes again inconsistencies between Jeremiah and Ezekiel and concludes that Ezekiel must have been written much later. He is critical that an exilic Ezekiel could describe a geographical distribution among the tribes in Palestine and mentions again with skepticism that an exilic author could provide a detailed building plan for the Temple. Again he concludes that Ezekiel must come from the Persian Period. He suggests that the name Ezekiel is invented and while we cannot know who the author of this book is, he must be counted among the post-exilic authors because of his language and modes of expression. Leopold Zunz, "Bibelkritisches," ZDMG 27 (1873) 678, 688.

³ Georg Heinrich Ewald, *Die Propheten des Alten Bundes erklärt 2* (Stuttgart: Adolph Krabbe, 1841) 207–9.

⁴ Chapters 33–36 describe the various dimensions of the certain salvation of the future; chapters 37–39 depict the completion, the bringing to perfection, of this salvation; chapters 40–48 follow this restoration of the individual and describe the restoration of the temple and the empire. Ewald, *Die Propheten des Alten Bundes erklärt 2*, 217.

⁵ Ewald, *Die Propheten des Alten Bundes erklärt 2*, 348.

bears noting in Ewald's theory is the misrepresentation of the true community of Israel as victorious over Gog. Israel only buries the bodies after the fact. The results of my study suggest that it is a significant point of Ezekiel's theology when the decisive battle of the sovereign God of Israel is waged and won by him alone, unaided by mortals.

In 1847 Ferdinand Hitzig published his commentary in response to Ewald's work six years earlier. He had no problem with Ewald's assessment ascribing the Gog pericope to the pen of Ezekiel, written as an integral part of what began in chapter 33.[6] He did, however, take issue with Ewald's conclusion that Gog, the enemy from the north, was a name given to a historical Chaldean (Babylonian) aggressor. In fact, Hitzig considered the disillusioning earth of the exile as fertile ground for the development of a hope which was increasingly supernaturalistic, not rooted in historical events.[7] Hitzig saw Ezekiel as theology. With his theological reflection on the book's supernatural hope, he was initiating a discussion, which would be continued and articulated more conclusively by Hermann Gunkel, Hugo Gressmann[8] and others whom we will look at below in the second period of critical study, linking the pericope to myth.

E. W. Hengstenberg's commentary *Die Weissagungen des Prophet Ezechiel*[9] was published over a two year period, 1867/68, just before his death in 1869. In it he describes chapters 38–39 as the last in a series of prophecies of consolation, chapters 33–39. In the Gog pericope, sharing

---

[6] It is clear to Hitzig *(Der Prophet Ezechiel erklärt* [KHAT 8; Leipzig: Weidmannsche, 1847] 288) that the Oracle must be understood in the context of the five chapters that preceded it. For him, these chapters are concerned with the rebuilding of the Kingdom of God and the Gog pericope finally secures this Kingdom from all external assaults.

[7] Johann Michel Schmidt, *Die jüdische Apokalyptik: Die Geschichte ihrer Erforschung von den Anfängen bis zu den Textfunden von Qumran* (Neukirchen-Vluyn: Neukirchener Verlag, 1969) 33–34.

[8] Hermann Gunkel, *Schöpfung und Chaos in Urzeit und Endzeit: Eine religionsgeschichtliche Untersuchung über Gen 1 und Ap Joh 12* (Göttingen: Vandenhoeck & Ruprecht, 1895); Hugo Gressmann, *Der Ursprung der Israelitisch-jüdischen Eschatologie* (FRLANT 6; Göttingen: Vandenhoeck & Ruprecht, 1905).

[9] Ernst W. Hengstenberg, *The Prophecies of Ezekiel Elucidated* (trans. A. C. Murphy & J. G. Murphy; Edinburgh: T. & T. Clark, 1869); originally published as *Die Weissagungen des Prophet Ezechiel erklärt* (Leipzig: Hinrichs, 1867/68).

a misperception similar to Ewald, Hengstenberg sees the community of the covenant, renewed by Yhwh, victoriously resisting all the assaults of the world. They had, in fact, no defense but Yhwh, as the text makes clear. Hengstenberg saw Gog as the product of fancy, not as an historical or supernaturalistic personage.[10] Regarded as a conservative scholar by Ewald,[11] he manifests a certain originality on this point.

In 1880 Rudolf Smend published his *Der Prophet Ezechiel*,[12] a revision of Ferdinand Hitzig's 1847 commentary. His research convinced him that the scheme of the arrangement, the logical progression of ideas, the recurrence of the same figures, themes, and idioms spoke of a unity.[13] Smend's commentary on chapters 38–39 reflects this same assurance that they are integrally related to the rest of the text. He sees the themes discussed as flowing clearly from what was explained by the prophet in chapter 36: to redeem the honor of his name, damaged by the fall of Jerusalem and the exile of his people, Yhwh must bring about the fall of Babylon (the Chaldean kingdom) which for Smend was represented by Gog.[14] Many today would challenge Smend's conclusion that Gog represents Babylon. Ezek 29:17–20 identifies Nebuchadnezzar, and consequently Babylon, as Yhwh's agent of judgment. Yhwh is not out to destroy the instrument of his judgment. Those who opt for an historical personage today choose Gyges of Lydia, not Nebuchadnezzar.

In 1884, Ludwig Seinecke published his second volume of *Geschichte des Volkes Israel*.[15] In it he again raised the issues presented by Zunz in 1832 and 1873, asserting, for the same reasons, that the book was a

---

[10] Hengstenberg, *The Prophecies of Ezekiel Elucidated*, 329–30.

[11] John W. Rogerson, "Ewald, Georg Heinrich August," in *Dictionary of Biblical Interpretation* (ed. John H. Hayes; Nashville: Abingdon, 1999) 363–64.

[12] Rudolf Smend, *Der Prophet Ezechiel* (KEHAT; 2d ed.; Leipzig: S. Hirzel, 1880).

[13] He saw no stages of development as did Ewald. It was his conviction that the book had been written down all at once, in one sitting. He said rather emphatically that no part could be removed without disturbing the whole structure and gave the date of the final redaction of the entire work (excepting the appendix in 29:17 ff, dated two years later) as that indicated in Ezek 40:1, the tenth day of the first month of the twenty-fifth year of the exile (sometime in March-April, 573). Smend, *Der Prophet Ezechiel*, XXI-XXII.

[14] Smend, *Der Prophet Ezechiel*, 293–94.

[15] Ludwig Chr. Seinecke, *Geschichte des Volkes Israel* 2 (Göttingen: Vandenhoeck & Ruprecht, 1884) 1–20.

pseudepigraph written during the Maccabean period.[16] Seinecke did accept the final redaction of the book as a unified literary work, but written four hundred years later.[17] He ends on a positive note saying that, when left to his own genius in chapters such as 19 and 37, the final editor's style is such that he takes second place to no prophet.[18] While Seinecke was not taken seriously by his contemporaries,[19] his conclusions and many of his bases for these conclusions would be more acceptable in the biblical community only fifty years later.

In 1886 Karl Cornill published his *Das Buch des Propheten Ezechiel*,[20] a careful study of the text based on versions, in which his primary concern was to critically improve the Hebrew text. His study of the text based on the various versions led him to see the book as a cohesive work whose final redactor was Ezekiel. He concluded, similar to Ewald, that Ezekiel completed his book at the time of the dating in Ezek 40:1, and he incorporated, at that point, earlier writings which, in Cornill's estimation, remained practically unchanged.[21] He does not question the relationship of Ezekiel 38–39 with what goes before it, nor is there any discussion of mythic elements.

In 1897 Alfred Bertholet published, at the age of 29, his first commentary on Ezekiel.[22] We will discuss his second commentary on Ezekiel (1936) during the second phase of the critical study of Ezekiel. His 1897 commentary patterns the movement of this first period and, when compared with his second commentary, will provide a graphic illustration of the 180 degree turn in Ezekiel studies that began at the turn of the century. In 1897 Bertholet strongly advocated for the origi-

---

[16] In the first twenty pages of his book he debunks Ezekiel as a prophet: "Ezekiel has announced nothing new but lives from the crumbs fallen from the table of earlier prophets. When the prophet is dated in a later period after the exile, it can be done with good reason." Seinecke, *Geschichte*, 2.

[17] The prophecies against Egypt for Seinecke (*Geschichte*, 12–13) speak of the defeat of the Ptolemies by Antiochus III; the loss of Edomite control of Hebron through the attack of Judas Maccabeus fulfilled the prophecies against Edom, and Gog was a cryptic personification of Antiochus Epiphanes. So exactly are Gog and his hordes depicted as Antiochus and his armies that Ezekiel must know the sovereign as his contemporary.

[18] Seinecke, *Geschichte*, 20.

[19] Karl Cornill, "Ezekiel, Book of," in *JEnc* 5 (ed. Isidore Singer; New York: Funk and Wagnells, 1907) 318.

[20] Karl Cornill, *Das Buch des Propheten Ezechiel* (Leipzig: Hinrichs, 1886).

[21] Cornill, "Ezekiel, Book of," in *JEnc* 5, 317–18.

[22] Alfred Bertholet, *Das Buch Hesekiel* (KHC 12; Leipzig/Tübingen: Mohr, 1897).

nal literary cohesiveness of the book.[23] In his treatment of chapters 38–39, he advances the hypothesis that chapters 33–37 would not be complete without the themes and message of 38–39 where God completely and finally destroys the enemy by his power against the heathens for the honor of his name. Bertholet, along with Hitzig, emphatically states that Gog is not a veiled reference to Babylon, but an unknown enemy in the future. Yhwh will proclaim his strength before the world, guaranteeing that any future attempts will lead to total annihilation of the enemy.[24] While I would agree with Bertholet on the majority of his conclusions, he falls somewhat short of the mark in his projected outcome of the pericope which for him focuses on Yhwh's ability to annihilate his opponents in the political arena. Is Ezekiel 38–39 rather a statement that divine judgment in the theological arena will never again sentence the purified exiles to a destruction like that wrought by Nebuchadnezzar? This present work explores bases for an affirmative answer to this question. That was Bertholet's position in 1897. In the introduction to his 1936 commentary he says: "I can almost say that no piece of the earlier work is left standing in this one."[25] We will treat that in the second (next) phase of the critical study of Ezekiel.

All the biblical scholarship presented thus far has been German. Three British scholars were also at work in this period. In 1892 A.B. Davidson published his commentary, *The Book of the Prophet Ezekiel* in Cambridge.[26] The Gog pericope is, for Davidson, an episode tied to the restoration of the people. With Hitzig, he sees it as an event which takes place far into the future. Gog was not a cryptic naming of Nebuchadnezzar. For Davidson, the Babylonians were an historical reality who would chastise Yhwh's people and humble ungodly nations like Egypt and Phoenicia. He notes with accuracy that Ezekiel's prophecies contain no threats against Babylon.[27] Davidson saw chapters 38–39 as flowing from chapters 33–37, in particular, as an illustration of what

---

[23] He acknowledged that some parts of the book had probably been introduced late into their present context, but he was convinced that the book had to be accepted or rejected as a whole. Bertholet, *Das Buch Hesekiel*, xx-xxii.

[24] Bertholet, *Das Buch Hesekiel*, 187.

[25] Alfred Bertholet and Kurt Galling, *Hesekiel* (HAT 13; Tübingen: Mohr, 1936) v.

[26] Andrew B. Davidson, *The Book of the Prophet Ezekiel* (CBSC; Cambridge: University Press, 1892).

[27] Davidson, *The Book of the Prophet Ezekiel*, 273–74.

was said in the last nine verses of chapter 37: that Yhwh would bring his people back to the land he had promised them so that the nations would know of Yhwh's power to sanctify his people. Davidson's conclusions clearly grasp the fact that Ezekiel's purpose was the writing of theology, not politics. The present work develops Davidson's conclusions further and seeks to confirm them by a study of the mythic elements in these nine verses and a discussion of how they are played out in part by chapters 38–39 and in part by chapters 40–48.

C. H. Toy's commentary of 1899[28] is representative of the scholarship of the period. Ezekiel is the final redactor of the book which is a unified literary work. He sees Gog as an historical figure. So convinced is he of the time frame that he mentions that two generations later Ezekiel would not have written the same prophecy.[29] He does not develop any theological or literary links of chapters 38–39 with other parts of the text. While some would opt for Toy's historical interpretation of the event, current scholarship in the main would see eschatology in the language of a text with phrases like "in the latter years" (Ezek 38:8). The present work asks if the fulfillment of this prophecy is not more solidly rooted in religious myth than history.

S. R. Driver published the first edition of his *Introduction to the Literature of the Old Testament* in 1891. In 1913[30] the ninth edition still contained his oft-repeated conclusion that the volume of Ezekiel's prophecies is arranged with such method that it must have been written by his own hand.[31] In the discussion of the book he includes chapters 38–39 in his section on chapters 33–39, but he does not discuss his reasons for linking them with chapters 33–37. The research in this work affirms anew Driver's conclusion that there is clear method and a strong editorial hand at work in the final form of Ezekiel, and it pro-

---

[28] Crawford H. Toy, *The Book of the Prophet Ezekiel* (The Sacred Books of the Old and New Testaments 12; London: James H. Clarke, 1899).

[29] The traumatic menace of the Scythian advance, as he describes it, will descend upon Israel in the near future. Toy *(The Book of the Prophet Ezekiel*, 173, 176–77) sees Ezekiel's prophecy as foretelling a period of unbroken peace. The destruction of the Scythian horde is a means on the part of Yhwh to lead Israel to true knowledge of the God of Israel.

[30] Samuel R. Driver, *An Introduction to the Literature of the Old Testament* (International Theological Library; 9th ed.; Edinburgh: T. & T. Clark, 1913).

[31] "No critical question arises in connection with the authorship of the book, the whole from beginning to end bearing unmistakably the stamp of a single mind." Driver, *An Introduction*, 279, 296.

poses a mythic groundwork laid in the text of chapters 34 and 37 of which the events of chapters 38–39 are part of a promised fulfillment. The second phase of modern biblical study of Ezekiel, beginning with the work of Richard Kraetzschmar published in 1900, radically departs from Driver's conclusions.

Second Phase: From 1900 to 1950

In 1900 Richard Kraetzschmar signaled a major shift away from those who shared Driver's view, with the publication of his *Das Buch Ezechiel*.[32] The idea that the entire book unmistakably bore "the stamp of a single mind"[33] became a notion of the past. Kraetzschmar challenged the authorial unity of the text.[34] Despite the apparent surface coherence, Kraetzschmar saw many incongruities in the accounts: the change in person, the interruption in the narrative at points, the repetition of various descriptions, the disorder of events in a story (he cites chapters 38–39 as an example).[35] Throughout his study of the book he sees parallel texts, and concludes the present book was made up of two separate recensions of Ezekiel's prophecies.[36]

Kraetzschmar sees the Gog pericope as an account of the mighty power of Yhwh, who, by destroying Gog and his hordes, manifests the holiness of his name before the nations. Consistent with his assessment of the discordant character of the book, he sees there rather disunity and incongruity.[37] Also of import, Kraetzschmar notes that Ezekiel

---

[32] Richard Kraetzschmar, *Das Buch Ezechiel* (HKAT 3; Göttingen: Vandenhoeck & Ruprecht, 1900).

[33] Driver, *An Introduction*, 296.

[34] For him it was an impossibility that the entire book came from Ezekiel. His first point of attack was the dating, arguing that not everything between two given dates was composed between those two dates. For him the date given only had validity for the first prophecy subsequent to the date. Kraetzschmar, *Das Buch Ezechiel*, XI.

[35] Kraetzschmar, *Das Buch Ezechiel*, XII.

[36] Indicative of this is the change in person, from first to third, in the course of the text. Kraetzschmar (*Das Buch Ezechiel*, XIII) saw the third person recensions as extracts from the first person recensions. Both were put together in a final form by a redactor who had formed the present whole.

[37] He makes use of chapters 38–39 to develop his theory of parallel recensions, comparing doublets between them. He cites chapters 38–39 as an example of the internal disunity of the text in the disordering of the events of the account. Kraetzschmar, *Das Buch Ezechiel*, XIV.

himself in 38:17 and 39:8 sees the pericope going back to older oracles which he suggests are probably lost to us forever. Gog is not for him a veiled allusion to an historic person, but rather he is the personification of an adversarial power opposed to Israel.[38] He relates the pericope to the plight of the exiles, but does not develop thematic connections to what precedes or follows. Kraetzschmar's assessment that Gog is the personification of an adversary opposed to Israel is a conclusion amplified in the discussion of Gog in chapters four and five of the current work. While the question of recensions receives demonstrable support from the text, so too, modern scholarship would say, does a unifying theme and a strong editorial hand in the composition of the final form. This, however, was not Kraetzschmar's focus. In comparison to those who immediately preceded him, he had set an exegetical course which would continue to escalate throughout this second phase of the modern study of Ezekiel.

Hugo Winckler published his *Altorientalische Forschungen*[39] in 1901. Winckler pointed out that during Ezekiel's time there had been no invasion of Palestine such as is described in Ezekiel 38–39. He rejected the notion that the passage was a reminiscence of the alleged Scythian invasion fifty to one hundred years earlier and sought a later historical context which corresponded more closely to the sequence of events described in the passage.[40] In his analysis of the text, he concludes that it reaches the climax of its promise to Ezekiel in chapter 37 and could easily close with that. In his assessment, chapters 38–39 are a later appendage.[41] Like Zunz and Seinecke before him, Winckler's findings were by and large dismissed by the scholarly community until thirty and forty years later when Torrey and Irwin used his same arguments to support their own research and conclusions.

Hermann Gunkel published his *Schöpfung und Chaos in Urzeit und*

---

[38] He also sees chapters 38–39 going on to have an effect on both the Book of Joel and later apocalyptic literature, and observes that the literary problem this point creates has hardly been touched. Kraetzschmar, *Das Buch Ezechiel*, XIV.

[39] Hugo Winckler, *Altorientalische Forschungen* 2 (Leipzig: Eduard Pfeiffer, 1901).

[40] Taking the description of Magog as an island kingdom to refer to Macedonia, Winckler (*Altorientalische Forschungen* 2, 161) suggested that Gog was Alexander the Great, and the inclusion of Macedonia in Gog's army led Winckler to date the Gog pericope to a period between Alexander's conquest of Asia Minor and his invasion of Palestine.

Endzeit: Eine religionsgeschichtliche Untersuchung über Gen 1 und Ap Joh 12 in 1895. Though he himself did not examine the Gog pericope, his writings would provide backdrop to help support Kraetzschmar's conclusion above, that the pericope goes back to older oracles, and even more so to understand Hugo Gressmann's work which follows. Gunkel's tradition-historical method gave balance to the *zeitgeschichtliche* method dominant at the time which attributed the characteristics of a literary work like the Gog pericope to disguised references to events in history.[42] For Gunkel, one could better understand these patterns as the endurance of mythic lore rather than as the result of one author's creative imagination.[43] Gunkel acknowledged the viewpoint that the characteristics of a narrative like the Gog pericope could refer to the concerns of history, but he set limits for treating the history in these texts. He believed that before searching for connections with historical events, one should see how the narrative correlates with the tradition. He also believed that if a reference to history was mediated by the tradition, it had to be understood as having made a forceful impression on people psychologically. Gunkel believed that one could better understand how mythic patterns such as those in chapters 38–39 were revered and passed on, after a long prior life in the tradition.[44] The present work argues that the final form uses the Gog pericope as part of its reframing of the Israelite creation myth, thereby illustrating Gunkel's insight.

In 1905 Hugo Gressmann published his *Der Ursprung der Israelitisch-jüdischen Eschatologie*. Though Gressmann worked closely with Gunkel in developing the tradition-historical method, in his own research he asserted that mythic patterns could be recognized in biblical texts without referring them back to specific authenticating myths for validation. This was a noticeable divergence from Gunkel's position. Through his study of patterns in earlier mythic texts, Gressmann was able to recognize these mythic patterns in biblical texts by pointing out incongruities of certain components within the story's context or by the stereotypic character of the account. He identified the Gog pericope as mythic in this manner by noting such indicators

---

[41] Winckler, *Altorientalische Forschungen* 2, 167.
[42] Gunkel, *Schöpfung und Chaos*, 202–5.
[43] Gunkel, *Schöpfung und Chaos*, 208–9.
[44] Gunkel, *Schöpfung und Chaos*, 216.

contained within it: the attack on the navel of the earth, the battle scene in 38:18–23 with all its cosmic elements, and the geographic vocabulary in chapter 39.[45] Gressmann's conclusion was that what we have in the biblical account is a fragmentary telling of the Gog myth as it once existed, though adapted to the monotheistic beliefs reflected in the final form of the text. He saw in the figure of the nations an army of gods attacking the mythic mountain which unites earth and heaven. Gressmann also highlighted the foe from the north as coming from the same myth. Looking at the plurality of gods suggested to him that the myth was probably not original to Israel.[46] The Combat Myth was, indeed, attested elsewhere in the region. Chapters two and four of this present work discuss the broad based regional parallels present as Israel developed its own religious myths.

In *Der Messias*,[47] published posthumously two years after Gressmann's death, and twenty-four years after *Der Ursprung*, Gressmann states more explicitly his conclusions on the relationship of the Gog pericope with the rest of the book. Despite his tracking the derivation of the Gog myth to sources prior to the exile, he ultimately did not attribute authorship of Ezek 38–39 to the prophet. The portrayal of the Eden-like existence after restoration (38:8, 12) did not allow him to date the unit to the exilic period or even the early period after the exile. He had reservations about attributing the invasion of Judah by chaotic forces to the exilic prophets. This was not characteristic of them for whom the exile had been the last catastrophe. If Ezekiel had been the author, he opined, would he not have declared reckoning against Babylon, rather than Judah?[48] Gressmann located the Gog myth historically in the late fifth, early fourth centuries B.C.E. nearer to the locust prophecy of Joel than to the exilic prophecies of Ezekiel.[49] He challenges and rejects the integral relationship of chapters 38–39 to the rest of the book, though the bases of some of his arguments for doing so can be challenged. Was the Gog pericope meant to be a depiction of a final disaster? There was in fact no loss of life, land or Temple on the part of Israel. It was, on the contrary, a great victory for the God of

---

[45] Gressmann, *Der Ursprung*, 185–86.
[46] Gressmann, *Der Ursprung*, 190–91.
[47] Hugo Gressmann, *Der Messias* (Göttingen: Vandenhoeck & Ruprecht, 1929).
[48] Gressmann, *Der Messias*, 123–24.
[49] Gressmann, *Der Messias*, 134.

Israel without any seeming disturbance to his people who emerged after it unperturbed from their dwellings to purify the land. Was it a pronouncement of judgment on either Babylon or Judah? As mentioned above, why would the prophet pronounce judgment on Babylon which he presented in the text as Yhwh's instrument? Second, why would he even pronounce judgment against Judah in this, the restoration sequence? That would make more sense prior to chapter 33. Does the story serve a different function than his arguments suggest he had given it? This present work will investigate the story's function more thoroughly in chapters four and five below.

Johannes Herrmann published his *Ezechielstudien*[50] in 1908, agreeing with Kraetzschmar that the book was not a cohesive literary work, but disagreeing with his conclusion. He pointed out that the books of Isaiah and Jeremiah contained collections of independent prophetic pieces belonging to these prophets. Why could it not be the same in the Book of Ezekiel? Herrmann, through systematic analysis of the book, determined that it was an anthology of smaller self-contained units which, for the most part, Ezekiel had put together and supplemented, editing and correcting as he worked. He cited chapters 4–24 and 33–39 as collections of unrelated materials. He also acknowledges that even this theory does not explain all the difficulties and consequently in some places the intervention of other hands must be assumed.[51] With this interpretation Ezekiel is no longer the creator of a planned and ordered book, but the genuineness of the individual prophecies is, for the most part, maintained.

In his exegesis of chapters 38–39, Herrmann determined that there was a complex structure of ten subunits.[52] Of these he only considered 38:17, 18–23 to be later reworkings, not editings by Ezekiel. Removing these, the Gog pericope could be read as the portrayal of a single event from different viewpoints.[53] Herrmann does not see a thematic relationship between chapters 38–39 and the rest of the text. He does support the findings of Gressmann that the Gog periocope is literarily influenced by myths known to Ezekiel. Herrmann developed the idea

---

[50] Johannes Herrmann, *Ezechielstudien* (BWAT 2; Leipzig: Hinrichs, 1908).
[51] Herrmann, *Ezechielstudien*, 4–6.
[52] 38:1–9, 10–16, 17, 18–23, 39:1–5, 6–8, 9–10, 11–13, 14–16, 17–20. Herrmann, *Ezechielstudien*, 39.
[53] Herrmann, *Ezechielstudien*, 41–42.

that myths could be used by prophets addressing their historical contexts. He interpreted Ezekiel 38–39 as authentically Ezekielian material and as a further development of the earlier, more historically based oracles against Israel and Egypt.[54] Hermann was correct in his insight that prophets used myths to address their historical contexts, but I take issue with his interpretation that the Gog pericope is a further development of more historically based oracles against Israel and Egypt. As mentioned above, it is not automatically apparent why the Gog pericope would be an oracle of judgment against Israel, since such an oracle would not make sense in the midst of the restoration chapters of the book. Nor is it clear on closer examination why the Gog periocope would be a further development of the Oracles against Egypt. The two sets of texts appear to have differing functions, which will be addressed in chapter five below.

In 1924 Herrmann published his long-awaited full commentary on the book: *Ezechiel übersetzt und erklärt*.[55] In it he maintains his position that chapters 38–39 are not thematically joined to 33–37.[56] In the end, Herrmann sees the book as a collection, an anthology written at different times, mostly by Ezekiel. In his view, chapters 38–39 do not show a thematic relationship with the rest of the book.

In 1922 George Ricker Berry published an article in the *Journal of Biblical Literature*[57] in which he denied Ezekielian authorship to chapters 38–39 for a number of reasons. While the author of these chapters wished them to be attributed to Ezekiel, Berry concluded that they actually belonged to a later time. His analysis of the style and syntax supported this thesis.[58] In his judgment, the final form does not present

---

[54] According to Herrmann (*Ezechielstudien*, 46–47) the use of myth in Ezekiel 38–39 was essentially no different from its use in the book's judgments against Israel and Egypt (Ezekiel 7, 29). In both of these oracles, the book presents an historical agent bringing the judgments of God on the Day of Yhwh. Herrmann suspected an historical figure may also have lain behind the figure of Gog even though chapters 38–39 were considerably more mythological in tone.

[55] Johannes Herrmann, *Ezechiel übersetzt und erklärt* (KAT 11; Leipzig: A. Deichertsche, 1924).

[56] He sees 37:26b–28 as a clear conclusion, ending with 39:25–29 which does not form part of the Gog pericope for him. Though he sees chapters 38–39 as a separate addition, he does not deny the pericope to Ezekiel. In fact he sees it as "absolutely possible" that Ezekiel placed them there. Herrmann, *Ezechiel*, XXIV, XXX.

[57] George R. Berry, "The Date of Ezekiel 38:1 - 39:20," *JBL* 41 (1922) 224–32.

[58] To Berry ("The Date of Ezekiel 38:1 - 39:20," 226, 228–30) the use of veiled language

a unified piece. Absent from his study is an accounting for the numerous textual links between chapters 38–39 and the rest of the book, which will be presented in chapter three below. These textual links weaken his argument that the final form was not concerned about presenting a unified piece of work. Over the course of this period Berry's conclusions were taken more seriously than the views of Zunz and Seinecke had been in the preceding century.

In 1914 Gustav Hölscher published *Die Propheten, Untersuchungen zur Religionsgeschichte Israels*.[59] The work shows Hölscher in metamorphosis in his stance on Ezekiel.[60] In 1922, in his *Geschichte der israelitischen und jüdischen Religion* [61] Hölscher's position is more fully developed. In chapter three, the Assyrian-Babylonian Period, he discusses the prophet Ezekiel ben Buzi. Speaking of the prophet, he notes that Ezekiel is influenced by mythology. Yet in this writing he has also concluded that there is nothing of the original prophet in chapters 38–39. In fact, he considers all restoration chapters (33–48) to be part of the pseudepigraphon. In this section of his book, Hölscher expresses his hope that he will be able to publish precise reasons for his opinion very soon.[62] In chapter four, on the Persian Period, Hölscher focuses on the book of Ezekiel which he describes as a pseudepigraphon written in the first half of the fifth century. For Hölscher, the book utilized some literary remains of the true Ezekiel and was subsequently added to by later hands.[63]

---

and exaggeration classified these chapters as apocalyptic and indicated an authorship during the Maccabean period. Through analysis of the text he determined the pericope to be referring to the time of Antiochus Eupator in 162 B.C.E.

[59] Gustav Hölscher, *Die Propheten, Untersuchungen zur Religionsgeschichte Israels* (Leipzig: J. C. Hinrichs, 1914) 298–315.

[60] For the most part his book maintains substantially traditional views. Yet he notes in a passing reference to the Gog pericope that it agrees in its most essential parts with the eschatological thoughts represented again and again in post-exilic prophetic literature. How much of it is Ezekiel himself speaking Hölscher (*Die Propheten*, 312) says is still not certain.

[61] Gustav Hölscher, *Geschichte der israelitischen und jüdischen Religion* (Giessen: Alfred Töpelmann, 1922).

[62] Hölscher, *Geschichte*, 114, 136.

[63] In his description of the book Hölscher (*Geschichte*, 136) presents the pseudepigraphon, from his own perspective, as a unified work in which the author-redactor elaborates on the poetry of the original prophet to present his own integrated message to the people in exile.

In 1924, shortly after the publication of Herrmann's full commentary, Hölscher published the work for which he is most noted, *Hesekiel, der Dichter und das Buch*.[64] He based his text analysis on the work of Cornill, Toy and others. In his view, some texts were severely damaged. These he determined to be the writings of the original prophet. Those texts which were better preserved he attributed to later redaction.[65] This early fifth century redaction served the agenda of the Zadokite priesthood, establishing their pre-eminence.[66] It was this later redaction according to Hölscher that made Ezekiel into the priestly writer laying out the ground plan of legalistic and ritualistic Judaism.[67] In fact, Hölscher concluded, the final form of the book as we have it is, in the main, the product of the later redaction, not of the prophet.

Hölscher's definition of prophecy also directed his conclusions on the Gog pericope. Hölscher's theory was based on *a priori* assumptions of style and form in Israelite prophecy.[68] For him the pericope was completely a literary product, not a prophecy. Working with material drawn from literature, a redactor created, according to Hölscher, a theological-exegetical hypothesis.[69] He does see the pericope as an integral part of the five chapters which precede it. Gog must be destroyed if the restoration described in chapters 33–37 is to be com-

---

[64] Gustav Hölscher, *Hesekiel, der Dichter und das Buch, eine literarkritische Untersuchung* (BZAW 39; Giessen: Alfred Töpelmann, 1924).

[65] To explain these observations, he developed his criteria, providing a basis for what in the text was original to the prophet and what was later addition. His conclusions drastically reduced the number of verses which he would attribute to the sixth century prophet Ezekiel. In Hölscher's criteria (*Hesekiel*, 5), the original prophet was a poet whose prophecy was inspired by God's Spirit. Apart from the poetry, he admits the call narrative and accounts of symbolic actions and visions as genuine to the prophet. Considering Ezekiel to be a poet, he judged much of the prose in the book not to be the work of Ezekiel (and also to be of poor quality).

[66] As mentioned above, the prophecies of restoration (chapters 33–48) were eliminated. He determined that the doctrine of individual responsibility was a post-exilic theme and the work of a redactor. Writings which seemed to exhibit influence of Deuteronomy or the Holiness Code were denied the prophet and attributed to the final redactor: a polemical writer from the Zadokite priesthood of fifth-century Jerusalem of the Deuteronomistic school. Hölscher, *Hesekiel*, 38.

[67] Hölscher, *Hesekiel*, 5–6.

[68] Hölscher, *Hesekiel*, 6.

[69] Hölscher, *Hesekiel*, 180.

plete. His destruction secures permanent peace and a purified temple cult worthy of Yhwh.[70] But is Hölscher correct that Gog's demise is part of establishing a permanent peace for Israel in the political arena, or is this peace part of the theology of the final form which would understandably seek to establish a peace beyond "peace at any price?"

Though Hölscher has presented chapters 38–39 as a unified part of chapters 33–48, he has not shown its coherence in the overall book as we have received it. It is not clear that Hölscher appreciates the skill employed in the final form's compilation in adding to the prophetic work. Hölscher distinguished, on the one hand, between the poetry of the prophet, composed under the impulse of God's Spirit, and, on the other hand, the theological-exegetical hypothesis (which he determines chapters 38–39 to be), written by a final redactor of the fifth century. Accordingly, Hölscher saw a gap, not unity, separating these two diverse literary expressions within the book. Hölscher speaks so forcefully in praise of Ezekiel's poetry and in critique of the redactor's poor prose that his use of the word unity in the final form would seem to refer more to juxtaposition than to literary skill. It is not, in fact, his purpose to show that the final form of the book was a cohesive literary work, and it is clear from his findings that he himself is not convinced that it is.

In 1930 Charles Cutler Torrey, a gifted philologist, published his *Pseudo-Ezekiel and the Original Prophecy*.[71] He proposed that the whole book was composed and redacted during the Seleucid period, in 230 B.C.E. as a pseudepigraphon written from the thirtieth year of the reign of Manasseh in the seventh century. The writer's intent was to show that the people were warned about the coming calamity upon Jerusalem and that it was well deserved. According to Torrey, the Babylonian exile and the Restoration were "a very ingenious reconstruction of history"[72] by the Chronicler to defeat the Samaritans in

---

[70] Hölscher, *Hesekiel*, 38.

[71] Charles C. Torrey, *Pseudo-Ezekiel and the Original Prophecy* (YOS Researches 18; New Haven: Yale University Press, 1930); republished with critical articles by S. Spiegel, C. C. Torrey and a Prolegomenon by M. Greenberg (LBS; New York: KTAV Publishing House, 1970).

[72] Subsequently a redactor worked over the book altering as little as possible with the purpose of giving it the appearance of the work of a prophet (Ezekiel) in Babylon during the captivity. The purpose of this editor according to Torrey (*Pseudo-Ezekiel*,

their claim of historical continuity. Torrey saw little proof of the drastic depopulation associated with the Babylonian exile. Redactors in the works of Jeremiah and Second Isaiah were also complicitous in this "reconstruction."[73] In Torrey's theory, the prophet Ezekiel became a literary creation of the seventh and sixth century and not a real person.

Torrey would attribute the Gog pericope to the first writer, discerning no additions or alterations by the redactor who soon followed with a different purpose for the text he would rework.[74] In Torrey's interpretation, Gog and his hordes are Alexander the Great and his armies. Judging the pericope to be of the apocalypse genre, he assigns it, along with Daniel and sections of Joel and Zechariah, to the third century.[75] There are inconsistencies in Torrey's thesis. He does not develop a literary basis demonstrating how the Gog pericope fits into the intent of the first writer or the redactor. If the first writer is calling the people to repentance before the religious persecution of the Seleucid royalty, the outcome of the pericope would not "sound the alarm." If the redactor was supporting a theology of Zion against leadership of or parity with the Samaritan cult, why did he have Gog's hordes come against the mountains of Israel rather than against Jerusalem which is not mentioned in the pericope? While he presents the book as a unified work, he does not provide a substantial basis to demonstrate this view, nor does he show that the Gog pericope is an integral part of the overall work. His scholarly efforts are directed toward discerning points of disunity. He sees the work as a literary invention to support a political polemic of the Jerusalem priesthood, not as a work to give hope to a people shaken by the trauma of a fallen Jerusalem and a destroyed Temple.

In 1931, James Smith published *The Book of The Prophet Ezekiel, A New Interpretation*,[76] essentially his doctoral dissertation which he had defended at the University of Edinburgh in 1929, under the title

---

103) was the establishment of pre-eminence and legitimacy of the Jerusalem priesthood over the Samaritan priesthood. In this redaction, the writer added the dates which reckon from the exile of Jehoiachin to those which reckon from the period of Manasseh.

[73] Torrey, *Pseudo-Ezekiel*, 58–61, 102–8.
[74] Torrey, *Pseudo-Ezekiel*, 108–12.
[75] Torrey, *Pseudo-Ezekiel*, 95, 97.
[76] James Smith, *The Book of the Prophet Ezekiel, A New Interpretation* (New York: Macmillan, 1931).

"The Non-Babylonian Oracles in the Book of the Prophet Ezekiel (I-XXXVII)."[77] What is of interest in this present study is Smith's understanding of the relationship of chapters 38–39 with the rest of the text. He does note that the author of Ezekiel 40–48 recognized that Ezekiel did not mean his temple to be built on the Jerusalem site. It was Smith's understanding that the author of chapters 38–48 was the redactor who put the prophecies of Ezekiel together at least 120 years after he was active in the northern kingdom.[78] For Smith, disunity was clearly evident in the text. It is not clear that, in his analysis, chapters 38–39 are thematically integral to the overall work.

Volkmar Herntrich followed James Smith in 1932 with *Ezechielprobleme*.[79] Disagreeing with Torrey and Smith, Herntrich saw Ezekiel as active during the period immediately prior to and during the early part of the Babylonian captivity, yet with them he asserts that the activity of the prophet took place in Jerusalem. His study of the text led him to conclude that the Book of Ezekiel began as the prophecies of a Jerusalem prophet delivered during the reign of Zedekiah, and at a later date they were reworked and edited within a Babylonian framework. To the Babylonian redactor he assigns 33:21–23 and chapters 40–48. The redactor's purpose was to validate the power of his God in opposition to the Babylonian pantheon. Apart from redactional elements, Herntrich assigns the remainder of the book to the prophet Ezekiel, active in Jerusalem. Herntrich acknowledges that, apart from these two major compositional efforts, later hands have expanded the text, particularly for chapters 40–48.[80] The book as he sees it represents the world of a genuine Judean prophet, and the world of the exilic redactor who constructs a framework around the genuine prophecy.

---

[77] Smith (*The Book of the Prophet Ezekiel*, 21, 90–91, 93. 98–100) believed that some parts of these thirty-seven chapters had a Palestinian origin and that some parts had a non-Palestinian origin, both artificially combined later by a redactor. The two authors of these thirty-seven chapters, according to Smith, were in reality one, for Ezekiel wrote the first part amongst the community in exile after 722. The second and larger part he wrote in northern Israel after his return in 691. Smith sees these two collections as the basis for Josephus' reference to Ezekiel's two books. The redactor re-worked the text so that it would appear to be a product of the Judean exile in Babylon.

[78] Smith, *The Book of the Prophet Ezekiel*, 66–67.

[79] Volkmar Herntrich, *Ezechielprobleme* (BZAW 61; Giessen: Alfred Töpelmann, 1932).

[80] Herntrich, *Ezechielprobleme*, 63–64, 124–26, 128.

While Herntrich would see chapters 38–39 as part of the prophecies of Ezekiel, he sees them as a contrast to chapters 33–37. Chapters 38–39 constitute a self-contained unit, standing only in loose connection with the preceding chapters. Obviously with later expansions, they derived in the main from Ezekiel. According to Herntrich, these chapters were written during the early exile by the prophet active in Jerusalem, and the use of ancient Near Eastern mythological themes is evident.[81] For Herntrich the themes of 38–39 are foreign to what precedes them. They are a disconnected unit of mythological themes inserted without purpose by the author in his work.

Alfred Bertholet, as mentioned above, began his career holding a rather traditional view of the text. By the time he published his commentary *Hesekiel* [82] in 1936, his position had shifted radically. In his second commentary, Bertholet assumed two periods in the prophetic activity of Ezekiel. The first, 593–586, took place in Jerusalem and is introduced by the vision of the scroll in 2:3–3:9, whereas the second took place in exile in 585, and began with the throne-chariot vision of 1:4–2:2. He supported Kraetzschmar's theory of doublets in modified form and attributed the compilation of the book to a later editor, who interpolated the work and who transferred the prophet's ministry wholly to Babylon.[83] Regarding chapters 38–39, Bertholet detects a parallelism which leads him to conclude that they are two accounts of the same story, and he sees a core of Ezekiel's words clearly revised and elaborated towards an apocalyptic understanding of the text.[84] He treats the Gog pericope as a unit separate from what precedes it. He does not develop thematic links between it and chapters 33–37, as he had in his 1897 commentary where he saw the pericope as the logical completion and conclusion of what went before it. This current work presents evidence of thematic cohesiveness through the textual links and mythic elements in Ezekiel's final form which disputes Bertholet's radically altered second position.

In 1936, George A. Cooke published *A Critical and Exegetical Commentary on the Book of Ezekiel*.[85] In his introduction Cooke notes the

---

[81] Herntrich, *Ezechielprobleme*, 119.
[82] Alfred Bertholet and Kurt Galling, *Hesekiel* (HAT 13; Tübingen: Mohr, 1936).
[83] Bertholet, *Hesekiel*, XIII-XV.
[84] Bertholet, *Hesekiel*, 129–31.
[85] George A. Cooke, *A Critical and Exegetical Commentary on the Book of Ezekiel* (ICC; Edinburgh: T. & T. Clark, 1936).

revolution which Ezekiel studies have undergone since Samuel Driver's assessment that the book bore the mark of a single mind. He also strongly rejected Herntrich's view that maintained the exclusive exilic activity of the prophet. He was at a loss for a rational explanation of Ezekiel's power to see what was going on in Jerusalem, but he was prepared to ascribe "second sight" to the prophet. While his view has more in common with older scholars of the nineteenth century, he did recognize a larger number of secondary expansions than they and he particularly marked a number of sections in the concluding chapters as expansions. His study of the text led to the conclusion that editorial hands had been at work throughout the entire book, disturbing Ezekiel's purpose and confusing the situation. Though in his exegesis he always demanded sufficient reason to question authorship, in the end he considers the Book of Ezekiel to be an anthology of prophetic oracles, delivered at various times and collected by editors into its present form.[86] This present work challenges the conclusion that the book is an anthology. Our research seeks to show that Ezekiel's final form is a crafted apologetic, showing in the first part of the book the justice of Yhwh's judgment against Israel, and in the second part of the book the hand of the Creator at work in bringing his cosmos to completion.

Cooke considered chapters 38–39 to be best explained as composed after Ezekiel's day. The sequence of events had analogies in later writings and did not fit into the prophet's plan for the future. In fact, Cooke saw the two chapters as undermining the whole tenor of Ezekiel's message in this period. He noted that no collapse of Babylon was mentioned in the book and he considered with Ewald that the absence was an indication that the oracles against Gog were a hidden attack on Babylon.[87] For Cooke these chapters could not be attributed to Ezekiel and are better considered a later intrusion into the plan of the book.

In 1943 with the publication of William Irwin's *The Problem of Ezekiel: an Inductive Study*,[88] the questioning of the text's unity reached its apogée. Irwin's position had not changed much from his review of Harford's book[89] on Ezekiel in 1936 where he says:

[86] Cooke, *A Critical and Exegetical Commentary*, V-VI, XX, XXIII-XXIV.
[87] Cooke, *A Critical and Exegetical Commentary*, XIX, 407–8.
[88] William A. Irwin, *The Problem of Ezekiel: An Inductive Study* (Chicago: University of Chicago Press, 1943).
[89] John Battersby Harford, *Studies in the Book of Ezekiel* (Cambridge: Cambridge University Press, 1935).

The book cannot be restricted to any two writers; in chapter after chapter it can easily be demonstrated that we deal with not two but three or even four whose views are pyramided in a series of comments upon comments. And there are sections that have no relations to any of these authors nor to one another . . . there is at least one important passage in the book that is demonstrably Maccabean. Moreover, we are not yet in a position to decide that the original kernel of the book was written in Palestine; that it seems primarily concerned with Palestine and Judea is too slight basis for rejecting the older view which saw herein the utterances of a homesick exile.[90]

In the 1943 text, he developed criteria based on a discrepancy which he found in chapter 15 between verses 1–5, a parable, and 6–8, its interpretation.[91] Proceeding from this conclusion, he was able to distinguish the 251 genuine verses in Ezekiel from among the 1273 verses in the book. Concurring with Hölscher, Irwin essentially limits the genuine material of the book to its poetic passages.[92] All of chapters 40–48 were in no way original to Ezekiel. He saw Ezekiel himself as active in Jerusalem from the days of Jehoiakim and continuing in his prophetic role after being taken into exile in 587.[93]

Regarding chapters 38–39, Irwin sees 38:1–4a as original to the oracle and considers the rest a late eschatological intrusion into the book.[94] He notes that the oracle against Gog, 38:1–4a, seems to reflect Babylonian life at the time, and this would support Irwin's theory that the prophet went into exile in 587.[95] Like others before him, Irwin focuses not on the unity of the text, but on its disunity, and this scholarly perspective consistently carries over into his exegesis of chapters 38–39, including its internal unity.

Reviewing the findings of this second phase in the modern study of Ezekiel, it is extremely different from the first phase's treatment of chapters 38–39 in relation to the book. Of the twelve scholars reviewed, three (Kraetzschmar, Hölscher and Torrey) spoke of unified literary

---

[90] William Irwin, "Harford, John Battersby, Studies in the Book of Ezekiel," *JR* 16 (1936) 209–10.
[91] Irwin, *The Problem of Ezekiel*, 33–36.
[92] Irwin, *The Problem of Ezekiel*, 283–86, 304.
[93] Irwin, *The Problem of Ezekiel*, 258, 322.
[94] Irwin, *The Problem of Ezekiel*, 172, 176.
[95] Irwin, *The Problem of Ezekiel*, 330.

work in the final form, but they did not present a case supporting that view, at least in regard to chapters 38–39. Kraetzschmar does not present chapters 38–39 as linked to the rest of the book. Hölscher suggests unity but critiques the text in a way that undermines his initial premise and affirmation of cohesiveness. Using either of Torrey's unifying themes, neither writer nor redactor successfully integrate the Gog pericope into the final unity. Seven commentators (Winckler, Gressmann, Berry, Smith, Bertholet, Cooke, Irwin) see chapters 38–39 as separated thematically from what precedes and follows them. Winckler describes the two chapters as a later appendage. Gressmann sees a clear break between Ezekiel 38–39 and what precedes them and dates both recensions of these two chapters to the post-exilic period. Berry also situates chapters 38–39 in a later time and does not credit the redactor with having presented their inclusion as a unified part of the whole. Smith does not present chapters 38–39 as a part of an integral work. Bertholet, in this period, treats chapters 38–39 as a unit separate from what precedes it. Cooke considers the two chapters to be a later intrusion and Irwin would say the same of all but 38:1–4a. Two writers, Herrmann and Herntrich, would characterize the book as an anthology of Ezekiel's writings which the prophet mostly put together and supplemented. For both scholars, chapters 38–39 were clearly not related to what preceded them. The third phase, even with efforts at moderation largely continues this approach.

Third Phase: From 1950 to the Present

While Umberto Cassuto would fit chronologically in the previous period, the thrust of his 1946 writing "The Arrangement of the Book of Ezekiel"[96] marks him more as an independent exception for this third period. It was Cassuto's contention that principles governing the organization of material in Eastern literature are not those underlying European notions of organization. He proposes that the method used for the organization of Ezekiel, one esteemed as an aid to memorization, arranged sections of the book on the basis of the association of ideas and words. Two verses show an associative connection between

---

[96] Umberto Cassuto, "The Arrangement of the Book of Ezekiel," in *Biblical and Oriental Studies, Vol 1: Bible* (trans. Israel Abrahams; Jerusalem: Magnes, 1973) 227–40.

the Gog pericope and what precedes it: "Behold, I will take the children of Israel from the nations among which they have gone, and will gather them" (37:21) and "that is gathered out of many people" (38:8).[97] For Cassuto, after the three main parts of the book were set up, the material within each of the three parts was placed to provide a mnemonic device for the memorizing of the text. This was the basis for giving the text its final form.

C. G. Howie's dissertation directed by W. F. Albright was published in 1950 under the title, *The Date and Composition of the Book of Ezekiel*.[98] As befits the influence of his director, Howie's conclusions were influenced by the findings of archeology with a strong preference for the traditional view. He attributed a greater part of the work to Ezekiel, prophesying in Babylon at the time specified in the book, but only chapters 1–32 were composed by Ezekiel, according to Howie. After the prophet's death, a disciple made a collection of his teachings. He began with these thirty-two chapters and then gathered other material from records and memory. He made chapter 33 into a literary link between what Ezekiel had written down and other independent material to which he then attached chapters 40–48, a well-known vision of the prophet.[99] For Howie, chapters 38–39 were independent material written by Ezekiel but gathered and appended, among other independent writings, by a disciple after the death of the prophet. My own study supports Howie's assessment of chapter 33 as a literary link, yet he seems to leave unexplained much textual and thematic evidence that would point to the literary cohesiveness of chapters 34 through 48. This present work asks if such evidence can be excluded from the discussion.

In 1952 Georg Fohrer submitted his *Habilitation* thesis, *Die Hauptprobleme des Buches Ezechiel*,[100] which includes his discussion of the book's unity. This was followed in 1955 with a commentary[101] on Ezekiel, replacing Bertholet's 1936 volume in the HAT series. Fohrer's

---

[97] Cassuto, "The Arrangement of the Book of Ezekiel," 228, 239.

[98] Carl G. Howie, *The Date and the Composition of the Book of Ezekiel* (SBLMS 4; Philadelphia: SBL, 1950).

[99] Howie, *The Date and the Composition*, 100–102.

[100] Georg Fohrer, *Die Hauptprobleme des Buches Ezechiel* (BZAW 72; Berlin: Alfred Töpelman, 1952).

[101] Georg Fohrer and Kurt Galling, *Ezechiel* (HAT 13; Tübingen: Mohr, 1955).

main focus in his commentary was the identification of secondary (non-Ezekielian) matter and the process of the book's compilation. In Fohrer's view, the book was the product of an editor, who collected Ezekiel's oracles after his death. The prophet himself wrote down his sayings which had been spoken, but he left them without arrangement by date or subject matter. Later an editor or editors built up the basic form of the book. Fohrer states clearly that he disagrees with the contention that the book is a unified literary work. For him it is a chronologically arranged collection.[102] Consistent with this position, Fohrer also argues that the placement of chapters 38–39 in the text resulted from a chronological grouping with other future restoration materials produced by later hands.[103] Their location in the book, for him, is not the result of the theological or literary development of the book. The discussion in the following chapters locates the basis for their placement in a cohesive literary pattern rooted in the religious myths of ancient Israel.

In 1953, Theodore Vriezen published his article "Prophecy and Eschatology."[104] For Vriezen the book of Ezekiel was brought together thematically by the theological schema of a totally inward and foundational renewal of the people of Israel. For him Ezekiel's theology focused on a most profound life of the spirit.[105] He sees chapters 38–39 as a later addition, alien to this unifying theme of a call to inner renewal. While he sees the book as unified, he views the Gog pericope as a discordant section later added by the final redactor. More recently scholars see the "Vision of the Dry Bones" in chapter 37 as a prophecy of national restoration, challenging Vriezen's conclusion that inner renewal is the unifying thematic. It would also suggest caution in

---

[102] He determined the compositional process to be the following: first the writings were placed together in view of similar content, i.e. ecstatic experiences, symbolic actions, catchwords. This formed eight collections as the basic core of the book. Remaining collections and single sections were inserted later based on considerations of chronology or similar content. A final transposition was brought about by moving the threats directed against the foreign nations from the end to the middle of the book, giving the four sections of the book, as Fohrer (*Ezechiel*, XI; *Die Hauptprobleme*, 48) would see them, in their present form.

[103] Fohrer, *Die Hauptprobleme*, 196.

[104] Theodore C. Vriezen, "Prophecy and Eschatology," in *Congress Volume, Copenhagen 1953* (VTSup 1; ed. G. W. Anderson, et. al.; Leiden: Brill, 1953) 199–229.

[105] Vriezen, "Prophecy and Eschatology," 216.

accepting Vriezen's arguments that chapters 38–39 are alien to what precedes them.

In 1956 Konrad von Rabenau published his "Die Entstehung des Buches Ezechiel in formgeschichtlicher Sicht."[106] In this form critical analysis of Ezekiel he addresses the issue of the unity/discordancy of the text, in particular the principle that shaped the construction of the text. Von Rabenau sees the unifying principle of the book, its distinguishing mark, centered around three literary structures: (1) the five visions; (2) the phrase "The Word of the Lord came to me saying" used forty-five times and (3) the sixteen times the prophet is addressed as "Son of Man." Von Rabenau uses these three features to separate the original composition from expansions.[107] While he does not consider the book to be an assemblage of independent collections, he also does not consider the book to be a unified literary work.

For von Rabenau, the only original composition in chapters 38–39 is 39:1–5. The remainder, except for two parts which he considers later additions by the original author, are for him gross distortions of the author's thought processes. He also states that later editors inserted related sayings which were originally unconnected. They do not fit their placement in the pericope, nor do they fit in their positioning in the book.[108] The Gog pericope for von Rabenau is part of a larger unity only because of the author's use of the recurring phrases (numbers 2 and 3 mentioned above). There is no literary thematic unity for him.

In the same year as von Rabenau's study, Otto Eissfeldt published the second edition of *Einleitung in das Alte Testament*.[109] In his opinion Ezekiel clearly contains a framework of passages deriving from Ezekiel. These most probably would include: (1) two biographical accounts, dated like diary entries which were compiled by Ezekiel himself, one referring to Jerusalem and Israel, and another containing the threats against Tyre and Egypt (1:1–3:15; 3:16a + 4–5; 8–11; 20; 24; 26;

---

[106] Konrad von Rabenau, "Die Entstehung des Buches Ezechiel in formgeschichtlicher Sicht," WZ 4 (1955–56) 659–94.

[107] Von Rabenau, "Die Entstehung des Buches Ezechiel," 680–81.

[108] Von Rabenau, "Die Entstehung des Buches Ezechiel," 676–77, 682.

[109] Otto Eissfeldt, *The Old Testament, An Introduction* (trans. Peter R. Ackroyd; Oxford: Basil Blackwell, 1965); originally published as *Einleitung in das Alte Testament* (3rd ed.; Neue theologische Grundrisse; Tübingen: Mohr, 1964).

29:1–16; 29:17–21; 30:20–26; 31:1–18; 32:1–16; 32:17–32; 33:21–22; 40–48); and (2) speeches and compositions of more general content also couched in biographical style. Eissfeldt does not specify the chapters and verses for this second group of passages, saying that it is not certain whether they are isolated passages, smaller or larger collections, in large number or of rare occurrence.[110]

Eissfeldt posits that these two sources of Ezekielian material were most probably combined by an editor, not by Ezekiel. He hesitates to say whether this happened before or after their expansion with undated passages. The compilation received various expansions by later hands, and these expansions, as in other prophetic books, particularly affected the threats against foreign nations and the promises for the people itself. This is particularly true of the Gog pericope which was much elaborated, though it was not entirely secondary. What is genuine Ezekielian material and what is not? Eissfeldt acknowledges that it is difficult to say, due first to the ability of editors to assimilate the characteristics of Ezekiel's style, and second because of the possibility that the core of genuine material was reworked so much, changing it almost beyond recognition.[111] Eissfeldt's concern is not the thematic unity of the text. Given his respect for editorial skill in assimilating characteristics of Ezekiel's style, he could possibly believe in thematic unity but he did not discuss it in depth himself.

In 1965–1966 Walther Eichrodt published his *Der Prophet Hesekiel*.[112] He sees in the book three collections of material by Ezekiel. This entire body of material is supplemented by this first redactor and others. For Eichrodt, the book clearly betrays much evidence of this subsequent elaboration, though he still considers the unique and characteristic style of the parts composed by Ezekiel to be so strong and dominant that this is the decisive factor determining the whole.[113]

---

[110] Eissfeldt, *Einleitung in das Alte Testament*, 380–81.
[111] Eissfeldt, *Einleitung in das Alte Testament*, 380–81.
[112] Walther Eichrodt, *Ezekiel, A Commentary* (trans. Cosslett Quin; OTL; Philadelphia: Westminster, 1970); originally published as *Der Prophet Hesekiel: übersetzt und erklärt* (ATD 22; Göttingen: Vandenhoeck & Ruprecht, 1965 –1966).
[113] One collection contains the oracles against the foreign nations in chapters 26–32. The second, derived from the first person reports of the prophet, contains his prophecies concerning Jerusalem and Judah. The third is a series of individual writings of the prophet which were put together and inserted by a redactor when he brought together the first two documents. Eichrodt, *Ezekiel, A Commentary*, 18, 21.

While Eichrodt considers chapters 38–39 to be generally well-preserved text, he also sees them as among the most difficult to interpret in the book. Finding no unity of conception he views the Gog pericope as a series of individual visions, impossible to combine with one another into an organic picture. He says that one could be tempted to consider 39:1–8 as an original prophecy but he clearly resists this view. For him both chapters are the completely independent work of redactors, written after the return from exile to deal with the agonizing problem of acknowledging the sovereignty of Yhwh while his people suffered diminished political circumstances.[114]

Eichrodt was the first scholar, since the first phase of the study of Ezekiel, to deal directly with the issue of the placement of chapters 38–39 in the book's final form. For Eichrodt they are an insertion contrary to the prophet's intentions, a disruption of the link between 37:28 and 40ff. The salvation of the new Israel which was described in chapters 34–37 is fittingly brought to its conclusion for him by the establishment of the new temple and the transformation of the land in chapter 40ff. In Eichrodt's opinion there would be no need to assert once again the superiority of Israel's God as is done in chapters 38–39, unless historically the final form answered the burning question for a generation sometime after the return from exile: why, after Yhwh had freed his people from captivity, did he not at the same time assert his dominion over the nations? The future victory of Yhwh in the Gog pericope provided an answer to this question. Looking for a place to insert the prophecy, the editor(s) of the final form placed it before the description of the new Temple and the new land.[115] Eichrodt's solution presupposes that the purpose for chapters 38–39 is to show Yhwh's superiority and dominion over the nations and that their insertion after chapter 37 is rather arbitrary. Can these be so easily assumed? He leaves unexplored the ramifications of the promised "Covenant of Peace" mentioned in 37:26, which forms part of the prophecy that sets Yhwh's sanctuary in Israel's midst in 37:26–28. How is that first part of the promise fulfilled and with what do the three verses form a link? This present work seeks to provide answers to these questions.

John Wevers published his commentary *Ezekiel*[116] in 1969. He starts his introduction to the commentary with a comment similar to Driver

---

[114] Eichrodt, *Ezekiel, A Commentary*, 519, 521.
[115] Eichrodt, *Ezekiel, A Commentary*, 519–20.
[116] John W. Wevers, *Ezekiel* (NCBC; London: Thomas Nelson & Sons, 1969).

that more than any other book in the canon of the Latter Prophets, the Book of Ezekiel shows evidence of intentional arrangement and a single editorial mind. Yet when he discusses chapters 38–39 in relation to the whole book, he departs from his initial assessment in noting that these chapters are more problematic than other sections. In fact, in chapters 33 to 39 he states that no clear principle of arrangement can be fully outlined. It was because of the many expansions which were eschatological in nature that the editor placed these two chapters at the end of the restoration section.[117] I agree with Wevers that these chapters were placed correctly in the restoration section. The study below presents a principle of arrangement based in Israel's reinterpretation of its creation myth after the devastating effects of the fall of Jerusalem and the Exile.

We close the decade of the 1960s with the publication of Walther Zimmerli's two-volume commentary, *Ezechiel*.[118] Zimmerli shows Ezekiel's interaction with a great deal of mythological, legendary and literary material. He identifies three stages in the composition of the book: (1) an oral delivery stage by the prophet; (2) Ezekiel's fixing his preaching in writing; and (3) a number of further phases of redaction and addition, the earlier ones attributable to the prophet himself, the later ones to a school of redactors. In this last stage original texts were reworked both by Ezekiel and his followers so that the earlier text could address the concerns of the later period. Zimmerli detects no indication of Persia's rise in the region or the return of the exiles in the book. As a consequence, he suggests about a thirty-year period when Ezekiel's disciples could work from Ezekiel's last prophecy to the defeat of Babylon by Cyrus. Zimmerli believes that the material written in this thirty-year period provides genuine access to the thinking of the prophet.[119]

---

[117] Wevers, *Ezekiel*, 1, 5.

[118] Walther Zimmerli, *Ezekiel I: A Commentary on the Book of the Prophet Ezekiel, Chapters 1–24* (trans. R. E. Clements; Hermeneia; Philadelphia: Fortress, 1979); originally published as *Ezechiel I* (BKAT 13/1; Neukirchen-Vluyn: Neukirchener Verlag, 1969); Walther Zimmerli, *Ezekiel II: A Commentary on the Book of the Prophet Ezekiel, Chapters 25 - 48* (trans. James D. Martin; Hermeneia ; Philadelphia: Fortress, 1983); originally published as *Ezechiel II* (BKAT 13/2; Neukirchen-Vluyn: Neukirchener Verlag, 1969).

[119] Zimmerli, *Ezekiel* 1.25, 41–42, 68, 70–71; Walther Zimmerli, "The Special Form and Traditio-Historical Character of Ezekiel's Prophecy," *VT* 15 (1965) 515, 527.

In his analysis of chapters 38–39, Zimmerli identified three independent units which constituted the original, three-strophe oracle characterized by direct address and elevated prose: 38:1–9 (minus later expansions), 39:2–5, 17–20. Zimmerli described the expansions as continuing theological reflection among Ezekiel's disciples, stating that the redaction of the Gog pericope strengthened the apocalyptic features of the prophet's preaching. He also noted that the expansions reflected the further cumbersome development of the text. In his comment on chapters 38–39, he attributes their ordering to Ezekiel, not the final form; for the prophet, the judgment of the enemy peoples in these chapters is not incorporated into the description of ultimate salvation in chapters 34–37 and chapters 40–48. Zimmerli goes on to state that, in the mind of Ezekiel, the sequence of the sixteen chapters is not to be systematized in terms of temporal sequence like the later apocalyptic development of the Gog prophecy.[120] Yet, are chapters 38–39 written as a judgment of enemy peoples as Zimmerli suggests? It is clear from Ezek 38:4 that Yhwh brought this army against Israel. Could Yhwh have done that for judgment against them or does their mustering, march and annihilation serve another purpose in the final form?

Jörg Garscha continued the task of reconstructing the redactional history of the book with the publication of his *Studien zum Ezechielbuch: Eine redaktionskritische Untersuchung von 1–39*[121] in 1974. According to Garscha only about 21 verses (parts of 1:1, 3; and parts of 17:1–10 and 23:2–25) derive from the prophet. The book's structure comes from an author working in the first half of the fifth century. Working in the first half of the fourth century, a redactor allowed his contribution to be colored by bitterness against those who were not taken into exile. He also set up the dating formulas and added the various versions of the "Recognition Formula": "And you (sg./pl.)/they shall know that I am Yhwh." The "sakralrechtlich" redaction took place at the end of the fourth century. Other parts were added during the third century and the work was completed by the end of the same century.[122]

---

[120] Zimmerli, *Ezekiel*, 1.70, 2. 296–98, 304, 310.

[121] Jörg Garscha, *Studien zum Ezechielbuch: Eine redaktionskritische Untersuchung von 1–39* (EHS 23.23; Bern: Herbert Lang, 1974).

[122] Garscha, *Studien zum Ezechielbuch*, 284–85, 287, 308, 310–11.

In the Gog pericope Garscha determined the same threefold structure as Zimmerli: three original "strophes" (38:1.9a, 39:1-5, 17-20). Written by the first redactor in the early fifth century, these were amplified with further material by Deutero-Ezekiel and redactors in the second century. For Garscha, a fundamental process which gives rise to themes is the reflection on future events by forming analogies with the past. The Gog pericope for him is a reflection on the earlier victory of Nebuchadnezzar, but this time with the reverse result.[123] I agree with Garscha's conclusion here that the Gog pericope is a replay of Nebuchadnezzar's earlier victory, but the second victory is more universal and permanent in scope, as determined by Yhwh's will. The present study will ask if both earlier and later victories should not be understood primarily as statements of Yhwh's disposition toward his people, not Yhwh's disposition toward Israel's enemies.

Michael Astour published his "Ezekiel's Prophecy of Gog and the Cuthean Legend of Naram-Sin"[124] in 1976. Cutha was a city 20 miles north-east of Babylon mentioned in a Naram-Sin inscription. At the fall of the northern kingdom when the Samaritans were deported to Assyria, the inhabitants of Cutha were settled in Samaria.[125] In his article Astour proposes that Ezekiel's source for the Gog pericope was the Cuthean Legend of Naram-Sin which the prophet would have known in Babylon during the exile. In one sentence in the article Astour asserts that as a dramatic climax chapters 38-39 quite naturally link with the preceding chapters. He does not, however, give any reasons for this part of his proposal, nor does he develop the point any further. It is not, in fact, the point of his article. Such a link will be, in part, the focus of this present work.

In 1977 Reuben Ahroni published "The Gog Prophecy and the Book of Ezekiel."[126] Ahroni argues that the entire text is a late, post-exilic insertion into the book. Interestingly, and in contrast with those who

---

[123] Garscha, *Studien zum Ezechielbuch*, 293, 303, 308.

[124] Michael C. Astour, "Ezekiel's Prophecy of Gog and the Cuthean Legend of Naram-Sin," *JBL* 95 (1976) 567-79.

[125] Alasdair Livingstone, "Nergal," in *Dictionary of Deities and Demons in the Bible* (ed. Karel van der Toorn, Bob Becking, Pieter W. van der Horst; 2d ed.; Leiden: Brill, 1999) 621.

[126] Reuben Ahroni, "The Gog Prophecy and the Book of Ezekiel," *HAR* 1 (1977) 1-27.

immediately preceded him, he does see the Gog Prophecy as a literary work possessing an essential unity and marked by common linguistic features, except for 39:25–29.[127] In fact, he sees the Prophecy as "an independent and self-contained entity which differs widely from the rest of the book of Ezekiel in content, form, mood and literary genre. The Prophecy is not only alien to the style and train of thought of the book, but also clearly interrupts the sequence and consistent chronological scheme of chapters 1–37 and 40–48."[128] This current work asks if, for a consistent chronological schema, chapters 40–48 could take place before what is accomplished in chapters 38–39? Based in the myths of Israel and the ancient Near East, the Book of Ezekiel would ask if the palace could be built before the decisive battle. This is developed more fully in chapter five below.

In the same year, Frank Hossfeld published *Untersuchungen zu Komposition und Theologie des Ezechielbuches*.[129] Similar to Garscha, Hossfeld focuses on the redactional history of Ezekiel. With Garscha and others he agrees that the original sixth century core of the book had been subjected to expansion over a considerable period and through a multitude of stages. Hossfeld sees six redactional strata and in his final comments characterizes Ezekiel as a "Book of Transitions." Hossfeld's book itself was not a commentary on the entire book.[130] His study focused on particular sections of Ezekiel, and it does not deal with thematic unity in the overall work.

Hossfeld determined the original oracle of the Gog pericope to be 38:1–3a and 39:1b–5. In a structural comparison of the original oracle within the Book of Ezekiel, he found great similarity between it and several oracles against the foreign nations. He notes that it is the classic example of a text that was further elaborated toward an eschatological understanding of itself. Hossfeld saw the reworking of the oracle as a response to the problem of unfulfilled prophecy. It was in fact the separation of the oracle from its original historical meanings which made the expansions possible. Though he focuses on the redactional layers in an effort to determine the original text of the prophet,

---

[127] Ahroni, "The Gog Prophecy," 5, 8.

[128] Ahroni, "The Gog Prophecy," 2.

[129] Frank Hossfeld, *Untersuchungen zu Komposition und Theologie des Ezechielbuches* (FB 20; Würzburg: Echter, 1977).

[130] Hossfeld, *Untersuchungen*, 9, 525–28.

unlike Garscha he does discuss the relationship of chapters 38–39 to what precedes and follows them. He sees them in stark contrast to both what precedes them and what follows them.[131] In the 1998 *Einleitung in das Alte Testament* of Erich Zenger, Hossfeld writes the chapter on the Book of Ezekiel and repeats his position: the Gog pericope breaks the connection between chapter 37 and 40–48. It speaks of the distant future and must be linked back into the context by 39:23–29.[132] While there are thematic similarities between the Gog pericope and the Oracles against the Nations, I disagree with Hossfeld in his seeing the former as an eschatological elaboration of the latter. As mentioned above in the discussion of Johannes Herrmann, the questions to be asked are the function each section serves and the role myth plays in identifying them. This will be examined more fully in chapter five below.

At the end of the decade, Paul Hanson published the second revised edition of his *The Dawn of Apocalyptic*.[133] While he does not look at the book as a whole, he does comment on chapters 38–39. He views them as later attempts at re-interpretation of Ezekiel 1–37 and 40–48. Yet this reconstruction involves a misreading of the pericope itself. Hanson sees redactors, a post-exilic circle, asking why the promises of the prophets have not been fulfilled and judging the reasons to be the people's need of further purification from the evil remaining in the land, hence the threatened destruction by the enemy from the north. More recently Hanson repeats this assertion of the dissonant nature of these chapters: "How rudely this triumphant movement is interrupted by chapters 38–39! They scream out that the glorious age would not unfold as originally pictured by the prophet. Affliction and devastation lay ahead that would outstrip in magnitude and horror anything previously experienced by the people."[134] I disagree with Hanson's interpre-

---

[131] Hossfeld, *Untersuchungen*, 405, 494, 496–97, 500–501.

[132] Frank Hossfeld, "Das Buch Ezechiel," in *Einleitung in das Alte Testament* (ed. Erich Zenger; 3d ed.; Kohlhammer-Studienbücher Theologie 1; Stuttgart: Kohlhammer, 1998) 453.

[133] Paul D. Hanson, *The Dawn of Apocalyptic, the Historical and Sociological Roots of Jewish Apocalyptic Eschatology* (rev. ed.; Philadelphia: Fortress, 1979).

[134] Paul Hanson, *The People Called: the Growth of Community in the Bible* (San Francisco: Harper & Row, 1986) 269. See also Paul Hanson, *Old Testament Apocalyptic* (Interpreting Biblical Texts; Nashville: Abingdon, 1987) 37.

tation that, for Ezekiel, further purification is needed for Israel. Does Yhwh's role in the battle, Israel's function as observer and the decisiveness of the victory demonstrate a need to further purify the people? The purpose of the two chapters must come from another motivation.

In the same year Brevard Childs published his *Introduction to the Old Testament as Scripture*, with Chapter Nineteen devoted to Ezekiel.[135] Distancing himself from the historical-critical method of exegesis, he proposes a new point of departure for the study of the OT, the canonical form of the text. The impact of Child's book on the biblical community is clear from the entire issue of JSOT with seven reviews of the work and a response from Childs.[136] In discussing the canonical shaping of Ezekiel he briefly touches on the placement of chapters 38–39. He notes that, in the final form of the book, they were separated from the Oracles against the Nations. In the Gog pericope these nations are now attacking a restored and forgiven Jerusalem.[137] While he attributes the placement to an expression of eschatological hope in the divine destruction of the enemy, he sees the Gog pericope as a final destruction of the historical enemies of the people of Israel. As noted above, such a conclusion is not clearly supported from the text and suggests that the final form is about writing political history rather than theology. Does the text manifest more political resolution or religious mythic covenant fulfillment? My research suggests the latter, not the former, as will be presented below.

Bernhard Lang published *Ezechiel: Der Prophet und das Buch* in 1981.[138] Working with the literary style and historical setting of the book as a whole, he finds a greater unity of viewpoint than do the scholars we have viewed thus far. In his writings he describes his position as similar to Zimmerli: any additions are a natural part of a redaction process which includes the prophet's own work as well as a school of Ezekiel's disciples.[139] That starting point contrasts with his discus-

---

[135] Brevard S. Childs, *Introduction to the Old Testament as Scripture* (Philadelphia: Fortress, 1979) 355–72.

[136] *JSOT* 16 (1980) with reviews by Bonnie Kittel, James Barr, Joseph Blenkinsopp, Henri Cazelles, George Landes, Roland Murphy, and Rudolf Smend.

[137] Childs, *Introduction to the Old Testament*, 366–67.

[138] Bernhard Lang, *Ezechiel: Der Prophet und das Buch* (ErFor 153; Darmstadt: Wissenschafliche Buchgesellschaft, 1981).

[139] Bernhard Lang, *Kein Aufstand in Jerusalem: Die Politik des Propheten Ezechiel* (2nd ed.; SBB; Stuttgart: Katholisches Bibelwerk, 1978) 126–27.

sion of chapters 38–39 which he considers to be a part of the Oracles against the Foreign Nations in chapters 25–32 and 35, even if they must be treated as a special case with many unresolved puzzles. He hypothesizes with Zimmerli that the pericope represents a cryptic word announcing a future invasion by Babylon in which a very different ending results than the first encounter in the early sixth century; this time there is a total defeat and annihilation of Israel's enemy. In that context, he considers it odd that this event which will happen at the end of years (38:8) would take place in the context of the Restoration spoken of in chapters 34–37 and 40–48.[140] Lang, despite his belief in the overall unity of the book, does not present persuasive reasons for the placement of the Gog pericope in its present location. By grouping the oracles in chapters 38–39 together with 25–32 and 35, he overlooks the possible distinct purposes of each in the final form.

The year after Lang published his work, Joachim Becker revived a position which seemed definitely to have been abandoned. In a Festschrift for Josef Schreiner in 1982 Becker stated that he considered the book to be a total pseudepigraph composed in the fifth century B.C.E.[141] In his work he does touch on the thematic unity of chapters 34–48. He sees the material within these chapters as sorted out thematically, but he discusses no thematic inter-relation between the chapters.[142] In an earlier work he does address the question of thematic inter-relation of chapters 38–39 with what precedes and what follows. He says that it is a question which does not have a place in a prophetic proclamation of salvation. Such proclamations do not perfectly integrate the accounts in their succession.[143] In Becker's mind the author of the pseudepigraph Ezekiel was not trying to create a unified literary work.

No review of literature on Ezekiel would be complete without mentioning Moshe Greenberg who differs sharply from exegetes like Zim-

---

[140] Lang, *Ezechiel*, 106, 111–12.

[141] Joachim Becker, "Erwägungen zur ezechielischen Frage," in *Künder des Wortes: Beiträge zur Theologie der Propheten* (ed. Lothar Ruppert, Peter Weimar, Erich Zenger; Würzburg: Echter, 1982) 138.

[142] Becker, "Erwägungen zur ezechielischen Frage," 141.

[143] Joachim Becker, *Ezechiele-Daniele* (trans. Gianni Poletti; Assisi: Cittadella Editrice, 1989) 141–42; originally published as *Der priesterliche Prophet, Das Buch Ezechiel* (SKKAT 12; Stuttgart: Katholisches Bibelwerk, 1971).

merli in that he seeks to make sense of the book, textually and structurally, as received in the MT rather than the LXX. Greenberg describes his approach as "holistic"[144] and regards the literary criteria used by exegetes like Garscha and Hossfeld as "simply *a priori*, an array of unproved modern assumptions and conventions that confirm themselves through the results obtained by forcing them on the text and altering, reducing, and reordering it accordingly."[145] Stressing the need to respect the literary integrity of the book, he argues that much of the work of revision and re-application was carried out by Ezekiel himself.[146] The third volume of Greenberg's commentary on Ezekiel in the Anchor Bible Series, covering chapters 38–48, has not yet been published. There, possibly, he will put into print his thoughts on the relationship of chapters 38–39 to the overall text.

In 1984 Aelred Cody published his commentary *Ezekiel*.[147] In his introduction he notes that the Book of Ezekiel has an orderly structure due to its editorial process which makes it fairly easy to distinguish the parts, each with their own characteristics. He also comments on the conceptual homogeneity of the book, to which the additions were made in such a way that the ideas of the basic text were developed and expanded by them. In his discussion on the Gog pericope, however, he does not seem to have resolved the relationship of chapters 38–39 to the overall text. For him, these chapters are unexpected, disconcerting, and chronologically out of place between what precedes and what follows. He asks about the placement of chapters 38–39 here. He notes that the lack of focus in the account would be more in place in a later time period. Dealing with the distant future as they do, why are they not placed after chapters 40–48? He closes his commentary on these two chapters noting that 39:25–29 form a natural link between the end of chapter 37 and the beginning of chapter 40.[148] In his own scholarly reflection, he appears unconvinced that chapters 38–39 were placed in

---

[144] For a full-development of Greenburg's holistic approach see "What are Valid Criteria for Determining Inauthentic Matter in Ezekiel?"in *Ezekiel and His Book* (ed. Johan Lust; BETL 74; Leuven: Leuven University Press, 1986) 123–35.

[145] Moshe Greenberg, *Ezekiel 1–20* (AB 22; New York: Doubleday & Co., 1983) 20.

[146] Greenberg, *Ezekiel 1–20*, 21.

[147] Aelred Cody, *Ezekiel with an Excursus on Old Testament Priesthood* (OTM 11; Wilmington, DE: Glazier, 1984).

[148] Cody, *Ezekiel*, 11, 13, 183–84, 189–90.

the book as part of a unified literary work. This present study asks if investigation of the final form's mythic frame of reference would not provide the unifying threads making chapters 38–39 integral to the overall work rather than the unexpected, disconcerting anachronism Cody describes.

Marco Nobile approaches the text from a starting point similar to Greenberg and Lang who see more unity than disunity in the book. Though he acknowledges redaction he is convinced of the unity of the final form, and speaks well of the benefits of synchronic exegesis of Ezekiel. Among recent authors, his hypothesis deals most directly with the focus of this work and so we will give it a fuller treatment. The extract of his doctoral dissertation[149] at the Biblicum, a 1986 article[150] he published in the BETL series *Ezekiel and His Book*, his *Introduzione all'Antico Testamento*,[151] and *Teologia dell'Antico Testamento*[152] show his position over sixteen years consistently maintaining the tripartite schema.

This tripartite liturgical literary schema, as constructed from his more recent 1995 *Introduzione all'Antico Testamento* and his 1998 *Teologia dell'Antico Testamento*, consists of: (1) theophany and introductory transition (chapters 1–3);[153] (2) combat against the enemies of Yhwh, including both Israel/Judah and the foreign nations, whose conquest forms the foundation for the erection of the Temple (chapters 4–32, 38–39);[154] and (3) erection of the Temple and establishment of the cult which includes a vision of the new creation and a future restoration/reestablishment of the twelve tribes of Israel in an ideal land (chapters 40–48).[155]

---

[149] Marco Nobile, *Una lettura simbolico-strutturalistica di Ezechiele* (Rome: Pontificio Istituto Biblico, 1982).

[150] Marco Nobile, "Beziehung zwischen Ezek. 32, 17–32 und der Gog-Perikope (Ezek. 38–39) im Lichte der Endredaktion," in *Ezekiel and His Book* (ed. Johan Lust; BETL 74; Leuven: Leuven University Press, 1986) 255–59.

[151] Marco Nobile, *Introduzione all'Antico Testamento* (Epifania della Parola Ns 5; Bologna: Edizioni Dehoniane, 1995).

[152] Marco Nobile, *Teologia dell'Antico Testamento* (LOGOS, Corso di Studi Biblici 8/1; Torino: Editrice Elle Di Ci, 1998).

[153] Nobile, *Introduzione all'Antico Testamento*, 103.

[154] Nobile, *Teologia dell'Antico Testamento*, 135.

[155] Nobile, *Introduzione all'Antico Testamento*, 103–4.

Nobile posits that the Gog pericope is a radicalization of the fight between God and the nations in chapters 25–32.[156] In this liturgical-literary schema chapters 38–39 constitute both a well-constructed preface to chapters 40–48, and a continuation and climax of chapters 25–32.[157] Chapters 40–48 are presented as an absolute future which would orient and organize human contingency and would call forth faith in a future realization allowing for the free intervention of God.[158] Chapters 38–39 are presented as the first of two complementary aspects of the same reality[159] and the events which these chapters present must take place before this absolute future of 40–48 can be realized.

With his primary focus on the re-establishment of the cult on Mt. Zion as the purpose of the book's final form, it is not clear how Nobile integrates the non-liturgical societal elements of these last nine chapters (chapters 40–48) into a cultual schema. In fact, he extends the purpose of the schema by referring to it as a true constitutional project.[160] Do the societal and liturgical/cultual agenda become one in the end? The specifics of the shift are not discussed. Cult and liturgy, the unifying schema of the final form, are not synonymous with civil government even if the government is a hierocracy.

While Nobile consistently re-affirms the literary unity of Ezekiel in its final form,[161] his tripartite schema leaves a very important section of the book (chapters 33–37) not clearly enough integrated into his explanation of the schema's unifying power for his case to be convincing.[162] We agree with his understanding that chapters 40–48 and 38–39 constitute a literary diptych whose parts are complementary expres-

---

[156] Nobile, "Beziehung zwischen Ezek. 32, 17–32 und der Gog-Perikope," 257–58; Marco Nobile, "Ez 38–39 ed Ez 40–48: i due aspetti complementari del culmine di uno schema cultuale di fondazione," *Anton* 62 (1987) 149.

[157] Nobile "Beziehung zwischen Ezek. 32, 17–32 und der Gog-Perikope," 255, 257.

[158] Nobile, *Una lettura simbolico-strutturalistica*, 144.

[159] Nobile, "Ez 38–39 ed Ez 40–48: i due aspetti complementari,"143.

[160] Nobile, *Introduzione all'Antico Testamento*, 103.

[161] Nobile, *Una lettura simbolico-strutturalistica*, 141; Nobile, "Beziehung zwischen Ezek. 32, 17–32 und der Gog-Perikope," 255; Nobile, *Introduzione all'Antico Testamento*, 101; Nobile, *Teologia dell'Antico Testamento*, 134.

[162] The 1984 *Biblica* article by Marco Nobile ("Ez 37, 1–14 come costitutivo di uno schema cultuale," *Bib* 65 [1984] 476–89) interprets the role of this section within the context of chapters 36–48. He does not, however, deal with the role of other sections of the restoration oracles in chapters 34–37 in detail.

sions[163] and necessary for bringing creation to completion, yet the undiscussed aspects of the final form show an undefended omission in his argument.

Not completely discussing the part played by chapters 33–37 in his schema also leaves the function of the Oracle against Edom in chapter 35 unexplained. The functions of the Oracles against the Foreign Nations in chapters 25–32, the Oracle against Edom in chapter 35 and the Gog pericope in chapters 38–39 are significant in understanding the final form of the book. Why are the Oracles in chapters 25–32 situated between the last announcement of the fall of the city and the actual fall of Jerusalem? Why is the Oracle against Edom in the middle of the Oracles of Salvation of Israel? Why is the Gog pericope located after these Oracles of Salvation and not immediately after the Oracles against Egypt? Leaving these questions unaddressed undermines the case for Nobile's tripartite liturgical literary schema.

Geschichtskonzepte im Ezechielbuch by Thomas Krüger,[164] a revised version of his doctoral dissertation presented to the University of Munich in 1986, appeared in 1989. It is a study of the changing conceptions of Israelite history found in Ezekiel. He isolates and discusses two conceptions in Israelite history through exegesis of four key texts, the first three (5:5–17, 16:1–43, 23:1–30) representing the first conception of history and the fourth (20:1–44) representing the second. His discussion of these two conceptions of Israelite history does not address indications of coherence in the overall literary work, particularly since the first conception of history stems from the early part of the prophet's career and the second conception comes after the Fall of Jerusalem in 587.[165] He does speak of the relationship of chapters 38–39 to what precedes and follows them. According to Krüger chapters 34–37 and 40–48 clearly did not originally include chapters 38–39; instead 38–39 are linked to 34–37 as a later reflection on the indestructibility of the restored Israel after the return from exile. The insertion of chapters 38–39 gives the impression that the restoration plan of 40–48 can only take place after Gog's attack and defeat in the latter years.[166] Yet

---

[163] Nobile, "Ez 38–39 ed Ez 40–48: i due aspetti complementari," 167.
[164] Thomas Krüger, *Geschichtskonzepte im Ezechielbuch* (BZAW 180; Berlin: de Gruyter, 1989).
[165] Krüger, *Geschichtskonzepte im Ezechielbuch*, 465–67.
[166] Krüger, *Geschichtskonzepte im Ezechielbuch*, 309–10.

seeing chapters 38–39 as a later reflection of the indestructibility of Israel does not make sense from the text because Yhwh is the only warrior in the battle. Israel does no fighting. The author must have another point.

In 1989 Ellen Davis published *Swallowing the Scroll: Textuality and the Dynamics of Discourse in Ezekiel's Prophecy*,[167] a revision of her Yale Ph.D dissertation. In it she breaks new ground in Ezekiel studies. Taking the position that Ezekiel's prophecies were first written down rather than seeing them as a deposit of orally delivered sayings written down later, she explores the impact of such a dynamic on the prophetic message. Ezekiel was, Davis acknowledges, transitional in that devices from oral prophecy produced a form of speech that could be recognized and assimilated by the audience. But it signaled a turning point in Israelite prophecy, charting a new course from which prophecy would never turn back. By writing prophecy down, prophetic activity shifted from an oral mode of production to prophecy as written record. The written record then assumes an independent existence from the writer. Encounter with the divine word as fixed in the text becomes the main event. Davis sees this shift as determinative for written tradition, developing in the subsequent centuries of Judaism.

Davis makes only brief reference to chapters 38–39. She does not take a position in the discussion on whether or not they form a cohesive part of the final form. She categorizes them as projected future history[168] and does not discuss mythic elements in them.

Joseph Blenkinsopp's commentary on *Ezekiel*[169] was published in 1990. In the introduction he notes both the basic authenticity of the work and his own assessment that the book may be read as a unified and well-rounded composition, independently of the question of authenticity. However when he discusses the Gog pericope, he asserts that the present position of the two chapters is something of a problem. While others have seen 39:25–29 as an editorial link between the end of chapter 37 and the beginning of chapter 40, Blenkinsopp takes a singular position among current scholars in seeing these verses as a

---

[167] Ellen F. Davis, *Swallowing the Scroll: Textuality and the Dynamics of Discourse in Ezekiel's Prophecy* (JSOTSup 78; Bible and Literature Series 21; Sheffield: Almond, 1989).

[168] Davis, *Swallowing the Scroll*, 119, 138.

[169] Joseph Blenkinsopp, *Ezekiel* (Interpretation; Louisville: John Knox, 1990).

prologue to chapters 34–37. Basing himself on a late LXX version found among the J. H. Scheide papyri, second to fourth century A.D., he places chapters 38–39 before the account of Israel's restoration in these four chapters.[170] The format and style of the series do not allow for a fuller development of his position. In a more recent 1996 publication,[171] he describes chapters 38–39 as being "spliced into the book at this point." He is not convinced that they are, in their present placement, integral to the unfolding of the final form.

Prior to the publication of the first part of his commentary on Ezekiel, chapters 1–19, in 1996, Karl-Friedrich Pohlmann published, in 1992, *Ezechielstudien*[172] which presented ten years of scholarly research to the exegetical community and laid the groundwork for the commentary which followed. Using redactional-critical methods, Pohlmann determined that there were at least four redactional layers which did not include the later addition of chapters 40–48. The present shape of the book was dominated by a favorable attitude toward the Golah, those taken to Babylon in 597. According to this redaction, those who went into exile in 587 had no real place in Yhwh's future plans. Included in this redaction were two earlier layers. The fourth layer was composed after the community had had adequate time to reflect on the events of 597. It was written comprehensively in an effort to redirect the message of the book to all who lived in the Diaspora, without giving the Israelites deported in 597 any privileged position. He was not sure what particular parts of the text could be traced to Ezekiel, and is skeptical that one man could have played so many roles.[173]

In relation to chapters 38–39 and their location in the book, Pohlmann does not think their present placement reflects their original position. He would place them more appropriately before chapter 37, introduced by 36:16–23a, bα. He cites their placement in Papyrus 967 which supports his conclusions. He sees chapters 38–39, along with

---

[170] Blenkinsopp, *Ezekiel*, 8, 180.

[171] Joseph Blenkinsopp, *A History of Prophecy in Israel* (rev. and enl. ed.; Louisville: Westminster John Knox, 1996) 178.

[172] Karl-Friedrich Pohlmann, *Ezechielstudien: Zur Redaktionsgeschichte des Buches und zur Frage nach den ältesten Texten* (BZAW 202; Berlin/New York: de Gruyter, 1992); Karl-Friedrich Pohlmann, *Der Prophet Hezekiel/Ezechiel 1–19* (ATD 22.1; Göttingen: Vandenhoeck & Ruprecht, 1996).

[173] Pohlmann, *Ezechielstudien*, 88, 124, 129–31, 217, 252–53.

36:16–23a, bα, as part of the fourth layer of redaction, a message to all who live in the Diaspora. It is the final intervention of Yhwh, showing his power to all the nations. He sees them and chapter 37 as bringing closure to what went before it in the book and as the introduction to chapters 40–48.[174] His redactional method did not lead him to a discussion affirming the literary cohesiveness of the final form of the text. For Pohlmann, chapters 38–39 are misplaced in their present position as they seem more logically linked to 36:16–23a, bα, and disruptive to the dual functions of chapter 37.[175] Pohlmann sees the present placement of chapters 38–39 as more discordant than concordant. Instead, he would re-arrange the text to achieve thematic coherence.

Friedrich Fechter published *Bewältigung der Katastrophe: Untersuchungen zu ausgewählten Fremdvölkersprüchen im Ezechielbuch*[176] in 1992. A study concerning the Oracles/Sayings about the Foreign Nations, his research objective is to learn the nature, purpose, date and relationship to the prophet of a few selected oracles contained within chapters 27–32 of Ezekiel. As such, he does not discuss chapters 38–39.

Leslie Allen published his Word Biblical Commentary, *Ezekiel 20–48*, in 1990 and followed up with *Ezekiel 1–19* in 1994.[177] The commentary primarily presents the book through the prism of its redaction. He describes chapters 38–39 as intervening after 37:25–28 which he considers as a heading for chapters 40–48. He sees the two chapters as an extension of the themes of 34:25–28 where it would have been better inserted, but because that too would be disruptive he sees its present location as its second best placement.[178] For Allen, chapters 38–39 envision a worst case scenario to allay fears of the final outcome if another invasion should take place. The Gog account "checks the security

---

[174] Pohlmann, *Ezekielstudien*, 86, 88, 107, 112, 122, 134.

[175] Pohlmann's chapter on the Book of Ezekiel ("Ezechiel oder das Buch von der Zukunft der Gola und der Heimkehr der Diaspora," in *Grundriß der Einleitung in die kanonischen und deutero-kanonischen Schriften des Alten Testments 2: Die prophetischen Werke* [ed. Otto Kaiser; Mohn: Gütersloher Verlagshaus, 1994] 82–102) makes no revision in these conclusions.

[176] Friedrich Fechter, *Bewältigung der Katastrophe: Untersuchungen zu ausgewählten Fremdvölkersprüchen im Ezechielbuch* (BZAW 208; Berlin: de Gruyter, 1992).

[177] Leslie Allen, *Ezekiel 20–48* (Word Biblical Commentary 29; Dallas: Word Books, 1990); Leslie Allen, *Ezekiel 1–19* (Word Biblical Commentary 28a; Dallas: Word Books, 1994).

[178] Allen, *Ezekiel 1–19*, xxxiii.

system and finds it more than adequate."[179] Allen is correct in his view that chapters 38–39 are thematically related with 34:25–28, yet my research led me to ask if they are not thematically related also to 37:25–28 and to ask if the Covenant of Peace mentioned in both 34:25–28 and 37:25–28 is not thematically related to what unfolds in chapters 38–39. That is the focus of the present investigation which follows.

In 1996 Ronald Clements published his Ezekiel commentary.[180] While Clements does not speak forcefully of the overall unity of the text, even more pronounced is his negative assessment of the location and purpose of chapters 38–39. In his introductory paragraph he describes them as "an unexpected and in most respects unwelcome aftermath to the bold and confident message of hope expressed in chapters 33–37 . . . it is a much later message, added at a time when Ezekiel's grand assurances still seemed unfulfilled and the prosperity they promised needed to be looked at afresh."[181] For Clements these chapters are not linked in any way to what precedes or follows them. Yet given the victorious outcome of the battle, won single-handedly by the God of Israel, can chapters 38–39 honestly be assessed in the final form as contradicting the message of hope expressed in chapters 33–37?

Lawrence Boadt would place his work in line with the commentaries of Moshe Greenberg, Marco Nobile, and Bernhard Lang. These scholars see a greater unity of viewpoint in the book than discordancy and approach the book as an organic whole. The majority of Boadt's scholarly publications treat the Book of Ezekiel.[182] While he has dealt with many sections of the book in his writings (the Oracles of Judgment, in particular the Oracles against Egypt, the Oracles of Salvation, to name a few), and touched on chapters 38–39 in various ways, he has not published an argument establishing the thematic unity of these two chapters with the overall book based in a study of mythic elements in the text. In fact, as we will see below, he stated clearly in a 1996 article[183] that this needs to be done.

---

[179] Allen, *Ezekiel 1–19*, xxxiii.
[180] Ronald Clements, *Ezekiel* (Westminster Bible Companion; Louisville: Westminster John Knox, 1996).
[181] Clements, *Ezekiel*, 170.
[182] See Bibliography for a partial listing of his works on Ezekiel.
[183] Lawrence Boadt, "Mythological Themes and the Unity of Ezekiel," in *Literary Structure and Rhetorical Strategies in the Hebrew Bible* (ed. L. J. de Regt, J. Je Waard and J. P. Fokkelman; Assen, The Netherlands: Van Gorcum, 1996) 211–31, esp. 223.

Daniel Block published the first volume of his commentary on Ezekiel in 1997, with the second volume following quickly after in 1998.[184] The two volumes provide a very extensive and valuable summary of information about Ezekiel. In the commentary, while he presents a detailed verse-by-verse exposition for each individual unit, he also establishes an argument for the overall coherence and intentionality of the whole book with a focused message. Concerning the question of mythic influence on the book, he often points out examples of mythic parallels with ancient Near Eastern myth, yet he stops short of interpreting the significance of their use mythically or metaphorically in the final form, in reformulating Israelite faith and hope after the traumatic events of Jerusalem's fall, the Temple's destruction and the exile. As an example which we will discuss below, he presents the ancient Near Eastern mythic affinities that the images of the Pharaoh in 32:1–10 would evoke and concludes that the chaos monster described in these parallels is a reference to a crocodile in Ezekiel.[185] In so doing, he drains the image of much of its power to convey the faith of Israel. He presents thematic coherence between chapters 34–48.[186] Where I disagree with Block, and the point that the next chapter of this present work will develop, concerns the significance of mythic elements in understanding the final form of the book.

Thomas Renz's *The Rhetorical Function of the Book of Ezekiel* was published in 1999.[187] The stated concern is the effect the Book of Ezekiel was designed to have upon its original audience by its author, and the means employed to achieve this effect. The goal of the study is to explore the rhetorical function of the Book of Ezekiel in its original context.[188] Renz's study examines the entire book in its final form in order to examine the suasive characteristics of the book in view of the audience addressed. At least in Renz's discussion of chapters 38–39, myth was not one of the means employed by the author to achieve this effect. He treats the decisive battle of the chapters, not as a necessary

---

[184] Daniel I. Block, *The Book of Ezekiel: Chapters 1–24* (NICOT; Grand Rapids: Eerdmans, 1997); Daniel I. Block, *The Book of Ezekiel: Chapters 25–48* (NICOT; Grand Rapids: Eerdmans, 1998).

[185] Block, *The Book of Ezekiel, Chapters 25–48*, 137.

[186] Block, *The Book of Ezekiel, Chapters 25–48*, 272.

[187] Thomas Renz, *The Rhetorical Function of the Book of Ezekiel* (VTSup 76; Leiden: Brill, 1999).

[188] Renz, *The Rhetorical Function*, 2, 11.

part of the drama, but as a confabulated story which tells the people that the events of 587 will never happen again.[189] By not acknowledging the use of myth in the text and its power for the audience, Renz ignores a key component of the rhetor's suasive power.

With the twenty-nine authors reviewed in this third phase, we may identify one individual and three groupings. The individual is Umberto Cassuto. He sees the entire book, including chapters 38–39, linked mnemonically for the sake of memorization.

The first group of scholars focused primarily on the many redactional layers which their research uncovered in the book. Here we list Fohrer, Eissfeldt, Eichrodt, Zimmerli, Garscha, Hossfeld, Allen and Pohlmann. Fohrer and Zimmerli see the basis of placement for chapters 38–39 as purely chronological. Eissfeldt does not treat the literary thematic relationship of the pericope to the text. Eichrodt sees the two chapters as an insertion into the text contrary to the dominant intentions of the prophet. Given the focus of their studies on the redactional history of the text, neither Garscha nor Pohlmann treat the literary thematic unity of the text. Hossfeld, however, does consider the placement of chapters 38–39 in the text and sees them to be in stark contrast with what precedes and follows them. Allen's commentary with its strong emphasis on redactional issues treats 38–39 as intervening between 37:25–28 and what most naturally follows in 40–48. Even in terms of connectedness with the text, Allen sees the current placement of chapters 38–39 as "second best," preferring their insertion immediately after 34:25–28.

The second and larger group of scholars identify clear evidence of redaction in Ezekiel, but also include other criteria in forming their conclusions on the placement of the Gog pericope. This group would include Howie, Vriezen, von Rabenau, Wevers, Astour, Ahroni, Hanson, Becker, Cody, Blenkinsopp, Childs, Krüger, Fechter, and Clements. Howie considered the pericope an independent work of Ezekiel added to the first thirty-two chapters which Ezekiel had assembled as a cohesive literary work. Vriezen saw the chapters as a discordant addition in the midst of a call to inner renewal. Von Rabenau, Becker and Blenkinsopp see the chapters as poorly placed. Wevers can find no clear principle of arrangement in chapters 33–39. Astour intuits

---

[189] Renz, *The Rhetorical Function*, 118–19.

thematic unity but offers no basis for his assessment as it was not the focus of his study. Ahroni views the pericope as an interruption of the schema of the entire book. Hanson, Cody and Clements characterize the two chapters as a rude interruption. Childs sees the pericope, a continuation of the Oracles against the Nations, as a destruction of Israel's historical enemies and offers no discussion of a mythical dimension to the battle. Krüger, discussing two conceptions of Israelite history separated by a space of years, suggests but does not develop links between the later addition of chapters 38–39 and that which precedes and follows them. Fechter sees the Gog pericope as a cryptic reference to Babylon, an Oracle against the Nations which is out of place.

The third group, consisting of Lang, Greenberg, Nobile, Davis, Block, Renz and Boadt, approaches the book as a work of greater unity of viewpoint than the twenty reviewed thus far in this phase. Even here, Lang considers the Gog pericope as misplaced. Greenberg has not published the third volume of his commentary which would deal with the chapters. Nobile developed one example of the pericope's thematic unity with one part of the book. Davis' focus supports greater thematic unity, but in minor references to chapters 38–39 she sees them as projected history, not religious myth. Renz' study deals with the cohesiveness of the book, that for him was geared to persuade the first audience who received the final form. It does not treat mythic elements. Block sees the book as a cohesive literary work, but always stops short of interpreting the use of mythic elements as being employed with the force of myth. Boadt opines the thematic unity of the two chapters with the book, but notes that a fully developed argument in its defense is needed.

The Present Project

In a more recent publication on Ezekiel,[190] Boadt suggests that much work has already been done on the relationship of chapters 40–48 to the overall book,[191] and that what needs to be done at this

---

[190] Boadt, "Mythological Themes," 223.

[191] Examples include: Moshe Greenberg, "The Design and Themes of Ezekiel's Program of Restoration," *Int* 38 (1984) 181–208; Jon D. Levenson, *Theology of the Program of Restoration of Ezekiel 40–48* (HSM 10; Atlanta: Scholars Press, 1986); Susan Niditch, "Ezekiel 40–48 in a Visionary Context," *CBQ* 48(1986) 208–24; Kalinda Rose Stevenson,

point is to demonstrate adequately the thematic unity of the Gog pericope with the rest of the book in its final form. It is from this comment that the present work developed. It is our contention that, based on a study of theological and mythic literary themes, it can be shown, in fact, that Ezekiel 38–39 is "part of a piece," part of a well-crafted, cohesive literary work, that it is placed where it is placed appropriately and for a reason, and that this reason is not mysterious, but demonstrable.

We will look at the book in its final form. Gerhard von Rad reminds us[192] of Franz Rosenweig's comment that the sign "R" should not only designate redactor, but should also be understood as *Rabbenu*, "our master, our teacher" because we are dependent on the final form, its compilation and its theology, for the message we receive in the book. It is our teacher and its theology is our teaching.[193] Though redaction critics would cite glaring inconsistencies in the text, this perhaps is a call to greater reflection to grasp the message. Gerald Sheppard wisely points out: "Semantic 'coherency,' as I have argued, depends partly on what vision one has of "the text" to be interpreted. An incoherent text under one envisioning of it may be coherent in the eyes and ears of another. Texts are unlikely to be preserved at all if they are not coherent to someone."[194] While there is clear benefit derived through redactional methods in the task of understanding the message, there is also benefit in looking at the final form which was crafted with its own message. H. G. M. Williamson reminds us that, in fact, we really have no way of knowing where each paragraph may once have stood. We don't know if any of the smaller units in the chapter were joined before they were given their present setting or whether the links between them are the product of the final form. We don't know to what extent

---

The Vision of Transformation: The Territorial Rhetoric of Ezekiel 40–48 (SBLDS 154; Atlanta: Scholars Press, 1996).

[192] Gerhard von Rad, *Genesis, A Commentary* (trans. John H. Marks; OTL; London: SCM, 1966) 41; originally published as *Das erste Buch Moses, Genesis* (ATD 2; Göttingen: Vandenhoeck & Ruprecht, 1956).

[193] Martin Buber and Franz Rosenzweig, *Scripture and Translation* (trans. Lawrence Rosenwald; Indiana Studies in Biblical Literature; Bloomington: Indiana University Press, 1994) 23; originally published as *Die Schrift und ihre Verdeutschung* (Berlin: Schocken, 1936).

[194] Gerald T. Sheppard, "The Book of Isaiah: Competing Structures according to a Late Modern Description of Its Shape and Scope," in *SBL 1992 Seminar Papers* (ed. Eugene H. Lovering, Jr.; Atlanta: Scholars Press, 1992) 566.

the final form intervened in the assembling of the texts to make them flow more smoothly, distorting their original shape.[195] To this I would also add that looking at the final form of the text does not require the implicit assumption of Ezekielian authorship for the whole book. To use Paul Joyce's words on that subject, we must "be content with a proper agnosticism about this."[196] What we do know is that the final form of the text as we have it is a literary work of integrity worthy of study. Stevenson's comments on chapters 40–48 are partially apt here for the book as a whole:

> Crazy-quilts are intentionally produced by stitching together different scraps of cloth, with the intention of producing a quilt. To reverse the process by taking the quilt apart to separate out the scraps would result in a pile of scraps and no more quilt—an engaging pastime, but not much comfort on a cold night. . . . the issue is not that someone pieced together scraps, but that someone wanted a quilt.[197]

This book is about looking at the "quilt" in Ezekiel's final form. It is our contention that the quilt is not, in its final form, "crazy." It is in fact methodically put together with a purpose that may be discerned through the myths of Israel and the ancient Near East.

---

[195] Hugh Godfrey M. Williamson, "Synchronic and Diachronic in Isaian Perspective," in *Synchronic or Diachronic? A Debate on Method in Old Testament Exegesis* (ed. Johannes C. de Moor; OTS 34; Leiden: Brill, 1995) 226.

[196] Paul M. Joyce, "Synchronic and Diachronic Perspectives on Ezekiel," in *Synchronic or Diachronic? A Debate on Method in Old Testament Exegesis* (ed. Johannes C. de Moor; OTS 34; Leiden: Brill, 1995) 126.

[197] Stevenson, *Vision and Transformation*, 7.

CHAPTER 2

The Significance of Myth in Itself and in Ezekiel

Hans-Peter Müller speaks of the universal content of religious speech and the significance of myth in that speech. In both biblical and extra-biblical literature, myth fulfills the function of dealing with the problems of human existence. For Müller, the integration of God into human history belongs to a mythical context, and to understand the God of history fully, one must commit to a conversation with the mythical.[1] Mark Smith, in an article in *Congress Volume* from the Oslo Meeting of the IOSOT in 1998,[2] notes in relation to biblical study of Israel:

> Ugaritic provides a distant backdrop or *Gestalt* for Israelite developments, both in their similarities and differences. Understanding the emergence of monotheistic statements in the seventh and sixth centuries involves a look at Judean society in general and the demise of the monarchy in particular; and both developments may be illumined by contrast and comparison with the Ugaritic texts presenting Ugaritic society and royal ideology.[3]

---

[1] Hans-Peter Müller, "Mythische Elemente in der Jahwistischen Schöpfungserzählung," in *Babylonien und Israel, Historische, Religiöse und sprachliche Beziehungen* (ed. Hans-Peter Müller; WF 633; Darmstadt: Wissenschaftliche Buchgesellschaft, 1991) 149–52.

[2] Mark Smith, "Ugaritic Studies and the Hebrew Bible, 1968–1998 (With Excursus on Judean Monotheism and the Ugaritic Texts)," in *Congress Volume, Oslo 1998* (ed. André Lemaire & M. Sæbø; VTSup 80; Leiden: Brill, 2000) 327–52.

[3] Smith, "Ugaritic Studies and the Hebrew Bible," 344.

While Müller and Smith do not address Ezekiel, their reflections are apt to the further understanding of its final form. In that setting, with the monarchy led away to Babylon, and hopes of its restoration uncertain, the Israelite worldview shifts and speaks of Yhwh, the Creator God, in a new key: the Israelite creation myth and the Israelite understanding of their God had to integrate new and devastating data.[4] The quintessential role of Israel's God came to center stage. The deities of other nations in this period were no longer truly considered deities. They were illusory. Yhwh alone was ruler of the cosmos. All the kings and their nations must submit to the authority of Yhwh who is the power beyond any power. Israel itself now became the bearer of Yhwh's covenant to the nations.[5] Foundational to this discussion is a look at Israel's myth in its relationship to ancient Near Eastern religions and in particular to its significance for Israel's religious faith after the fall of Jerusalem and the destruction of the Temple.

I

Basic to all religion is a unique experience of confrontation with power not of this world. It is the human response to this experience that constitutes religion.[6] Myth's efforts to evoke response to this experience of supra-human powers are central to religious thought. The central religious myths of a people reveal what they consider essential in the supernatural experience. They point beyond themselves and yet remain within this world, wholly human and culturally conditioned.

What is a working definition of myth? In his *Myth in Old Testament Interpretation* published in 1974, Rogerson defined myth as stories expressing the faith and worldview of a people which speak of people's intuitions of transcendent reality.[7] In 1987 Kees Bolle defined myth as an expression of the sacred in words: it reports realities and events

---

[4] Norman Cohn, *Cosmos, Chaos, and the World to Come, The Ancient Roots of Apocalyptic Faith* (New Haven: Yale University Press, 1993) 154; Frank M. Cross, "The Development of Israelite Religion," *Bible Review* 8.5 (1992) 18–29, 50.

[5] Smith, "Ugaritic Studies and the Hebrew Bible," 346–49.

[6] Thorkild Jacobsen (*The Treasures of Darkness, A History of Mesopotamian Religion* [New Haven: Yale University Press, 1976] 3–5) treats this topic; also Müller, "Mythische Elemente," 115–17.

[7] John W. Rogerson, *Myth in Old Testament Interpretation* (BZAW 134; Berlin: de Gruyter, 1974) 174.

from the origin of the world and the renewal of that origin which remain valid for the basis and purpose of all there is.[8] More recently, in 1992, Batto in his book *Slaying the Dragon,* defined myth as a narrative concerning fundamental symbols that are constitutive or paradigmatic of human existence, pointing to reality beyond itself that cannot be directly symbolized.[9] In a 1996 publication in *UBL,* Wyatt defined myth as narrative theology, dealing with life and death, metaphysics and morals.[10] Put succinctly, myths are tales which express the beliefs of a people seeking to explain the world of powers and forces beyond their own which cannot be seen but whose effects are experienced. While myth is popularly seen as lacking in veracity, a fantastic confabulation of facts beyond the real, it must be clearly asserted that myth is the bearer of its own unique truth, beyond the measurable, quantifiable, perceptible world in which we live.[11] Though not scientifically verifiable, myth seeks to articulate what is true for a people in their experience of forces beyond the physical world perceived with their senses.

Fontenrose began his famous study *Python* with the words: "every god has his enemy, whom he must conquer and destroy."[12] The struggles of Baal against Yamm and Yhwh against Leviathan belong to this genre of divine conquest. They belong to a very important genre of divine conflict dispersed widely and found in India, Mesopotamia, Anatolia, Greece and Europe.[13] The motif of a decisive battle against an evil force has exerted a powerful effect on the religious imagination of many ancient peoples, beginning with early Mesopotamian mythology. In the late third and early second millennium, it is present in the Sumerian Myth of Gilgamesh's defeat of Huwawa.[14] The Sumerian

---

[8] Kees Bolle, "Myth, An Overview," in *EncRel* 10 (ed. Mircea Eliade; London: Collier Macmillan Publishers, 1987) 261, 264.

[9] Bernard F. Batto, *Slaying the Dragon, Mythmaking in the Biblical Tradition* (Louisville: Westminster/John Knox, 1992) 11.

[10] Nick Wyatt, *Myths of Power* (UBL 13; Münster: Ugarit-Verlag, 1996) 117.

[11] Hans-Peter Müller, *Jenseits der Entmythologisierung* (2d ed.; Neukirchen-Vluyn: Neukirchener Verlag, 1979) 9.

[12] Joseph E. Fontenrose, *Python: A Study of Delphic Myth and Its Origins* (Berkeley: University of California Press, 1959) 1.

[13] Wyatt, *Myths of Power,* 127.

[14] Hallo, William W., ed. *The Context of Scripture 1: Canonical Compositions from the Biblical World* (New York: Brill, 1997) 458–60.

Myth of the annihilation of Zu by Ninurta from the same period[15] and its later Assyrian counterpart again reflect this motif, as does the Sumerian Myth of the battle and victory of Ninurta over the Azag Demon,[16] this latter having significant parallels with the Gog pericope. In the late second millennium the Babylonian legend of Tiamat in all her darkness defeated by Marduk, the god of light, traces this same pattern,[17] and, from the same period, the West Semitic myth of the victory of Baal, the storm god who provided fertility to the earth with his rain, over Yamm, the sea god of chaos and disintegration and the enemy of the good order of nature,[18] and later over Mot, the personification of the ultimate power behind wickedness and death itself, has analogous themes.

The Combat Myth narrative posits a basic opposition, before and after: when the enemy ruled there was chaos; when the divine king rules there is order. The combat narrative begins with a statement of the fundamental conflict or opposition of some kind which the champion's victory will eliminate. The villainy of the opposition is portrayed, in some cases just by a simple enumeration of his characteristics: greedy, tyrannical, etc. There is always an attack in which the evil representative of chaos causes mayhem. The hero of the myth is usually a representative of his people (their king or their god), and he resolves matters of the State. The hero must organize the chaos into some type of acceptable structure. This result is represented as the triumph of the protagonist.[19] Forsyth in his study discerns a twelve part schema representing significant incidents in the plot structure of the Combat Myth.[20] Four of the twelve aspects are always present: villainy, battle, victory, and a triumph which itself could include several

---

[15] James B. Pritchard, ed. *ANET* (3d ed. with suppl.; Princeton: Princeton University Press, 1969) 514–17. In those cases where a myth is not available in translation in either volume of the more recent publication *The Context of Scripture, ANET* will be used. The "Ninurta-Anzu-Bird Myth" is the first of these.

[16] Samuel N. Kramer, *History Begins at Sumer* (3d rev. ed.; Philadelphia: The University of Pennsylvania Press, 1981) 170–72; originally published as *From the Tablets of Sumer* (Indian Hills, CO: Falcon's Wing, 1956).

[17] *The Context of Scripture*, 1.391–99.

[18] *The Context of Scripture*, 1.241–74.

[19] Neil Forsyth, *The Old Enemy, Satan and the Combat Myth* (Princeton: Princeton University Press, 1987) 447–52.

[20] Forsyth, *The Old Enemy*, 448–51.

components. Without these four parts, the narrative would not be a combat. The other eight parts of the twelve-fold schema may be absent or shortened at times without changing the basic structure of the narrative.[21] Such is the standard plot line of the Combat Myth.

This myth has been of marked importance in all the civilizations of this vast region. It is concerned with the maintenance of the cosmos, whether by war or only by invoking the gods to provide supernatural assistance, which might then take practical and political form. The god himself is addressed and adjured to repel the forces of chaos. Primitive myths state this very succinctly, even abruptly at times. The versions of Ugarit and Babylonia are later elaborations of the primitive myth, extending its range and application. The Ugarit version is the oldest narrative form, distinct from earlier allusions and applications.[22] Why did this myth enjoy such a long and influential life?

The peoples of the ancient Near East understood the world as a reflection of the world of the gods. Eliade notes that when one penetrates the authentic meaning of a myth, it clearly shows its recognition of a situation of cosmic dimension.

> Objects or acts acquire a value, and in so doing become real, because they participate, after one fashion or another, in a reality that transcends them. . . . archaic man acknowledges no act which has not been previously posited and lived by someone else, some other being who was not a man. What he does has been done before. His life is the ceaseless repetition of gestures initiated by others. . . . these are facts which help us to understand how and why, for the man of the pre-modern societies, certain things become real.[23]

The king in the ancient Near East was considered the mediator of divine realities to human society, and it was believed that his life acts

---

[21] Richard J. Clifford (*Creation Accounts in the Ancient Near East and in the Bible* [CBQMS 26; Washington, D.C.: The Catholic Biblical Association of America, 1994] 9) notes that the ancients had a great tolerance for several versions of a single basic plot. Each approach handles new data. Nuance and perspective were conveyed by the selection and omission of narrative detail. As I will discuss in greater detail below, no one version of any tale that has come down to us is more "original" or more "true" than any other version.

[22] Wyatt, *Myths of Power*, 127, 133–34.

[23] Mircea Eliade, *Cosmos and History, The Myth of the Eternal Return* (New York: Harper, 1954) 5.

out the mythological acts of the gods. The ruler on earth has power only in reference to his divine status and to his recapitulation of divine victory.[24] The Enuma Elish is a foreshadowing of Babylon's and Marduk's rise to rulership over a united Babylonia, but projected back to the mythical times and made universal; it is a story of world origins and world ordering which includes the monarchy, but grounded in divine power and the divine will.[25] The enthronement motif in the Baal Cycle, Smith notes, points to the same central theme, the legitimation of the political institution. The divine kingship of Baal mirrors and reinforces the human kingship of the royal patron of the Baal Cycle.[26] It exalts the divine king as well as the limits of Baal's kingship, and in turn it reinforces the parallel situation in his earthly kingdom. The importance of the myth then was not only the glorification of the divine world of the gods, but also the presentation of a paradigm replicated on earth. An author can give authority to the writing in the eyes of readers by describing the events of history in the context of myth.

The divine action of the *Chaoskampf* motif is foundational for the king's power. It is for this reason that victory, any victory, was given its greatest force when it was described and celebrated in the mythic genre because it gave divine authority to and legitimized the political victory. The king's military action will be expressed in terms of mythic combat to give it greater force and legitimacy. The *Chaoskampf* myth was a model and a goal from the primordial deeds of the god. It is concerned with primordial events which themselves constitute cosmos while at the same time it is properly timeless or cyclical or eschatological in character.[27] It raises a political theme to a supernatural level. No victory is as important as the *Chaoskampf* victory. It is the paradigm of all victories.[28] Its playing out in human history is the realization of what the gods had already created in their own world. As the king can show his victory to be a reflection of the *Chaoskampf* victory, he establishes a firmer foundation for his own right to rule.

It was, in fact, its political application which made the *Chaoskampf*

---

[24] Wyatt, *Myths of Power*, 120, 155–56.

[25] Jacobsen, *The Treasures of Darkness*, 191.

[26] Mark S. Smith, *The Ugaritic Baal Cycle, Volume I: Introduction with Text, Translation and Commentary of KTU 1.1–1.2* (VTSup 55; Leiden: Brill, 1994) 109.

[27] CMHE, viii and 120.

[28] Wyatt, *Myths of Power*, 155–56.

myth so serviceable and it was the application rather than the narrative line in itself which explains its continued transmission down the centuries in a variety of contexts. All myths have histories, and no one version of any tale as it has come down to us is more original or more "true" than any other version.[29] Rather, they reflect the social order. If a world view slips radically out of line with the general experience of the way things are, it would cease to be effective. So long as the myth is alive, it is changing even while it is still felt to be the same myth.[30] This is the process of mythopoeism, the remaking of a myth, integrating new data.

Mythopoeism means "myth-making." It is a process by which new myths are created or old myths are extended to include new dimensions. Mythopoeism uses the human faculty of imagination rather than reason. In doing this myth-makers gave non-rational pre-scientific but true answers to the original human dilemmas. It was through mythopoeic speculation that the biblical authors reflected theologically about the activity of God and their relationship with God. The concept of mythopoeism in Levy-Bruhl's theory on myth has been highly criticized because it is clearly not only characteristic of primitive societies. In fact, the mythopoeic process can be operative in any society. Attributing it only to primitive societies is possibly the product of a biased first-world mentality.[31] If myth is defined as preconscious and unreflected thought, then obviously there is no authentic myth in the Bible, any more than in modern Western society. But this is hardly an adequate definition of myth.

Mythopoeic must be distinguished from mythopoetic which is a metaphoric or symbolic use of mythic images in artistic literary compositions. Mythopoetic language uses well-known images and words from popular myths as metaphors and allusions. The mythopoetic remains a literary ornament. In mythopoetic usage, the mythic elements have lost their value as operative myths and survive only as lit-

---

[29] Peter Munz, *When the Golden Bough Breaks; Structuralism or Typology?* (London & Boston: Routledge & Kegan Paul, 1973) 27.

[30] Bolle, "Myth, An Overview," 263; Mary K. Wakeman, *God's Battle with the Monster* (Leiden: Brill, 1973) 4–5.

[31] Batto, *Slaying the Dragon*, 6–7, 12–13; Boadt, "Mythological Themes," 217–18; Hans-Peter Müller, *Vergleich und Metapher im Hohenlied* (OBO 56; Freiburg, Switzerland: Universitätsverlag; Göttingen: Vandenhoeck & Ruprecht, 1984) 53.

erary symbols or images, vestiges of their original mythic function.[32] These are no longer the carriers of community values and community faith. Mythopoeic activity, on the other hand, describes new divine activity in categories with which primordial divine activity has been described.[33] The force of mythopoetic usage is not completely understood if it has not been experienced in its mythopoeic dimension. The impact of the Oracles against the Foreign Nations which contain many examples of mythopoetic language was felt by those for whom the prophetic book was written precisely because of the active influence of the mythical (the mythopoeic) in their religious faith. For metaphor is more than simile. Metaphors have, in fact, real cognitive content which only the metaphor itself can give.[34] We will see more examples of the use of metaphor in the Oracles against the Nations further in chapter five below.

When any myth ceases to function as the carrier of the community's beliefs, it is abandoned. Significantly the Combat Myth enjoyed a vitality in the literary and cultic communities at least from the late third millenium to the early second century after Christ in the Near East. The Combat Myth provided imagery and conceptual framework for explaining divine rule over the world, and for assuring that meaningful existence was possible within this chaotic world.[35] This Combat Myth, this *Chaoskampf* myth had significant impact on the biblical writers. It had, in fact, mythopoeic significance for them. Through it, events of history were given foundation in the divine world. We turn now to look at its influence there.

II

The scientific study of myth, including the possible presence of mythical elements in the Bible, has occupied scholars since the first half of the nineteenth century. The definition of myth as stories about

---

[32] Batto, *Slaying the Dragon*, 6–8; Boadt, "Mythological Themes," 219.

[33] Batto, *Slaying the Dragon*, 3, 12; Boadt, "Mythological Themes," 219.

[34] Carol A. Newsom, "A Maker of Metaphors—Ezekiel's Oracles Against Tyre," *Int* 38 (1984) 151–64.

[35] Batto, *Slaying the Dragon*, 11–12; Richard J. Clifford, "The Roots of Apocalypticism in Near Eastern Myth," in *The Encyclopedia of Apocalypticism*, *1* (ed. John J. Collins; New York: Continuum, 1998) 3, 34.

the gods, made popular by Jacob and Wilhelm Grimm, was accepted by many and presented an obstacle to movement in the discussion until the mid-twentieth century. If myth is about polytheism, it can't be present in the monotheistic testimony which is the Bible. Such was the assumption which conditioned the entry point into the discussion.

The breakthrough came when Rudolph Bultmann saw myths as ways in which a culture expresses a certain understanding of human existence, that the world and human life have their ground and their limits in a power which is beyond all that we can calculate or control.[36] G. Henton Davies similarly moved the discussion forward when he defined mythology as a way of thinking about the divine rather than a way of thinking about a number of gods.[37] B. S. Childs permanently put to rest the Grimm Brothers' definition with the publication of *Myth and Reality in the Old Testament*.[38] In his book Childs notes the real damage done by the continued reliance upon the Grimm Brothers' definition because myth is defined too exclusively as a literary product rather than as a cultural phenomenon. From this he goes on to discuss myth in a way similar to Bultmann as an understanding of reality.[39]

In 1973, F. M. Cross's *Canaanite Myth and Hebrew Epic* expressed the polar opposite of the stance that was fearful of undermining the biblical monotheism by acknowledging the presence of myth. Here Cross positively develops a mythic pattern discernible in the OT. He uses as prime example the pattern of the *Chaoskampf* motif, a Canaanite cosmogonic myth precisely because it shows up frequently in biblical literature, in fragment or in full form. The pattern contains four components: (1) a battle between a divine warrior and a chaotic sea god; (2) the victory of the divine warrior; (3) the proclamation of this warrior as king, and (4) the completion of his sanctuary.

The old traditions were sources of great riches and wisdom, and it was precisely because of the power and significance of their symbolism that they continued to be used and adapted to similar Israelite and

---

[36] Rudolf Bultmann, *Jesus Christ and Mythology* (New York: Scribner, 1958), 19.

[37] G. Henton Davies, "An Approach to the Problem of Old Testament Mythology," *PEQ* 88 (1956) 88.

[38] Brevard S. Childs, *Myth and Reality in the Old Testament* (SBT 27; London: SCM, 1960).

[39] Childs, *Myth and Reality*, 15–17.

Judahite contexts. Myth, for the authors of the OT, was a reservoir of symbols which contained the hopes and fears of the faith of Israel,[40] but, as with all myth, outmoded aspects of the combat myth dropped out. New written attempts in the Hebrew Bible enlarged, adapted and transformed the standard elements in the Semitic Combat Myth to develop a point about the unique character of the God of Israel. Myth-making in biblical and non-biblical writings was not a question of repeating ancient stories, but rather of a vibrant process of growth. The mythopoeic attempts to persuade the audience that God is truly creating something new as in the day of primordial creation.[41] The biblical authors themselves make free use of the ancient images without being bound by the structure of the myth.

As the head god of a national pantheon was addressed and adjured to repel the forces of chaos, in the same way Yhwh was similarly invoked in the Bible.[42] This theme of a decisive battle surfaces in OT books besides Ezekiel: Zech 14:1–5 and Dan 11:40–45. A definitive battle where all Yhwh's enemies are finally destroyed is attested also in *1 Enoch* 90:20 ff., *2 Esdras* 13:5, 8 ff., and the *Assumption of Moses* 10:1ff. In the literature of Qumran, the *War Scroll* develops the theme of the final battle into a full-scale military description with detailed maneuvers and battle standards. The antagonist here is called Belial.[43] The primeval myths make it clear that God's final act of world ordering is not an act which is self-evident, unthreatened, and extant from all eternity. Rather it is something won, something dramatic, something exciting. In the Baal Cycle Baal's kingship is glorious but fragile. The kingship of Baal is a hard-won reign.[44] It is this unfinished quality of world ordering which makes the *Chaoskampf* struggle a part of the act of creation.

---

[40] Wyatt, *Myths of Power*, 124–25.
[41] Boadt, "Mythological Themes," 219.
[42] Thomas Podella, *Das Lichtkleid JHWH's, Untersuchungen zur Gestalthaftigkeit Gottes im Alten Testament und seiner altorientalischen Umwelt* (FAT 15; Tübingen: Mohr, 1996) 271.
[43] Florentino Garcia Martínez, *The Dead Sea Scrolls Translated: The Qumran Texts in English* (New York: Brill, 1994) 95, 98, 110–15.
[44] Norman Girardot, "Chaos," in *EncRel* 3 (ed. Mircea Eliade; London: Collier Macmillan, 1987) 216; Jon D. Levenson, *Creation and the Persistence of Evil* (San Francisco: Harper & Row, 1988) 9; Smith, *The Ugaritic Baal Cycle*, 104–5.

Amidst the cognitive dissonance caused by the exile, the final form of Ezekiel sees this decisive battle coming "in the latter years" (Ezek 38:8). Other biblical texts see such a conquest as coming at a future time. Isa 27:1 gives witness to this: "On that day, the Lord will punish with His great, cruel, mighty sword Leviathan, the elusive serpent — Leviathan the twisting serpent, He will slay the dragon in the sea." This quote presupposes that the powers of chaos have not yet been eliminated or completely domesticated. These still threaten, and human evil can provoke a disaster. So long as Israel's ancient and by now archetypal enemy endures, the full realization of Yhwh's creation cannot be realized. It will remain *in potentia*.[45] The decisive battle is the mythopoeic statement of belief that the ancient and enduring opposition to the full realization of creation will ultimately be brought under Yhwh's dominion in the final times.

In his *Urzeit und Endzeit*, Gunkel shows that the *Chaoskampf* battle with the monster was connected with creation and came to have eschatological significance as an allegory of the battle that would precede the New Age.[46] Levenson, ninety years later, notes at greater length that the Combat Myth of Creation has been projected onto the onset of the future era. This decisive victory must be interpreted in the light of the painful historical experiences which Israel had endured: the destruction of worship sites, the absence of miracles, the sacred name profaned, what appeared to be the unraveling of Yhwh's covenant and promise, and the general collapse of his mastery over the world. He notes that Psalm 74 expresses a theology that can no longer accept the hymnic language of primordial creation as a given, but rather draws attention to the painful gap between the liturgical affirmation of the God's absolute sovereignty and the empirical reality of evil triumphant and unchecked. On the one hand, the author cannot deny the discrepancy between his experience and the faith tradition he has received. On the other he refuses to abandon the affirmation of the God's world-ordering, and his power to defeat even the primeval personifications of chaos and to fashion the world as he sees fit. Any past triumphs are incomplete. There must be more.[47] Cognitive dissonance was in this case an impetus to faith, not its undoing.

---

[45] Levenson, *Creation and the Persistence of Evil*, 36–38.
[46] Gunkel, *Schöpfung und Chaos*, 84, 87.
[47] Levenson, *Creation and the Persistence of Evil*, 19–22, 27.

Batto states the case well. For the biblical authors the primeval myth functioned to authenticate the ancestral faith of Israel that their God was truly sovereign Creator both in heaven and on earth, despite the evil in what seemed to be a world coming apart. Creation for Israel will come to completion only when the people are gathered again under a covenant of peace around the Lord's cosmic mountain throne in Zion.[48] This is not a novelty in view of the understanding of the meaning of creation in the ancient Near East in the biblical period.

Interestingly though, the power of evil seems not to be eliminated in the myth but brought under the dominion, tamed to be a contributing member of the generativity of creation.[49] Ezek 47:1–12 would seem to suggest that the cosmic waters of chaos were brought under Yhwh's dominion. The power of evil was not eliminated but somehow brought within bounds which allowed it to participate in the generativity of creation.

While the *Chaoskampf* myth did have its own independent literary existence,[50] it also belonged to a broader schema, found in the various ancient Near Eastern myths of cosmogony. This schema provides a fuller context for understanding the Book of Ezekiel. Cosmogony is the fundamental myth, paradigmatic in a special way because of the many things to which its sheer force as a model is able to give birth. Consciously or unconsciously, the fundamental and founding power of the creation myth was acknowledged and experienced in the ancient Near East when it was recited on the occasion of the enthronement of the king or at the time of the renewal of life and of kingship in the New Year festival. The use of Sumerian in the telling of the creation myth in Babylon long after Sumerian had ceased its vernacular existence also bears witness to the power of myth.[51] The *Enuma Elish* is fundamentally an account of how the world is ruled. It is a story of world origins and world ordering which is the product of the conscious creative intelligence of Marduk. It was he who created the physical world

---

[48] Batto, *Slaying the Dragon*, 3, 164, 166–67.

[49] Batto (*Slaying the Dragon*, 167) posits that before the covenant of peace can come, the power of evil must be eliminated completely from the heart and fabric of creation. This seems not to be the case at least in the final chapters of Ezekiel and in other myths as well. Mot, for example, reappears in the story line after having been slain by Anat. *The Context of Scripture* 1.270, 272.

[50] Claus Westermann, *Genesis* 1 (BKAT 1.1; Neukirchen-Vluyn: Neukirchener Verlag, 1974) 39–46.

[51] Bolle, "Myth, An Overview," 265–66.

where the inhabitants of the ancient Near East dwelt and provided the gods with divine rest by creating humans to do slave labor. His victorious battle against Tiamat takes place in that broader context of cosmogony. World order in the *Enuma Elish* is grounded in divine power and divine will.[52] The myth gives more tangibility to the belief that the universe is a moral and meaningful expression of a creative intelligence with valid purpose: order and peace and prosperity. In Ugarit, the process of cosmogony begun by El is completed by Baal's action presented in the *Chaoskampf* motif. *Chaoskampf*, here too, is part of the broader schema of cosmogony. These two, in fact, include a third element: Temple building. Conflict, kingship, ordering of chaos, and temple building are all parts of the overarching theme of creation.[53] In Babylonia, the creation of the world results from Marduk's victory over his enemies, and this victory brings about his enthronement. In Ugarit, the building of a temple is related after the victory of Baal.

The many functions of El and Baal, of Ea and Marduk are mentioned side by side in the OT for the polemical purpose of showing that Yhwh's power is absolute. The Israelite creation myth and its final act, the combat myth, have the same choreographer: Yhwh.[54] Both Sarna and Cassuto have determined the existence of a popular and independent creation myth in ancient Israel in which the struggle between God and the mutinous forces of primeval chaos was inextricably interwoven with the Hebrew ideas of creation. Cassuto even reconstructs the myth from OT passages and discusses the mythopoeic process it underwent from the myths extant in the ancient Near East.[55]

---

[52] Jacobsen, *The Treasures of Darkness*, 191.

[53] Richard J. Clifford, "The Unity of the Book of Isaiah and Its Cosmogonic Language," CBQ 55 (1993) 8; Loren Fisher, "Creation at Ugarit and in the Old Testament," VT 15 (1965) 316, 320; Thomas Römer, "La redécouverte d'un mythe dans l'ancien testament: la création comme combat," ETR 64 (1989) 563, 568; Moshe Weinfeld, "Sabbath, Temple, and the Enthronement of the Lord — The Problem of the *Sitz im Leben* of Genesis 1:1–2:3," in *Mélanges bibliques et orientaux en l'honneur de M. Henri Cazelles* (ed. A. Caquot et M. Delcor; AOAT 212; Neukirchen-Vluyn: Neukirchener Verlag, 1981) 507.

[54] Oswald Loretz, *Ugarit und die Bibel* (Darmstadt: Wissenschaftliche Buchgesellschaft, 1990) 159.

[55] Nahum Sarna, "The Psalm for the Sabbath Day (Ps 92)," *JBL* 81 (1962) 160; Umberto Cassuto, *The Goddess Anath: Canaanite Epics of the Patriarchal Age* (trans. Israel Abrahams; Jerusalem: Magnes, 1971) 72–74; originally published in Hebrew (Jerusalem: Magnes, 1953).

Von Rad sees this same connection between creation and redemption in Israel's theology. Isaiah 51:9 speaks of splitting Rahab in the cosmogonic battle which led to creation and 51:10 shifts without pause to the miracle at the Red Sea where Yhwh held back the waters for the redeemed to pass through. Von Rad notes: "Here creation and redemption almost coincide, and can almost be looked on as one act of dramatic divine saving action in the picture of the struggle with the dragon of Chaos."[56] In fact, the world is about to be transformed, by an act as wondrous as its original creation.[57] Preuss arrives at similar conclusions as von Rad: "Yahwistic faith, whether active in its own formulation or in its transformation of ancient Near Eastern statements, does not shape an isolated, separate creation theology. Rather, this faith of Israel reasons about works of creation and acts of salvation in the entwinement of creation and history."[58] Prov 8:22–29 is perhaps the most specific of all the passages which associate combat and creation. At the very outset of the cosmogonic process, the passage relates how God constrained the depths and confined the sea. Creation means precisely the transformation of chaos into cosmos, and the combat myth implies the victory of stability and order over the forces of destruction that would negate creation. Human wickedness is seen as endangering the very cosmos itself, but the God of Israel who is Creator of the past, the present and the future describes the redemption of the exiles in terms of creation. God's creatorship and his mighty acts of deliverance of his people are one.[59] Ps 74:12–17 attests eloquently to an Israelite myth of combat between Yhwh and aquatic beasts, leading to the ordering of the world.[60] In Exod 15:1–18, 21 the constituent parts of the *Chaoskampf* motif are present. Verse 13 clearly presents a redemption theme and v. 16 presents a creation theme: Yhwh invoked as the

---

[56] Gerhard von Rad, *Old Testament Theology, Volume One: The Theology of Israel's Traditions,* trans. D. M. G. Stalker (New York: Harper & Row, 1962) 137–38; originally published as *Theologie des Alten Testaments, Bd. 1: Die Theologie der geschichtlichen Überlieferungen Israels* (Munich: Chr. Kaiser, 1957).

[57] Cohn, *Cosmos, Chaos, and the World to Come,* 153.

[58] Horst Dietrich Preuss, *Old Testament Theology* 1 (trans. Leo G. Perdue; OTL; Louisville: Westminster John Knox, 1995) 235; originally published as *Theologie des Alten Testaments* 1 (Stuttgart: Kohlhammer, 1991).

[59] See, for example, Isa 41:20, 42:16; 43:19, 44:23 as cited in Marjo C. A. Korpel, "Creator of All," in *Dictionary of Deities and Demons in the Bible* (ed. Karel van der Toorn, Bob Becking, Pieter W. van der Horst; 2d ed; Leiden: Brill, 1999) 209–10.

[60] Cohn, *Cosmos, Chaos, and the World to Come,* 152.

Creator of a people.[61] In this passage, victory, redemption and creation, are linked. Justifiably Levenson[62] notes that the defeat by Yhwh of the forces that seek to interrupt the order of creation is intrinsically an act of creation. In fact, *Chaoskampf* completes cosmogony.

It is important to remember that throughout the ancient Near Eastern world, including Israel, the point of creation and the truth to which creation myths bear testimony was not only the creation of the cosmos with its mineral, vegetable, animal and human life forms, but also the power of the gods to effect the emergence of a stable community in a benevolent and life-sustaining order.[63] Del Olmo Lete has recently published a series of fragmentary Ugaritic texts which he proposes as a minor Baal Cycle. In one text, Baal and the gods of the desert, Baal is initially slain by the desert gods in vengeance for confronting them over an injustice to the other sons of El. A consequence of his death is the paralysis of all human activity and the suspension of the social order, not just the natural order.[64] Both Ugaritic and Babylonian cosmogonies see not only El and Ea as creators. Baal and Marduk in their triumphs present a very real second act analogous to the creation event. The victories of Baal and Marduk assure political stability and fertility for the community. They bring peace and order for the world and its peoples.[65] The order that comes out of chaos in the ancient Near Eastern cosmogonies is not only the ordering of the physical creation, rather cosmogony completed for them includes the benign and successful working together of elements that promote human life.

Whether order is being restored or created in ancient Israelite culture, they were two parts of one piece. The sustaining of creation through victory over the powers of evil has its own broad influence on biblical texts.[66] Preuss notes that creation faith in the OT leads to hope

---

[61] Wyatt, *Myths of Power*, 179.

[62] Levenson, *Creation and the Persistence of Evil*, 12, 33–34.

[63] Richard J. Clifford, "The Hebrew Scriptures and the Theology of Creation," *TS* 46 (1985) 508–12, and (by the same author) "Cosmogonies in the Ugaritic Texts and in the Bible" *Or* 53 (1984) 201; Preuss, *Old Testament Theology*, 1.235–36; Römer, "La redécouverte d'un mythe," 569; Westermann, *Genesis*, 1.128.

[64] Gregorio del Olmo Lete, *Mitos, leyendas y rituales de los semitas occidentales* (Pliegos de Oriente, Serie Proximo Oriente; Madrid: Editorial Trotta S.A., 1998) 137.

[65] Loretz, *Ugarit und die Bibel*, 155, 157–58.

[66] Levenson, *Creation and the Persistence of Evil*, 12; Loretz, *Ugarit und die Bibel*,

in a new creation that will complete the history of Yhwh's salvation for his people and his world. Creation is bound up with the eschatological fulfillment of the new temple, the new Jerusalem and the new Davidic ruler. The theology of creation, product of the vital needs of a community reflecting in faith on its situation, is included in the historical journey of Yhwh leading to the perfection of his lordship and the perfection of humanity.[67] The product that emerged from the process of creation was not only a physical universe, but also a people in a life-sustaining order and right relationship with their Creator.

Two final points need to be discussed to understand the influence of myth on the Bible. The first is the relationship of myth and history. F. M. Cross would suggest that Israel had a concern with the "historical," which was unique and particular to Israel. In epic narrative, according to Cross, people and their god or gods interact in the temporal course of events. His definition of Epic comes from an effort to set apart Israel's use of myth as it serves "primarily to give cosmic dimension and transcendent meaning to the historical, rarely functioning to dissolve the historical."[68] While Israelite faith is certainly distinct, Cross's effort to set Israelite faith apart as distinct in this way is a misuse of the term epic. Epics as such do not have the authority of myths. They are, in fact, the first clear signs of a process of secularization of myths.[69] Cross's placement of Israelite faith in the category of epic in this context becomes problematic.

Both Albrektson[70] and Clapham[71] challenge the distinctiveness of

---

159; Marvin H. Pope, *Probative Pontificating in Ugaritic and Biblical Literature* (ed. Mark S. Smith; UBL 10; Münster: Ugarit-Verlag, 1994) 86.

[67] Clifford, "The Unity of the Book of Isaiah," 8; Preuss, *Old Testament Theology*, 1.236; Römer, "La redécouverte d'un mythe," 572.

[68] *CMHE*, vii–ix, 90.

[69] For a discussion of this see Bolle, "Myth, An Overview," 264–65. In an earlier article, Charles Conroy ("Hebrew Epic: Historical Notes and Critical Reflections," *Bib* 61 [1980] 1–30) also challenges Cross's use of the literary term Epic. Analyzing the uses of the term in contemporary literary criticism, he concludes that the application of the term Epic to the JE *Vorlage*, except as a description of certain literary qualities, is inaccurate.

[70] Bertil Albrektson, *History and the Gods: An Essay on the Idea of Historical Events as Divine Manifestations in the Ancient Near East and in Israel* (ConBOT 1; Lund: CWK Gleerup, 1967).

[71] Lynn Clapham, "Mythopoeic Antecedents of the Biblical World-View and Their Transformation in Early Israelite Thought," in *Magnalia Dei, The Mighty Acts of God*

Israel's concern with history and the interaction of a god or gods in the political affairs of mortals. Esarhaddon's Inscriptions note that the defenders of a city against which he had set a siege sprinkled a siege ramp with a flammable substance and tried to set it on fire. He notes that "at the order of Marduk, the king of the gods, the north wind, the pleasant breeze of the lord of the gods, blew and turned the tongue of the increasing fire against Uppume; it . . . burned down (the city's) wall and left it in ashes."[72] This description of divine intervention is not a whole lot different than Exod 14:21, "And Yhwh drove the sea back by a strong east wind the whole night and made the sea dry land, and the water was divided." Esarhaddon's successful attack of the city came about through divine intervention affected through the word of Marduk.[73] Another example of such involvement of a god in the affairs of mortals is *Muwatalli's Prayer to the Assembly of Gods Through the Storm-God of Lightning*.[74] The prayer begins with a confession of offenses and sins to the Storm-god. The body of the prayer consists of a systematic search for the cause of the Storm-god's anger and the king's solemn promise to make amends. It concludes with a final appeal to the Storm-god to restore his grace upon the Land. It would seem from this prayer that Muwatalli expected the Storm-god's involvement in history. These examples are not unique. In fact, it is clear that ancient rulers and nations often interpreted their historical and political fortunes with direct reference to the role played in them by deities of the Divine Warrior type.

In Ugaritic literature, the Keret and Aqhat myths show that the events were understood to be shaped by El, Baal, Anat, Mot and Yamm who divide and govern affairs in heaven, earth, sea, and the underworld. These gods are active in the seasonal cycle and daily affairs of human society. They form a political assembly whose decisions, loves, intrigues and conflicts directly affect human life and nations and determine the seasonal and daily fluctuations of nature.

(ed. F. M. Cross, Werner E. Lemke and Patrick D. Miller, Jr.; Garden City: Doubleday, 1976) 108–16.

[72] Riekele Borger, *Die Inschriften Asarhaddons Königs von Assyrien* (AfO 9; Graz: Ernst Weidner, 1956) 104.

[73] Albrektson, *History and the Gods*, 59.

[74] Itamar Singer, *Muwatalli's Prayer to the Assembly of Gods Through the Storm-god of Lightning (CTH 381)* (Atlanta: Scholars Press, 1996).

These deities embody powers of nature but they have added political or historical dimension. Important among these deities, understandably, are those possessing special abilities in divine warfare and executive power.[75] While there is doubt that Gilgamesh himself existed as a historical figure, the content of the Epic gives testimony to the fact that non-Israelite cultures of the region considered the divine involvement in human affairs to be an ordinary part of the course of events.

Ezek 21:26 (MT) mentions Nebuchednezzar's divination to choose between two possible routes at a fork in the road by shaking arrows, by consulting the *teraphim* and by inspecting the liver. He was not alone in believing deities could guide him in the events of history through the medium of divination. Atamrum, having turned down an offer to assist Babylon, is en route to Mari to hold negotiations with Zimri-Lin, and must choose a route. "He will arrive either via Saggaratum or via Terqa [or via Ma]ri. Concerning the three routes [ ] he is going to arrange [an oracular inquiry] and [if the gods render their consent], it is that (particular) route which shall be seized and he will arrive at my lord. May my lord [know about it]!"[76] He believed the gods would indicate their preference.

Liver divination was widely known and used in both Mesopotamia and Palestine. In Assyria, Shamash, the sun god, was asked through extispicy: "O Shamash, great lord, on the matter about which I ask you, answer me a firm assent . . . for these hundred days and hundred nights, the period stipulated for this extispicy, . . . Will either . . . the troops of the Cimmerians, or the troops of the Medes, or the troops of the Mannaeans, or any enemy whatever, Strive and plot (against me)?"[77] Clay models of livers, marked as keys for hepatoscopy, have been found in Mari, Ebla, Hazor, Ugarit, and Megiddo among other places. In the palace of Mari alone, they found thirty-two clay livers to be used for divination.[78] As the chief priest consulted the Urim and

---

[75] Clapham, "Mythopoeic Antecedents," 117.

[76] Abraham Malamat, "New Light from Mari (ARM XXVI) on Biblical Prophecy (III-IV)," *Storia e Tradizioni di Israele Scritti in Onore di J. Alberto Soggin* (ed. Daniele Garrone e Felice Israel; Brescia: Paideia Editrice, 1991) 188.

[77] Daniel Luckenbill, *The Annals of Sennacherib* (The University of Chicago Oriental Institute Publications 2; Chicago: University of Chicago, 1924) 140; Henry W. F. Saggs, *The Encounter with the Divine in Mesopotamia and Israel* (Jordan Lectures in Comparative Religion 12; London: The Athione Press, 1978) 130.

[78] James B. Pritchard, ed., *ANEP* (Princeton: Princeton University Press, 1969) 196, 321; Jan-Waalke Meyer, "Lebermodelle," in *Reallexikon der Assyriologie und*

Thummim (Num 27:21; 1 Sam 14:41; 28:6) to determine God's response to questions asked by the leader of the people, Mesopotamian kings are known to have consulted diviners to learn the will of the gods before important undertakings. The answer they received from the diviner was regarded as a communication from supernatural forces.[79] Though it is not clear whether the consultation of the Urim and Thummim required only a "yes" or "no" response from Yhwh or were capable of giving answers to more complex questions,[80] it is clear that Israelite kings and other ancient Near Eastern rulers posed questions to deities with the expectation that they would involve themselves in the affairs of humans. In fact, during the second millennium, the period traditionally considered the patriarchal period, the time of Moses, and the early Tribal League, religious custom in the ancient world exhibited belief in the deities' historical involvement in human affairs, similar to those of the worldview found in biblical texts.

This relationship of history and myth, the involvement of deities in the affairs of humankind, is related to what Paul Ricoeur would describe as the second meaning of history. For history is not only the narrative of events. It is also history as humans and deities make these events or are affected by them. In a given culture, historiography may be intended to provide only partial explanations that make no claim to be comprehensive, while the broader question involving the meaning of history is left to myths. In this sense history is a type of knowledge and a type of discourse which is distinct from the mythical mode of thought[81] even as it originated from and ultimately serves the purposes of myth in a different way. In this sense history and myth are part of a

---

Vorderasiatischen Archäologie 6 (Berlin: de Gruyter, 1982) 523; André Parrot, *Babylone et l'Ancien Testament* (Cahiers d'Archéologie Biblique 8; Paris: Neuchatel, 1956) 113; Yigal Yadin, "Explorations at Hazor, 1958, Preliminary Communique," *IEJ* 9 (1959) 83–84.

[79] Albrektson, *History and the Gods*, 58.

[80] Wayne Horowitz and Victor Hurowitz ("Urim and Thummim in Light of a Psephomancy Ritual from Assur [LKA 137]," *JANES* 21 [1992] 114) would see them as only providing answers to "yes" or "no" questions, similar to the psephomancy ritual practiced in Assyria; Jacob Milgrom *(The JPS Torah Commentary, Numbers* [Philadelphia: The Jewish Publication Society, 1990] 484–86) sees them as needing to be capable of more than a "yes" or "no" answer. Neither article presents their position as definitive.

[81] Paul Ricoeur, "Myth: Myth and History," in *EncRel* 10 (ed. Mircea Eliade; London: Collier Macmillan, 1987) 274–75.

continuum of literary genres.[82] For Ricoeur,[83] this relationship led to the historicization of myth which is present in the Hebrew Bible "for it is only as a broken myth that the archaic myth is reasserted within the gravitational space displayed by the historiography of the monarchic period."

A further point that needs to be discussed is the relationship of myth and cult. The influence of cult on myth and myth on cult came about through a growing awareness in many circles of the central importance of ritual acts for ancient peoples and of the accompanying texts, the myths. The Myth and Ritual School saw the words accompanying these ritual acts as inseparable from the acts. The proponents of the theory based their position on the work of Hermann Gunkel who firmly rooted the study of the OT in the cultic practices of the ancient Near East.[84] How did myth and cult interact with each other? Was myth reconstituted in the cult or was it something that was newly actualized?

In fact, the participants in the cult have been decisively shaped by the defining activity of Yhwh in their own time and in previous history and not primarily or only by its cultic actualization and representation. The cult is rather an opportunity through the work of Yhwh for the new actualization of the divine. It is also true that Yhwh's salvation experienced by cult participants in their present was interpreted differently. The religious myths in Israel's salvation history: the exodus from Egypt, the wandering in the wilderness, the election of Zion and the Temple, the Sinai event, were certainly celebrated in the cult of Israel. Some more universal myths like the *Chaoskampf* myth were not reenacted or actualized in Israel's cult, yet Israel's New Year's festival is an example of one celebration that contained many elements that were constitutive for the festival's celebration in Ugarit and Mesopotamia.[85]

The main criticism of the Myth and Ritual School is the scope of its focus. The story of creation appears in association with ritual acts, but

---

[82] Ricoeur, "Myth: Myth and History," 276.

[83] Ricoeur, "Myth: Myth and History," 281.

[84] Walter Harrelson, "Myth and Ritual School," in *EncRel* 10 (ed. Mircea Eliade; London: Collier Macmillan Publishers, 1987) 282.

[85] Horst Dietrich Preuss, *Old Testament Theology* 2 (trans. Leo G. Perdue; OTL Louisville: Westminster John Knox, 1996) 212–13, 231; originally published as *Theologie des Alten Testaments* 2 (Stuttgart: Kohlhammer, 1992).

it also has a life outside its ritual use. The great prayers and hymns of the ancient world and of Israel are cultic texts to be used as the community participates in the re-creation and reestablishment of its world and of the cosmos, but these prayers and hymns too have a life of their own. They reflect fundamental realities on which the social existence of the people depended.[86] Cult is not the genesis of myth. Myth is that which inspired cult.

Israel came to understand its faith in a dialectic process of reflection on both Yhwh's saving action in its history and the myths which formed the religions which surrounded it during the centuries of its own faith's formation.[87] The interpretation of Yhwh's saving action in the history of Israel, particularly the re-interpretation of that history after the exile, was shaped strongly by inherited mythic patterns and language which belonged not only to the nations which surrounded it, but also to Israel. It was the context in which Israel discerned the uniqueness of its faith.[88] The OT comes from a firmly mythical environment in Israel and so myth is the most helpful horizon for understanding OT phenomena.[89] It would not have been surprising for early Israelite audiences to have been able to fill out the brief allusions to these myths with the larger story so familiar to them.[90] The mythic parallels mentioned show correlation with ancient Near Eastern cultures, yet given the mythic heritage of Israel it is unnecessary to posit

---

[86] Harrelson, "Myth and Ritual School," 285.

[87] Any number of authors discuss this theme: Boadt, "Mythological Themes," 216–19; Brevard S. Childs, *Myth and Reality,* 13–16; *CMHE,* viii; and more recently F. M. Cross, "The Development of Israelite Religion," 18–29, 50 and "Israelite Origins," *Bible Review* 8.4 (1992) 23–32, 61–62; Aarre Lauha, *Zaphon, der Norden und die Nordvölker im Alten Testament,* 72; Tryggve N. D. Mettinger, "Fighting the Powers of Chaos and Hell Towards the Biblical Portrait of God," *ST* 39 (1985) 21–23; Robert A. Oden, Jr., *The Bible Without Theology* (New Voices in Biblical Studies; San Francisco: Harper & Row, 1987) 48–51; Annmarie Ohler, "Die Gegenwart Gottes in der Gottesferne," *BibLeb* 11 (1970) 87; Preuss, *Old Testament Theology* 1, 247–48; Rolf Rendtorff, "El, Ba'al und Jahwe," *ZAW* 78 (1966) 277–78.

[88] Hans-Joachim Kraus, *The Theology of the Psalms* (trans. Keith Crim; Minneapolis: Augsburg Publishing House, 1986) 134–35; originally published as *Theologie der Psalmen* (BKAT 15/3; Neukirchen-Vluyn: Neukirchener Verlag, 1979); Preuss, *Old Testament Theology,* 1.217.

[89] Müller, *Jenseits der Entmythologisierung,* 9.

[90] It is through the Ugaritic and similar materials that we are able to get a sense of the full dimensions of the old myth and its continuing vitality in Israel.

influence or dependence. The point of this work is not what particular myths the final form of Ezekiel is taken from. The point of this work is that the final form of Ezekiel is about presenting a new mythic conclusion to the Israelite cosmogonic myth to give hope to Israel. In the course of constructing this myth, the final form overturns the mythic gods of the other nations and reveals the emptiness of their threat before the power of the Creator, the God of Israel. This new cosmogonic myth of Ezekiel will provide a structure for understanding the placement of chapters 38–39 in the final form.

Müller considers prior knowledge of the mythic elements of the religions of the region by the people as the first criterion for studying the influence of these myths on the religious worldview of Israel.[91] The findings of archaeology give support to Israel's knowledge of the religious myths of the region and the influence of these myths on the people. The significant number of human and animal figurines found in the soil of Iron Age Palestine is notable, and, of these, the significantly larger number found in Jerusalem and Samaria as compared to other sites. According to Gösta Ahlström, the figure for Jerusalem totaled 597 figurines, as opposed to 159 in Samaria, 28 in Bethel, 22 in Shechem, 64 in Gibeon and 44 in Hazor.[92] Jerusalem's and Samaria's attachment to these religious figurines at non-cultic sites, including a much greater predominance of female figurines over male figurines, seems to be pronounced and is worth our consideration in studying the religious faith of Israel and Judah.

Some background to give context would be helpful. Such terra cotta figurines or stone artifacts employing iconographic portrayals are not a major feature of the "Establishment" sanctuary or shrine of either the united or divided monarchy.[93] Holladay's reflection on the archaeological findings of Iron II period excavations in the region notes that the actual organization and practice of religion in ancient Israel and

---

[91] Müller, "Mythische Elemente," 115.

[92] Gösta Ahlström, *Royal Administration and National Religion in Ancient Palestine* (Studies in the History of the Ancient Near East 1; Leiden: Brill, 1982) 82–83; John S. Holladay, "Religion in Israel and Judah Under the Monarchy: An Explicitly Archaeological Approach," in *Ancient Israelite Religion, Essays in Honor of Frank Moore Cross* (ed. Patrick D. Miller, Jr., Paul D. Hanson, S. Dean McBride; Philadelphia: Fortress, 1987) 265.

[93] Holladay, "Religion in Israel and Judah," 297.

Judah seems to exist on two levels. The dominant religious structure paralleled the political structure of the state, confirming and complementing the state government with the stipulations, sanctions, and blessings of the true ruler of the universe. In this regard, the religious structure could no more suffer religious heterodoxy than the political structure could. Alternative forms of religious expression sprang up when individuals or groups would find themselves at odds with the religious establishment. These dissenting groups were not entirely divorced from the dominant state religion, yet a great many people took care to propitiate and supplicate the powers of the universe on more than one level. Consequently, archaeologically recoverable evidence for more than one community of believers at each level of political organization was in evidence.[94] These facts give rise to a question: was Israel's tradition truly aniconic?

The answer to the question is both yes and no. Helpful to the interpretation is the distinction between *de facto* tradition and programmatic tradition. Mettinger notes that the late explicit ban on images is a programmatic formulation, prior to which existed a much older *de facto* tradition of aniconism in which aniconism was perhaps a conventional observance, but not linked to the iconophobia present at the time of the exile.[95] The *de facto* aniconism permits a greater degree of tolerance. According to the archaeological findings, the officially sanctioned religious praxis of Israel and Judah seems to have been basically aniconic during the divided monarchy.[96] A totally different form of religious expression is witnessed during the divided monarchy, both north and south, by small clusters of cultic artifacts, heavily biased toward the iconographic, discontinuously distributed, spatially and temporally, throughout domestic quarters and through large clusters of restricted chronological span centered on extramural locations near major cities (Jerusalem and Samaria). These cult areas are character-

---

[94] Holladay, "Religion in Israel and Judah," 249, 266–67.

[95] Tryggve N. D. Mettinger, *No Graven Image? Israelite Aniconism in Its Ancient Near Eastern Context* (ConBOT 42; Stockholm: Almqvist & Wiksell International, 1995) 14, 37.

[96] Holladay, "Religion in Israel and Judah," 295. The discussion here is of archaeological findings. Ezekiel considered polytheism to have been widespread and recorded it in his book to be at every level of Israelite society: in the homes of the poor, in the royal palace and in the Temple itself.

ized by the presence of a significant quantity of figurines, dominated by female figurines as opposed to male figurines, dominated in the overall by statuettes of animals.[97] Even outside the city gate at Tel Dan, site of the northern sanctuary of the northern kingdom, two bronze plaques were found in the 1997 and the 1998 excavation seasons. They are both ninth century B.C.E. adoration scenes depicting deities.[98] Monotheistic faith in Yhwh seems to have had much to contend with and made headway slowly.

The worship of other deities along with the worship of the patron god of the city or nation was a common practice in ancient Near Eastern societies. For Israel to worship other deities did not take away from the unique honor given to Yhwh. What was unique was the denunciation of polytheism by some of Israel's prophets and their insistence that Israelites should worship Yhwh alone.[99] The formulation of an express veto on images is closely linked with this insistence on worship of Yhwh alone and there was no such express veto on images among other Semitic peoples of the ancient world. The express veto on images does belong then to what became specifically different about the practiced institutional faith of Israel, and in Israel, aniconism developed into an extreme programmatic anti-iconic attitude.[100]

The vocabulary of Ezekiel itself supports these findings for the late Iron Age. גלולים, a noun always appearing in the plural, belongs to a group of words used in mocking polemics against idols, and is the predominant word for foreign gods in Ezekiel. In the book it is used mainly to denote a sin of idolatry committed by Israel in the past and also in the exilic present. Ezekiel brands such apostasy as an abomination to Yhwh, and that which is totally foreign to Yhwh.[101] The word גלולים is found 48 times in the OT and 39 of these are in Ezekiel.[102] Idolatry is, in fact, *the* sin of Israel, *the* stumbling block (see Ezek 14:7). This has implications for the impact of ancient Near Eastern myth on Israel and on Ezekiel as well.

---

[97] Holladay, "Religion in Israel and Judah," 274, 281.

[98] Avraham Biran, "Two Bronze Plaques and the Ḥuṣṣot of Dan," *IEJ* 49/1–2 (1999) 52–54.

[99] Cohn, *Cosmos, Chaos, and the World to Come*, 141.

[100] Mettinger, *No Graven Image?*, 196–97.

[101] Horst Dietrich Preuss, "גלולים," in *TWAT* 2 (Stuttgart: Kohlhammer, 1977) 1–3.

[102] Ezek 6:4, 5, 6, 9, 13 (twice); 8:10; 14:3, 4 (twice), 5, 6, 7; 16:36; 18:6, 12, 15; 20:7, 8, 16, 18, 24, 31, 39 (twice); 22:3, 4; 23: 7, 30, 37, 39, 49; 30:13; 33:25; 36:18, 25; 37:23; 44:10, 12.

Ezekiel's final form was a revision of Israel's religious myth for a new generation, presenting a perception of Israel's faith story. After a the faith shattering crisis of Jerusalem's destruction and the uprooting of exile, the final form presents the paradigmatic myth of a society that would be replicated on earth. The final form of Ezekiel sees included in cosmogony not only the recounting of the origins of the intelligible universe, but also the recounting of the completion of that same universe as created anew in the future. Ezekiel, a product of the theology of its time, presented the belief that the definitive victory of the Creator over chaos is not so much a primeval event as an eschatological hope. In this sense, the Book of Ezekiel is a cosmogony presenting the completion of Yhwh's act of creation.[103] It made mythopoeic use of the Combat Myth in chapters 38–39 as part of an unfolding articulation of faith in chapters 34–48 that the Creator God of Israel would bring his act of creation to completion and the Reign of God would come. Ezekiel proclaims this, grounded in the authority of myth, a language whose message and import the audience would understand. We will look at this more thoroughly in chapters four and five of this work, but in the next chapter we will first look at the textual links which show chapters 38–39 as an integral part of the final form textually.

---

[103] Benjamin Uffenheimer, "Theodicy and Ethics in the Prophecy of Ezekiel," in *Justice and Righteousness: Biblical Themes and Their Influence* (ed. Henning G. Reventlow and Yair Hoffman; JSOTSup 137; Sheffield: JSOT, 1992) 202.

CHAPTER 3

Textual Links between the Gog Pericope and Other Sections of Ezekiel

While this study focuses mainly on the foundational role of ancient Near Eastern myth in understanding the significance of chapters 38–39 in the final form of Ezekiel, it is also important to note the textual links of chapters 38–39 with the rest of the book which give clear testimony that in the final form, these chapters were understood as part of the whole. These textual links are most noticeable in two areas: formulaic usage and similarities in phrases used in both the Gog pericope and the Oracles against Egypt. But before we look at these, we will examine other examples of textual links between chapters 38–39 and the remainder of the text that could be missed by a more cursory reading.

I

When one studies the vocabulary used in the final form of Ezekiel, the number of words which appear both in chapters 38–39 and in other sections of the book, either unique to Ezekiel, rarely used in the OT apart from Ezekiel, or used frequently enough in the final form to be significant, one sees not a disparate effort in the composition of the text's final form, but rather clear textual connections between chapters

38–39 and the rest of the book. The following list of twenty-six instances[1] demonstrates this clearly.

(1) משך, תבל: "Meshech and Tubal," these two geographical locations appear in the OT only five times and only in Ezekiel. They appear three times in the Gog pericope, 32:2, 3; 39:1 as well as in the Oracle against Tyre (27:13) and in the Oracle against Egypt (32:26).

(2) מכלול, "completeness, perfection," occurs only twice in the Hebrew Bible: Ezek 23:12 and 38:4.

(3) קהל רב, "a great company," appears eight times in the OT, four of those in Ezekiel, twice in the Gog pericope, 38:4, 15. The other two times, as above, occur in the Oracle against Tyre (26:7) and in the Oracle against Egypt (32:3).

(4) מגן and כובע, "shield and helmet," a combination which appears only twice in the OT, both in Ezekiel, 27:10 and 38:5.

(5) אגף, "army," a usage unique to Ezekiel, appears six times in the book, 12:14, 17:21 and four times in chapters 38–39: 38:6, 9, 22 and 39:4.

(6) תגרמה, "Togarmah," is mentioned twice in Ezekiel, 27:14 and 38:6 and in the Table of Nations, Gen 10:3 and I Chron 1:6.

(7) מקבצת, "gathering," applied to the dispersed, appears in 38:8, 39:27 and similarly in 39:28. This theme of regathering, discussed below in the Oracles against Egypt, recurs throughout the book: 11:16–17; 20:34, 41; 28:25–26; 34:13; 36:24; 37:21 plus the three occurrences in chapters 38–39.

(8) הרי ישראל, "the mountains of Israel," a phrase appearing fourteen times in Ezekiel and unique to him, appears four times in the two chapters: 38:8; 39:2, 4, 17. Prior to the pericope it appears in 6:2, 3; 19:9; 33:28; 34:13; 35:12; 36: 1, 4, 8; 37:22.

(9) חרבה, "desolate place," is also characteristic of Ezekiel. Appearing twice in the Gog pericope (38:8, 12), this word or a variation of the tri-consonantal root conveying the same sense precedes twelve times in the book: 5:14; 13:4; 25:13; 26:20; 29:9, 10; 33:24, 27; 35:4; 36:4, 35, 38.

---

[1] While I have deleted, modified and added to his list, I'm grateful for the initial prior research of Stephen Cook (*Prophecy and Apocalypticism: The Postexilic Social Setting* [Minneapolis: Fortress, 1995] 98–103).

(10) כבוד, "glory" meaning the presence of the all-powerful deity. It is thematic to Ezekiel, appearing nineteen times: 1:28; 3:12, 23; 8:4; 9:3; 10:4 (twice), 18, 19; 11:22, 23; 28:22; 31:18; 39:13; 43:2, 4, 5; 44:4. Significantly, one of those times is in the Gog-Magog passage.

(11) אדמת ישראל, "the land of Israel," occurs seventeen times in the book: 7:2; 11:17; 12:19, 22;13:9; 18:2; 20:38, 42; 21:7, 8; 25:3, 6; 33:24; 36:6; 37:12; 38:18, 19. It is a phrase unique to the Book of Ezekiel, including its two occurrences in the Gog pericope as noted in the verse listing.

(12) ישב לבטח, "live securely," or a similar usage appears nine times in Ezekiel, with five of these occurrences in the pericope: 38:8, 11, 14; 39:26 and similarly 39:6. Preceding these uses, it occurs in 28:26; 34:25, 28; and similarly 34:27 and is in continuity with the theology of his book.

(13) כענן לכסות, "like a cloud to cover," appears four times in Ezekiel, twice in the pericope, 38:9, 16, and with similar usage in 30:18, 32:7.

(14) שבא, דדן, and תרשיש, "Sheba, Dedan and Tarshish," are also mentioned in the trade list in chapter 27. These same cities occur again in 38:13.

(15) קהל גדול וחיל רב, "a great assembly and a mighty army," occurs in the pericope once (38:15) and earlier with a similar usage in 17:17.

(16) ידע הגוים, "the nations" as the subject of the verbal element of the recognition formula appears five times in the two chapters: 38:16, 23 and 39:6, 7, 23. A similar usage of this more narrowly defined usage ("the nations will know") of the recognition formula appears seven other times in Ezekiel, 36:23, 36; 37:28; 26:6; 29:6; 30:6 and similarly in 21:10.

(17) בהקדשי לעיניהם, with "God" as subject + "before the eyes" ("I shall sanctify myself before (their) eyes"); this and similar usage (once it appears in the hithpaʻel rather than niphal form) appear seven times in Ezekiel, three times in the pericope, 38:16, 23; 39:27, and also 20:41; 28:25; 36:23 and similarly 28:22.

(18) קנאה + דבר, "speak in (angry) zeal," occurs four times in Ezekiel: 5:13; 36:5, 6; 38:19.

(19) עברה + אש, "blazing wrath," a combination which is an Ezekiel expression, appears once in the Gog periocope (38:19) and three other times in the book: 21:36; 22:21, 31.

(20) גשם שוטף, "torrential rain," a combination which occurs once in the pericope, 38:22, and only twice elsewhere in the Hebrew Bible, Ezek 13:11, 13.

(21) אלגביש, "hail," is a term peculiar to Ezekiel in the Hebrew Bible, occurring once in the pericope 38:22 and two other times: 13:11, 13.

(22) נתתיך לאכלה, to "give for food" to wild animals appears twice in the pericope, 39:4, similarly 39:17, with similar usage ten other times in Ezekiel: 15:4, 6; 29:5; 33:27; 32:4, 5;.34:5, 8; and 35:12.

(23) צפור כל כנף, "birds of every wing," appears in 39:4, 17 and 17:23. Apart from Ezekiel the phrase appears only in Deut 4:17.

(24) טהר, "to cleanse, to purify," appears in 39:12, 14, 16. In Ezekiel it also appears in 36:25, 33; 37:23; 43:26.

(25) שבעה, "satiety," in its feminine form appears in the OT only seven times. Three are in Pss 88:4 ; 123:4; 30:16. The fourth is in Isa 56:11. The other three are in Ezekiel: 16:28, 49; 39:19.

(26) שלחני, "my table," with Yhwh as antecedent appears in the OT only twice, and both instances are in the Book of Ezekiel, 39:20 and 44:16.

These examples are presented to illustrate the ways that the vocabulary, language and phraseology of chapters 38–39 echo those of the other sections of the book. The repeated usage of particular phrases and of recurrent wording, especially that which is specific to Ezekiel, demonstrates clear textual links between the Gog pericope and the remainder of the book.

II

The major formulas are very striking stylistic characteristics used throughout the book including chapters 38–39. These would suggest that the Gog pericope was integrated into the formation of the final form. Of the many formulas[2] used frequently in the final form, eleven appear in chapters 38–39. As a basic schema[3] for these eleven we will

---

[2] A summary listing and explanation of these seventeen formulas is presented in Ronald Hals' commentary (*Ezekiel* [FOTL 19; Grand Rapids: Eerdmans, 1989] 359–63).

[3] The organizational schema of the formulas in Block (*The Book of Ezekiel, Chapters 1–24*, 30–35) is helpful in this regard,

look first at forms of address, secondly at direct speech markers, thirdly at prophetic commands, and lastly at a theological formula very significant to the Book of Ezekiel.

When Yhwh is addressed by the prophet, he is addressed with the title אדני יהוה, "Lord, Yhwh." This form of address appears more than 200 times in the book. It is employed both before and after chapters 38–39. It is used fifteen times[4] in the Gog pericope. The double title is significant because it identifies the God of Israel, Yhwh, as Lord: the sovereign, Creator God, above all gods. A second form of address, almost[5] unique to Ezekiel is the title of address to the prophet: בן־אדם, "son of man." It underscores the prophet's creaturely status, his humanity, before the Creator. It appears 93 times in the book,[6] in chapters before and after the Gog pericope and four times in the Gog pericope.[7] It establishes the prophet's stance solidly among the people. Lastly, the final form's preferential title of address for the people, בית ישראל, "house of Israel,"[8] used more than sixty times throughout the book, appears five times in chapters 38–39, and in chapters preceding and following.[9] Ezekiel's preference for this over the title "sons of Israel" stresses the unity of the nation based on kinship and consanguinity.[10] In the Gog pericope, it is the House of Israel who is called upon to bury the bodies and so to purify the land to be a fit space for the habitation of the community.

The first of the direct speech markers is the Prophetic Word Formula, ויהי דבר יהוה אלי לאמר "and the word of Yhwh came to me saying." Appearing almost forty times in Ezekiel before the Gog pericope, it opens the Gog pericope in 38:1. It is a statement preceding divine prophetic speech, signaling that what follows is the word of the sovereign Creator. The Messenger Formula, כה אמר אדני יהוה, "Thus says the Lord God," occurs 122 times in Ezekiel, both before and after

---

[4] 38:3, 10, 14, 17, 18, 21; 39: 1, 5, 8, 10, 13, 17, 20, 25, 29.

[5] It also appears in Dan 8:17, though Eichrodt (*Ezekiel*, 61) sees that as having been influenced by Ezekiel.

[6] Block, *The Book of Ezekiel, Chapters 1–24*, 30.

[7] 38:2; 38:14; 39:1; 39:17.

[8] For a full development of the usage of this term see Daniel Block, "Israel's House: Reflections on the Use of בית ישראל in the Old Testament in the Light of Its Ancient Near Eastern Environment," *JETS* 28 (1985) 257–75.

[9] 39: 12, 22, 23, 25, 29.

[10] Block, "Israel's House," 275.

the Gog pericope and seven times in the Gog pericope.[11] Its use authenticates the prophet as speaking in the prophetic divine voice. The last of the direct speech markers, the Prophetic Utterance Formula, נאם אדני יהוה, "Oracle of the Lord God," concludes an oracle or a section of an oracle. It appears 81 times in Ezekiel, in the chapters preceding and following chapters 38–39 and eight times in these two chapters.[12] Whether occurring at the end of an oracle or at the end of a section of an oracle, it acts as a signature of the authority of the speaker. Once again it highlights the subservient role of the prophet. It is the word of Israel's God, Yhwh who is Lord.

The Commissioning Formula, most commonly in Ezekiel . . . הנבא ואמרת, sometimes ואמרת . . . אמר, appears thirty-five times up to and including the Gog pericope. Four of these occurrences are in the Gog pericope: 38:2, 14; 39: 1, 17. This stylistic pattern of prefacing the verb with another verbal command is distinctive to Ezekiel.[13] With a function similar to other formulas, it is an authoritative charge to the prophet to deliver a message in the name of the sovereign Lord. אני דברתי, "I (Yahweh) have spoken," the Conclusion Formula for divine speech, is a frequent marker in Ezekiel, stressing the power of God's word, appearing in 39:5 and fifteen other times in the book: 5:13, 15, 17; 17:21, 24; 21:22, 37; 22:14; 24:14; 26:14; 28:10; 30:12; 34:24; 36:36; 37:14. Zimmerli finds this formula particularly characteristic of Ezekiel.[14] הנני אליך (עליך), "Behold, I am against you," the Challenge to a Duel Formula, appears twenty-two times in the Hebrew Scriptures, fourteen of these in Ezekiel and twice in the Gog pericope, 38:3; 39:1. This challenge to a duel is imitated by the prophets in announcements of punishment, usually in a context dominated by imagery of battle.[15] The last of the ten, the Hostile Orientation Formula, שים פניך אל, "set your face against," occurs six times in the chapters preceding chapters 38–39. The phrase begins the Gog pericope, 38:2. A common idiom throughout the ancient Near East,[16] it is used to introduce a prophecy

---

[11] 38:3, 10, 14, 17; 39:1, 17, 25.
[12] 38:18, 21; 39:5, 8, 10, 13, 20, 29.
[13] Block, *The Book of Ezekiel, Chapters 1–24*, 34.
[14] Zimmerli, *Ezekiel*, 1.26–27.
[15] Hals, *Ezekiel*, 359.
[16] Scott Layton, "Biblical Hebrew 'to set the face' in the Light of Akkadian and Ugaritic," *UF* 17 (1986) 169–81.

against a particular group, reflecting Yhwh's hostile disposition toward them.

The last of the examples of formulaic usage which shows textual linkage between chapters 38–39 and the remainder of the book is a very significant theological formula in Ezekiel, what has been called the Recognition Formula. The Recognition Formula highlights and reinforces Yhwh's role and prerogatives as Creator. That Yhwh's sovereignty as Creator would be known by Israel and the nations is one point that is clear and sounded, like a metered cadence, in the seven uses (38:16, 23; 39:6, 7, 22, 23, 28) of the Recognition Formula in chapters 38–39. It is the second largest concentration[17] of the formula's 79[18] occurrences[19] including variations, in the entire Book of Ezekiel. It is significant, and to be discussed further in chapter six, that chapter 39 is the last chapter in which the Recognition Formula is used.

Such formulaic replication would lead one to conclude that an effort was made, at least in stylistic characteristics of the final form, to purposefully present a unified text in which 38–39 were linked textually both to what preceded and what followed. Another curious textual link between chapters 38–39 and the overall book is the eight similarities in text between the Oracles against Egypt and the Gog pericope. We will present the similarities briefly here as they do clearly indicate an effort at a purposeful integration of chapters 38–39 into the overall text. We will discuss their significance in chapter five when we discuss

---

[17] It occurs in the fifteen verses of chapter 25 six times: 25:5, 7, 9, 11, 14, 17.

[18] Zimmerli (*I Am Yahweh* [trans. Douglas W. Stott; ed. and intro. Walter Brueggemann; Atlanta: John Knox, 1982] 30–31, 143–44) cites 78 occurrences though his listing repeats 6:13 twice and does not mention 25:5. To these I added, in agreement with Block (*The Book of Ezekiel, Chapters 25–48*, 430), 39:23. Zimmerli himself considers the heart of the recognition formula to be the recognition of Yhwh and of his unique activity (Zimmerli, *I Am Yahweh*, 31). Verse 23 is clearly about the recognition of Yhwh in his unique activity. Odell would include 39:21 ("Are You He of Whom I Spoke By My Servants the Prophets? Ezekiel 38–39 and the Problem of History in the Neo-Babylonian Context" [Ph.D. diss., University of Pittsburgh, 1988; available from Harvard University] 148). Yet given the significance of the Hebrew verb ידע in its use in the recognition formula and the use of ראה in v. 21, it seemed beyond the limits of a variation.

[19] 2:5; 5:13; 6:7, 10, 13, 14; 7:4, 9, 27;11:10, 12; 12:15, 16, 20; 13: 9, 14, 21, 23; 14:8, 23; 15:7; 16:62; 17: 21, 24; 20:12, 20, 26, 38, 42, 44; 21:5; 22:16, 22; 23:49; 24:24, 27; 25: 5, 7, 9, 11, 14, 17; 26:6; 28:22, 23, 24, 26; 29: 6, 9, 16, 21; 30: 8, 19, 25, 26; 32: 15; 33:29, 33; 34:27, 30; 35: 4, 9, 12, 15; 36:11, 23, 36, 38; 37:6, 13, 14, 28; 38:16, 23; 39:6, 7, 22, 23, 28.

the differing functions of the Oracles against the Nations and the Gog pericope.

Both accounts do present amazing similarities in text.[20] Both Pharaoh and Gog are presented as mere puppets of Yhwh, who puts hooks in their jaws at will: 29:4; 38:4. Both peoples will be gathered from the peoples among whom they have been scattered, and they will be restored to their lands after a time: 29:13; 38:8; 39:27. Both armies will fall in the open field and on the mountains where the birds of the air and wild beasts of the field will gorge themselves on their carcasses: 29:4f.; 39:4, 5, 19. In both cases Yhwh will make the enemies' weapons fall (נפל) from their hands, 30:22; 39:3. The theme of being given into the hand of the enemy by Yhwh appears in both passages, though with the use of different verbs: 30:10, 12, 25; 31:11; 39:23. The return of the captives recurs in 39:25 in reference to Israel, an echo of the return of captives to Egypt in 29:14. The Challenge to a Duel Formula (הנני אליך) repeats itself twice in each passage: 29:10, 30:22; 38:3; 39:1. The use of the same two verbs of similar meaning (בזז, שלל) to intensify the image of devastation surfaces again in the Gog pericope after it was used in the Oracle against Egypt: 29:19; 38:12. Lastly, the recurrent theme of "the many peoples" (עמים רבים) repeats itself no less than eight times in the two passages, appearing only twice in the rest of the book: 3:6 and 27:33.

The massive textual linkage in Ezekiel supports the position of a strong editorial hand in the formulation of the final form. The book is primarily about writing a theology, not a political history. Myth serves as the frame of reference for writing such a theology that would inspire a defeated people with hope in their God and enkindle again the fire of their religious imagination in Yhwh's possibilities. Let us proceed then to investigate the mythic elements in the book and see where they lead us.

---

[20] Lawrence Boadt, *Ezekiel's Oracles Against Egypt, A Literary and Philological Study of Ezekiel 29–32* (BibOr 37; Rome: Biblical Institute Press, 1980) 177 n. 16.

CHAPTER 4

Ezekiel 38–39, Cosmogony Completed, A Covenant of Peace Fulfilled

Apart from the Book of Ezekiel, Gog and Magog make their appearance frequently in literature after the exile. In later literature specific reference to them surfaces in the Sibylline Oracles (Book III, lines 319 ff. and 512 ff.). They are also mentioned very often in rabbinic literature. Besides chapters 38–39 of the *Targum of Ezekiel*, they occur in the *Babylonian Talmud*, the *Mishna*, the *Midrash Rabbah*, *Pesikta*, and *Sifre*,[1] and they regularly appear in Jewish Legend.[2] The theme of the

---

[1] Roger Le Déaut, trans., *Targum du Pentateuque 3: Nombres* (Sources chrétiennes 261; Paris: Editions du Cerf, 1979) 110; Roger Le Déaut, trans.,*Targum du Pentateuque II: Exodus et Lévitique* (Sources chrétiennes 256; Paris: Editions du Cerf, 1979) 311; Abramo Alberto Piatelli, trans., *Targum Shir Ha-Shirim* (Textus biblici 1 001; Rome: Barulli, 1975) 80; Samson H. Levey, trans., *The Targum of Ezekiel* (Aramaic Bible 13; Edinburgh: T. & T. Clark, Ltd, 1987) 105–9; Harry Freedman, trans., *The Babylonian Talmud, 3: Shabbath* (London: Soncino Press, 1987) 118a; Jacob Shachter & Harry Freedman, trans., *The Babylonian Talmud, 19: Sanhedrin* (London: Soncino Press, 1987) 17a; A. Mishcon and A. Cohen, trans., *The Babylonian Talmud, 21: Abodah Zarah* (London: Soncino Press, 1988) 3b; Judah Goldin, trans., *The Fathers According to Rabbi Nathan* (YJS 10; New Haven: Yale University Press, 1955) 141; Hubert Danby, trans., *The Mishnah* (London: Oxford University Press, 1958) 426; Harry Freedman, trans., *Midrash Rabbah, Genesis I* (London: Soncino Press, 1983) 292; Simon M. Lehrman, trans., *Midrash Rabbah, Exodus* (London: Soncino Press, 1983) 3, 144, 182, 285, 367; J. Israelstam and Judah Slotki, trans., *Midrash Rabbah, Leviticus* (London: Soncino Press, 1961) 113,

final battle is a very prominent feature of the NT Book of Revelation which mentions Gog and Magog by name in Rev. 20:7–10 and by clear allusion in 19:17–21.[3] The Gog/Magog account also makes its appearance in two *sura's* of the Qur'an (18:93–111 and 21:96–105).[4]

It is the faith of the Jewish and Christian traditions that as long as the forces of evil exist unchecked, God is not altogether God: his sovereign power is not yet fully realized. "In the latter years," Ezek 38:8, is now interpreted to mean that the ancient and enduring opposition to the full accomplishment of God's sovereign power is destined to be brought under conclusive dominion at the end of history.[5] This unfinished element was present in the *Chaoskampf* myth as well. The possibility of Tiamat's split-open body growing together again is a continuing threat. The myth makes clear that the energy of life resists regulation,[6] and can move to chaos at any time. Most significant in understanding the themes of chapters 38–39 will be the mythological accounts of the decisive battle, but before looking at these links, let us

---

136, 356, 387; Judah Slotki, trans., *Midrash Rabbah, Numbers II* (London: Soncino Press, 1961) 499, 664; Harry Freedman and Maurice Simon, trans., *Midrash Rabbah, Esther, Song of Songs* (London: Soncino Press, 1961) 6, 101, 211, 227 f.; William G. Braude, trans., *Pesikta Rabbati: Discourses for Feasts, Fasts, & Special Sabbaths* (YJS 18; New Haven: Yale University Press, 1968) 688; William G. Braude and Israel J. Kapstein, trans., *Pĕsikta dĕ-Rab Kahana: Compilation of Discourses for Sabbaths & Festal Days* (London: Routledge & Kegan Paul, 1975) 183; Jacob Neusner, trans., *Sifré to Numbers, An American Translation and Explanation 2: Sifré to Numbers 59–115* (Atlanta: Scholars Press, 1986) 47; Reuven Hammer, trans., *Sifre, A Tannaitic Commentary on the Book of Deuteronomy* (YJS 24; New Haven, London: Yale University Press, 1986) 354.

[2] Louis Ginzberg, *The Legends of the Jews, Vol. 1* (Philadelphia: Jewish Publication Society of America, 1961) 167–70; *Vol. 2, 3* and *4* (Philadelphia: Jewish Publication Society of America, 1954) 2:347, 356–57, 3:45–50, 251–52, 443–46, 452–62, 4:65–72, 266–70, 270–77; *Vol. 6* (Philadelphia: The Jewish Publication Society of America, 1959) 57–58, 266–67.

[3] In Rev. 19:17–21 the birds of the air and wild beasts of the field are invited to come for a victory feast where they will "eat the flesh of kings, the flesh of captains, the flesh of the mighty, the flesh of horses and their riders." It clearly parallels Ezekiel 39:17–20.

[4] For a comparative discussion of the Hebrew Bible use of the Gog/Magog account and the later Qur'anic use, the reader may refer to John Kaltner, "The Gog/Magog Tradition in the Hebrew Bible and the Qur'an, Points of Similarity and Dissimilarity," *USQR* 49 (1995) 35–48.

[5] Levenson, *Creation and the Persistence of Evil*, 38.

[6] Wakeman, *God's Battle with the Monster*, 24, 42.

first meet the narrative as it appears in the text and theology of chapters 38–39 apart from the mythic elements.

I

Efforts at understanding the structural division of the narrative's final form yield inconclusive and unsatisfying results.[7] While formulas elsewhere in Ezekiel often suggest stages of an unfolding plot, they lack the consistency to do so here. Reviewing the work of scholars, it is difficult to offer an unproblematic explanation on the division of text.[8] The final form of the text uses some other principle of arrangement than its formulas; these seem not to have been placed in the final form

---

[7] I found Allen's outlining (*Ezekiel 20–48*, 202–4) of the discussion very helpful.

[8] Using a sevenfold division based on the Messenger Formula, כה אמר אדני יהוה ("Thus says the Lord God") in 38: 3, 10, 14, 17; 39: 1, 17, 25 does not provide uniform outcome. Both Allen (*Ezekiel 20–48*, 202) and Blenkinsopp (*Ezekiel*, 180) note that such a division limps because 38:17 is clearly not the beginning of a sub-unit within the oracle. The material in 38:18–23 is separate from it, and vv. 23–24 belong with vv. 25–29. The Messenger Formula clearly has an intermediate role within a larger sub-unit. Allen sees the use of the Messenger Formula as only a stylistic technique. Henry van Dyke Parunak ("Structural Studies in Ezekiel" [Ph.D. diss., Harvard University, 1978; available from University Microfilms, Ann Arbor, MI] 490–91) and Robert R. Wilson ("Ezekiel," *HCBC* [San Francisco: HarperSan Francisco, 2000] 620–21) would both suggest a fourfold structure based on the Commissioning Formula, בן אדם הנבא ("Mortal, prophesy), in 38:2, 14; 39:1, 17. But this is not supported by the text. As Hossfeld (*Untersuchungen*, 406) notes, 38:14 beginning with "therefore" is clearly dependent on what precedes it, part of a larger sub-unit and does not begin anything. Both Zimmerli (*Ezekiel 2*, 296–99), and Garscha (*Studien zum Ezechielbuch*, 237) basically come up with a redactional core of three sections by eliminating Parunak's second division. To this three part redactional core later material was added. Yet such a division itself can be challenged by noting that the third division is of a very different nature than the first two which are marked by extensive parallelism (Allen, *Ezekiel 20–48*, 203). Block (*The Book of Ezekiel, Chapters 25–48*, 425) notes that using the Prophetic Utterance Formula, נאם אדני יהוה ("... says the Lord God"), which appears eight times in the two chapters: 38:18, 21; 39: 5, 8, 10, 13, 20, 29 does not furnish a structure. While it is usually placed at the end of a unit or a major section within a unit, in only three instances (39:10, 20, 29) here is it used to conclude oracle sub-units in which it is located. Wevers (*Ezekiel*. 285) concludes that the Recognition Formula, וידעו כי אני יהוה ("And they will know that I am Lord"), does not give structure to the two chapters. Its expanded forms are used seven times in the Oracle, 38:16, 23; 39:6, 7, 22, 23, 28, yet in only two uses does it conclude what would seem to be a sub-unit in the chapters.

for the purpose of organization. I suggest that the retelling of myth provides the structure for chapters 38–39.

The narrative can be divided into three blocks of material which are useful in grasping a sense of the plot's dynamics. After being introduced by the Ezekielian prophetic word formula in v. 1, three parts follow; each one primarily describes one key player in the drama. The primary focus of the first part, 38:2–17 (sixteen verses), is Gog. The second division, 38:18–39:8 (fourteen verses), introduces the Creator God of Ezekiel. The final division, 39:9–20 (twelve verses), looks at the response of creation after the battle. This divides the Gog pericope into three groups of 16, 14, and 12 verses respectively. These are followed by a conclusion in 39:21–29 directed not to Gog but to the audience addressed by the narrative.

Ezekiel 38:2–17

Ezekiel 38:2–17 introduces Gog, but the actual identity of Gog is far from clear. The broad consensus of scholars who would try to discern an allusion to an historical figure settles on Gyges of Lydia who lived in the middle of the seventh century, B.C.E.[9] The military record of Gyges, however, does not seem to justify such a comparison. With similar successes and setbacks as other rulers of comparable power, he was eventually killed in a raid by the Cimmerians,[10] the very people who forced him to seek foreign alliance with Ashurbanipal earlier in his career.[11] He was hardly the quintessential model of the archetypal

---

[9] Zimmerli (*Ezekiel* 2.305) suggests that if Gog is the name of a reference to a former ruler, his "hiddenness" could be compared to the "hiddenness" of the future David.

[10] Eduard Lipiński ("Gyges et Lygdamis d'après les sources neo-assyriennes et hebraïques," *XXXIV International Assyriology Congress* [Turk Tarih Kurumu yayinlari. XXVI dizi 3: 159–65; Ankara: Türk Tarih Kurumu Basimevi, 1998] 162) actually cites the Cimmerian defeat of Gyges as that which was evoked and projected into a future era when Gog was supposed to have reappeared. Yet given Yhwh's single-handed defeat of Gog in chapters 38–39 without any human support troops, it seems a weak parallel at best and not supportive of the sovereignty of the Creator so thematic to *Ezekiel*.

[11] *ARAB* 2: *Historical Records of Assyria From Sargon to the End* (ed. J. H. Breasted; Ancient records, 1st series; Chicago: University of Chicago Press, 1927) 297–98, 326, 351–52; Hartmut Schmökel, *Geschichte des alten Vorderasien* (HO 2.3; Leiden: Brill, 1957) 280.

enemy depicted in the person of Gog by the final form of chapters 38–39.

It is suggested that Gog is compared not to the Gyges of history but to the Gyges of legend. Some would cite his mention in Herodotus' *Histories*. This, however, is far from convincing. The allusion in Herodotus refers to a successful palace *coup*, but his achievement was due more to subterfuge in the royal bedroom than to prowess on the battle field. Herodotus ends the account observing that Gyges achieved nothing else of significance in his thirty-eight years as king.[12] Plato's *Republic* also mentions Gyges and his coup d'etat. In the *Republic* Gyges accomplished the *coup* through a ring that made him invisible and allowed him to slay the king in bed without being observed. Plato then goes on to discuss this ring's great power when used by either a good or an evil person.[13] This ring could have given Gyges a reputation of more legendary dimensions. Yet Gog was quite visible, outstanding in arrogance, without need of artifice, or so he thought.

Others would see Gog's name as derived from the Sumerian *gug*, meaning darkness, with Magog meaning the land of darkness.[14] Though Albright summarily dismisses this as an etymology that "need not be taken very seriously,"[15] his basis can be challenged. It is not automatically to be assumed, as he does, from Genesis 10:2 that Magog is a real ethnic name, nor do we know that the compiler did not himself take the name from the Book of Ezekiel.[16]

The image of Gog's army as a cloud covering the land in vv. 9 and 16 is an image of darkness, and would re-enforce such a hypothesis. He and his hordes are seen as a pall, engulfing the whole land with no escape. In laments such opacity signifies total inaccessibility to the

---

[12] Herodotus, *The Histories* 1:12, 14 (trans. Robin Waterfield; Oxford World's Classics; Oxford: Oxford University Press, 1998) 8.

[13] Plato, *The Republic* 2:359–60, in *The Collected Dialogs of Plato* (ed. Edith Hamilton and Huntington Cairns; Bollingen Series 71; Princeton: Princeton University Press, 1963) 607.

[14] Paul Heinisch, *Das Buch Ezechiel übersetzt und erklärt* (HSAT 8.1; Bonn: Peter Hanstein, 1923) 183; Alban van Hoonacker, "Eléments sumériens dans le livre d'Ezechiel?" ZA 28 (1914) 336.

[15] William F. Albright, "Gog and Magog," *JBL* 43 (1924) 381.

[16] Astour, "Ezekiel's Prophecy of Gog," 569.

deity.[17] Here this dark obscurity describes the overwhelming incursion of Gog's army.

The imagery of Gog coming "from the farthest corners of the north" (38:6, 15; 39:2) also supports this interpretation. Childs notes the historical shift in interpretation of the enemy from the pre-exilic passages of Jeremiah to later occurrences. The pre-exilic passages consistently maintain Gog's character as an historical human agent with no sign of mythical interpretation. In his exilic/post-exilic understanding, first appearing in Ezekiel 38–39, Gog is presented as the trans-historical representative of the cosmic powers of returned chaos.[18] On this point, both Zimmerli and Lauha concur in their findings.[19] Given the focus of Gog's attack on the mountains of Israel at the center of the earth (38:12), this image of the remotest parts of the north becomes the point on earth most removed from there. Gog comes from a region that lies at the fringes of creation, and his presence means the undoing of that creation. This image presents Gog as the antithesis of creation.[20] Gog of Magog is the ultimate symbol of anti-creation and all that stands in opposition to the divine sovereign. It is characteristic of the *Chaoskampf* myth that darkness accompanies the reign of the monster.[21] The evidence does not support Albright's dismissal of the derivation of Gog's name from the Sumerian *gug*.

The origins of Gog's identity will perhaps never be clear. This itself may indicate something. There is a danger in over-determination. Whatever evil force is personified, one consistent characteristic may be, in fact, its indeterminacy. The vagueness of its form expresses the nature of the monster: the spirit of disorder. Wakeman notes that while the monster is often given a name and physical attributes, its form does

---

[17] David N. Freedman and B.E. Willoughby, "עָנָן," in *TWAT* 6 (Stuttgart: Kohlhammer, 1989) 272–73.

[18] Brevard S. Childs, "The Enemy From the North and the Chaos Tradition," *JBL* 78 (1959) 192, 195–96.

[19] Zimmerli (*Ezekiel* 2.303) notes that while the passage has many of the markings of the foe from the north in Jeremiah's oracles, it is clear that the motivation for Jeremiah's event has here been abandoned. Gog has not come as an instrument of Yhwh's judgment on Israel, but acts for another purpose. See also Aarre Lauha, *Zaphon, der Norden und die Nordvölker im Alten Testament* (AASF B49; Helsinki: Der Finnischen Literaturgesellschaft, 1943) 70.

[20] Batto, *Slaying the Dragon*, 159–62.

[21] Wakeman, *God's Battle with the Monster*, 80.

not fit into "natural" categories. While the most common appellation given to the monster designates it as sea, various names associated with dry land are given to monsters as well.[22] The very vagueness of Gog's form is expressive of the disorderly nature of the monster. He is a godless power who is evil incarnate, universal in scope and absolute in character.[23] Precisely because formlessness is intolerable, Gog is given a name and physical attributes, but the threat he poses is acknowledged in his often composite form which doesn't fit into any "natural" category. The arguments in favor of the interpretation of Gog as darkness, given his characterization, are more convincing than others. It is, in fact, the potential for such chaos, disorder and darkness embodied in enemy nation states which needs to be definitively undone if the promised covenant of peace in chapters 34 and 37 is to be established forever between Yhwh and his people.

It is arguable that Gog represents the personification of evil which Yhwh will engage in battle at some future time. There will come into Gog's mind (38:10) the evil desire to commit an atrocity against the defenseless to be attacked when they least expect it. Without provocation, solely for the purpose of seizing spoil and carrying off plunder, Gog and his hordes go against the people, now home from many nations, living safely on the mountains of Israel in unwalled villages without bars on their gates. Booty and plunder are Gog's sole motive and consuming passion. Especially highlighted is Gog's capacity to exploit opportunity without regard to ethical or moral principle. His aim is to bring calamity on the land. Precisely when the people are finally enjoying security, Gog will pounce on the unsuspecting victim in order to satisfy his greed and enrich himself with the possessions of the defenseless and the weak. Gog's character was entirely offensive and an affront to Yhwh in the eyes of the righteous.[24] He was the quintessential threat to the restored nation of Israel living securely in unwalled villages without bars on their gates in the latter years. He represents the possibility that must be permanently eliminated so that the events of 597/587 may never happen again.

---

[22] Wakeman, *God's Battle with the Monster*, 44–45, 117.

[23] Cohn, *Cosmos, Chaos, and the World to Come*, 161; Nobile, *Introduzione all'Antico Testamento*, 103; Wakeman, *God's Battle with the Monster*, 45.

[24] Block, *The Book of Ezekiel, Chapters 25–48*, 445–50.

These verses depict the conscription of Gog and the mass deployment of troops in preparation for this war that will end all wars. The inventory of Gog and allies, with their battle attire and their arms, indicates that they are a well-equipped force, highly efficient against their prey. Gog's allies include Meshech, Tubal, Gomer and Beth-Togarmah in the north and Paras, Cush and Put in the south. Analysis of these nations indicates that they comprise the northern and southern limits of the world as Israel knew it.[25] Gog, coming out of the north, assumes the proportions of an international plot against Yhwh's people, and his allies allow him to totally envelop their victim. This was to be a battle of cosmic proportions. Assembled for battle through the instrumentality of Yhwh who put thoughts into Gog's mind to lead such a force into battle against a defenseless nation, this is a gathering, deployment (and obliteration) of any forces that could ever possibly be a threat to Israel in the future.

Part of Gog's horde will never see battle but stand to profit more than any who do soldiering. Sheba, Dedan and Tarshish are all mentioned in the listing of the commercial nations in chapter 27.[26] As Gog's allies come from the southern and northern extremes of the world known to Israel, Block notes that this listing too is a merism from east to west of all the nations involved in international commerce. Their slave traders are eager for the market of human merchandise which will become available as a result of Gog's campaign. Their commercial merchants have their eyes on the silver, the gold, the livestock and movable property that will be plundered (v. 13).[27] With Gog and his hordes they challenge the sovereign God by seeking to make a profit through trafficking in his people.

The site of Gog's attack is both diffuse and focused at once. The battle will take place on the mountains of Israel, upon a people living at the center of the earth. It is not an accident that the attack is not made explicitly on Jerusalem. Though the author twice refers to Jerusalem indirectly in the two chapters (38:12; 39:16), he never mentions Jerusalem or Mt. Zion openly. Rather, the field of battle, the sight of the victory feast and the purification of the land all take place on

---

[25] Block, *The Book of Ezekiel, Chapters 25–48*, 439–42; Lauha, *Zaphon, der Norden und die Nordvölker*, 70; Odell, "Are You He of Whom I Spoke," 101, 103, 107–8.
[26] Ezek 27:22, 20, 12.
[27] Block, *The Book of Ezekiel, Chapters 25–48*, 448–49.

הרי ישראל, "the mountains of Israel." This phrase appears four times in the two chapters (38:8; 39:2, 4, 17), and is there to convey a message. Boadt suggests[28] that the final form demonstrated a certain disaffection with the temple practices of its day and looked forward to a day when God would consecrate the whole land, not merely the city of Jerusalem. Yet the heart of Gog's profanation is his attack on "my" people, Yhwh's people, living securely at the center of the earth.[29] In this context they hold a unique importance because the nations of the world, from its farthest limits, now conspire to destroy them. Such an attack against Yhwh's people living securely without walls would overturn the order of creation once again in a manner as devastating as the events endured by those who survived Nebuchadnezzar's defeat of Jerusalem.

Not only does the geographical situation of this battle have significance. Its temporal location is important as well. According to Ezek 38:8, the appearance of Gog falls "in the latter years." In 38:16 it is "in the latter days." Both these references indicate that the events described have passed from the plane of history and entered the eschatological age. The battle against Gog is the final stage before the coming of the new age.

The crucial verse 17 states: "Thus says the Lord God: Are you he of whom I spoke in the former days by my servants, the prophets of Israel, who in those days prophesied for years that I would bring you against them?" This verse has long been problematic and the object of lengthy discussion by exegetes.[30] Given its significance for the completion of cosmogony and the fulfillment of the covenant of peace, we will discuss it in detail.[31] The verse involves four issues. First, is it a question or a declarative statement? Second, who are the prophets

---

[28] Lawrence Boadt, "Rhetorical Strategies in Ezekiel's Oracles of Judgment," in *Ezekiel and His Book* (ed. Johan Lust; BETL 74; Leuven: Leuven University Press, 1986) 190–93, and, by the same author, "The Function of the Salvation Oracles in Ezekiel 33–37," *HAR* 12 (1990) 18; Boadt concurs with Zimmerli, *Ezekiel* 1.53–55, 59.

[29] This is the first of the three indirect references to the city of Jerusalem. See Richard J. Clifford, *The Cosmic Mountain in Canaan and in the Old Testament* (HSM 4; Cambridge, MA: Harvard University Press, 1972) 190.

[30] Daniel I. Block ("Gog in Prophetic Tradition: A New Look at Ezekiel XXXVIII:17." *VT* 42 [1992] 158) reviews the discussion of more than a century.

[31] The research of both Daniel I. Block ("Gog in Prophetic Tradition") and Margaret S. Odell ("Are You He of Whom I Spoke," 115–16) was very helpful to me in this.

spoken of? Third, who is the "you" addressed? Fourth and finally, does the verse demand a positive or a negative answer? Let us look at these four questions in turn, and then draw some conclusions.

In the past, v. 17 has been translated as an affirmative statement rather than a rhetorical question, supported by the texts in the LXX and the Vulgate, but not by MT. Among more recent editions, the Tanakh version translates v. 17 as an affirmative statement. The NRSV translates v. 17 as a rhetorical question, but notes below: "It is preferable to read with Greek (Septuagint) and Latin (Vulgate) an indicative sentence, 'You are he of whom I spoke. . . .'"[32] Recent scholarship suggests that this is not automatically to be assumed.

Zimmerli, among others, sees the Hebrew interrogative particle *ha* here as a dittograph.[33] The expression האתה־הוא while unique in the Bible has syntactic parallels.[34] These parallels all involve a direct encounter between two persons and, as requests for clarity concerning a person's identity, they are interrogative.[35] In the final analysis, against the recommendation of the BHS,[36] there is no reason to depart from MT. MT frames the address as an interrogative noun clause: "Are you the one?" As an interrogative statement it raises questions about the identity of Gog.

In regard to the question who these "prophets of Israel, who in those days prophesied?" (Ezek 38:17) are, two conclusions can be determined from the text. The phrase "my servants the prophets" is used in the Deuteronomistic history of those who spoke the true word of God [37] which is to say they are not false prophets. Furthermore, by referring to them as prophets of Israel, they are clearly not foreign prophets. As scholars suggest,[38] these are a reference to the prophecies of Isaiah and Jeremiah.

---

[32] *The Harper Collins Study Bible*, NRSV (ed. Wayne A. Meeks; London: Harper Collins Publishers, 1993) 1284.

[33] Zimmerli, *Ezekiel* 2.288.

[34] Odell, "Are You He of Whom I Spoke," 226. A partial list of her results: Gen 27:21; Judg 13:11; 2 Sam 2:20; 9:2; 20:17; 1 Kgs 13:14; 18:7, 17.

[35] Odell, "Are You He of Whom I Spoke," 115.

[36] Elliger, Karl, and Wilhelm Rudolph, eds. *BHS*, 3d ed. (Stuttgart: Deutsche Bibelgesellschaft, 1987) 968, critical apparatus 17c.

[37] Odell, "Are You He of Whom I Spoke," 115; Zimmerli, *Ezekiel* 2.312.

[38] Ahroni, "The Gog Prophecy and the Book of Ezekiel," 11–12; Blenkinsopp, *Ezekiel*, 186; Eichrodt, *Ezekiel*, 525.

Who is the "you" addressed in the question? Is he the one mentioned by the prophets who would be brought against Israel? What is Gog's role in relation to the prophecies in the prophetic tradition? The phrase "that I would bring you against them" has a tradition history stretching through 1–2 Kings, Jeremiah and Ezekiel.[39] It is used in descriptions of impending disaster and in oracles of judgment which are pronounced due to disobedience. The formula describes punishment of the people for infidelity.[40] The author is asking whether or not Gog is the agent of divine wrath proposed in earlier prophecies as punishment for Israel's infidelities.

Now we move to the fourth issue: the answer, affirmative or negative. If the answer is affirmative, then Gog is the fulfillment of earlier prophecy. Those supporting this position[41] suggest that the verse refers to prophecies of Isaiah or Jeremiah with their allusions to the foe from the north. Yet Isa 14:24–25 was concerned with the Assyrians who were clearly out of the picture before the time of the exile, and Jeremiah himself understood Jeremiah 4–6 to have been fulfilled by Nebuchadnezzar and the Babylonians.[42] For Jeremiah, his prophecy of the invasion from the north had been accomplished.

Block asserts correctly that v. 17 is a reinterpretation of an old oracle on the basis of new realities. This is an example of the content of a tradition which has been adapted, transformed and reinterpreted.[43] There is actually no reason to insist on a positive answer to the question, "Are you he of whom the prophets spoke?" As Block points out, an example of a similar rhetorical question with a negative answer occurs in 2 Sam. 7:5 where Yahweh instructs Nathan to ask David, "Are you the one who should build me a house to dwell in?"[44] The answer expected to that question is certainly negative.

A negative answer changes Gog's role dramatically. If the answer

---

[39] Odell, "Are You He of Whom I Spoke," 227. A partial list: 1 Kgs 9:9; 21:21, 29; 2 Kgs 21:12; 22:16, 20; Jer 4:6; 5:15; 6:19; 11:11; 19:3; 31:8; 32:42; 35:17; 48:8; 49:5; 51:64; Ezek 6:3; 26:7; 28:7; 29:8.

[40] Odell, "Are You He of Whom I Spoke," 116.

[41] Some notable examples are Ahroni, "The Gog Prophecy and the Book of Ezekiel," 11–12; Blenkinsopp, *Ezekiel*, 186; Eichrodt, *Ezekiel*, 525.

[42] Block, "Gog in Prophetic Tradition,"168–69; Odell, "Are You He of Whom I Spoke," 34–36.

[43] Block, "Gog in Prophetc Tradition,"168–69.

[44] Block, "Gog in Prophetic Tradition," 170.

were affirmative, it would mean that he was Yhwh's agent predicted by the prophets. However if the answer is negative,[45] then Gog is not the one spoken of earlier by the prophets. Interpreting the verse with a negative answer, opens up the passage that follows to understand Gog in his fundamental purpose: to be an instrument which Yhwh could use in the future to unloose his anger against Israel again. Gog was a potential weapon of Yhwh's chastisement of Israel at a later time. Gog's fate in this passage would have significant implications for the exiles. Would Jerusalem and her Temple, the pinnacle and most outstanding accomplishment of Yhwh's act of creation, be undone again as they were at the hands of Nebuchadnezzar?

In summary, v. 17 is not a declarative statement, but a rhetorical question. The prophets were true prophets of Israel whose prophecies were accessible to the author. The rhetorical question was: "Are you, Gog, the enemy spoken of by former prophets whom I will bring against Israel?" And the answer demanded by the rhetorical question was negative. Gog was not Yhwh's instrument to chasten Israel as in the events of 597/587. God brings Gog to Israel for an entirely different purpose. Gog's role will become clear in chapter 5 below when we look at Yhwh's covenant of peace in Ezekiel 34 and 37.

The comments about Gog in these sixteen verses also tell us something about Yhwh and his people. While Gog is the enemy, it is clear who exercises control over him. In v. 4, Yhwh will turn Gog around, he will put hooks in his jaws and he will bring (Hiph'il causative) Gog to the land that he might vindicate his holiness. In vv. 7–9 Yhwh even announces the military strategy Gog is to pursue. This use of the Hiph'il causative appears again in v. 16 where, despite the first three verbs in vv. 14–16 denoting Gog's self-propulsion ("you will rouse yourself," "you will come from your place out of the remotest places of the north," and "you will come up against my people Israel,"), v. 16 indicates clearly that Yhwh is the power behind the attack: "I will bring you." The Creator who creates by fiat is made manifest again by his action: he creates the situation where his power will be demonstrated and not by any human agency. We could ask ourselves, and well ought we to, why the Creator would bring enemy nations against Israel who

---

[45] Dominique Barthélemy (*Critique Textuelle de l'Ancien Testament* 3 [OBO 50; Göttingen: Vandenhoeck & Ruprecht, 1992] 306) asserts the same conclusion: the implicit answer is "no."

is here depicted as keeping the Covenant so faithfully. Why would God destroy his own creation when they are finally living together in such a benign and successful way in the promotion of human life? The significance of Yhwh's action will become clear and even more sharply defined below in the comparison of mythic elements here with other attested myths.

The people are regathered. A ruined land has once again been populated and, having recovered from war, they have resettled securely within the land, are prospering with abundant livestock and are living at peace. The signs of Yhwh's blessing are evident. The phrase living securely, ישבו לבטח (see vv. 38:8, 11, 14; 39:26, variations consonant with textual context) describes the security offered by Yhwh when the blessings of the covenant are operative and the divine patron stands guard over them.[46] The inhabitants have taken no defensive precautions. They have trusted in Yhwh's promises of eternal peace and prosperity. God is their security. Situating this pacific scene in the context of ancient Near Eastern myth, as we shall see below, will uncover this message's added force for a people who have known defeat and exile.

Ezekiel 38:18–39:8

In the next fourteen verses, 38:18–39:8, the Creator God of Israel does battle against Gog and his hordes. Yhwh's action is that of the Divine Warrior. His universal victory will show him to be holy, sovereign, having ultimate superiority to be faithful to his creation and to subdue the forces of chaos that war against it. The skillful employment of biblical imagery and parallels discussed shortly below present a battle whose proportions and implications will become clear in the discussion further below devoted to the mythopoeic use of these elements to give vivid expression to this decisive conclusion of Israel's new creation myth.

Verses 18–23 describe the beginnings of this decisive conflict concluded in 39:1–8. They have been considered by many as a secondary expansion, an interruption between 38:17 and 39:1. I propose, rather, that in the final form, it was not an interruption but the first part of two where the forces of nature go to war at the bidding of their Cre-

---

[46] Block, *The Book of Ezekiel, Chapters 25–48*, 444.

ator against the powers of chaos, paralleled by its counterpart in 39:1–8, the military defeat by Yhwh. Such an understanding of Yhwh, the Creator, with all the forces of nature at his disposal and his own effortless defeat of the forces of chaos in favor of his people, living securely without walls, having no bars or gates in their land are two panels of one piece in the ancient Near Eastern frame of reference discussed below.[47] In fact both parts are very necessary for the book's message. In the first part, creation itself passes judgment on Gog at the command of its Creator. The second panel is the final judgment of Yhwh himself on any forces that would undo the order of his creation. In fact, when this battle is over there will be no enemy left to threaten ever again Yhwh's people living securely and without walls.

The outrage of the Creator at the advance of chaos, we are told, will erupt visibly "in the face of God" and physically in "the great shaking" of the earth and all creatures that inhabit it. Ezek 38:18 announces the rage of God. MT describes God's rage as being "in my face": his face is visibly flushed. The LXX does not have that phrase and the NRSV follows the LXX. That is a loss. This visible rage harkens back to the rage of the holy war described by the Israelite narrators, Josh 8:14 ff.; Judg 4:14 ff.; 5:4; 20; 1 Sam 7.7 ff.; 14:15 ff.; 2 Sam 5:20 ff.[48] It dramatically heightens the sense of the profanation of the Creator's covenant people living in right order and relationship, and the anger of their defender.

Verse 19 declares the "great shaking" in Israel initiated by God's anger in the previous verse. This verb (רעש) is associated with the manifestation of Yhwh revealing his power over creation, and his defeat of primeval chaos.[49] In this conclusive battle Yhwh manifests the powers to shake the earth. The final form's use of the phrase "on that day" signals the decisive battle which will complete cosmogony.[50] The cosmic powers are enlisted in the service of God to introduce the legal proceeding which issues in judgment in the form of cosmic upheaval: plagues, blood, rain, hailstones, fire and brimstone (v. 22). This judg-

---

[47] Richard J. Clifford (*Creation Accounts in the Ancient Near East*, 7–10, 169–72) discusses the interrelation of these two seemingly dichotomous partners.

[48] Eichrodt, *Ezekiel*, 525.

[49] Childs, "The Enemy from the North," 189.

[50] Lawrence Boadt, *Ezekiel's Oracles Against Egypt, A Literary and Philological Study of Ezekiel 29–32* (BibOr 37; Rome: Biblical Institute Press, 1980) 63.

ment among the nations is a recurring feature of the rule of God in the eschatological time. It can be characterized either by a royal or legal act or by a military victory.[51] Here God judges in favor of the vulnerable, the defenseless, keeping the covenant in harmony and peace. The returned exiles are to know that when they live faithfully according to the covenant they will not come up short in the balance of the scales of justice, and the powers of chaos will be decisively undone and brought under the dominion of their Creator.

It is v. 23 that contains the ultimate meaning of the conflict: Gog serves the revelatory purposes of Yhwh whose glory is set among the nations acknowledging their Maker. In exercising his wrath before the nations, God proves his true identity: Sovereign Creator and Lord of history. Yhwh will now become known in the eyes of many nations. No enemy ever comes against Yhwh's people counter to his will and after this battle of cosmic proportions there will be no enemy left among the nations for Yhwh to employ.

Ezekiel 39:1–8 takes the form of a battle account between two champions. The magnitude of Gog's army portrayed in the first division of the narrative will yield in these verses to the magnitude of God's victory. As in 38:2–17, it is very clear that Gog's attack takes place under Yhwh's hand who controls the battle and the outcome. The four verbs in 39:2 assert that Yhwh is the ultimate power behind the attack: "I will turn you around": שבבתיך, "I will drive you forward": ששאתיך, "I will bring you up": העליתיך, "I will lead you against": הבאותך. Several meanings offered for the second verb highlight Gog's passivity. Zimmerli suggests a translation of "I will lead you by the nose."[52] Koehler and Baumgartner suggest "I will lead you along on a rope."[53] Rosenberg proffers "I will entice you."[54] And though the third and fourth verbs are used earlier in vv. 8 and 9 in the Qal conjugation, here they are used in the Hiphʻil form to convey Yhwh's causative power: the whole journey from the farthest north to the mountains of Israel is

---

[51] Blenkinsopp, *Ezekiel*, 187.

[52] Zimmerli, *Ezekiel*, 2.290.

[53] Walter Baumgartner, et al., eds., *The Hebrew and Aramaic Dictionary of the Old Testament* 4, trans. and ed. Mervyn E. J. Richardson (Leiden: Brill, 1994–2000) 1664; originally published as *HALAT*, 1–6 (Leiden: Brill, 1967–96).

[54] Abraham J. Rosenberg, *Ezekiel* 2 (New York: Judaica Press, 1991) 334.

under Yhwh's guidance. Gog is overcome by Yhwh's person as Yhwh knocks the weapons from his hands and renders him defenseless.

In v. 4 Gog becomes an unburied battle casualty and is given as food to the birds of prey and the wild beasts of the field. Such an end would be abhorrent to the people of Israel and fitting in their eyes for Gog who would so profane God's name (v. 7). The text uses the prophetic perfect in v. 4 to anticipate fulfillment: the result is decreed, authorized and as good as completed.[55] The exiles are assured of this. Verse 6 contains the image of fire, a symbol of destruction drawn from ancient and modern practices of razing conquered cities, which often appears in descriptions of final judgment,[56] and here it is clear that it is a judgment in favor of Yhwh's people. Verse 8 begins with the exclamation: "Behold! It has come, it has happened," הנה באה ונהתיה. This day is the day of Yhwh's decisive intervention on behalf of his creation, the day on which he frees Israel from all its foes and breaks the rod of his anger forever.

Ezekiel 39:9–20

The next twelve verses (39:9–20) deal with creation's response to the victory. This last part of the Gog pericope has as its implicit emphasis the obedience of the new people who live in right relationship with their Creator and with one another. This is fundamental to cosmogony which when completed includes the benign and successful working together of elements that promote human life. Purified by the exile and restored to their land, they are a people radically transformed in a re-established covenant with their God. It reinforces Israel's ability to follow the ordinances of this re-established covenant which Yhwh has made with them. The land of Israel is now the site where God's power and the people's obedience meet. It is the land of restored creation. The purification of the land becomes the task of this people purified by Yhwh.[57] The verses begin with the residents of the land disposing of the weaponry and the bodies of Gog and his army. This is, in fact, the first time the Israelites have entered the picture directly. Untouched by Gog's invading forces, the dwellers in the cities of Israel emerge to dis-

---

[55] Boadt, *Ezekiel's Oracles Against Egypt*, 52.

[56] Cook, *Prophecy and Apocalypticism*, 95.

[57] Margaret S. Odell, "The City of Hamonah in Ezekiel 39:11–16: The Tumultuous City of Jerusalem," *CBQ* 56 (1994) 487–89.

pose of the weapons of the annihilated enemy by fire. A fair question to be asked by the reader at this point is "Why in the final form is Israel not involved in its own defense until it comes time for the 'clean-up operation'?" Why was it Yhwh's war alone?

For seven months they will bury the bodies, and for seven months they will search for any they have not found initially. This purification was prescribed by Yhwh for a week of months, not a week of days as in Numbers 19, not only because of the number of bodies, but also out of concern to render the land absolutely holy.[58] This concern for scrupulous burial of the enemy gives witness to Israel's passion for the purity of the land and to Israel's fidelity to her new found security in Yhwh, her Creator. The site of burial itself will serve as a permanent memorial to the destruction of the enemies of Yhwh and Israel. The name will recall the event, but the reference to the nearby city's name will recall much more: וגם שם־עיר המונה, "a city Hamonah is there also." In 7:12–14 Jerusalem's name is referred to as המונה: riotous and rebellious. In 5:7 Jerusalem's המון, her refusal to follow covenant demands and all kinds of abominations exceeded that of the surrounding nations. Later in 23:40–42, the surrounding nations are invited by her to bring their boisterous behavior into the city of Jerusalem itself. Hamonah is not only the resting place for Gog. It is also the resting place for the nation's past infidelities.[59] Where once Yhwh's people exceeded the nations in their arrogance and rebellion, now they give witness to Yhwh by their passion to adhere to the order of creation which he has established. The biblical purification fulfilled in this "scouring of the land" is given mythic proportion that it might fit in context, as we shall see below, and a people in a life-sustaining order and right relationship with their Creator is now the promised restoration for the exiles.

Yhwh's triumph is celebrated with a victory feast. The verses are cast in the form of an official invitation to special guests to attend a grand banquet hosted by Yhwh. The birds of the air and beasts of the field are to be the diners. The abundance of the meal is signified by the participants' eventual satiation and drunkenness at Yhwh's own table, noted in distinction from a table prepared in Yhwh's honor. Yhwh is the host. The abundance of the banquet speaks of his bounteousness and the enormity and totality of the victory Yhwh celebrates. The sac-

---

[58] Block, *The Book of Ezekiel, Chapters 25–48*, 470.
[59] Odell, "The City of Hamonah," 482–84, 486.

rificial feast takes place "on the mountains of Israel." It is worthy of note that it was the actual battle field which became the table for the sacrificial meal in the account. This also is indicative of the enormity of the defeat: as mentioned above, it is of mythic proportions.

Two aspects of the Gog pericope are frequently critiqued by commentators. One is the seemingly disordered juxtaposition of the burial of the enemy followed by the victory feast in which the national leaders, ranking military, brave warriors and their horses are consumed by the birds of prey and the wild animals in this victory feast.[60] A careful reading of the text renders other explanations for this seemingly disordered juxtaposition[61] yet when viewed in its mythic context, as in the next section, the ordering becomes more comprehensible.

Another reason that the passage is so enigmatic is that it is inimical to Israelite religious practice which according to Lev 3:16–17 stated the fat and blood of the sacrifice must be given to Yhwh. A careful reading of the stated text again helps to clarify,[62] yet the mythic parallels give the greatest understanding.

---

[60] Allen, *Ezekiel 20–48*, 203; Zimmerli, *Ezekiel*, 2.298.

[61] It is not clear from MT that such is the course of events. The verbs in vv. 11–16 are all in the imperfect tense or the *waw* consecutive perfect except for one verb in v. 15 which is in the perfect tense because of the time sequence set up with the verb which precedes it, by the preposition which introduces it. To give someone a place for burial is not to bury the person. Mention is only made of an apportionment of space for Gog's burial. It is not clear that the burial itself happened prior to the feast, after which, bones could be buried.

Also to be considered is the existing parallel between the possible burial and then devouring of Gog and his hordes and, in chapter 32, the eating of Egypt's cadaver by scavengers followed by its consignment to Sheol. Both Gog and Egypt suffer a double "doing-in" so to speak. Batto (*Slaying of the Dragon*, 154–57, 166) develops this structural parallel which cautions against judging this passage in logical categories.

[62] This is a sacrificial meal, זבח. Here in contrast with the human worshiper slaughtering animals in Yhwh's presence, Yhwh offers slaughtered humans to animals who gather for this festive celebration on the mountains of Israel where they eat fat until they are filled and drink blood until they are drunk. Gen 9:1–6 forbids the eating of human flesh by humans (v. 4). It also forbids the taking of human life by animals (v. 5) but it is Yhwh who took life in the battle and there is no prohibition in the text, contrary to Block's assertion (*The Book of Ezekiel, Chapters 25–48*, 477) against animals eating human flesh and drinking the blood of those already dead. This is not a new concept in the book. In both 29:5 and 32:4 the same fate is assigned to Egypt. It is the punishment to befall the survivors in Judah in 33:27. In fact, if Yhwh were to give a victory feast of the slain, he could not invite the Israelites. He could only invite the birds of prey and wild beasts.

Also helpful in understanding the choice of menu for the meal are the references to Yhwh's victory feast in Jewish apocryphal/deuterocanonical and intertestamental literature. There the fare of the victory banquet was to be precisely those over whom Yhwh had been victorious. In *2 Esdras* 6:52, *2 Baruch* 29:4, *1 Enoch* 60:24,[63] and *Baba Bathra* 75a[64] it is specifically Leviathan and Behemoth who are to be devoured. While it seems an unusual selection, there were proponents of the theme who provided comparable offerings for the feast even in the OT, Ps 74:14: "You will give him (Leviathan) as food for the people." Other aspects of a feast, which might at first reading seem bizarre, will also become clearer when we look at mythological elements in the narrative.

Ezekiel 39:21–29

In the exegesis of chapters 38–39, the relationship of vv. 21–29 to the whole has often been challenged. While the focus of the present work is the final form of the text, not its redactional history, it is important to study this issue to understand the intent and purpose of the final form.[65] If there are stylistic phenomena in the present text that raise the question of its unity, they are not necessarily explained by proposing the existence of later additions not integral to the final form's purposes. Some would propose redactional strata from v. 25,[66] some from v. 23,[67] some from v. 21,[68] some from v. 17.[69] Wherever one would

---

[63] The citation from *1 Enoch* actually stops half way through v. 24: "These two dragons are prepared for the great day of the Lord and will nourish. . . ." The text is mutilated. André Dupont-Sommer and Marc Philonenko, eds. (*La Bible. Écrits Intertestamentaires.* [Bibliothèque de la Pleiade 337; Paris: Gallimard, 1987] 582–83) would complete its sense as ". . . will nourish the just in the banquet which will be served to them at the end of time," based on the citations from *2 Bar* 29:4 and *2 Esdr* 6:52.

[64] Isidore Epstein, ed. *The Babylonian Talmud, Seder Nezikin* (London: Soncino Press, 1935) 299.

[65] Daniel I. Block's discussion ("Gog and the Pouring out of the Spirit, Reflections on Ezekiel xxxix 21–29," VT 37 [1987] 257–70) was very helpful in this section.

[66] Eichrodt, *Ezekiel,* 251; Smend, *Der Prophet Ezekiel,* 295

[67] Fohrer, *Ezechiel,* 218; Hossfeld, *Untersuchungen,* 484, 508–9, and "Das Buch Ezechiel," 450, 453; Zimmerli, *Ezekiel,* 2.319.

[68] Herrmann, *Ezechiel übersetzt und erklärt,* XXX, 251; Wevers, 285, 294.

[69] Cooke, *A Critical and Exegetical Commentary,* 407–8, 421–22; Hölscher, *Hesekiel, der Dichter und das Buch,* 178, 186–87.

propose redactional strata, the final verses of chapter 39 in their present context do in fact represent a conclusion to the Gog oracle, unless we assume that these verses are part of a random arrangement of various segments. What evidence is there for interpreting the last verses of chapter 39 as an intentional part of and conclusion to the Gog oracle?

The dating in 40:1 and the Prophetic Utterance Formula at the end of 39:29 clearly indicate the *terminus ad quem* of the unit. Some would separate v. 25 and what follows from what precedes it because of the word לכן. It is a divider yet it also provides coherence between the succeeding and preceding material. Hossfeld notes that it can sometimes function rhetorically to draw attention to the resumption of an idea.[70] It does not, then, seem likely that this would intentionally be a new section in the final form. Verses 21–22 seem to refer directly to what precedes them. The revelation of Yhwh's judgment to the nations in v. 21 is the result of what goes before it. מן־היום ההוא, "from that day forward," in v. 22 would seem to refer to what introduces it as well. The reference to "that day" requires an antecedent.

The issue then is the relationship of vv. 23–24 to what precedes and follows them. How are these two verses linked to their present context? One of the frequently used stylistic literary devices in the final form of Ezekiel, the "halving pattern,"[71] may help answer this question. In "halving" the second part of the set of verses develops or expands in some way the ideas expressed in the first half. This pattern can detect the progression of thought from one section of a unit to another by examining internal consistencies. Ezek 39:21–29 seems to be an example of this type of progression of thought.[72] There is a discernible break at verse 25, yet, as mentioned above, לכן can also function to draw attention to a repetition or a resumption of an idea. The halving pattern in this instance unfolds as follows:

---

[70] Hossfeld, *Untersuchungen*, 406–7.

[71] Block in "Gog in Prophetic Tradition, " 157, and Greenberg in *Ezekiel 1–20*, 25–26, 137–38 discuss "halving" as a characteristic literary device used in *Ezekiel*. Greenberg cites this as the organizing principle in the oracles in chapters 6, 7, 13, 18 and 20. Block considers chapters 38–39 as an example of "halving" themselves, one of the most impressive, in fact, with Panel A consisting of 365 words and Panel B, 357.

[72] Block, *The Book of Ezekiel, Chapters 25–48*, 479–80; Odell, "Are You He of Whom I Spoke," 150–52.

God acts	21a	25
(1) The Nations and (2) Israel respond	21b	26/27
The Recognition Formula	22	28
(1) The Nations and (2) Israel know the truth of the exile and the Creator's sovereignty.	23/24	29

In the first half, by Gog's defeat, the Israelites will know that the Lord is God, and in this knowledge will be born the full realization of the covenant relationship. And the nations will know through the defeat of Gog that Israel's captivity was a sign of the sovereign God's chastisement for Israel's contempt of and treachery towards the covenant relationship. In the second half, the message shifts to a promise for Israel. And אשיב את־שבית, "I will restore the fortunes," is a very significant promise for it says that the judgment of exile will be reversed, the people will be restored to the land and Yhwh will no longer hide his face. He will forget their shame and their treachery and will pour out his Spirit on the house of Israel.[73] It is a total restoration of his covenant.

In the second half (vv. 25–29) we can see a clear expansion and development of the ideas of the first half (vv. 21–24). The two halves mirror one another yet they diverge, representing two different sides of Yhwh's treatment of Israel in which the second is a reversal of the first. The first describes Yhwh's action of judgment in response to Israel's rebellion, while the second describes Yhwh's salvific activity on Israel's behalf through the permanence of the restoration. Where Yhwh hides his face from them in the first half (vv. 23, 24), he promises in the second half never to hide his face again (v. 29). Verses 23–24 are part of the overall thematic progression of the nine verses.

What is still needed is an understanding of how these nine verses are related to the Gog pericope as a whole. There are clear thematic links between these verses and the pericope. As discussed above, vv. 21–22 need an antecedent for what precedes them to make sense. The theme of setting Yhwh's glory among the nations in v. 21 echoes the reference to his glorifying himself in 39:13. Yhwh's jealousy for his holy name in v. 25 is a reflection of 39:7. So too the seven references to future time in

---

[73] John M. Bracke, "*šûb šĕbût*: A Reappraisal," *ZAW* 97 (1985) 240, 244.

the narrative (38:8, 10, 14, 16, 18, 19, 39:11) are in a relationship of contrast to the use of עתה, "now," in v. 25.

Verses 21–29 provide a satisfactory conclusion to the Gog oracle. They highlight the revelatory impact of Yhwh's defeat of Gog, first on the nations and then on Israel. The Gog oracle is put in the context of Yhwh's covenant relationship with Israel in the land which he has given them. The pouring out of the spirit in 39:29 is a sign and seal of that covenant on his creation. The time relationship between the oracle and its conclusion can help us here. The pericope, while speaking of the future, also functioned as a consoling guarantee to the exiles for the present.[74] God's everlasting covenant would last forever, as the final reversal of the Gog pericope testifies. God's chastisement was not rejection. The Creator God would complete his creation and he would do that through the restoration of his chosen people. The covenant could be trusted now, in the context in which the final form was written. The promised Covenant of Peace foretold in chapters 34 and 37 would hold true. Chapters 38–39 are meant to give hope for the present as well as the future. They do just that.

II

Looking at chapters 38–39 through the prism of the ancient Near Eastern *Chaoskampf* myth, cosmogony's completion, brings the final form theology of the two chapters into sharper focus. It also gives elements that are seemingly disparate in the discussion above a greater cohesiveness. The essential characteristics of the *Chaoskampf* myth are present in the two chapters. Also significant in the discussion are aspects of this ancient Near Eastern Combat Myth which are lacking in the two chapters. These speak of development within Israelite faith. Let us look first at these as they show the mythopoeic reformulation of the Israelite creation myth.

Many myths of Israel and the ancient Near East contain a "consultation episode" where the divine council or the elders meet among themselves or appeal to the hero from the gods.[75] In Ezekiel's

---

[74] Block, "Gog and the Pouring Out of the Spirit," 265–67; Odell, "Are You He of Whom I Spoke," 155.

[75] In the Baal-Yamm sequence, Baal challenges Yamm's right to rule, charging him with presumption. Yamm sends a message to El's council of the gods, gathered at their mountain height place of convocation and demands that Baal be given over to him and

monotheistic retelling of the myth, there is, in fact, quite the opposite of a consultation. Yhwh announces quite clearly: "I am against you, O Gog." Yhwh decides when the confrontation will be, and who will be sent. At the end of the consultation in other accounts, one among the gods is chosen to do battle.[76] In the Gog pericope the Creator God of Israel will not send anyone in his place. He is the divine warrior God, the God of armies. He speaks in thunder and shoots lightning (Exod 19:16–19; 20:18). He is present in fire and uses it as his weapon (Exod 13:21; 1 Kgs 18:38). He has control over the waters of the earth — the sea (Exod 14:21), the rivers (Josh 3:16–17), and the rain (Gen 2:5; 1 Kgs 17).[77] He does not delegate the battle to another.

Verses 14–16 speak of Gog's journey to the mountains of Israel. The journey undertaken by the hero to the dwelling place of the villain may figure in the Combat Myth.[78] Here, it is quite the reverse, and consistent with the faith in the sovereignty of the Creator which is expressed in the final form of Ezekiel. It is Yhwh who conscripts Gog and his army to meet him at the site chosen for the confrontation. As noted above, Gog is depicted as a pawn: his march is generated by Yhwh. Of the twenty-two uses of the Hiph'il in these two chapters, sixteen refer to activity generated by Yhwh in his campaign. The Creator brings the enemy to judgment on the mountains of Israel from which the order of his creation emanates. Gog is summoned from the periphery to the center for judgment. The Creator does not go to Gog.

The final missing aspects of the Combat Myth in the Gog pericope speak to the conclusion of the two chapters. There, in prophetic divine speech, the Creator declares that he was the one to send Israel into exile because of the iniquity of the people. In some ancient Near Eastern myths, the hero is initially defeated.[79] In this context, the second

---

that his own lordship be acknowledged. The "consultation episode" follows (*The Context of Scripture* 1.246). A similar "consultation" takes place among the gods in the Ninurta-Anzu-Bird Myth immediately after Anzu-Bird stole the Tablet of Destinies (*ANET*, 113).

[76] See again *The Context of Scripture*, 1.246 and *ANET* 113 for the continuation of the narration begun in preceding footnote.

[77] Cross, "The Development of Israelite Religion," 26, 29.

[78] In "Gilgamesh and the Land of the Living" it is Gilgamesh who travels to Huwawa. *The Context of Scripture*, 1.458.

[79] Forsyth, *The Old Enemy*, 446–47.

and more successful battle is seen in terms of the first.[80] The final form makes it clear that this was not the pattern with the Creator God of Israel. Everything that was done, was done in fulfillment of the Creator's will.

The four core components of the Combat Myth motif are villainy (38:2–17), battle and victory (38:18–39:8), and triumph (39:9–20).[81] The opening section of the narrative depicts the villainy of Gog. Like his counterparts from the earliest, Gog embodies the power of chaos and disintegration; with Tiamat he is threat to the order of creation.[82] Through his malevolence the stable and life sustaining society of those "living without walls and having no bars or gates" (Ezek 38:11) could be undone. He comes against those who are defenseless and unprepared for his attack. These verses are the statement of the fundamental situation common to combat myths which determines the subsequent events and which the champion's victory will liquidate. The number of nations amassed against Israel is seven,[83] to be noted, given that the seven heads of the dragon and the seven heads of the beast are traditional ancient Near Eastern mythic characteristics.[84]

The Combat Myth plot gives a deeper understanding to Gog's

---

[80] In the Ninurta-Anzu-Bird Myth, Ninurta's first attack is repulsed by Anzu-Bird. Ninurta must seek help from the wily god Ea to conquer (*ANET*, 515–16); in the battle of Ninurta against the Azag Demon, there is also a moment when Ninurta seems to be defeated and flees like a bird. See Samuel N. Kramer, *History Begins at Sumer*, 170–72 and, by the same author, *Sumerian Mythology* (Wesport, CT: Greenwood, 1988) 80–81.

[81] Forsyth, *The Old Enemy*, 446.

[82] *The Context of Scripture*, 1.393.

[83] In v. 2 Gog is addressed in the English translation of the oracle as "chief prince of Meshech and Tubal." Some would see the word ראש as a proper noun, a third nation over which Gog was prince, James D. Price ("Rosh: An Ancient Land Known to Ezekiel," *GTJ* 6.1 [1985] 88–89) being a strong proponent of this position. The construct pointing of the MT favors this, yet Râshu/Rêshu/Arashi proposed by Price is located far to the east of the kingdoms of Meshech and Tubal, and grammatically in the citing of geographical place names, the conjunction would precede Meshech if ראש were a proper noun; see Jan Simons, *The Geographical and Topological Texts of the Old Testament* (Studia Francisci Scholten memoriae dicata, 2; Leiden: Brill, 1959) 81. Given the sense of the text and the mythic significance of the number seven which we will cover below, I would see ראש rather as a common noun.

[84] Adela Yarbro Collins, *Cosmology and Eschatology in Jewish and Christian Apocalypticism* (JSJSup 50; Leiden: Brill, 1996) 122, and, by the same author, *The Combat Myth in the Book of Revelation* (HDR 9; Missoula, MT: Scholars Press, 1976) 77–79.

malevolent arrogance. In the Ninurta-Anzu-Bird Myth,[85] the rebellion of Anzu-Bird was one of making himself equal to Enlil when he seized the Tablet of Destinies, taking away the Enlilship. Just as Anzu-Bird plotted aggression ("The removal of Enlilship he conceives in his heart"[86]), so too did Gog when thoughts came into his mind and he devised his evil scheme (v. 10). Interesting addition to the plot in the final form, it is the Creator who puts the thoughts in Gog's mind. Once again, the sovereignty of the Creator God of Israel is paramount.

Gog comes from "the remotest parts of the north," ירכתי צפון (38:6, 15; 39:2). Dietrich and Loretz assert that clearly the biblical authors have taken the formulation "from the remotest parts of the north" out of an Ugaritic-Canaanite source.[87] The translation could also be interpreted as "from the summits of Zaphon," which is how it is interpreted the only other two times the phrase appears in MT, Ps 48:3 and Isa 14:13.[88] The summits of Mt. Zaphon are the home of Baal. There the "Rider of the Clouds" builds his palace: "in the fastness of Zaphon, a thousand fields the house shall cover."[89] "The summits of Zaphon" is a valid translation of the text.[90] This leaves us with two questions.

---

[85] *ANET*, 112–13.

[86] *ANET*, 112.

[87] Manfried Dietrich and Oswald Loretz, "Ugaritisch ṣrrt ṣpn, ṣrry und hebräisch jrktj ṣpwn," UF 22 (1990) 85.

[88] This is true in the NRSV translation. It is also true in *Lexicon Hebraicum et Aramaicum Veteris Testamenti*, ed. Franciscus Zorell (Rome: Pontificium Institutum Biblicum, 1984) 699–700. F.M. Cross contests this translation of the Isaiah verse both in *CMHE*, 38 and, more recently, in *From Epic to Canon: History and Literature in Ancient Israel* (Baltimore: Johns Hopkins Press, 1998) 86–87. He sees it as best translated "in the distant north," citing the translation of ירכתי צפון in Ezek 38: 6, 15; 39:2 in support of that and noting that both Isaiah and Ezekiel refer to Mt. Amanus, the abode of El. He rejects the possibility of conflation of Baal and El elements in the Isaiah verse. Yet in using the three Ezekiel verses to support his translation of the Isaiah verse, he himself is conflating the mythic imagery in chapters 38–39 where the enemy from the north is clearly a warrior which Cross himself would cite as a distinct mode of revelation for Baal, not El (*CMHE*, 174). It is not clear from his own argument how "the enemy from the distant north" in 38:6, 15 and 39:2 with its accompanying imagery would be coming from Mt. Amanus. The imagery is that of Baal, the divine warrior, and the commonly rendered translation of Isa 14:13 for ירכתי צפון would be equally applicable to 38:6, 15 and 39:2.

[89] Dennis Pardee, trans., "The Ba'lu Myth," in *The Context of Scripture*, 1.261.

[90] Jörg Jeremias, *Theophanie: die Geschichte einer alttestamentlichen Gattung* (rev. and enl. 2nd ed., WMANT 10; Neukirchen-Vluyn: Neukirchener Verlag, 1977) 116–17.

First, is "the enemy from the remotest parts of the north" a veiled reference to Baal? Or for the first hearers/readers, not such a veiled reference? Second, Lipiński postulates[91] that Yhwh's dwelling on Mt. Zion is patterned after Mt. Zaphon. Is the final form suggesting that this final battle will be a battle between two well-known players, legitimate and otherwise, in Israel's new creation myth? I suggest that the reference is deliberately ambiguous. Gog's hordes coming from the remotest parts of the North are referred to in v. 6 as the עמים רבים, the many peoples. The Hebrew resembles phonetically and morphologically the מים רבים, the many waters of primordial chaos.[92] This is to be a battle between the Creator God of Israel and the forces of evil.

This battle will take place on the mountains of Israel, upon people living at the center or navel of the earth. In Mesopotamian mythology this reference to the center of the earth represents the cosmic center of the universe. This center, symbol of all that sustained harmony in the universe, will be assaulted by all the forces of chaos, these forces knowing, as they do, the significance of their victory for destroying the order of the cosmos as established by its Creator.[93] This war fought at the center of the earth has, from its location, other significances, as well. First, it was initially used to refer to Mt. Zaphon where Baal fights and defeats his enemies.[94] After the battle of these two chapters, Mt. Zaphon will be subordinate in significance to the navel of the earth located in the mountains of Israel. Second, this location represents a decisive event for Israel, a decisive event in the cosmogony of Israelite faith. Gog in his hubris strikes at the heart, the center point of ordered creation as Yhwh's people knew it. His defeat will be all the more climactic.

The battle scene in chapters 38–39 spans two chapters. As noted earlier, some commentators suggest that the battle is only in the first part of chapter 39 and see vv. 18–23 as an inappropriate interruption. Yet the fact that Yhwh has at his command the forces of nature, and is able to marshal them at will in this combat, is a significant theme in the

---

[91] Eduard Lipiński, "צפן," *TWAT* 6 (ed. Helmer Ringgren and Heinz-Josef Fabry; Stuttgart: Kohlhammer, 1989) 1099.
[92] Nobile, "Ez 38-39 ed Ez 40-48: i due aspetti complementari," 147.
[93] Clifford, *The Cosmic Mountain*, 190; Loretz, *Ugarit und die Bibel*, 160; Nobile, "Ez 38-39 ed Ez 40-48: i due aspetti complementari," 147.
[94] Clifford, *The Cosmic Mountain*, 175.

Combat Myth. In the Ninurta-Anzag-Demon myth, Ninurta, harnessing and controlling of the forces of nature after his victory, organizes the complex irrigation system of Mesopotamia.[95] In the Sumerian version, Gilgamesh is aided by Utu, the sun God who immobilizes seven destructive weather phenomena.[96] In the Babylonian version, Shamash, the sun god, is explicitly responsible for Gilgamesh's victory.[97] In the creation account of the *Enuma Elish,* after Marduk's victory over Tiamat, though he sets the sun, the moon and the stars on a course of their own, he reserves the phenomena of winds and storms for himself.[98] Marduk, the "rider-on-the-clouds," controlling wind, cloud and lightning, resembles Israel's Creator God in this, "deploying the four winds that none of (Tiamat) may escape, . . . raising the Deluge, his great weapon, . . . mounting the terrible chariot, the unopposable storm demon."[99] Verses 38:18–23 give much greater force[100] to the battle described in 39:1–8. It is through these verses that all the nations will know the full extent of Yhwh's lordship: his dominion over creation includes the deployment of all the forces of creation to defeat primeval chaos and bring it under his dominion.

The third core component of the Combat Myth, the victory, is seen in the Gog pericope in 39:1–8. In some of the epics, the hero conquers by guile or deceit. Gilgamesh convinces Huwawa that he is only there to offer his older sister in marriage and his younger sister as servant so Huwawa lays down his armor and is then subdued.[101] Other divine warriors do not win with guile (e.g., Baal and Anat). Similarly, Yhwh is not a trickster who outwits Gog. He needs no artifice. For Israel, he is all-powerful Creator. In the battle scene Yhwh's mystifying power: "I will strike your bow from your left hand and make your arrows drop out of your right hand" is reminiscent, even in its reversal, of

---

[95] Kramer, *History Begins at Sumer*, 171.

[96] *The Context of Scripture*, 1.458.

[97] *ANET*, 80.

[98] John Day, *God's Conflict with the Dragon and the Sea: Echoes of a Canaanite Myth in the Old Testament* (University of Cambridge Oriental Publications 35; Cambridge: Cambridge University Press, 1985) 185; Jacobsen, *The Treasures of Darkness*, 179.

[99] *The Context of Scripture*, 1.397.

[100] *CMHE*, 105–6 sees the cosmic elements as giving mythic depth to the historical events. They become a mythopoeic vehicle for the motif of the cosmic warrior in the Hebrew Epic.

[101] Jacobsen, *The Treasures of Darkness*, 200.

Anzu-Bird's successful initial defeat of Ninurta where the arrow could not approach Anzu but was turned back.[102] Korpel and de Moor interpret the texts to say that Baal lacks strength in the final battle with Mot.[103] The all-powerful Creator God of Israel here, in contrast, demonstrates emphatically his mighty arm. Israel's sovereign is not without strength as he completes his cosmogony. In fact, Yhwh defeats his enemy alone and unaided in battle without the help of Israel. Day notes[104] that Behemoth and Leviathan cannot be captured by man but only by God.

The fourth core component in the Combat Myth is the triumph. In vv. 9–20 his chosen people are involved in the "clean-up" after the battle and a victory feast is served. As mentioned above the burial of the vanquished prior to their being served as the feast in vv. 9–20 has often been criticized yet, if this is in fact a disordering, examples abound in the ancient Near Eastern myths of that which would not fit into logical categories. The reappearance of Mot in the story line after he has been slain by Anat[105] is one example. Mythical time does not work in the categories of the rational mind.[106] The logical structure of our world, our causation is not necessarily applicable.[107] A coherent and logical system is not always present in myth.

After the purification of the land the victory feast is played out in the Gog pericope in vv. 17–20. In the Marduk-Tiamat myth, the gods are invited to sit down for a banquet of delights. In the Baal-Yamm myth, a great temple and a palace are built to honor Baal in his victory, and a victory feast is held to celebrate the triumph.[108] In the same text, Anat may enjoy a bloody feast of defeated warriors. This triumphal banquet in vv. 17–20 is not without its ancient Near Eastern roots.

---

[102] *ANET*, 516.

[103] Marjo Korpel and Johannes C. De Moor, Review of *God's Conflict with the Dragon and the Sea* by John Day in *JSS* 31 (1986) 243–45.

[104] Day, *God's Conflict with the Dragon and the Sea*, 181.

[105] *The Context of Scripture*, 1.270, 272.

[106] W. F. Albright ("The Place of the Old Testament in the History of Thought," *History, Archaeology and Christian Humanism* [New York: McGaw-Hill, 1964] 95) notes that it is characteristic of myth that it lacks precision. The writers were "trying to create a vague, changing outline in order to make the picture shimmer, so to speak, in the mind of the listener."

[107] Wyatt, *Myths of Power*, 121.

[108] *The Context of Scripture*, 1.401, 261–62.

Gressmann, before the discovery of Ugarit, in his 1905 study on the grisly meaning of זבח as sacrificial meal in the texts of Zeph 1:7, Ezek 39:17–20, Isa 25:6–8 and 34:5–8 notes :

> (The idea) must have entered from a tradition known at that time, but unknown to us. We must ask further how he (the prophet) had access to this tradition and how it looks as we grope in the darkness. It doesn't come from the books which the ancient prophets transmitted to us. Whether it was handed on in oral or written form, it doesn't matter. I have no doubt that a rich literature on the Day of Yhwh is presupposed and must have been lost to us.[109]

The Ugaritic cognate (*dbḥ*) of זבח is found both in the Baal Epic and the Legend of King Keret.[110] In the former we read:

> For two kinds of *banquets* Baʿal hates, three the Rider of the Clouds: A *banquet* of shamefulness, a *banquet* of baseness, and a *banquet* of handmaids' lewdness.[111]

In the Legend of King Keret:

> Lift up thy hands to heaven, *Sacrifice* to Bull, thy Father El;
> Honor Baʿal with thy *sacrifice,* Dagon's Son with thine oblation.[112]

The invited guests, too, are partially explained by an analogous feasting in the Baal Epic. After Anat seizes, cleaves, winnows, burns, grinds, and sows Mot in a field, "birds eat his remnants, consuming his portions, flitting from remnant to remnant."[113] When we consider the significance of Mot as death, the context in which Gog, the consummate personification of chaos, is offered as food to the birds of the air and the wild animals becomes more understandable.

Not of little significance in their possible mythic referents are the items on the menu. Blenkinsopp[114] sees in the fare a veiled reference to Leviathan, the seven-headed dragon slain by Anat.[115] Connections

---

[109] Gressmann, *Der Ursprung,* 137–38.
[110] Block, *The Book of Ezekiel, Chapters 25–48,* 475.
[111] *The Context of Scripture,* 1.258.
[112] *The Context of Scripture,* 1.334.
[113] *The Context of Scripture,* 1.270.
[114] Blenkinsopp, *Ezekiel,* 189.
[115] Michael D.Coogan, *Stories from Ancient Canaan* (Philadelphia: Westminster, 1978) 92.

could be made with Leviathan and Behemoth through Rabbinic literature as we have seen above. Gressmann suggests that Gog, a choice human sacrifice, has been placed on a level with the most valuable slaughter animals: those who have been newly sheared for the first time.[116] More recent research using Ugaritic materials not available to Gressmann would indicate parallels in Canaanite literature.

> Frequently animal names were used metaphorically as designations or titles for leaders or nobles of some sort or for warriors. This is especially true of poetic materials. . . . Generally such designations are simply metaphor, poetic language. . . . The chieftains or princes who receive such designations may or may not be regarded as inimical to the poet and his people. . . .[117]

Miller notes that the list of animals in v 18, cited with warriors and princes, probably secondarily reflects the custom of designating such categories of personnel by animal names. In the Ugaritic literature "rams" commonly denotes noblemen, chiefs, leaders; "bulls" is often used to designate dignitaries or warriors.[118] The *Targum of Ezekiel* interprets each of the names in this verse rather than translating them: "kings, rulers and governors, all of them mighty men, rich in possessions."[119] These terms, it would seem, are paralleling the Ugaritic practice, animal designations for nobility. This would fit, coming from the description of the nations amassed against Israel in 38:3–6.

There is an interesting contrast here in the fare of the two feasts. Baal, for his feast, slaughters cattle, bulls, fatlings, rams, calves, lambs and kids, and feeds them to his brethren, the seventy children of Asherah: the gods and goddesses.[120] In the Gog account, in an interesting reversal, the animals are invited to feast on those who would put themselves in the position of a god. As noted earlier, Behemoth and Leviathan are to be consumed in the Jewish tradition at the victory banquet.

In the passage the birds of the air and beasts of the field are served food (the fat and the blood) which was ritually forbidden for any but

---

[116] Coogan, *Stories from Ancient Canaan*, 139.

[117] Patrick D. Miller, Jr., "Animal Names as Designations in Ugaritic and Hebrew," *UF* 2 (1970) 177.

[118] Miller, "Animal Names as Designations in Ugaritic and Hebrew," 182, 184.

[119] *The Targum of Ezekiel*, 108–9.

[120] *The Context of Scripture*, 1.262.

Yhwh (Lev 3:16–17). Gressmann suggests that such a violation of ritual law would be an indication of a foreign provenance.[121] Von Soden[122] is more specific and says that such violation of ritual law is an indication of the influence of the Baal cult, where, in imitation of the banquet offered by Baal, it is mentioned that the guests sated themselves with fat foods in the feast.

There is also a characteristic of this feast of Yhwh which parallels what is characteristic of the banquets given by the gods, Baal in particular on Mt. Zaphon. Verses 17 and 19 mention "my feast" and v. 20 mentions "my table." Especially from the last designation of "my table," it is clearly not a feast in Yhwh's honor. It is a feast hosted by Yhwh. In the Baal Epic, Baal is also a host.[123] As mentioned above in the first section of chapter three, Ezek 39:20 and 44:16 are the only places in the OT where the phrase "my table" is used.

Cassuto notes that it was through the use of the Israelite Creation Myth, shared with the surrounding nations of the ancient Near East and reworked, that the prophets brought tidings of consolation regarding the ultimate dominion of evil at a future time.[124] Yhwh, the Creator and the divine warrior, in the process of delivering his people, has destroyed forever any nation which could ever be used by him in the future in judgment against Israel as Babylon was used through Nebuchadnezzar. The stage is now set for the establishment of Yhwh's enthronement and universal rule in his Temple at the center of the earth which he created.

In the next chapter we will look at ancient Near Eastern mythic parallels in chapters 1–37 and 40–48. Our focus will be specifically myths used in the reformation of a new Israelite creation myth as discussed in chapter two. Through these patterns, the integral nature of the Gog pericope in the final form of the book will emerge and be complemented by the mythic enthronement of a victoriously sovereign Yhwh in his restored Temple.

---

[121] Gressmann, *Der Ursprung*, 137–38.
[122] Wolfram von Soden, "Trunkenheit im babylonisch-assyrischen Schriftum," in *Bibel und Alter Orient* (ed. Hans-Peter Müller; ZAW 162; Berlin: de Gruyter, 1985) 193.
[123] *The Context of Scripture*, 1.261–62.
[124] Cassuto, *The Goddess Anath*, 75.

CHAPTER 5

Mythic Elements and Cosmogony in Ezekiel 1–37 and 40–48

Significant mythic elements and cosmogonic themes throughout Ezekiel's final form engage the religious imagination of its readers. The book calls upon the images of Israelite and other ancient Near Eastern myth from the very first chapters, restoring hope in Israel's all-powerful Creator. The mythic elements in the Oracles Against the Nations show the sovereignty of Yhwh bringing order out of chaos among the nations and lead naturally to the chapters on the Restoration of Israel: monarchy, people, and Temple. These elements and their impact on a people who had known the sack of their capital city and the destruction of their God's dwelling give a greater depth of understanding to a context. With good reason, the *Chaoskampf* myth became an essential part of cosmogony after the events of 587 B.C.E. Treatment of all the mythic elements prior to and following chapters 38–39 would be overly repetitious. Below I will discuss the mythic referents most foundational in understanding the Gog/Magog account as integral to the text in its final form.

Ezekiel 1:4–28

In Israel's tradition which proscribed the worship of graven images (Exod 20:2–6; Deut 5:6–10), Ezekiel's record of the prophet's vision of

Yhwh in the throne chariot makes it stand out, though not singularly (cf. Isaiah 6, Zechariah 4). The prophet assists at a spectacle of the power of God himself in the two constituent elements of Creator and judge[1] who will come in judgment to bring his act of creation to fulfillment. Keel does not believe there was an actual Yhwh iconography in Israel or Judah yet he notes that the process of imagining occurred in a region that was filled with literary and iconographic images.[2] Through the use of the words "like"(17 times), "form"(17 times), "appearance"(15 times), analogous referencing portrays the grandeur of the God of Israel in the text. In fact, the use of such varied imagery gives semantic depth to the prophet's image of God.[3] It is understandable that Israel would conceive of their God in images. The final form of Ezekiel uses these images mythopoeically to convey the vision of the Creator whose sovereignty is not surpassed.

For our purposes, the vision can be divided into four components: (1) the elements of the storm theophany; (2) the physical description of the four living beings; (3) the platform and the throne; and (4) the divine being. There is the unmistakable presence of mythic elements and cosmogonic themes in the four components of the vision which parallel other ancient Near Eastern texts. The first of these, the storm theophany, sets the stage for the vision: a tempestuous wind comes out of the north, bearing a great cloud with brightness around it and fire flashing forth continually from within. Within the fire were burning coals and torches moving to and fro. Lightning issued from the fire, and lightning was characteristic of the living creatures within. The movement of the living creatures is like the sound of mighty waters, like the thunder of the Almighty. The splendor surrounding the throne chariot was like a bow in the clouds on a rainy day revealing within the כבוד יהוה. The rainbow here is used by the author to describe the indescribable, the glory of the Lord.

These elements of fire, lightning, thunder and shining cloud are not new to OT theophany accounts, cf. Exod 19:16–20; Judg 5:4–5; Nah

---

[1] Nobile, *Teologia dell'Antico Testamento*, 120.

[2] Othmar Keel and Christoph Uehlinger, *Gods, Goddesses, and Images of God in Ancient Israel* (trans. Thomas H. Trapp; Minneapolis: Augsburg Fortress, 1998) 405; originally published as *Göttinnen, Götter und Gottessymbole* (Quaestiones disputatae 134; Fribourg: Herder, 1992).

[3] Podella, *Das Lichtkleid JHWH's*, 273.

1:3–8; Hab 3:8–15. The stormy wind propelling the cloud appears in Isa 19:6; Jer 23:19; 30:23; Zech 9:14; Job 38:1; 40:6. The appearance of the fiery presence of God to his people is also an element of tradition: Exod 16:10; Num 14:10; 16:19. Other texts of storm theophany (Pss 18:14, 144:6) speak as well of lightning, paralleling them with the arrows of the divine warrior.

All these occurrences share in the mythic traditions of the ancient Near East. They are all intimately bound together in descriptions of the theophany of the storm god or of the attack of the divine warrior. One Babylonian mystical text describes the universe as consisting of three heavens and three earths.[4] The closing formula of the text notes that this description of the universe is a secret of the great gods.[5] The initiate may reveal it to another initiate, but the uninitiated are not allowed to see it. In the middle heaven is the Lord Marduk. He is above the lower heaven of stars, and seated in his throne room on a throne of lapis lazuli, surrounded by the gleam of *elmēšu*, amber. The parallels to Ezekiel's vision, where the Lord is seated above the lowest heaven of stars on a throne made of lapis lazuli and illuminated by the gleam of amber, are self-evident.

A second curious similarity is the importance in both traditions that the transmission remains a closely guarded secret. The four creatures in Ezekiel's vision bear striking resemblance to four equally mysterious creatures described by Philostratus as hanging from a celestial dome of lapis lazuli in the king's judgment chamber in Babylon.[6] These creatures have fiery bodies. They seem to be burning fire, and run out from and return to the god like flashes of lightning. They speed out with messages from the Supreme Father and return to him.[7] Such a title, Supreme Father, would imply that it was from him that all life generates, that he is Creator of all.

Chapter three above, in the discussion of ירכתי צפון, noted the significance of "the north" as the home of Baal. It is at first curious that

---

[4] Alisdair Livingstone, *Mystical and Mythological Explanatory Works of Assyrian and Babylonian Scholars* (Oxford: Clarendon, 1986) 83.

[5] Peter Kingsley, "Exile by the Grand Canal: between Jewish and Babylonian Tradition," *JRAS* 3rd Series, 2 (1992) 339–46.

[6] Loretz, *Ugarit und die Bibel*, 214–15; Flavius Philostratus, *Das Leben des Apollonios von Tyana*,1.25 (trans. Vroni Mumprecht; Munich: Artemis, 1983) 81.

[7] Philostratus, *Das Leben des Apollonios* 1.25, 81; Hans Lewy, *Chaldean Oracles and Theurgy* (Paris: Études Augustiniennes, 1978) 133, 163–64.

Yhwh would come from Zaphon rather than Sion, his dwelling. It is unlikely that it is suggesting that Yhwh lived on Mt. Zaphon, the site of Baal's palace. It is not meant to be a conflated reference to Sion-Jerusalem which in fact lies west of Babylon. Rather, the point is that Yhwh can come from any direction he pleases, even that which is supposed to be the home of the storm deity.[8] It reflects Yhwh's sovereign freedom as Creator.

Greenberg[9] suggests very convincingly that the wind out of the north could be based in the experience of the *shamāl*, a persistent and regular northwesterly wind over the whole of Iraq occurring from May throughout the summer and producing dust and sandstorms. He seems to suggest that the experience of *shamāl* would negate the possibility of mythical elements, yet he does not allow the possibility that the *shamāl* could be the event which triggered a mystical experience which was clearly more than a sandstorm. His observation does not exclude such an experience based in natural phenomenon. Given the extent of the mystical experience described, even if triggered by the experience of a sandstorm, Greenberg's consideration is a moot point.

One of the words frequently discussed in Ezekiel is the word חשמל, translated in the NRSV as "amber." Garfinkel, Greenberg and Kingsley all[10] note its probable correspondence with the Akkadian word *elmēšu*, a brilliant stone of some type. Its Akkadian use is attested in mythological contexts reminiscent of its use in Ezekiel: "I (Ishtar) have established your throne under the great heaven; I watch (over you) from a golden abode in the midst of the heaven; I light the lamp of *elmēšu*-stone before Esarhaddon." It is used as well as a descriptor for Nergal "whose upper cheeks are *elmēšu*, his lower cheeks flash constantly like lightning."[11]

This image of cloud-rider in the storm theophany appears also in the Ugarit texts where Baal is given this image. Thunder and lightning reflect Baal's role as storm god.[12] Baal drives his chariot of clouds,

---

[8] Block, *The Book of Ezekiel, Chapters 1–24*, 92; Ohler, "Die Gegenwart Gottes," 86; Pohlmann, *Der Prophet Hesekiel/Ezechiel 1–19*, 58.

[9] Greenberg, *Ezekiel, 1–20*, 42–43.

[10] Stephen P. Garfinkel, "Studies in Akkadian Influences in the Book of Ezekiel" (Ph.D. diss., Columbia University, 1983) 81–82; Greenberg, *Ezekiel, 1–20*, 43; Kingsley, "Exile by the Grand Canal," 340.

[11] Greenberg, *Ezekiel, 1–20*, 43.

[12] Pope, *Probative Pontificating*, 74.

both as warrior god and as one going out to distribute rain.[13] Loretz describes "Cloud-Rider" as one of the essential aspects of the weather god Baal. Baal's chariot on the clouds makes the coming of rain possible. The coming of the chariot is always accompanied by storm, lightning, thunder and, most important of all, rain. Baal as "Cloud Rider" rides his chariot in or above the rain clouds.[14] In Hos 6:3 Yhwh's appearance is connected with rain, which is to say he is depicted in the same role as Baal. The implied message, though not the main point of the vision, is clear. It is Yhwh, the Creator, who provides the rain, makes the earth to produce vegetation and has the elements of nature at his disposal to do that.

The second component of the theophany is the physical description of the four living creatures in the middle of the cloud. Legs straight and feet like calves, they sparkled like burnished bronze. Each of the creatures had two sets of wings, one spread out touching the other creatures and the other set covering their bodies. Under the wings were human hands. The creatures each had four faces, of a human, a lion, an ox and an eagle. In the midst of the creatures was something that looked like burning coals of fire, like torches, moving to and fro. The fire was bright and lightning came forth from the fire. The creatures themselves moved like lightning. The fiery appearance of Yhwh's messengers and the fiery substance moving among them, flashing lightning, partakes of Yhwh's own fiery nature.[15] Their wings made a sound like mighty waters, like the thundering of Shaddai, like the sound of the tumult, like the sound of a mighty army.

It is clear that the cherubim depicted in the Solomonic Temple (1 Kgs 6:24; 7:29, 36) represented a design with good ancient Near Eastern parallels.[16] Cherubim, for example, appeared on the watchtowers before

---

[13] Wolfgang Herrmann, "Rider Upon the Clouds," in *Dictionary of Deities and Demons in the Bible* (ed. Karel van der Toorn, Bob Becking and Pieter W. van der Horst; 2nd ed.; Leiden: Brill, 1999) 704.

[14] Eichrodt, *Ezekiel*, 56; Oswald Loretz, "A Hurrian Word for the Chariot of the Cloud Rider?" in *Ugarit, Religion and Culture, Proceedings of the International Colloquium on Ugarit, Religion and Culture* (ed. Nick Wyatt, W. G. E. Watson, and J. B. Lloyd; UBL 12; Münster: Ugarit-Verlag, 1996) 173–74; Nobile, *Teologia dell'Antico Testamento*, 120.

[15] Carol Newsom, *Songs of the Sabbath Sacrifice: A Critical Edition* (HSS 27; Atlanta: Scholars Press, 1985) 315.

[16] Pohlmann (*Der Prophet Hesekiel/Ezechiel 1–19*, 57) notes that the four components structuring the כבוד יהוה in the vision: the living creatures, the dome, the throne

each royal building in Babylon.[17] Ps 104:4 speaks of fire and flame as Yhwh's ministers. The combination of theophany and the language of fire appears also in Ps 18:7 ff. where Yhwh rides forth from his palace as a devouring warrior: "devouring fire went forth from his mouth; glowing coals flamed forth from him." He does so in response to his servant David whom he draws from the mighty waters (v. 16). Ps 46:3–4 sees in the roaring of the sea the continued rebellion of the armies of the monster of chaos.[18]

The four living creatures with their four wings, four faces and calves feet have parallels in the ancient Near Eastern iconography of northern Mesopotamia and Syria from as far back as the fourteenth century, B.C.E., aiding in the interpretation of the biblical cherubim, and serving in precisely the same function.[19] The living creatures in chapter 1 are identified in chapter 10 of Ezekiel as cherubim. At least since the fourteenth century, ancient Near Eastern iconography represented these living creatures as divine beings. As the living creatures carry the throne and the divinity, so too do their ancient Near Eastern contemporaries. Pohlmann notes that in their position of carrying the throne places, the cherubim hold a status inferior to the God of Israel. Implied in the image is the service of other gods to Yhwh.[20] They are in an inferior status to him.

Their wings suggest that the four creatures probably embody the four cosmic winds with the lion standing for the south, the ox for the north, the eagle for the east and the human for the west. These four

---

and the enthroned deity have been present in the religious art of Mesopotamia and Anatolia since the third millenium B.C.E. and on into the Persian Period, and that they signal to the reader that the God of Israel is enthroned over the firmament, omnipowerful and omnipresent.

[17] Rüdiger Bartelmus, "Die Tierwelt in der Bibel II," in *Gefährten und Feinde des Menschen* (ed. Bernd Janowski, Ute Neumann-Gorsolke, Uwe Gleßmer; Neukirchen-Vluyn: Neukirchener, 1993) 302–3.

[18] Zimmerli, *Ezekiel* 1.131.

[19] Tryggve Mettinger, "Cherubim," in *Dictionary of Deities and Demons in the Bible* (ed. Karel van der Toorn, Bob Becking and Pieter W. van der Horst; 2d ed.; Leiden: Brill, 1999) 190.

[20] Othmar Keel, *Jahwe-Visionen und Siegelkunst* (SBS 84/85; Stuttgart: Verlag Katholisches Bibelwerk, 1977) 271; Othmar Keel, *The Symbolism of the Biblical World: Ancient Near Eastern Iconography and the Book of Psalms* (trans. Timothy J. Hallet; New York: The Seabury Press, 1978) 171; originally published as *Die Welt der altorientalischen Bildsymbolik und das Alte Testament: Am Beispiel der Psalmen* (Neukirchen: Neukirchener Verlag, 1972); Pohlmann, *Der Prophet Hesekiel/Ezechiel 1–19*, 58.

cosmic forces carry the ruler of the world who has their service at his command,[21] accentuating his absolute superiority and sovereignty. It is in the context of the storm god that the final form makes reference to the roaring of many waters to describe the noise of the wings of the cherubim.[22] That the movement of their wings sounded like the thunder of Shaddai has its background in the lightning and thunder which accompany the theophany of the storm god.[23] Fire is intimately associated with those divine beings who attend the great gods, and the fire appears to be a sort of weapon.[24] The messengers of Yamm appear as warriors, flaming with swords: "fire, burning fire, doth flash." These incendiary characters inspire dread in the deities who see them.[25] In his sovereignty, the divine warrior has under his dominion even those messengers who serve Yamm, the chaos god Sea.

The third component of the vision: a dome like shining crystal upon which was a throne, something like sapphire, is supported by these creatures. The luminous quality of the firmament under the throne of God is similarly described in Exod 24:10. Next to each of the creatures was a wheel, gleaming like beryl and the wheels moved as the creatures moved, the spirit of the living creatures being in the wheels. The rims of the wheels contained eyes all around. The wheels are a symbol of the divine sovereignty over the whole world, to see all and be everywhere effortlessly.[26] The wheels serve to connect the cloud and the chariot in a number of texts. Ps 77:19 reads "the crash of your thunder was in the wheel." Ps 104:3 states: "who makes the clouds your chariot." Such references make it meaningful to talk of the theophanic cloud chariot of the Lord.[27]

Pohlmann sees here strong parallels in the throne chariot with the

---

[21] Pohlmann, *Der Prophet Hesekiel/Ezechiel 1–19*, 58–59; Nobile, *Teologia dell' Antico Testamento*, 120.

[22] Herbert G. May, "Some Cosmic Connotations of *Mayim Rabbîm*, Many Waters," *JBL* 47 (1955) 17.

[23] *CMHE*, 58.

[24] Patrick D. Miller, Jr., "Fire in the Mythology of Canaan and Israel," *CBQ* 27 (1965) 259.

[25] *The Context of Scripture*, 1.246.

[26] Moshe Greenberg, "Ezekiel's Vision: Literary and Iconographic Aspects," in *History, Historiography and Intepretation: Studies in Biblical and Cuneiform Literatures* (eds. H. Tadmor and M. Weinfeld; Jerusalem: Magnes, 1984) 166; Nobile, *Teologia dell'Antico Testamento*, 120; Zimmerli, *Ezekiel* 1.129.

[27] Tryggve Mettinger, *The Dethronement of Sabaoth* (ConBOT 18; Lund: Wallin & Dalholm, 1982) 105.

Assyrian and Persian Divine Chariot which accompanied the royal leader into battle empty, as symbol of the presence of the deity in the battle with the king and his army. The wheels of these chariots were, as described in Ezekiel, a wheel within a wheel, and the rims were crafted with nails whose heads could have inspired the image of wheels with eyes.[28]

The fourth component is the figure seated on the throne whose form was only partially anthropomorphic: a human upper body and a radiant lower body. Above "something that had the appearance of"[29] his loins, he appeared as gleaming amber. He was enclosed in fire and down from his loins there was fire all around. This depiction is a shift to a more transcendent divinity than the fully anthropomorphic description appearing in Isa 6:1[30] where "the hem of his robe filled the Temple." The place of honor on the throne has been given to the כבוד יהוה, the glory of the Lord. Yhwh is portrayed as Lord of the cosmos,[31] Creator and supreme sovereign.

By the time of the exile and after, Baal had evolved into the "Lord of Heaven." He had moved beyond his range of concerns as weather god. As "Lord of Heaven," he was still responsible for rain, but his majesty was now expressed in the increasing range of his territory as well as his combined solar and celestial characteristics. Parallel biblical images in Ps 104:1–4 and Ezek 1:4–28 suggest that aspects of a weather god and a sun god converge with images depicting a creator god, in a portrait of Yhwh, ruling as Creator in a Baal-type figure:[32] "you are wrapped in light as in a garment, . . . you set the beams of your chambers on the waters, you make the clouds your chariot, you ride on the wings of the wind, . . . fire and flame are your ministers."

---

[28] Pohlmann, *Der Prophet Hesekiel/Ezechiel 1–19*, 60.

[29] Marjo Korpel (*A Rift in the Clouds, Ugaritic and Hebrew Descriptions of the Divine* [UBL 8; Münster: Ugarit Verlag, 1990] 95–96) notes that despite the early traditions attributing a visible form to God, the OT shows much more restraint in speaking of the body of God than Ugarit. No text mentions the nakedness of God. The Book of Ezekiel is very careful not to report that the prophet saw the loins of the divinity.

[30] Mark S. Smith, "Mythology and Myth Making in Ugaritic and Israelite Literature," in *Ugarit and the Bible: Proceedings of the International Symposium on Ugarit and the Bible, Manchester, September 1992* (ed. George J. Brooke, Adrian H. W. Curtis and John F. Healey; UBL 11; Munster : Ugarit-Verlag, 1994) 322.

[31] Keel, *The Symbolism of the Biblical World*,171.

[32] Keel and Uehlinger, *Gods, Goddesses, and Images of God*, 261.

The description of the enthroned figure in Ezek 1:26–27 sharply distinguishes between its upper half which glitters like electrum and its lower half which was like fire. This resembles the representation of the god Ashur in his solar disc. The disc itself is decorated with tongues of flames and the head and torso of the god exhibit recognizably human features, while his lower parts seem to consist of flaring fire.[33] Keel notes parallels with a second figure of a creator god of heaven giving blessing from the same period, "not to be distinguished from the Assyrian sun god," whose upper body protrudes from lotus buds and blossoms that surround a disk.[34] It is also similar to a seal found in Jerusalem on which is depicted a god whose upper body is shown coming out of a nimbus cloud.[35] In these images and Ezekiel's depiction, the upper bodies are plainly outlined while the lower part is out of view. Furthermore, Ezekiel's depiction places Yhwh over the heavens.[36] The relationship of Yhwh to the other creatures is one of superiority. [37] As Creator, he rules over the remaining powers.

The four components of the vision, with their comparable ancient Near Eastern analogues, create an image of the God of Israel that compares with the God of the exodus from Egypt. The tradition of the exodus incorporated within it the imagery of the storm god defeating his enemies. The vision proclaims the כבוד of Yhwh who also led his people through the desert and manifested himself to them in a fiery cloud, Exod 16:7, 19:16ff., 24:16f., 40:34f. The images perhaps recall images of the wilderness narratives of the Pentateuch.[38] This כבוד יהוה in its mobile throne chariot is not tied to the Temple precinct but went before the people to lead them forward. The final form is evoking these associations for a very particular reason: the desert wanderings themselves had cosmogonic significance for Israel. As Yhwh led his people forth from Egypt to the Promised Land he was in the process of forming them as a stable life-sustaining community to bring his work of creation to completion. The God of Ezekiel's Inaugural Vision is the Creator God of Israel who created his chosen people, led them out of

---

[33] *ANEP*, 180, 314.
[34] Keel and Uehlinger, *Gods, Goddesses, and Images of God*, 402.
[35] Keel and Uehlinger, *Gods, Goddesses, and Images of God*, 295–96.
[36] Keel, *Jahwe-Visionen und Siegelkunst*, 271–72.
[37] Bartelmus, "Die Tierwelt in der Bibel II," 303.
[38] Greenberg, *Ezekiel 1–20*, 54; Zimmerli, *Ezekiel* 1.121.

Egypt and who has not yet concluded his act of creation. The readers of the final form would see continuity between the God of Ezekiel and the God who initiated their cosmogonic formation in the desert centuries before.

An aspect of the כבוד יהוה developed in the vision of the throne chariot is God's function as judge.[39] The act of judgment is intimately bound with the harmony to be restored by the Creator. Purification from all the obstacles of chaos and evil must take place if the good order of creation is to be re-established.[40] While neither the words שפט, nor משפט appear in the throne chariot theophany, the vision announces the impending judgment of Yhwh. Many exegetes from St. Jerome onward assume a positive purpose to the vision: that Yhwh is present with his people even in their exile.[41] A closer look will show basis for this consolation in Yhwh's judgment which Ps 98:8–9 cites as cause for cosmic jubilation: "Let the floods clap their hands; let the hills sing together for joy at the presence of the Lord for he is coming to judge the earth."[42] Yhwh's judgment is cause for such jubilation because it is prefatory to re-creation.

The passage itself is an interweaving of themes of the storm theophany and the throne theophany. While the storm theophany is used to depict Yhwh coming as a warrior to conquer the foes of his people, it is also used to convey Yhwh's intervention to bring judgment on Israel.[43] In the throne theophany in Isaiah 6 we see that the function of the vision is to prepare for Isaiah's vocation as a prophet of judgment.

---

[39] Davidson, *The Book of the Prophet Ezekiel*, 4; Kraetzschmar, *Das Buch Ezechiel*, 21; Smend, *Der Prophet Ezechiel*, 7. More recently, W. H. Brownlee (*Ezekiel 1–19* [Word Bible Commentary 28; Waco: Word Books, 1986] 18) sees the import of the vision as "the cosmic Lord of the universe . . . intervening in history to judge Israel and warn them through one man, Ezekiel."

[40] Hans-Peter Müller, *Ursprünge und Strukturen alttestamentlicher Eschatologie* (BZAW 109; Berlin: Alfred Töplemann, 1969) 120; Nobile, *Introduzione all'Antico Testamento*, 103.

[41] *S. Hieronymi Presbyteri Opera 1: Opera exegetica 4: Commentarium in Hezechielem libri 14* (Corpus Christianorum, Series Latina 75; Turnholt: Brepols, 1964) 7; Bertholet and Galling, *Hesekiel*, 9; Eichrodt, *Ezekiel: A Commentary*, 54, 58–59; Fohrer and Galling, *Ezechiel*, 14–16; Hals, *Ezekiel*, 16; Ralph Klein, *Israel in Exile*, (Overtures to Biblical Theology 6; Philadelphia: Fortress, 1979) 74–75; Toy, *The Book of the Prophet Ezekiel*, 96; Zimmerli, *Ezekiel* 1.140.

[42] Ellen Davis, "Psalm 98, Rejoicing in Judgment," *Int* 46 (1992) 173–74.

[43] Cf. Amos 1:2; Micah 1:2–7, Isa 59:15–20; Mal 3:1–5. Jeremias, *Theophanie*, 130–32.

Yhwh has judged his people and Isaiah is invited to deliver the verdict.[44] Similar to Greenberg's reflection on Ezekiel, O. H. Steck[45] suggests that this vision of God as judge legitimates Isaiah as prophet of judgment.

The vision itself is part of a larger unit which includes the prophetic call of Ezekiel. Ezekiel is commissioned as a prophet of judgment. In the account, Israel is designated as those who have rebelled against Yhwh (Ezek 2:3), an accusation which warrants divine judgment. Ezek 2:4 concludes with the Messenger Formula and 2:5 assures Ezekiel they will know a prophet has been among them "whether they hear or refuse to hear." This indicates that at least some of the Oracles to be spoken will be Oracles of Judgment. When Ezekiel eats the scroll, he is told that it contains "words of lamentation, mourning and woe." This too suggests judgment. Verses 16–21 also emphasize Ezekiel's role as prophet of judgment, supporting the evidence, at least in its final form, that the vision in chapter one was a vision of a God of judgment. If the vision is to prepare Ezekiel for the commission which follows, it would most logically reveal Yhwh as judge.

The theophany on Sinai (Exodus 19–20) is a comparable OT example of God appearing in judgment. He comes amidst lightning flashes, thunder claps, wrapped in a dark cloud. Yhwh descends on the mountain in fire and his anger, demonstrated predominantly through aspects of the storm, burning like fire. V. Hamp notes that it is in theophanies of judgment exhibiting a strong mythological hue where we encounter such motifs of fire.[46] The vision in Ezekiel 1 employs many such mythic elements of judgment. Fire, a representation of Yhwh's wrath and a weapon of destruction, appears in 1:4, 13 and 27. There is fire flashing forth continually from the midst of the creatures, like burning coals and torches moving to and fro. Fire surrounded the human form on the throne with fire descending down from the loins. D. N. Freedman and B. E. Willoughby note that the final form links clouds with storm, thunder and the powerful forces of nature to describe God's fury against his enemies.[47] Ezekiel 1 is about the glory of the Lord come to

---

[44] Leslie C. Allen, "The Structure and Intention of Ezekiel 1," *VT* 43 (1993) 155.

[45] Odil H. Steck, "Bermerkungen zu Jesaja 6," *BZ*, NF 16 (1972)195 n. 22.

[46] Vincenz Hamp, "אש IV. Feuer in Verbindung mit Gott," *TWAT* 1 (Stuttgart: Kohlhammer, 1973) 460.

[47] Freedman and Willoughby, "ענן," *TWAT* 6 (Stuttgart: Kohlhammer, 1989) 273.

judge. In this sovereign capacity he will create even out of the tragedy of the exile "a stable community in a benevolent and life sustaining order."[48] But before the restoration portion of this post-exilic remake of Israel's creation myth, there must come the judgment of Yhwh's people, the purification from all the obstacles of chaos and evil mentioned above, in order that the good order of creation may be re-established.

This image of Yhwh as judge itself has mythic foundations in ancient Near Eastern myth. Yhwh as just judge of the whole world is an attribute which is also affirmed of Shamash, the sun-deity inherited from the Babylonian tradition.[49] In the Epic of Tukulti-Ninurta I, Tukulti-Ninurta declares that he is reading out his complaint to the divine overseer of such matters, Shamash whose verdict will emerge from the ordeal of battle.[50] The attributes of Shamash were also attributed to Marduk who is referred to as "the sun god of gods" by Babylonian theologians. He is characterized by rays issuing from his shoulders, by a saw with which, as supreme judge, he "cuts decisions" and by his attitude with one foot on a mountain.[51] Two late compilations explain Shamash as a name of Marduk. Shamash is referred to as the Marduk of justice and the Marduk of the law suit.[52]

The elements of the theophany in Ezekiel 1 have a cosmogonic bearing, comparable to the first action of the Creator God when he conquered chaos, creating the world and initiating the beginning of the history of salvation of Israel and the world. It is his cosmogonic power which creates all things new, begun in judgment to purify all things first, and restore all to right relationship with their Creator, responsive to the presence and will of its Maker. For God's judgment requires nothing less than this absolute clarification of human identity with respect to God's will.[53] Such clarification, which takes place in the first

---

[48] Clifford, "Cosmogonies in the Ugaritic Texts," 201.

[49] Temba L. J. Mafico, "Judge, Judging," *ABD* 3 (New York: Doubleday, 1992) 1196.

[50] Peter B. Machinist, "Literature as Politics: The Tukulti-Ninurta Epic and the Bible," *CBQ* 38 (1976) 458.

[51] Wakeman, *God's Battle with the Monster*, 119.

[52] Wilfred G. Lambert, "Trees, Snakes and Gods in Ancient Syria and Anatolia," *BSOAS* 48 (1985) 439.

[53] Davis, "Psalm 98, Rejoicing in Judgment," 173–74; Nobile, *Teologia dell'Antico Testamento*, 120, 135.

half of the book, must be "in place" before cosmogony can be brought to conclusion. These two constituent elements of the God of Israel foreshadow in this first vision the two central themes of the entire book, the bringing to fulfillment of Yhwh's creation and its prerequisite corollary of judgment.

Pohlmann would go so far as to say that all statements in the vision which seem puzzling and mysterious in their occurrence derive from a concern to characterize the God of Israel as the sole and sovereign God of heaven.[54] While that would depend on what one would consider puzzling and mysterious, it is the understanding of the mythic elements which solves the puzzle, reveals the mystery and proclaims the power of the Creator God of Israel.

Ezekiel 8–11

In 592 B.C.E., the midpoint between the two Babylonian invasions, Ezekiel, who had been exiled to Babylon after the first invasion, is transported back to Jerusalem in a divine vision which is recorded in chapters 8–11. In this vision Yhwh abandons his Temple. Chapter eleven speaks of the disastrous effects that would attend this abandonment, the departure of the כבוד יהוה from the city; in the last three verses, he brings it to pass.

It was the common belief in the ancient Near East that no temple was destroyed except when its god had abandoned it, whether reluctantly under coercion of a higher decree, or in anger because of the offenses of the worshipers.[55] Chapters 8–11 present Yhwh's divine abandonment of his Temple as a severe judgement with cosmogonic implications for the people. The chapters respond to the "cognitive dissonance" caused by the destruction of the Temple and the exile of Jerusalem's inhabitants[56] and through mythopoeic use of the myths known to their author(s), they give answer to Israel's devastated faith. In fact, it is the distinctions between the departure of other gods of the

---

[54] Pohlmann, *Der Prophet Hezekiel/Ezechiel 1–19*, 61.
[55] Moshe Greenberg, "The Vision of Jerusalem of Ezekiel 8–11: A Holistic Interpretation," *The Divine Helmsman* (ed. J. L. Crenshaw and S. Sandmel; New York: Ktav, 1980) 159.
[56] Tryggve N. D. Mettinger, "The Name and the Glory: The Zion-Sabaoth Theology and its Exilic Successors," *JNSL* 24 (1998) 2.

region from their dwellings and the departure of Yhwh from his, that make it clear, neither his sovereignty nor power as Creator are diminished by this divine abandonment. Rather, Yhwh's departure from his dwelling confirms and asserts his sovereignty.

Key to understanding the Creator's undiminished sovereignty even in the departure from his Temple is the final form's use of כבוד יהוה. It is, in fact, a theme in Ezekiel, appearing eighteen times.[57] Significantly, one of those times is in the Gog-Magog passage. Primarily it appears in the three visions: Ezekiel's Call, the Judgment of Jerusalem, and the New Temple.

The word כבוד can have many meanings from heavy or weighty to the glory and honor manifesting itself in history and in creation. The noun כבוד appears frequently with the meaning "power" or "might." It is defined in fact by Rendtorff as "that aspect of the activity of Yhwh in which he himself is revealed in his power."[58] Ps 145:11 states: "They shall speak of the כבוד of your kingdom, and tell of your power." Ps 3:4 proclaims: "You, O Lord, are a shield around me, my כבוד, and the one who lifts up my head." Listed among the synonyms for כבוד is עז, power, Ps 29:1, "Give to the Lord glory and power"; Ps 63:3, "So I have looked upon you in the sanctuary, beholding your power and your glory." In Akkadian literature, kings and gods are clothed and girded with *melammu*, terrifying radiance. Crowns and sacred weapons are surrounded by *melammu*. In Egypt and Assyria the crown was endowed with power and considered a source of awe and terror, overthrowing the enemy.[59] Yhwh's כבוד has this same sense. The description of the כבוד יהוה as a blazing fire in the Call Vision of chapter 1 is certainly an image not just of the awe and majesty of Yhwh, but also of power which can go wherever Yhwh pleases. Exod 24:17 speaks of the כבוד יהוה as a "devouring fire." In Deut 5:25, the people were afraid of being consumed by the great fire blazing forth from the כבוד יהוה. In the context of these passages, the word denotes the personal presence

---

[57] 1:28; 3:12, 23; 8:4; 9:3; 10:4 (twice), 18, 19; 11:22, 23; 28:22; 31:18; 39:13; 43:2, 4, 5; 44:4.

[58] Rolf Rendtorff, "The Concept of Revelation in Ancient Israel," *Revelation as History*, trans. David Granskou (ed. Wolfhart Pannenberg; New York: Macmillan, 1968) 37; originally published as "Die Offenbarungsvorstellungen im Alten Israel," *Offenbarung als Geschichte* (ed. Wolfhart Pannenberg; KD 1; Göttingen: Vandenhoeck & Ruprecht, 1961).

[59] Moshe Weinfeld, "כבוד," *TWAT* 4 (Stuttgart: Kohlhammer, 1984) 28–29.

of the all-powerful deity.[60] This כבוד יהוה, the presence of the God of Israel among his people, was not bound to a particular location. He not only leaves his Temple; he also appears at the river Kebar in Babylon.

The focus of the first part of the Book of Ezekiel is judgment: whose failure brought about the exile? The focus of the second part is creation: what Yhwh will do in the future about this regression to chaos? Mythic elements in chapters 8–11 highlight, as we shall see, this כבוד יהוה, Yhwh's sovereignty as Creator whose departure is judgment.

In the vision shown to Ezekiel by God Jerusalem is in a state of religious collapse; cultic abominations are being practiced in the Temple itself. Given the evidence in Jeremiah, it is probable that what Ezekiel reports as apostasies were going on in Jerusalem at that time.[61] Yhwh's agents of judgment will be sent through the city killing all who are guilty of such abominations. Yet even here in judgment Israel's hope is not lost. The Creator is laying the ground work for the completion of his creation: the creation of a people. A remnant is to be spared. Right relationship is to be restored between Yhwh and his people. This execution described in Ezekiel has roots in the birth process of an earlier Israelite cosmogony: the Passover tradition knew of the destroying angel who slew the first-born of the Egyptians.[62] Similar to the markings of the lamb on the doorposts of the Israelite dwellings in Egypt, so too here, Yhwh commands a man clothed in linen to mark with the letter "ת" (which in archaic cursive script had the form of an "x")[63] the foreheads of those who sigh and groan over all the abominations committed in the city. This judgment, too, will bring God's creation to fulfillment.

There are mythic elements in the apostate worship taking place within the temple as S. Ackerman and M. S. Smith well describe.[64] I

---

[60] Zimmerli, *Ezekiel* 1.123–24.

[61] Jer 7:16–8:3; 13:27; 17:1–4, 19–27; 19:1–13; 32:34–35 are all descriptions of religious apostasy in sixth century Jerusalem. Fohrer (*Die Hauptprobleme des Buches Ezechiel*, 169–70) notes that Jehoahaz, Jehoiakim, Jehoiakin, and Zedekiah are all guilty of acts of religious apostasy in 2 Kgs. 23:32, 37; 24:9, 19.

[62] Eichrodt, *Ezekiel*, 131; Greenberg, *Ezekiel 1–20*, 177; Zimmerli, *Ezekiel* 1.246.

[63] Block, *The Book of Ezekiel, Chapters 1–24*, 310–14.

[64] Susan Ackerman, *Under Every Green Tree: Popular Religion in Sixth-Century Judah* (HSM 46; Atlanta: Scholars Press, 1992) 55; Susan Ackerman, "A Marzēaḥ in Ezekiel 8:7–13?" *HTR* 82 (1989) 280; Mark S. Smith, "The Near Eastern Background of Solar Language for Yhwh," *JBL* 109 (1990) 29–39.

will not discuss these here. We are dealing with ancient parallels to Yhwh departing from his Temple. The mythic aspects of the Throne Chariot and the Cherubim mentioned in Ezekiel 10 were discussed in the preceding section, 1:4–28, and will not be developed further.

That a god would abandon his "turf," so to speak, is not a new theme in ancient Near Eastern literature[65] whose myths provide numerous examples and justifications for it. Historical records indicate that Ezekiel is not the only literary work wrestling to come to understand political outcomes in the context of this theme. In the second millennium, "The Curse of Agade"[66] struggles to understand the irreversible devastation of that city, deprived of human friendship, filled with wailing and lamentation, its holy places destroyed, fraught with rampant starvation and desolation, a place unfit for human habitation. In the recounting, all this occurs when Inanna acts in accordance with the word of Enlil and abandons her shrine. She does this when, according to the account, Naram-Sin, the king of Aggad attacks and sacks Ekur, Enlil's holy shrine in Nippur. Inanna allows the destruction of her city in retaliation for such a desecration. In the Tukulti-Ninurta I Epic, the author cites the abandonment by the gods of their native sanctuaries out of anger with the Babylonian ruler, Kashtiliash, as indication of vindication of Tukulti-Ninurta I and the Assyrian cause.[67]

Spoliation of divine images as a politico-military policy is attested in neo-Assyrian inscriptional evidence. This was meant to portray the abandonment of the conquered by their own gods in submission to the might of the conquering god. Neo-Assyrian spoliation of an enemy's gods lasted as long as it took to secure guarantees of loyalty from the defeated.[68] Such a spoiliation is even referred to in the fall of the northern kingdom of Israel to Sargon II when he says in his Nimrud prism: ". . . the gods, in which they trusted, as spoil I counted."[69]

Other accounts of divine abandonments describe them from a theo-

---

[65] Daniel I. Block, *The Gods of the Nations: Studies in Ancient Near Eastern National Theology* (Evangelical Theological Society Monograph Series 2; Jackson, MS: Evangelical Theological Society, 1988) 125–61.

[66] *ANET*, 646–51.

[67] Machinist, "Literature as Politics," 458.

[68] Morton Cogan, *Imperialism and Religion: Assyria, Judah and Israel in the Eighth and Seventh Centuries B.C.E.* (SBLMS 19; Atlanta: Society of Biblical Literature and Scholars Press, 1974) 40–41.

[69] Mettinger, *No Graven Image?*, 136.

logical perspective. In Sumerian literature, not long after the events they record, two lamentations commemorate the destruction of the capital city of Ur in ancient Sumer. These second millennium laments date from 1925 B.C.E.[70] The purpose of these laments was to soothe the heart of the city-god, Nanna, ensuring his support in the restoration of his temple and his successful efforts in the future to prevent its happening again. The first [71] of these is dedicated to Ninlil, the consort of Nanna. In the initial of eleven cantos, the author enumerates with metaphor the major cities and temples of the land which were abandoned by their respective gods and devastated. When Ningal is unable to attain the assurance of An and Enlil that they will spare her city, the enemy attacks as a merciless "storm" to destroy the city. She flees from her temple like a bird flying away from her ravaged nest, and continues to lament over the city and its people. Her temple and that of Nanna are destroyed by the axes of the enemy. In the last canto Nanna himself pleads both that he might return to his city and rebuild it, and that this destructive "storm" might never happen again.

The second lament for Ur's destruction is dedicated to Nanna himself. After pleading with Enlil to no avail, he abandons the city, allowing the enemy to take it over. This lamentation names very clearly the cities of Sumer abandoned by their gods before the onslaught of the enemy: Marda, Erech, Umma, Gaesh, Ashshu, Ennigi, Gishbanda, Eridu, Kisiga and finally Ur. It describes the destruction of the cities and houses, the drying up of rivers and canals, the sterility of fields and steppes, the disruption of family life and the removal of kingship to a foreign land.[72] In these two accounts, the gods flee in fear, not in a sovereign choice.

In two other second millennium accounts, the gods are not so impotent in their abandonment. In "Lamentation Over the Destruction of Nippur," the gods do not flee in fear. In fact, they have ceased to care for it; the lord of the city has turned away from it, allowing its temple to be despoiled and destroyed.[73] A fourth Sumerian lament for a city is

---

[70] W. C. Gawaltney Jr., "The Biblical Book of Lamentations in the Context of Near Eastern Lament Literature," in *More Essays on the Comparative Method* (ed. William W. Hallo, James C. Moyer, Leo G. Perdue; The Context of Scripture 2; Winona Lake, IN: Eisenbrauns, 1983) 196.

[71] *The Context of Scripture*, 1.535–39.

[72] *ANET*, 611–19.

[73] Samuel N. Kramer, "Lamentation Over the Destruction of Nippur," *EI* 9 (1969) 91.

"The Eridu Lament."[74] In this lament, Enki and Damgalnunna seem powerless and lament their city as a "roaring storm covered it like a cloak, spread over it like a sheet" and destroyed it.[75] The other gods, however, are portrayed as being the aggressors in demolishing and destroying their cities. Mullil destroys Kiur. Aruru, his sister, destroys her city of Urusagrig. Nanna and Ashimbabar destroy the city of Ur. Ashananna destroyed her city of Uruk as Eanna destroyed Uruzeb.[76] This divine abandonment expressed sovereignty on the part of the gods.

This theme of divine abandonment also appears in Babylonian literature of the first millennium. The background for the Marduk prophecy[77] is the reign of Nebuchadnezzar I (1125–1104 B.C.E.). Of all the events of this period, the one that had the greatest impact on the literature of the time was the victory against Elam and the recovery of the Marduk statue. The removal of the statue of Marduk by the Assyrians was a great humiliation for the people of Babylon. Their cities had been destroyed and their gods had abandoned them.[78] The text begins by proclaiming that Marduk is wont to traverse the universe. He dwelt for a while among the Hittites and then returned to Babylon. Curiously, he was brought back to Babylon by military means. It would seem that his departure was not a free and sovereign choice. Marduk then mentions a stay in Assyria which country he blessed by his presence. However such a blessing was not in store for Elam where he states that Nebuchadnezzar will smash Elam, its cities and dismantle its fortresses, even though Marduk also notes that he and all the gods went to Elam because he, Marduk, ordered it.[79] His anger rises at the Elamites for the devastation they have spread and for their carrying off

---

[74] Margaret Green, "The Eridu Lament," *JCS* 30 (1978) 137, 141.

[75] The date of the composition of the lament cannot be determined directly since the king responsible for the restoration which the lament celebrates is not named. The attacking force, unknown, is symbolized as a violent storm. Green, "The Eridu Lament," 127–28, 133.

[76] Green, "The Eridu Lament," 139.

[77] Riekele Borger, "Gott Marduk und Gott-König Šulgi als Propheten. Zwei prophetische Texte," *BO* 28 (1971) 16–17.

[78] Tremper Longman III, *Fictional Akkadian Autobiography: A Generic and Comparative Study* (Winona Lake, IN: Eisenbrauns, 1991) 138–40.

[79] Benjamin R. Foster, *Before the Muses: An Anthology of Akkadian Literature 1: Archaic, Classical, Mature* (Bethesda, MD: CDL Press, 1993) 304–7.

of the gods. The author connects Nebuchadnezzar with Enmeduranki, an antediluvian king of Sippar in order to enhance Nebuchadnezzar's prestige.[80]

There are similarities between the first millennium Mesopotamian laments and Ezekiel's account of Yhwh's departure in chapters 8–11: (1) the power and majesty of the gods; (2) the wrath of the gods; (3) the ultimate cause of the cities' fall is not the political enemy, but the gods' decision; (4) the abandonment of the cities by their gods; and (5) the gods are called upon to return to their abandoned cities.

The departures of other gods from their dwellings differ from Yhwh's departure from his abode most clearly in two ways. The mythopoeic process at work in the divine abandonment theme in Ezekiel contrasts with the same theme as it appears in other ancient Near Eastern myths. The theme of divine abandonment as it appears in Ezekiel may be, in fact, regarded as a transformation of its Mesopotamian prototypes.[81] There is firstly a difference in causality. In the Mesopotamian laments, the emphasis is on the power of the divine, not the rightness of the decision. The humans have committed no particular sin or crime which moves the gods to wreak such devastation. It is not a judgment on evil humans. In the "Eridu Lament" the storm possesses neither kindness nor malice. It does not distinguish between good and evil.[82] In chapters 8–11 Yhwh clearly judges evil behavior on the part of his people in the cultic abominations presented.

Second, in contrast to other national deities who were thought to dwell within their images, Yahwism became officially an aniconic religion: the Temple housed no image of Yhwh. It was not a graven image or a talisman that left the Temple but the כבוד יהוה.[83] Yet the power of the God of Israel withdraws from the Temple, and the final form in its vocabulary makes it clear that it is a distinct juncture in Yhwh's relationship with his people. The phrase אדמת ישראל occurs seventeen times and only in the Book of Ezekiel.[84] It is ארץ ישראל, used to desig-

---

[80] Wilfred G. Lambert, "Enmeduranki and Related Matters," *JCS* 21 (1967) 126–27.

[81] Kramer, "Lamentation Over the Destruction of Nippur," 90; Samuel N. Kramer: "Sumerian Literature and the Bible," *AnBib* 12 (1959) 201.

[82] Gawaltney, "The Biblical Book of Lamentations," 207.

[83] Podella, *Das Lichtkleid JHWH's*, 267.

[84] Ezek 7:2; 11:17; 12:19, 22; 13:9; 18:2; 20:38, 42; 21:7, 8; 25:3, 6; 33:24; 36:6; 37:12; 38:18, 19.

nate "the land deserted by the glory of Yhwh."[85] The use of אדמת ישראל begins in chapter seven and ends in chapter thirty-nine. If anything drove Yhwh from his sanctuary, it was not the approaching enemy as in the Sumerian accounts, but the infidelity of his people. The Divine Presence need not remain in its sanctuary if the sanctuary loses its sense and function, when Yhwh's people do not keep Covenant.[86] Otherwise, there would be no possibility of spoliation by the enemy. This was significant. While the gods of other nations appear to leave their dwellings freely, in fact, underlying these accounts are enemy invasions and the spoliation of the deities' image.[87] On the other hand, the Creator's sovereignty in Ezekiel is never in doubt. He departs in five stages (9:3, 10:4, 10:18, 10:19, 11:23) when and however he chooses to leave. And in exile, as 11:16 aptly puts it, Yhwh himself became their sanctuary.[88] Because the Temple is not the exclusive location of God's presence, the element of mobility allows his presence to be associated with Israel in exile.[89] The loss of the Temple was not an obstacle to Yhwh's presence to his people.

Loretz notes the emphasis in the restoration chapters on the kingship of Yhwh and asserts that the departure of Yhwh in Ezek 11:23 forms the expectation of his return as a future horizon.[90] Neither his sovereignty nor his identity as Creator are put into question here. Rather, the profanations presented in chapters 8 and 9 place the judgment squarely on Israel for Yhwh's departure in chapter 11. It lays the foundation for Israel's eventual acceptance of responsibility for the fall of Jerusalem and the exile, and it sets the stage for the Creator to undo forever the gnawing potential of chaos' resurgence, complete his act of

---

[85] B. Keller, "La terre dans le livre d'Ézéchiel," *RHPR* 55 (1975) 489.

[86] Nobile, *Introduzione all'Antico Testamento*, 104; Nobile, *Una lettura simbolico-strutturalistica di Ezechiele*, 143.

[87] Block, *The Gods of the Nations*, 154.

[88] Andreas Ruwe, "Die Veränderung tempeltheologischer Konzepte in Ezechiel 8–11," in *Gemeinde ohne Tempel, Community without Temple* (ed. Beate Ego, Armin Lange, Peter Pilhofer; WUNT 18; Tübingen: Mohr-Siebeck, 1999) 10.

[89] John F. Kutsko, *Between Heaven and Earth, Divine Presence and Absence in the Book of Ezekiel* (ed. William Henry Propp; Biblical and Judaic Studies from the University of California, San Diego 7; Winona Lake, IN: Eisenbrauns, 2000) 77, 99; Mettinger, "The Name and the Glory," 20; Nobile, *Una lettura simbolico-strutturalistica di Ezechiele*,143; Podella, *Das Lichtkeild JHWH's*, 269–70.

[90] Oswald Loretz, *Ugarit-Texte und Thronbesteigungspsalmen, Die Metamorphose des Regenspenders Baal-Jahwe* (UBL 7; Münster: Ugarit-Verlag, 1988) 448.

creation and return to his Temple "in the latter days" as described in chapter 43.

The severity of divine judgment, with its cosmogonic implications, is clear when one considers the significance of the Temple in Israelite theology. It cannot be seen in purely historical and geographical terms, instead it must be understood in the light of mystic concepts to grasp their significance for Ezekiel's final form. The Temple is a mythopoeic realization of heaven on earth, Paradise, the Garden of Eden. Here, order was established at creation and was renewed and maintained through rituals and ceremonies. It was the sacred center where Yhwh established his dwelling, where the three foundational elements of creation, kingship and Temple come together.[91] Here there is security, inviolability and a peace which no event in history can thwart. Only an understanding of the Temple's significance for creation can bring home the severity of Yhwh's judgment in abandoning his dwelling. Yhwh's departure from his Temple signalled, in this instance, Yhwh's declaration that the ritual and ceremony were no longer establishing, renewing and maintaining the order of creation. The first purpose of judgment was to re-establish right relationship between creature and Creator. This had to begin in the Temple. The Temple was a symbol of "divine promise, of assurance of things humanly impossible and yet hoped for, of a grace which works a change in the very structure of human character."[92] E. Davis reminds us[93] that judgment is a positive and passionate assertion of God's will for his creation, beginning with the foundation of his rule in the human heart. The abominations taking place in the precincts of the Temple itself make it clear that regression to chaos was complete. The judgment of Yhwh, leading to a transformed perception of the dimensions and goal of human life, must start from this very place.

Ezekiel 26:1–28:19; 29:1–32:32

Significant to Ezekiel's message and to the final form's use of myth to communicate that message are the Oracles against the Nations. They comprise chapters 25–32. While there is broad agreement that a

---

[91] Levenson, *The Theology of the Program of Restoration*, 8; Lawrence Stager, "Jerusalem as Eden," *BAR* 26.3 (2000) 37, 39.

[92] Levenson, *Theology of the Program of Restoration*, 161.

[93] Davis, "Psalm 98: Rejoicing in Judgment," 173.

threefold division governs the material of the book as a whole (1–24, 25–32, 33–48), this division alone does not explain the prophetic purpose. The Oracles against the Nations are criticized by significant Ezekiel scholars[94] for interrupting what would seem to be an organized unfolding of the book, in that the foreign oracles separate the warning of Jerusalem's immanent collapse (24:15–27) from the notice that it has occurred (33:21–22). The Book of Ezekiel is not alone in such an ordering. The same pattern appears in Zephaniah and the LXX version of Jeremiah. Yet Eichrodt refers to the placement of the oracles in Ezekiel as a "ruthless disturbance of the organic arrangement."[95] We will see in fact that the Oracles against the Nations do not interrupt anything, but rather substantiate and give force to the judgment of the Creator on Israel: the immanent fall of Jerusalem is the natural consequence of violating the right order of creation, as these nations have done.

The absence of Babylon from among the seven nations mentioned suggests that the list serves a different function than that which some scholars propose:[96] as a roll of Israel's enemies. In fact, Tyre and Egypt were Israel's fellow rebels against Babylon prior to the fall of Jerusalem. They were Babylon's political opponents, not Judah's. With her, they were the only other nations holding out against Nebuchadnezzar. This is not a list of enemies as is the case in the other prophetic books. The final form is using the particularities of one historical period to communicate a message translatable to other historical periods: Ezekiel sees Nebuchadnezzar and Babylon as Yhwh's instruments. Opposition to their advance was implicit rejection of Yhwh and a refusal to acknowledge the designs of the Creator. Davis concludes from this insightful analysis[97] that these foreign nations are presented

---

[94] Zimmerli, *Ezekiel* 2.3; Eichrodt, *Ezekiel*, 352.

[95] Eichrodt, *Ezekiel*, 352.

[96] Batto *(Slaying the Dragon*, 158) as one example, parallels the Oracles Against the Nations with the Oracle against Gog of Magog, the former as a destruction of earthly powers opposing the establishment of the people of God, the latter as a destruction of the meta-historical power of evil; Bernard Gosse ("Le recueil d'oracles contre les nations d'Ezéchiel XXV-XXXII dans la rédaction du livre d'Ezechiel," *RB* 93 [1986] 535–62) suggests a personal vendetta of Yhwh against these nations for their treatment of Israel. His conclusions miss the primary focus of the Oracles here: the nations violate their creaturely status and sin against Yhwh.

[97] Newsom, "A Maker of Metaphors," 154; Davis, "And Pharaoh Will Change His Mind," 226–28.

as an object lesson to Israel: when Ezekiel confronts the nationalistic absolutism of the foreign nations, the book is implicitly challenging Israelite absolutism as well, to show her the consequences that will be meted out for violating the primacy of right relationship with the Creator. The twenty occurrences[98] of the Recognition Formula throughout the Oracles of the Foreign Nations ground the purpose of the oracles in the acknowledgment on the part of Israel and all the nations of Yhwh as Creator of world history.[99] This is not a message with temporal or spatial limits.

The function of these Oracles in the final form of the book is distinct from the function served by chapters 38–39. Nobile includes chapters 38–39 as an integral part of these Oracles against the Foreign Nations. In his own assessment, given the thematic unity of these ten chapters, Nobile attributes the insertion of chapters 38–39 after the first Oracles of Salvation to the time elapsed between the proposed enacting of Yhwh's vengeance on the nations in chapters 25–32 and the predicted defeat of chapters 38–39 which takes place ביום ההוא, "in that day" (38:10, 14, 18, 19; 39:21).[100] I propose that, while this line of reasoning is understandable and indicative of a fundamental difference between chapters 38–39 and chapters 25–32, a more solid basis for the final form of the text can be found in the religious mythic elements in the work and the reasons for their mythopoetic (25–32) or mythopoeic (38–39) use. Chapters 38–39 serve a different function in the final form of the book. They are truly mythopoeic,[101] describing new divine activity in categories with which primordial divine activity has been described. The Oracles against the Nations, on the other hand, are mythopoetic, used as an object lesson for Israel whose fall will be announced in chapter 33. The nations, each in their own turn, are a metaphor for Israel, and the use of myth in these chapters is metaphoric. As we unpack the mythic references, we do so to understand the impact of their metaphoric use on those who receive the message of the book. As

---

[98] 25: 5, 7, 9, 11, 14, 17; 26:6; 28:22, 23, 24, 26; 29: 6, 9, 16, 21; 30: 8, 19, 25, 26; 32: 15.
[99] Davis, "And Pharaoh Will Change His Mind," 229.
[100] Nobile, "Ez 38-39 ed Ez 40-48: i due aspetti complementari," 149.
[101] On this conclusion I would disagree with Lawrence Boadt ("Mythological Themes," 223; "The Function of the Salvation Oracles," 17) who sees chapters 38–39 as mythopoetic. As chapters 38–39 describe Yhwh's act of creation brought to conclusion even in light of the devastating events of the exile, I see them as divine activity, mythopoeic activity.

Boadt reminds us, the Book of Ezekiel is rooted in a prophetic tradition which hurled threats at his own nation and not only at the enemy. Ezekiel's formulation of the Oracles against the Nations involved a combination of the standard curses which included re-application of judgment motifs already applied to Israel herself. [102] And this with a purpose! As Davis puts it so well,[103] Ezekiel counters the mythic religious beliefs of the other ancient Near Eastern faiths, judging their false perception of reality implanted in foreign mythologies, so that it can establish a renewed myth for the religious faith of Israel. The comparison with Israel is implicit, fitting to the nature of a metaphor, but is demonstrable from the text as we will show, specifically in relation to the Oracles against Tyre and Egypt.

Ezekiel 25, Oracles against Ammon, Moab, Edom, Philistia, and Sidon

The Oracles against the Foreign Nations with mythic elements are those directed against Tyre and Egypt, but I will begin with the nations mentioned in Chapter 25 and Chapter 28:20–24 because the indictments against Ammon, Moab, Edom, Philistia, and Sidon corroborate Ezekiel's message in the Oracles against Tyre and Egypt and are connected thematically with them. While each of the oracles against the five nations focuses on that nation's enmity to Israel, it is an enmity based in its political arrogance considered an offense to the God of Israel. Edom and Philistia both acted with revenge toward the house of Judah and offended Yhwh by taking vengeance on his people. From the perspective of the Book of Ezekiel, to pit one's nation against Yhwh is to be delusionally impressed with one's importance. Moab's offense is that they accused the house of Judah of being "like all the other nations" (Ezek 25:8). This phrase in the two other OT verses (Ezek 20:32 and 1 Sam 8:5) suggests a claim to autonomy apart from the covenant relationship with the Lord. To suggest that Judah is "like all the other nations" is to suggest that Judah worships gods of wood and stone, which is a contemptuous and short-sighted estimation of the God of Israel. Ironically, as the oracles will show, Judah was "like all

---

[102] Boadt, *Ezekiel's Oracles against Egypt*, 176.
[103] Davis, "And Pharaoh Will Change His Mind," 228.

the other nations," but the sin of Moab was not an inaccurate "sizing up" of Judah, but rather an offense against the majesty and power of their Creator God. Sidon treated Israel with contempt as did Ammon who is prophesied against because it said: "Aha," over the Lord's sanctuary when it was profaned, over the land of Israel when it was made desolate, and over the house of Judah when it went into exile (Ezek 25:3). Such derision can only be based in hubris. Such hubris is disruptive to the harmony of creation and a denial of the proper relationship between the Creator and his creation.

Ezekiel 26–28, The Oracles against Tyre

As Carol Newsom notes,[104] the Oracles against Tyre comprise four separate oracles grouped by the use of a concluding refrain into three units, 26:1–21; 27:1–36; and 28:1–19, which pairs to two different oracles, 1–10 and 11–19. The use of myth in these oracles focuses principally on three elements: its locus in the midst of the sea in chapter 26, the metaphor of Tyre as ship in chapter 27 and the arrogance of the king in chapter 28.

The action prophesied in chapter 26 is primarily the attack of the nations against Tyre. Yet choice of vocabulary cues the reader to best view this attack as object lesson for Israel. Davis notes incisively that the phrase צחיח סלע "bare rock" is used twice to describe Jerusalem in the chapter preceding the Oracles against the Nations (24:7, 8) where God brings down vengeance upon her, exposing her shed blood on bare rock. The Oracle in chapter 24 is dated on the very day when Nebuchednezzar laid siege to Jerusalem. Tyre, exposed to the ravages of the nations is twice described in her devastated state as צחיח סלע "bare rock" (26:4, 14).[105] Though the metaphor is implicit, the vocabulary is telling. Let Israel be forewarned!

Verse 16 describes the mourning of the princes of the sea at Tyre's fall: "Then all the princes of the sea shall step down from their thrones; they shall remove their robes and strip off their embroidered

---

[104] Newsom, "A Maker of Metaphors," 154.
[105] Davis, "And Pharaoh Will Change His Mind," 227; Newsom ("A Maker of Metaphors,"154–56) also discusses Ezekiel's use of this metaphor.

garments. They shall clothe themselves with trembling and they shall sit on the ground." It parallels the mourning of El when Baal died at the hands of Mot: "We arrived at where Baʻlu had fallen to the earth: Dead was Mighty Baʻlu, perished the prince, master of the earth. Thereupon the Gracious One, the kindly god, descends from the throne, sits on the footstool, (descends) from the footstool, sits on the earth."[106] Boadt notes[107] the influence of Tyre in the introduction of Baal's cult (1 Kings 17–21) into Israelite devotional practices. The parallelism between the mourning over Tyre's fall and the mourning over the death of Baal, cleverly recalls and subverts the impotence of Baal to save even as it attacks the arrogance and pretension of Tyre.

In 26:19 the text speaks of Yhwh bringing the deep over Tyre and the great waters covering her. The parallelism in the verse between great waters and the deep suggest that it is not just a simple image of the waters of the Mediterranean swallowing the island of Tyre. These verses present the deep as an instrument of Yhwh's vengeance. תהום refers to the great primeval sea. In ancient Near Eastern cosmology, the earth was considered to be afloat in the midst of terrifying cosmic waters.[108] The many waters, the deep, become Yhwh's agent of destruction.[109] This "stirring up of the sea" is part of the standard vocabulary of the Combat Myth, occurring in the same connection in Jer 31:35, Isa 51:15 and Job 26:12.[110] In ancient Near Eastern literature, the cosmic waters were also an instrument of judgment. The alternative epithet at Ugarit for "Prince Sea" was "Judge River."[111] Such judgment by water is spoken of commonly in the Psalms. "Let not the Flood Waters sweep over me. Let not the deep swallow me" (Ps 69:15). "He reached from on high and took me. He delivered me out of the many waters" (Ps 18:16). Such cries have their roots in the water judg-

---

[106] *The Context of Scripture*, 1.267.

[107] Boadt, "Mythological Themes," 226.

[108] Bernard Batto, "The Reed Sea: *Requiescat in Pace*," *JBL* 102 (1983) 31; Choon L. Seow, "The Deep" *ABD* 2 (New York: Doubleday, 1992) 125.

[109] Block, *The Book of Ezekiel, Chapters 25–48*, 47; May, "Many Waters," 18; H. J. van Dijk, *Ezekiel's Prophecy on Tyre (Ez. 26:1–28:19), A New Approach*, BibOr 20 (Rome: Pontifical Biblical Institute, 1968) 11; Wakeman, *God's Battle with the Monster*, 128; Zimmerli, *Ezekiel*, 2.39.

[110] Sarna, "The Psalm for the Sabbath Day (Ps 92)," 162.

[111] P. Kyle McCarter, "The River Ordeal in Israelite Literature," *HTR* 66 (1973) 404–6, 412.

ment of ancient Near Eastern myth. The myth of the cosmic flood has been used to give expression to Yhwh's total judgment over a city.[112] In Israel it is Yhwh who stirs up the waters and delivers the suppliant from them.

Efforts in chapter 27 to suggest that the significance of the metaphor of Tyre as ship is similar to the cosmic ship[113] of Egyptian mythology seem at first glance to limp. The metaphor of Tyre as ship in chapter 27 is an image of only one nation. Despite its extensive and impressive record of world trade listed in the chapter, to suggest that the text is comparing the significance of that trade to the significance of the nightly journey of the Bark of Re in Egyptian mythology is to credit the final form with either trivializing the cosmic Bark of Re or mocking the pretensions of Tyre and her king. Yet placing the chapter in context, mockery, in fact, is the point. As Newsom notes "Ezekiel was not a public relations agent hired by the Tyre Chamber of Commerce."[114] The very vacuousness of the image of Tyre as cosmic ship in comparison to the cosmic Bark of Re makes Tyre's pretensions all the more ludicrous.

The final form develops the image of Tyre as ship at great length, describing its construction, its staffing and the extensive trade. The list of trade cities itself is not entirely germane to Ezekiel. In the Sumerian myth of Enki and Ninhursaga there is a list describing the trade of the port city of Dilmun and the list of countries, T. Jacobsen notes,[115] covers similar extremes, but of the world as known by the average Sumerian. The list is strikingly comparable to Ezekiel's list in chapter 27, and the extremes of east and west express in a very vivid way Tyre's worldwide connections.[116] This is a list of the outermost zone of the inhabited world that would have been known to ancient Israel. After twenty-five verses developing Tyre's expansive world relations, listing its many partners and patrons, Ezekiel sinks the "great ship of state"

---

[112] Zimmerli, *Ezekiel* 1.39.

[113] John B. Geyer, "Ezekiel 27 and the Cosmic Ship," in *Among the Prophets, Language, Image and Structure in the Prophetic Writings* (ed. Philip R. Davies and David J. A. Clines; JSOTSup 144; Sheffield: JSOT, 1993).

[114] Newsom, "A Maker of Metaphors," 157.

[115] Thorkild Jacobsen, *The Harps That Once . . . Sumerian Poetry in Translation* (New Haven: Yale University Press, 1987) 188–89.

[116] Moshe Greenberg, *Ezekiel 21–37* (AB 22A; New York: Doubleday, 1997) 566–67.

in one verse[117] and plunges it into the "heart of the seas," an image we will explore in the discussion of chapter 28. Verse 27 continues to describe the debacle: ". . . your mariners, your pilots, your caulkers, . . . all your warriors within you, with all the company with you, sink into the heart of the seas. . . ." The forces of nature obedient to the Creator's command speak his judgment.

Another element which recalls the *Chaoskampf* myth for the reader appears in 27:26, the reference to the east wind wreaking havoc on Tyre in the heart of the seas, this, again, in parallel construction with the great waters mentioned above in chapter 26. It is the east wind which Yhwh employed to drive back the waters (Exod 14:21), turning the sea into dry land for the Israelites to cross dry-shod in their exodus from Egypt.[118] In the same way that the great waters of the Red Sea and the east wind became the instruments of Yhwh to destroy Pharaoh and his army, and lead Israel to safety, so too here, the great waters destroy Tyre, propelled by the east wind, both images recalling the Exodus event so familiar to the book's audience, with the variation that here, Yhwh is not pitted against the sea, but rather enlists this element of his creation in his judgment of Tyre whose arrogance set the order of creation askew.

The oracles against Tyre conclude in chapter 28 with two oracles, vv. 1–10 and 11–19: the first focuses on the hubris of the king of Tyre that leads to the fall of his city, the second is a subsequent lament. The chapter itself is one of the most difficult texts in the book[119] and a lack of scholarly consensus to support arguments oftentimes cautions against dogmatism in interpreting the details. That being said, there are mythic elements which can be established with significant support.

Two recent works[120] posit the existence of a myth which is indirectly reflected in the literature of the ancient Near East including the OT,

---

[117] Newsom, "Maker of Metaphors," 157.

[118] Aloysius Fitzgerald (*The Lord of the East Wind* [CBQMS 34; Washington, DC: The Catholic Biblical Association of America, 2002]) devotes an entire chapter to the east wind in the account of the crossing of the Red Sea.

[119] Bertholet, *Hesekiel*, 100; Block, *The Book of Ezekiel, Chapters 25–48*, 88; van Dijk, *Ezekiel's Prophecy on Tyre*, 113.

[120] Hugh R. Page, *The Myth of Cosmic Rebellion: A Study of its Reflexes in Ugaritic and Biblical Literature* (VTSup 65; New York: Brill, 1996); Nick Wyatt, "The Hollow Crown: Ambivalent Elements in West Semitic Royal Ideology," *UF* 18 (1986) 421–36.

influential in the formation of royal ideology. Each work outlines a similar five fundamental elements of the myth and both see various parts of this myth played out in the two oracles in Ezekiel 28, and in other passages of the OT.[121] Reviewing these five elements is a good introduction to the key issues of the two oracles.

First, in the original myth the protagonist against the high god of the pantheon was himself a god in the divine council.[122] The title of king, Wyatt posits, at least in the minds of the people of the ancient Near East, is as much a divine title as a designation of royal office.[123] Mettinger regards the king of Tyre as having a mythical identity. He is the visible, earthly manifestation of the god Melqart and the spouse of Melqart's Astarte.[124] The research of Widengren,[125] at least, would suggest otherwise. Engnell suggests a modified stance: "That the king is god, implies, in my opinion, above all two things: the king is the human maintainer of the divine ideology — the king as law-king-sky-god in Hocart's terminology — and the king has — as executive king — to represent, especially in the cult, one or several divine characters."[126] Whether the king is divine or isn't is the pivotal issue in the two oracles.

Second, this mythical figure would ascend to heaven: "With the Cherub I set you, on the holy mountain of god you were, in the midst of 'firestones' you walked," Ezek 28:14. The assembly of the gods was where El and his council would gather to deliberate the affairs of men and the king was understood to be present at, if not actively participating in, their deliberations. This participation was a common motif of ancient Near Eastern myth. The ruler is endowed by the gods with surpassing knowledge and heavenly wisdom. In Assyrian mythology, for example, Sennacherib was supposed to have possessed the wisdom of the primordial king, Adapa, which was divine knowledge, and he

---

[121] Gen 2:4b–3:24; 6:1–4, Isa 14, Ps 82, Job 38, Dan 11–12 (Page, *The Myth of Cosmic Rebellion*, 204); Wyatt, "The Hollow Crown," 424.

[122] Page, *The Myth of Cosmic Rebellion*, 203.

[123] Wyatt, "The Hollow Crown," 425.

[124] Mettinger, *No Graven Image?*, 98–99.

[125] Geo Widengren, *The Ascension of the Apostle and the Heavenly Book* (UUÅ 1950:7; Uppsala: A. B Lundequistska, 1950).

[126] Ivan Engnell, *Studies in Divine Kingship in the Ancient Near East* (Uppsala: Almqvist & Wiksells, 1943) 31.

was carefully guided along the paths of righteousness by the gods themselves. [127]

Third, the king would live at the center of Paradise.[128] His dwelling would be at the center of the world, the point of intersection of heaven and earth and the nether world. It is not by accident that Solomon built his palace beside the Temple. In building the Temple and his palace there, he believed he was fulfilling a divine order to create a cosmic center where he would rule according to God's command. This configuration of contiguous Temple and Palace was common to the region of northern Syria and Canaan and based in the theological underpinnings of royal ideology.[129] It is from a frame of reference of this contiguous configuration out of which the two oracles in chapter 28 come: Ezek 28:2, "I am sitting on the throne of God in the heart of the seas," and Ezek 28:13, "You were in Eden, the garden of God."

Fourth, a verbal or physical attack would be made against the chief-god.[130] The danger of hubris was always present for a king. He possessed legitimate grandeur, wisdom, skill and wealth. All this was coupled with physical perfection. "You are indeed wiser than Daniel; no secret is hidden from you; by your wisdom and understanding you have amassed wealth for yourself, and have gathered gold and silver into your treasuries," Ezek 28:3–4. But in the myth this led to overweening arrogance. The king considered himself a god which is an overturning of the ordering of creation and, thus, a reduction of the cosmos to chaos. This point of hubris is the point of connection with the rhetorical question asked of Keret: "What ails Keret, that he weeps, the gracious one, heir of El, that he groans? Does he desire the kingship of the Bull, his father, or dominion like the Father of Man?"[131] Ezek 28:6 is an indictment against such royal pretensions: "You compare your mind with the mind of a god."

Fifth and finally, royalty is punished with expulsion, leading to his descent from heaven.[132] Here, the king is cast down from the height to which he aspires: "They will throw you into the Pit, and you will die a

---

[127] Widengren, *The Ascension of the Apostle*, 12–16.
[128] Wyatt, "The Hollow Crown," 426.
[129] John Monson, "The New 'Ain Dara Temple, Closest Solomonic Parallel," *BAR* 26.2 (2000) 35; Stager, "Jerusalem as Eden," 47.
[130] Page, *The Myth of Cosmic Rebellion*, 203
[131] Wyatt, "The Hollow Crown," 421, 428.
[132] Wyatt, "The Hollow Crown," 428–29.

shameful death," Ezek 28:8 and "I have thrown you down from the mountain of god," Ezek 28:16. This descent can either occur through the instrumentality of foreign enemies, as in the first case, or through the intervention of God himself, as in the second instance. The point of the descent is the king's removal from the center to the periphery.

This is the schematic pattern of both oracles and it suggests the possibility that one myth has assumed varied forms. Various agenda helped to shape the mythopoetic course it took in its development. Ezek 28:1–10 deals with the abuses of wisdom and the excesses of princely ambition. Ezek 28:11–19 treats offenses of authority stemming from wealth and pride.[133] We will now consider each oracle in turn.

Though he does not support the arguments put forward in the main by Wyatt, Loretz,[134] among others, acknowledges the presence of a prior mythic tradition in the first oracle. One need not look far for contested mythic reference in the oracle. It appears in 28:2 where, through prophetic divine speech, the author has Yhwh indict the king: "Your heart has grown proud and you have said 'אל אני.'" How is "אל אני" to be understood? Is it "I am a god," or "I am El"? The word is ambiguous in Hebrew. It is possible that the text is using the ambiguity to imply both meanings in the oracle.[135] Scholars opposed to the interpretation of אל as El cite two reasons.[136] First, they see it as a doublet of v. 9 where the author uses אלהים. Yet is it a doublet? Verse 2 is an accusation through declarative statement of fact. Verse 9, however, a question, begins with the infinitive absolute, האמר, which is used to strengthen an impassioned or indignant question.[137] They are not doublets. Verse 9 is effectively translated: "Will you then even say: 'I am a god'?" The tone is that of sarcastic mockery, asking what the king would say before his executioners.[138] Second, they see אל in the phrase

---

[133] Page, *The Myth of Cosmic Rebellion*, 203.

[134] Oswald Loretz, "Der Wohnort Els nach ugaritischen Texten und Ez 28, 1–2.6–10," *UF* 21 (1989) 266.

[135] *CMHE*, 44; Marvin H. Pope, *El in the Ugaritic Texts* (VTSup 2; Leiden: Brill, 1955) 98–99.

[136] Dijk, *Ezekiel's Prophecies on Tyre*, 95; Oswald Loretz, "Der Sturz des Fürsten von Tyrus (Ez 28,1–19)," *UF* 8 (1976) 456–57; Zimmerli, *Ezekiel* 2.77–78.

[137] Wilhelm Gesenius, *Gesenius' Hebrew Grammar* (ed. E. Kautzsch; 2d English ed.; trans. A. E. Cowley; Oxford: Clarendon, 1910) 343.

[138] Fechter (*Bewältigung der Katastrophe*, 161) describes the response as almost cynical.

וּלֹא־אֵל as being parallel usage with אָדָם immediately preceding it. Yet it could still be parallel usage if it were interpreted as El. We would interpret it as El for two reasons. First, those who argue against this interpretation mention but don't deal with a significant fact: the only two places where אֵל is used in the entire final form of Ezekiel is in this verse. This fact would weigh in favor of the translation El as opposed to "a god." Certainly אֵל in this context can be taken two ways. If these are the only two places in the book where the final form uses אֵל in place of אֱלֹהִים which it also uses twice in this verse, with Cross and Pope, we see intentional ambiguity as the reason. Where the king "stacks up" in relation to the high god of the pantheon, how divine he actually sees himself to be, is precisely the question being pursued in the two oracles. Suggesting that he sees himself as אֵל, El, rather than אָדָם illustrates his hubris all too well. Second, the final form is written from a monotheistic stance. As Fechter rightly points out the purpose of the oracle is really a confrontation between the unique sovereign claims of the Creator and the claims of the self-deified king of Tyre.[139] The issue at stake for the king of Tyre is one of usurping, but for the readers of the final form there was no council of the gods of which the king could become a member. He could only usurp the position of the high god of Israel: Yhwh. The final form wanted the "audience to draw connections with their own life situation and its unique Yahwistic theological underpinnings."[140] The issue for Israelite faith would be the political arrogance and pretensions of their own king. For them the issue would be supplanting the high god because there was only Yhwh.

Those who argue [141] that it should be understood as El of Canaanite and Phoenician myth argue correctly in their interpretation for other reasons, as well. The fact that reference is made to the dwelling of the god as being in the heart of the seas is a strong indicator that it refers to El. The gods do not dwell in the heart of the seas but only on the mount of assembly. The allusion can only be to a specific god who

---

[139] Fechter, *Bewältigung der Katastrophe*, 161.

[140] Page, *The Myth of Cosmic Rebellion*, 15, 141–42.

[141] Cassuto, *The Goddess Anath*, 57, 142, 145; Clifford, *The Cosmic Mountain*, 168–70; Otto Eissfeldt, "El and Yahweh," *JSS* 1 (1956) 28; Wolfgang Hermann, "El," in *Dictionary of Deities and Demons in the Bible* (ed. Karel van der Toorn, Bob Becking and Pieter W. van der Horst; 2d ed.; Leiden: Brill, 1999) 278; Newsom, "A Maker of Metaphors," 158; Pope, *El in the Ugaritic Texts*, 98; Wyatt, "The Hollow Crown," 428.

dwells in watery environs. And who could this be but El whose dwelling is at the springs of the two rivers, midst the channels of the deeps.[142] Clifford and Page both note that the reference to El's abode has here the double meaning of Tyre geographically in the midst of the seas and El's abode.[143] The quote is put on the lips of the king of Tyre for whom El is the high god in their pantheon.[144] While others have discounted this conclusion, the arguments that the king is not employing a common appellative: "a god," but rather saying that he is a particular god, "El," have greater force. This a mythic reference to El.

Whether Ezekiel has the king appropriate to himself the status of high god of the pantheon or not, it is clear that the king is claiming to be divine. He asserts himself to be one with divine authority and divine intelligence, seated on the throne of the gods, he regards his heart/mind as the heart/mind of a god (v. 2). These claims alone are the product of the ancient Near Eastern myths concerning the source of the king's authority: the assembly of the gods. It is a distinctive trait of the royal ideology of the region that the ruler is endowed by the gods at his enthronement with surpassing knowledge and heavenly wisdom. One Mesopotamian royal hymn describes the king as "the holy one, knowing everything."[145] The ruler receives the Tablets of Destinies which decide the destiny of the Universe, express the law of the whole world, and contain the mystery of heaven and earth. To the king is revealed the hidden knowledge possessed by the gods. He receives his commission from the high god.[146] In an early second millennium palace of the Old Babylonian kingdom centered in Mari, a wall painting at the entrance to the throne room depicts the goddess Ishtar, a warrior with weapons strapped to her shoulders, scimitar in one hand and the ring and rod in the other, presenting the emblems of authority to the king.[147] The ruler who believes these myths thinks himself endowed with authority by god and credits himself as something of a god by enthronement (cf. Ps 45:7). He runs the risk of over-identifying with the gods from whom he received his power. The prophecy does

---

[142] *The Context of Scripture*, 1.254.
[143] Clifford, *The Cosmic Mountain*, 170; Page, *The Myth of Cosmic Rebellion*, 142.
[144] Dijk, *Ezekiel's Prophecies on Tyre*, 95; Newsom, "A Maker of Metaphors," 158.
[145] Widengren, *The Ascension of the Apostle*, 12.
[146] Widengren, *The Ascension of the Apostle*, 11, 17.
[147] Stager, "Jerusalem as Eden," 39.

not castigate the king for his shrewdness or for his amassed wealth. Neither of the two is reprehensible. The problem with the king of Tyre arises with his response which is one of hubris, of over-identifying himself with El. The king's interpretation of the mythic beliefs needed a corrective. The frame of reference from which the king's faulty conception came was the religious myth of his region. This will play into the religious myth the final form is constructing. The religious myths of divine kingship and the purpose of creation in Tyre are directly opposed to what the final form presents as the proper myth for Israel: that Yhwh alone creates and rules all things.[148] Israel should learn from Tyre.

Often the subject of scholarly debate in the second oracle is the relationship of Ezek 28:11–19 to Genesis 2–3. Some would see the author representing the king of Tyre as an "Adamic" figure.[149] The explicit reference to "Eden, the garden of God" in v. 13, the reference to "the day you were created" in the same verse, the appearance of the guardian cherub in v. 14, the motif of sin and expulsion in vv. 15–17, all make one think of this. Is the final form presenting here an alternative version of the narrative of Genesis 2–3? Gunkel, in *Schöpfung und Chaos in Urzeit und Endzeit,* discusses mythic elements in Ezekiel 28.[150] In his commentary on Genesis in 1901 he suggests that Ezekiel is adapting the myth to his own purposes,[151] an example of the process of the mythopoetic, in this case, at work.

Many authors after Gunkel have concurred with him that both the oracle and the Genesis account are related to an earlier mythological tradition.[152] What that myth is, is not clear. There is, as yet, no basis for reconstructing a primitive myth about a Primal Man who is the origin and patriarch of both humankind in general and the king in particular. There is no indication in Ezek 28:11–19 that the oracle is about the first man. In its present context, the oracle is about a primal royal

---

[148] Boadt, "Rhetorical Strategies," 192–93.

[149] Newsom, "A Maker of Metaphors," 160–61.

[150] Gunkel, *Schöpfung und Chaos,* 148–49.

[151] Hermann Gunkel, *Genesis übersetzt und erklärt* (HAT 1; Göttingen: Vandenhoeck & Ruprecht, 1901) 34–35.

[152] Cooke, *A Critical and Exegetical Commentary,* 315; Eichrodt, *Ezekiel,* 392; Newsom, "A Maker of Metaphors," 160; Page, *The Myth of Cosmic Rebellion,* 157; Pope, *El in the Ugaritic Texts,* 102–3; John van Seters, "The Creation of Man and The Creation of the King," ZAW 101 (1989) 333–41; Anthony J. Williams, "The Mythological Background of Ezekiel 28:12–19," *BTB* 6 (1976) 50; Zimmerli, *Ezekiel* 2.95.

figure and speaks of the origins of royalty but not of humanity in general. The similarities lie in two motifs: the figure is placed in Eden, the garden of God, and he is expelled from the divine garden, after his sin is discovered. However, in Genesis the royal figure is no longer royalty. They were naked and their sin was depicted as the curiosity of the young.

Verses 13–14 introduce mythological elements: "You were in Eden, the garden of God; every precious stone was your covering, carnelian, chrysolite, and moonstone, beryl, onyx, and jasper, sapphire, turquoise and emerald; and worked in gold were your settings and your engravings. On the day that you were created they were prepared. *You were a wing-spread guardian cherub;*[153] you were on the holy mountain of God; you walked among the stones of fire." This oracle reflects a typical lament structure, with its first part describing past glory, and its second part narrating subsequent disaster. The verses portray an expansive picture of the king of Tyre as the glorious protector in the dwelling of God. The use of the word ברא in v. 13 poignantly draws in themes of the primal creation,[154] only to reinforce the undoing of creation in the verses that follow. Deftly there is mention made of the mountain of God. This is the only instance in the Hebrew Bible where the garden of God and the holy mountain of God have been unmistakably associated, obliquely joining primal creation themes with the creation of Yhwh's covenanted people. Accordingly, they may learn from Tyre's downfall, the object lesson which will come in the following verses. Yhwh's judgment is a judgment of cosmogony undone.

Eden, the garden of God, has its origin in the Semitic word עדן, meaning "abundant, lush."[155] The king is identified with the cherub. This is a reference to the figure of the king and not to a specific king. It

---

[153] The words in italics are my emendation of the NRSV translation of v. 14a, translating את as a second person masculine singular pronoun as supported both by Gesenius (*Gesenius' Hebrew Grammar*, 106) and Paul Joüon (*A Grammar of Biblical Hebrew* [Trans. and rev. Takamitsu Muraoka; 2 vols.; Subsidia Biblica 14/1; Rome: Pontifical Biblical Institute, 1991] 121). The translation of ממשח is supported by Ugaritic and Akkadian etymology as noted by Mitchell J. Dahood ("Ugaritic Lexicography," *Mélanges Eugène Tisserant* 1: *Écriture sainte - Ancien Orient* [Studi e testi 231; Vatican City: Biblioteca apostolica vaticana, 1964] 95). I also chose not to give a function to the cherub based on הסוכך, but rather to use it as a descriptor of the cherub.

[154] Fechter, *Bewältigung der Katastrophe*, 207.

[155] Alan R. Millard, "The Etymology of Eden," *VT* 34 (1984) 103–6.

comes out of the Tyrian royal myth.[156] Müller and Block see the verses as having analogues in the Gilgamesh Epic.[157] There is a passage in the Gilgamesh Epic which describes the arrival of the hero in the garden of the gods. Its parallels are striking.

> He went directly to the [ ] of the garden of the gods in order to admire (it), as its fruit it carries carnelians, vines are climbing (there) — beautiful to look at — (with a) foliage (made) of lapis lazuli. The(ir) grapes — a pleasure beyond — [are made of . . . -stones].
>
> [Break of about 23 lines]
>
> [ ] cedar [ ] its [. . . are made of] white ston[es] . . . The sea-laruš [its . . . are made of] sâsu-stones. Instead of thistles (?) and thorny shrubs [their . . . are made of] (red) AN.GUG-stones, (and) the harubu-thorns [their . . . are made of] abarummu-stones. Sabû-stones are haematite [are], [ ] -ri-e and pearls (?) [are]. Instead of [are made of] agate (?), of the [ ]sea [ ] While/when Gilgamesh was walking [through the . . . of] this [garden?] he looked up [and] this [ ].[158]

No mention of kingship is made in Genesis however except in a veiled way in the giving of dominion over the whole of creation. Furthermore, v. 14b, "You were on the holy mountain of God," clearly infers more than the Genesis account and implies the ascension spoken of above where the king enters the assembly of the gods to be invested with the divine wisdom which comes from receiving the Tablets of the Destinies. In Ezek 28:11–19, the primal man addressed is more than the "Adamic" figure of the Genesis account.

Another ancient Near Eastern myth contains a description of human origins with even more remarkable similarities to Ezek 28:11–19. This account of the creation of humanity (for the purpose of doing the labor of the gods) is unique among texts in that the divine pair of the mother goddess and Ea are to make a king quite distinct from the rest of humanity:

---

[156] David N. Freedman and Michael Patrick O'Connor, "כבוד," *TWAT 4* (Stuttgart: Kohlhammer, 1984) 327.

[157] Block, *The Book of Ezekiel, Chapters 25–48*, 115; Hans-Peter Müller, "Parallelen zu Gen 2f. und Ez 28 aus dem Gilgamesch-Epos," *ZAH* 3 (1990) 178.

[158] A. Leo. Oppenheim, "Mesopotamian Mythology II," *Or* 17 (1948) 47–48.

Ea began to speak, he directed his word to Belet-ili, "Belet-ili, Mistress of the great gods, are you. You have created the common people, now construct the king, distinctively superior person. With goodness envelop his entire being. Form his features harmoniously; make his body beautiful!" Thus did Belet-ili construct the king, a distinctively superior person. The great gods gave the king the task of warfare. Anu gave him the crown; Enlil gave him the throne. Nergal gave him weapons; Ninurta gave him glistening splendor. Belet-ili gave him a beautiful appearance. Nusku gave instruction and counsel and stands at his service.[159]

In this account the bestowal of physical beauty at birth and the vestiture of the king are combined and placed mythologically back at the time of creation, to legitimize kingship. The myth of creation in this account includes the creation of kingship. This myth speaks specifically of the creation of a king. What is distinctive about Ezekiel is the introduction of the prophetic judgment that the hubris of kings and nations leads to their downfall. Such hubris is antinomian to the kingship which will be presented in chapter 34 where the model of human leadership is set forth for a viable life-sustaining community created by Yhwh.

Similar to Loretz above, Pope, and Wilson[160] suggest that the myth in Ezek 28:11–19 is based in theomachy in which El and his champion (Prince Sea) and his cohorts were defeated and banished to the netherworld. With the influx of new cultural and ethnic groups, the inhabitants of a region could displace one god by another and reconstruct a myth accordingly. The struggle between El and Baal for dominance in Ugarit took place over several centuries, but eventually Baal was victorious. One thing that weakens the suasive strength of this argument as the basis for the myth of the fall of the king is the fact that the struggle between El and Baal was in fact a struggle between two gods, not a god and a mortal. If both the Gilgamesh Epic and the royal ideology where the king ascends to the dwelling place of the gods to receive divine wisdom could be created, a myth for the fall of a king could be

---

[159] Seters, "The Creation of Man," 337.

[160] Pope, *El in the Ugaritic Texts*, 103; Robert R. Wilson, "The Death of the King of Tyre: The Editorial History of Ezekiel 28," in *Love and Death in the Ancient Near East* (eds. John H. Marks and Robert M. Good; Guilford, CT: Four Quarters Publishing Co., 1987) 213.

created as well. I see Loretz, Pope and Wilson overextending the schema of theomachy in applying it to the fall of the king. Fechter notes that the core meaning of the images and fate of Tyre in 28:11–19 in many ways reflect the core meaning of the images and fate of Judah in chapter 19.[161] I concur with this for Tyre is object lesson for Judah.

Wyatt sees both oracles explained by two Ugaritic myths thematically related to them.[162] The first myth is the Keret story from Ugarit in which El appears to the king in a dream and says:

> What ails Keret, that he weeps, the gracious one, heir of El, that he groans,
> Does he desire the kingship of the Bull, his father, or dominion like the Father of Man?[163]

The significance of this story is found in the relation of El to the primal royal figure of the king. According to Wyatt, Keret is rebelling against his lot, by longing for a greater rule than is appropriate to his station. The story alludes to a kingship myth which Wyatt notes[164] appears thematically in four OT passages: Isa 14:4–21, Ezek 28:2–10 and 28:12–19 and Gen 2:4b–3:24. And he suggests that there is evidence of another myth which shows the motif to be integral to its understanding of the place of the king in relation to the gods.

The second myth which supports the first is structurally similar to the passages in Ezekiel 28 and takes place in the Baal Cycle during the period when Baal is held captive in the netherworld, a victim of Mot, the god of death.[165] It too portrays an overly ambitious and inappropriate self-aggrandizement in the role of kingship as does the King of Tyre in chapter 28. In the myth, the gods seek to provide a substitute, a god who has knowledge and intelligence. Lady Asherah chooses Ashtar the Tyrant who then ascends to the recesses of Zaphon to sit on the empty throne of the Powerful Baal, but his feet did not reach the footstool and his head did not reach the top. Ashtar, in fact, is a parody of kingship. He is squat and does not measure up to Baal's throne. And so he declares: "I will not reign from Zaphon's fastness," and down he goes from the throne of the powerful Baal and rules

---

[161] Fechter, *Bewältigung der Katastrophe*, 206.
[162] Wyatt, "The Hollow Crown," 421.
[163] Wyatt, "The Hollow Crown," 421.
[164] Wyatt, "The Hollow Crown," 424.
[165] *The Context of Scripture*, 1.266–67.

instead on El's earth below. He is not equal to the role Baal fills and so he chooses a place to rule that suits him, the earth below.

While it is clear that Ezek 28:11–19 comes from an older myth, it is difficult to say what features of the lament belonged to the original myth. Complicating the search is the very real factor of mythopoetic activity present in the final form. From these mythic elements, what can we conclude would be the author's message to Israel, to whom, in fact he was addressing these oracles? One can only think of the request of the people to Samuel in 1 Sam 8:5: "Appoint for us, then, a king to govern us, like other nations." The king of Tyre was not presented in this oracle as wicked or malevolent. His fault was crossing the thin line of the myth of royalty in the ancient Near East and seeing himself as El. The final form presents the stance of the king as contradictory to the relationship established at creation by God between him as Creator and his creatures.[166] As mentioned above, this proper relationship will be articulated more clearly in chapter 34.

Close to the end of the oracle in 28:18, Ezekiel uses economics as a primary arena to visibly demonstrate the self-idolatry of the king. Tyre's ruler has elevated his commercial success to the status of primordial myth.[167] In doing so it has undone the harmonious schema of the Creator. "Through the greatness of your iniquity, by the dishonesty of your trade, you desecrated your sanctuaries. And I brought forth fire from within you; it consumed you. And I turned you to dust on the earth, before the eyes of all who see you," Ezek 28:18. Unfortunately, Israel will become just such an example of merited devastation herself. In fact, by the time this Oracle was read, she had become such an example. Those who do not learn from history, it seems, do repeat it.

Ezekiel 29–32,
The Oracles against Egypt

We turn now to the Oracles against Egypt, the lengthiest treatment given to any of the seven nations. Batto suggests that Egypt is the personification of historical evil, the embodiment of the power that stands in opposition to Yhwh God.[168] In fact, the most potent example of

---

[166] Boadt, "Rhetorical Strategies," 192.
[167] Davis, "And Pharaoh Will Change His Mind," 232.
[168] Batto, *Slaying the Dragon*, 162–63.

arrogant pretensions to replace the Creator among the seven nations does come last. Ezekiel directs seven oracles against Egypt, more than against any of the other six nations. Mythic reference is present in the first, fifth, sixth, and seventh oracles. We will look at these and their cosmogonic implications and also, at the end, discuss the overall mythic significance of the seven oracles as a whole.

In the first oracle, Ezek 29:1–16, the oracle against Pharaoh, the final form uses mythopoetic language to describe the Pharaoh as the great dragon of the Nile, a sea monster lurking in the river which he claims to have made, and God hauls him out on a fishhook. But Pharaoh is, it must be remembered, a representative of his people and his country. He is more than a single personality.[169] Egypt's sin which caused her to stand out in bold relief against her neighbors is stated in these first verses of chapter 29: she is found guilty of being the chaos monster itself, the embodiment of all that would undo Yhwh's act of creation. The great dragon in v. 3 is the primeval chaos monster of the *Chaoskampf* myth. Some would argue that this is only a reference to a crocodile with an unclear mythological allusion.[170] They would see any mythological referent as being thoroughly historicized, comparing Pharaoh to a dragon-like creature. Yet we would counter by asking if תנין is historicized or if the Pharaoh is given mythic dimensions in terms of the evil which motivates him? תנין is used other places in the OT to describe the chaos monster.[171] The dragon is said to have made the streams in v. 3, which would only apply to the chaos monster, himself the personification of the primeval deep which feeds streams.[172] תנין is used in poetic contexts in the OT celebrating Yhwh's victory over the forces of evil.[173] Such is the case here. תנין here is not a reference to a crocodile. To suggest this is to lessen the force of the oracle.

When Pharaoh suggests that he made the Nile for himself, he is identifying himself as the creator, overturning the order of creation.

---

[169] Fohrer, *Ezechiel*, 166.

[170] Block, *The Book of Ezekiel, Chapters 25–48*, 137; Fohrer, *Ezechiel*, 166; Greenberg, *Ezekiel 21–37*, 601–2; Zimmerli, *Ezekiel* 2.159.

[171] Isa 51:9 and Isa 27:1 for example.

[172] Batto, *Slaying the Dragon*, 163–64; Day, *God's Conflict with the Dragon and the Sea*, 94–95; Gunkel, *Schöpfung und Chaos*, 74–75; May, "Some Cosmic Connotations of Mayim Rabbîm," 15; Wyatt, *Myths of Power*, 122.

[173] Block, *The Book of Ezekiel, Chapters 25–48*, 137; Gunkel, *Schöpfung und Chaos*, 73.

Ezekiel annuls the Pharaoh's self-exaltation by declaring him to be the chaos monster incarnate. Such mythic images would have been very clear to the audience. Pharaoh is charged with hubris for usurping the authority of the true Creator. He prevents authentic creation from occurring, and in 29:10–12 Yhwh sentences Egypt to non-creation.[174] Such hubris had consequences of which Egypt must be aware.

He is described as one who dwells in dark watery depths. The underworld dwelling of Osiris, god of the nether world in the Egyptian pantheon, was originally a desert, a Land of Silence, with no water, no air, cavernously deep, dark and lacking. There Osiris made from the blood, pus and corruption descended from his head a swamp and a land of marshes where the shadowy ones would dwell.[175] This is something like the dwelling place of Mot in the Ugaritic Baal Cycle which it parallels. There Baal was taken to Mot's home: "They left, they did not turn back; then they headed toward El's Son death, to the midst of his city, the Swamp, Muck, his royal house, Phlegm, the land of his inheritance."[176] Yhwh will draw the great dragon out of the water and disperse the body parts into the open field where they will lie, not to be gathered or buried. The phrase, "to fall in the open field," is associated, in four of its other locations in Ezekiel, 29:5, 32:4, 33:27, 39:5, with the Lord's judgment of death which falls on the accursed where they will fall and be devoured by bird and beast.[177] Such imagery has older models. It is Baal who drives Yamm from his throne and expels him. As mentioned above in chapters 38–39, the "open-field" motif parallels Anat's doing-in of Mot: "She seized the son of El, Mot. With a sword she split him, with a sieve she winnowed him, with fire she burned him up, with double mill stone she ground him, in the field she sowed him."[178]

Eventually, in forty years, Yhwh will gather up Egypt from where it has been scattered and return it to its land. Never again will Egypt challenge Yhwh's creation (Ezek 29:13–16). The significance of this

---

[174] Batto, *Slaying the Dragon*, 164; Seters, "The Creation of Man," 339.
[175] *The Context of Scripture*, 1.28–29, 31.
[176] Coogan, *Stories from Ancient Canaan*, 107.
[177] Frank H. Gorman, Jr., *The Ideology of Ritual* (JSOTSup 91; Sheffield: Sheffield Academic Press, 1990) 170.
[178] Boadt, *Ezekiel's Oracles against Egypt*, 71–72; Wakeman, *God's Battle with the Monster*, 123.

regathering comes clear in the light of a series of other very similar addresses to Israel in Ezekiel: 11:17–20, 16:59–63, 20:39–44, 28:24–26, 34:11 ff., 36:22 ff., 37:11 ff., 39:25–29.[179] This regathering in the Oracle against Egypt presents the same theology of covenant as is presented in the texts on Israel. It is significant because it implies a shift to universalism. Yhwh directs the history of the nations as well. If the nations are unfaithful, they too must be punished, but that punishment is not the last word. The nations will know restoration as well.[180] He is not only the God of Israel. It foreshadows what must take place in chapters 38–39 before the restoration of the Temple in chapters 40–48.

The textual links between the Oracles against Egypt and the Gog pericope come chiefly in chapter 29.[181] Let us deal with their significance here. It was noted earlier in the Oracles against Tyre and will be noted below in the fifth Oracle against Egypt that textual links also connect the Oracles of Judgment on Israel, chapters 1–24, and the Oracles against the Nations. The instances from the Oracles against Tyre and Egypt are four of the examples, chosen because of their relationship with myth. There are others.[182] It would seem that the author(s)

---

[179] Walter Vogel, "Restauration de l'Egypte et universalisme en Ezek 29, 13–16," *Bib* 53 (1972) 476.

[180] Batto, *Slaying the Dragon*, 165; Boadt, "Mythological Themes," 227.

[181] The eight similarities in text, as noted above in chapter three, are as follows: (1) Both Pharaoh and Gog are puppets of Yhwh who puts hooks in their jaws to play with them at will: 29:4; 38:4; (2) Both peoples will be gathered from among the nations where they have been scattered and they will be restored to their lands after a time: 29:13; 38:8; 39:27; (3) Both armies will fall in the open field and on the mountains where the birds of the air and wild beasts of the field will gorge themselves on their carcasses: 29:4f.; 39:4, 5, 19; (4) The theme of being given into the hand of the enemy by Yhwh appears in both passages: 30:10, 12, 25; 31:11; 39:23; (5) The return of the captives recurs in 39:25 in reference to Israel, an echo of the return of captives to Egypt in 29:14; (6) The Challenge to a Duel Formula (הנני אליך) repeats itself twice in each passage: 29:10; 30:22; 38:3; 39:1; (7) The use of the same two verbs of similar meaning (בזז, שלל) to intensify the image of devastation surfaces again in the Gog pericope after it was used in the Oracle against Egypt: 29:19; 38:12; (8) Lastly, the recurrent theme of "the many peoples" (עים רבים) repeats itself no less than eight times in the two passages, appearing only twice in the rest of the book: 3:6 and 27:33. Boadt, *Ezekiel's Oracles Against Egypt*, 177, n. 16.

[182] Boadt (*Ezekiel's Oracles Against Egypt*, 176) notes nine more: גאון עזה, "proud might," 7:20, 24; 24:21; 30:18; שים פניך, "set your face," 6:2; 13:17; 21: 2, 7; 29:2; כרת אדם ובהמה, "cut from man and animal," 14:13, 17, 19, 21; 29:8, 11; 32:13; פתחון, "opening" (in reference to the mouth), 16:63; 29:21; ריק חרב, "draw the sword," 5:12, 14; 30:11; עשה

of Ezekiel's final form has consciously linked the Judgments against Israel and the Judgments against the Foreign Nations, just as the Judgments against the Foreign Nations are linked with the Gog pericope. Boadt notes that the judgments against Israel, against the seven foreign nations, and against the consummate and ultimate foe are linked.[183] The linkage between the first and the second categories functions to strengthen the implicit comparison of the metaphor which presents the nations as a mirror image of Israel in its failing. The linkage between the second and the third continues this mirror image to reflect back to Israel the extent of their evil ways. As Pharaoh's hubris, in seeking to unseat the Creator himself, is a metaphor for the sin of Israel, so too is the victory in chapters 38–39 a suprahistoric reflection of the undoing of the evil that enveloped Egypt and Israel in their infidelity. The powers of evil are overturned and brought under the dominion of the Creator forever in chapters 38–39. Not only does this eliminate the power of the foreign nations who would supplant the Creator. It also eliminates such a possibility of evil arising against Israel in the future. It is the flip side of the creation by fiat in chapter 37. Not only is the nation restored; it will never fall again.

In the fifth oracle, the doom of the pharaonic tree, 31:1–18, the mythic elements continue. Egypt is compared to a giant cedar whose top towered among the clouds and whose roots reached down into the Abyss (תהום). Nourished by the waters of the deep, the tree towered above all the trees of the forest and became so great that "all the birds of the air" could nest in its boughs, and "all the beasts of the field" brought forth their young beneath its branches, while in its shade "all the many nations" dwelt (v. 6). The broad expanse of its far reaching branches, attributed to the "many waters" of the deep (v. 7), gives it beauty and greatness and makes it a place of shelter and source of life for many. Its beauty surpassed the "beauty of all the trees in the "garden of god" (v. 8). It was the envy of all the trees of "Eden" (v. 9). But also in v. 9 the plot thickens. While the preceding verses extol the majesty of the recipient of such grandeur, it is clear who is the Creator/donor of these gifts: "I (Yhwh) made it beautiful with its mass of branches" (v. 9). The tree,

---

שפטים, "execute judgments," 5:10, 14; 11:9; 16:41; 23:10; 30:14, 19; נתן ביד, "give into the hand," 6:14; 14:19, 13; 16:27; 30:25; בין עבתים צמרתו, "between the boughs of its top branches," 19:11; 31:3, 11, 14; הרים/אפיקים, "mountains/water channels," 6:3; 34:13; 36:4, 6; 31:12; 32:5.

[183] Boadt, *Ezekiel's Oracles Against Egypt*, 177.

overly proud of stature (v. 10), was given over to foreigners (v. 12), but ironically remained a shelter for birds and animals (v. 13) even after all taint of civilization had disappeared (v. 12): a tragic ending for such a mighty tree. Before we look at what all this means, let us clarify two points.

As it appears in MT, v. 3 would be translated as "Look at Assyria." This is frequently emended by adding ת before אשור which would yield the word cypress, providing a parallel to cedar.[184] Yet with others[185] I favor the translation "Look at Assyria" for several reasons. It is critically certain and has been read thus by all the ancient versions.[186] It is not clear that an emendation is helpful to understanding the choice of metaphor, and translating MT as it is would be helpful. As Greenberg notes, the metaphor is awkward when it is begun with a reference to both a cypress and a cedar. The מי of v. 2 indicates that the Pharaoh is compared to a person, not a thing.[187] Metzger notes rightly that comparing the Pharaoh to a cedar or a cypress is an odd choice. The historic trading links of Egypt with Lebanon in the importation of cedars notwithstanding, comparison of the Pharaoh to a palm tree which is indigenous to Egypt would have been a better choice of metaphor by far. The palm tree plays a large role in Egyptian iconography.[188] Therefore, the past tense narrative is better viewed as a reference to the past fall of Assyria.[189] In chapter 26, the fall of Tyre and its descent into Sheol are described as in the future, as are the events of chapter 32 describing the fall of Egypt.[190] The cedar served the purposes of the final form for a very particular reason.

---

[184] Boadt, *Ezekiel's Oracles against Egypt*, 96; Baumgartner, *The Hebrew and Aramaic Dictionary of the Old Testament*, 4.1677; Zimmerli, *Ezekiel* 2.141. It is even suggested by Elliger and Rudolph, BHS, Critical Apparatus, 952.

[185] Greenberg, *Ezekiel 21–37*, 637, 646–47; *The Harper Collins Study Bible*, NRSV, 1271; Irwin, *The Problem of Ezekiel*, 197; *The Jerusalem Bible* (ed. Harold Fisch; Jerusalem: Koren Publishers Jerusalem Ltd., 1983) 648; Paul Joüon, "Notes philologiques sur le texte hébreu d'Ézéchiel," *Bib* 10 (1929) 309.

[186] Joüon, "Notes philologiques," 309.

[187] Greenberg, *Ezekiel 21–37*, 646; Joüon, "Notes philologiques," 309.

[188] Martin Metzger, "Zeder, Weinstock und Weltenbaum," *Ernten, was man sät, Festschrift für Klaus Koch zu seinem 65. Geburtstag* (ed. Dwight R. Daniels, Uwe Glessmer und Martin Rösel; Neukirchen-Vluyn: Neukirchener Verlag, 1991) 211.

[189] Joüon, "Notes philologiques,"309.

[190] Greenberg, *Ezekiel 21–37*, 646.

Egypt in this oracle is an object lesson for a wayward Israel whose royal stock was compared to the mighty cedar earlier in the book in 17:3. Boadt notes that both passages share a number of specialized words rarely used elsewhere: צמר ("wool") referring to the top growth of the tree, 17:3, 31:3; דליות ("bough"), 17: 6, 7, 23 and 31:7, 9, 12; מטע (seed bed), 17:7, 31:4; and there are other semantic links, as well: the height of the tree, 17:22, 31:3, the nesting of the birds in its branches, 17:23; 31:6, the envy of the other trees, 17:24, 31:4, 5 and the bringing down of the tree in its arrogance, 17:24, 31:11–12. Whether Zedekiah in chapter 17 or Pharaoh in chapter 31, the final form uses mythological images in a mythopoetic way to establish the betrayal of Yhwh by living out a false faith typical of the pagan states that surrounded Israel.[191] Though cedar is perhaps a strange metaphor for Egypt in most cases, here the audience could not miss the point that was being made.

The final form, borrowing from an extant tradition or originally composing precisely because of the religious significance of the cedar, chose a cedar as its metaphor. That is clear. Comparing the Pharaoh to Assyria makes this oracle an object lesson within an object lesson. Though Assyria fell at the end of the seventh century, it still represented the ultimate in oriental despotism centuries after her demise, becoming an epithet for the Persian Empire.[192] The author presents Assyria as a symbol of imperial greatness with which Egypt could be compared. Assyria is also paired with Egypt in Isa 19:23, Hos 7:11 and Zech 10:11. She was a potent object lesson of political arrogance for both Egypt and Israel. Assyria is presented as a great cedar, whose hubris, as we will see below, is an offense to the Creator.

Block suggests that the allegory of the cosmic tree in chapter 31 is a political statement rather than a mythological one,[193] yet he notes in his reflections on the theological implications of the passage that it reiterates Yhwh's sovereignty over history: "Nations are not self-made; they draw their vitality from resources built into the universe and they derive their place by divine appointment."[194] That a nation would draw its vitality from resources built into the universe, as a

---

[191] Boadt, "Rhetorical Strategies," 193–94.
[192] Boadt, *Ezekiel's Oracles against Egypt*, 96.
[193] Block, *The Book of Ezekiel, Chapters 25–48*, 188.
[194] Block, *The Book of Ezekiel, Chapters 25–48*, 196.

cedar would be nourished by the waters of the deep till its height reached the heavens, this is the "stuff" of which religious myth is made. He notes further that "pride in human accomplishments draws the fury of God."[195] Verse 11 speaks of a punishment meted out by God: "I gave it into the hand of the prince of the nations." It is difficult to understand chapter 31 as a political rather than theological statement as if the ancient Near East (including the final form of Ezekiel), had clearly established a frame of reference separating "church and state." We would see this satirical allegory in chapter 31 as employing myth to make a statement on the disastrous consequences of political arrogance as it disturbs God's creation. To understand the power of the satire we will discuss further the myth of the cosmic tree.

The cedar in chapter 31 is clearly no ordinary cedar. It has cosmic significance. This cosmic tree in its greatness tames the terrifying cosmic waters of the deep and harnesses them for good, giving nourishment for the trees there (31:4). It was believed that the layers of the universe were kept distinct and in place by a world tree running through the exact center of the cosmos. It is a symbol of continuous renewal, cosmic regeneration, universal fertility, and the sacrality of the world.[196] As mentioned above the lofty cedar is a good metaphor for pride, yet it was chosen also for mythopoetic reasons. It was the image of the cedar which came to mind when one spoke of the religious myth of the cosmic tree. And the cosmic tree, also called the Tree of Life, is known all over the ancient Near East from the fourth millennium to the first millennium B.C.E.[197] The Tree of Life in turn is significant as it relates to immortality, kingship and divinity.[198] What primarily concerns us here is its relationship to divinity and kingship.

The gods were often associated with trees. The cedar forests of Lebanon were referred to as "the luxurious forest of Marduk . . .

---

[195] Block, *The Book of Ezekiel, Chapters 25–48*, 197.

[196] Mircea Eliade, "Lebensbaum," *RGG* 4 (ed. Kurt Galling; Tübingen: Mohr, 1960) 251; Pamela R. Frese and S. J. M Gray, "Trees," in *EncRel* 15 (ed. Mircea Eliade; New York: MacMillan, 1987) 27; May, "Some Cosmic Connotations of *Mayim Rabbîm*," 19–21; Seow, "The Deep," *ABD* 2 (New York: Doubleday, 1992) 125.

[197] Eliade, "Lebensbaum," 251; Metzger, "Zeder, Weinstock und Weltenbaum," 211; John Strange, "The Idea of Afterlife in Ancient Israel: Some Remarks on the Iconography in Solomon's Temple," *PEQ* 117 (1985) 35.

[198] Boadt, *Ezekiel's Oracles against Egypt*, 100; Strange, "The Idea of Afterlife in Ancient Israel," 35–36.

where mighty cedars planted by Anu grew."[199] Baal himself is depicted with a cedar branch in one hand and a bolt of lightning in the other.[200] In the *Poem of Erra* before Erra meets Marduk he says: "Where is the *mesu* tree, the flesh of the gods,[201] the ornament of the king of the universe? . . . whose roots reached as deep down as the bottom of the underworld: a hundred double hours through the vast sea waters; whose top reached as high as the sky."[202]

The Tree of Life plays an important role in the idea of divine kingship in Mesopotamia. The king is both gardener and the Tree of Life, itself. The royal scepter is sometimes regarded as a branch from the Tree of Life. In an ancient Near Eastern kingship myth the legendary Enmeduranki at his enthronement was given a scepter of cedar by the gods.[203] By means of this branch the Mesopotamian monarch is able to impart life to his subjects who kneel as suppliants before him.[204]

In fact, the cosmic tree, the bond between heaven and earth, was understood in the religious mythic mentality of the ancient Near East to be identical with the king.[205] In the early Babylonian Period, Ishmedagan of Isin states: "I am a shoot of cedar . . . exuding a sweet fragrance. I am the tallest of the trees which are the flesh of the gods with wide roots. With my broad branches I cover Sumer with my shadow."[206] In one Sumerian hymn to King Shulgi he is praised: "A cedar rooted by abundant waters, of pleasant shade thou art." In the same source listing the titles for the king, he is referred to as cedar oil, and in a blessing over Esarhaddon it is said: "We were dead dogs, the

---

[199] *ANET*, 307.

[200] Boadt, *Ezekiel's Oracles against Egypt*, 102; Lambert, "Trees, Snakes and Gods," 435–66.

[201] Luigi Cagni (*The Poem of Erra* [SANE 1.3; Malibu: Undena, 1977] 35) notes that the trees that formed the "flesh of the gods" served to form the internal part, the body of the divine statues.

[202] Cagni, *The Poem of Erra*, 32.

[203] Eliade, "Lebensbaum," 251; Strange, "The Idea of Afterlife in Ancient Israel," 35–36; Geo Widengren, *The King and the Tree of Life in Ancient Near Eastern Religion* (UUÅ 1951:4; Uppsala: Lundequistska, 1951) 20–22.

[204] Widengren, *The King and the Tree of Life*, 29, 32.

[205] Ilse Seibert, *Hirt - Herde - König; zur Herausbildung des Konigtums in Mesopotamien*. (Deutsche Akademie der Wissenschaften zu Berlin. Schriften der Sektion für Altertumswissenschaft 53; Berlin: Akademie-Verlag, 1969) 21.

[206] Willem H. Römer, *Sumerische Königshymnen der Isin-Zeit* (DMOA 13; Leiden: Brill, 1965) 52–53.

Lord-King gave us life, he placed the plant of life under our nose": in this example the king has in his possession the power of life.[207] Even the shadow of the king's cedar scepter was thought to provide protection and welfare. It was a cause of reverence and even fear. In this context of reverent fear the Sumerian king is extolled: "Select cedar, ornament in the courtyard of Ekur, Urninurta, the country of Sumer shyly admires your shadow. You are the Good Shepherd of all countries."[208] Such are the images that would be evoked in the audience when they were presented with the image of the great cedar, the cosmic tree. Given its significance, Egypt's pretensions to be the cosmic tree exceed Tyre's hubris in its pretensions to be the cosmic ship.

The satire comes in v. 10 of the oracle when the praise shifts to judgment. Assyria (read: Egypt) considered itself to have the grandeur, majesty and power of the cosmic tree. Given the significance of the cosmic tree, one could say Assyria saw itself as the linchpin of creation. So too Pharaoh's divine pretensions disordered the harmony of creation, and Egypt[209] must pay the price. Just as the ship of Tyre was sunk into the deep because of its arrogance so the Pharaoh, like the sturdy cedar of Assyria, will be cut down in his arrogance. As Tyre, Assyria and Egypt refused to be aware of their assigned role in the created order and suffered the consequences, so too Israel will suffer its consequences for its infidelity to Yhwh in the Fall of Jerusalem which comes in chapter 33 after the Oracles against the Foreign Nations. The hymnic quality reflected in "Whom are you like in your greatness?" (v. 2) slowly changes throughout the chapter to become a political lament (v. 18): "Now you shall be brought down with the trees of Eden to the world below; you shall lie among the uncircumcised. . . . This is Pharaoh and all his horde."[210] The mighty cedar, a failure as an object lesson to Egypt, would became an object lesson of failure to Israel as well.

In the sixth oracle, the doom of the pharaonic monster, 32:1–16, the final form returns to the image of Egypt as the chaos monster who, like Tiamat, writhes in mire in its watery abode: "You are like a dragon in

---

[207] Engnell, *Studies in Divine Kingship*, 27–29.

[208] Seibert, *Hirt - Herde - König*, 21.

[209] Greenberg (*Ezekiel 21–37*, 637) notes that the reference to Pharaoh represents the personification of the people in their king.

[210] Horst Dietrich Preuss, "דמה," *TWAT* 2 (Stuttgart: Kohlhammer, 1977) 271.

the seas; you thrash about in your streams, . . . I will throw you on the ground, on the open field I will fling you, . . . I will strew your flesh on the mountains and fill the valleys with your carcass" (Ezek 32: 2, 4, 5).[211] Chapter 32 shares many mythic themes with chapter 29. Here, too, the final form plays on the theme of the mythological defeat of Yamm for rule over creation. With two maces, "Driver" and "Expeller," Baal drives Yamm from his throne, twirls him around like a hawk in his fingers, strikes him on the shoulder with the first mace and finishes him off with the second mace. As Yamm goes slack and falls to the ground, Baal grabs his body and begins dismembering it.[212] Paralleling also the Mesopotamian combat myth, Yhwh, like Marduk in battle with Tiamat,[213] captures the dragon in his net and slays it, apparently severing two arteries (32:3, 6):[214] "Thus says the Lord God: . . . I will throw my net over you; and I will haul you up in my dragnet. I will drench the land with your outflow, to the mountain-heights with your blood, and the watercourses will be filled with your vital fluids." The תנין had fouled the waters. This is remedied by cutting him up so that his vital fluids filled the water courses.[215] God's power over the monster is made manifest through his use of the monster to regenerate his creation. So too, in the exile, Israel will be, figuratively, cut into pieces and scattered on the earth.

Block suggests that the monster has been thoroughly historicized.[216] This seems to understate the significance of the mythic elements and the mythopoetic character of the passage. In fact, the author uses the religious myths of the time to unmask the seriously miscalculated political pretensions of one who in his arrogance would seek to reorder creation according to his own designs.

---

[211] Batto, *Slaying the Dragon*, 165; as was mentioned above in relation to the first oracle, some would suggest here as well that תנין is a reference to a crocodile. We reject this for the same reasons given above and to that we add the note that in 32:2 תנין dwells in the seas which would not fit a crocodile but would fit the chaos monster. See Day, *God's Conflict with the Dragon and the Sea*, 94–95.

[212] *The Context of Scripture*, 1.248–49.

[213] "They locked in single combat, joining for the fray. The Lord (Marduk) spread out his net, encircled her. . . ." *The Context of Scripture*, 1.398.

[214] Batto, *Slaying the Dragon*, 165; Boadt, *Ezekiel's Oracles against Egypt*, 131; May, "Some Cosmic Connotations of *Mayim Rabbîm*," 15; Wyatt, *Myths of Power*, 122.

[215] Gunkel, *Schöpfung und Chaos*, 77; Wakeman, *God's Battle with the Monster*, 78.

[216] Block, *The Book of Ezekiel, Chapters 25–48*, 202.

The imagery of these myths must have been impressive to the religious imaginations of ancient Near Eastern kings who compared their victories to those of Marduk in their inscriptions.[217] Tiglath Pileser I also records: "Like a storm demon I piled up the corpses of their warriors on mountain ledges (and) made their blood flow into the hollows and plains of the mountains." Ashurnasirpal II chronicles: "With their blood I dyed the mountain red like red wool, (and) the rest of them the ravines (and) torrents of the mountains with their corpses."

Slaying the chaos monster, Yhwh shows himself to be completely victorious. Yhwh then casts the body of the dead monster into the field to be devoured by scavengers (32:4–5). This parallels Baal's slaughter of Yamm: "Ba'lu grabs Yammu and sets about dismembering (him), sets about finishing Ruler Naharu off. 'Attartu intervenes. By name 'Attartu reprimands (him): Scatter (him), O Mighty [Ba'lu], scatter (him), O Cloud-Rider, For Prince [Yammu] is our captive, [for] Ruler Naharu is our captive. Ba'lu carries out the order, mighty Ba'lu disperses him."[218] Yhwh causes the land of Egypt to revert completely into the pre-creation state of a night as dark as the underworld itself. In 32:7 Yhwh is the Creator of darkness,[219] (32:7–8): "I will cover the heavens when you are snuffed out, and I will darken their stars. The sun with a cloud I will cover, and the moon will not give forth its light. All the great lamps of heaven I will blacken out because of you, and I will allow darkness over your land!" God's power includes subsuming the powers of the monster. Ironically, in this darkness Egypt's many waters will now become settled and clear (v. 14). The streams of Egypt will run like oil, similar to the plenty of the Ugaritic Baal Cycle: "In a vision of the Creator of creatures, the heavens will rain down oil, the wadis will run with honey."[220] With the elimination of the chaos monster, the power of the authentic Creator is no longer veiled.

The seventh oracle against Egypt, its descent into Sheol (32:17–32), places Egypt in the deepest part of the Pit. Ezekiel's universe, as in

---

[217] Albert K. Grayson, *Assyrian Royal Inscriptions* 2 (RANE; Weisbaden: Otto Harrassowitz, 1972) 9, 14–15, 135.

[218] *The Context of Scripture*, 1.249; Peter J. van Zijl, *Baal, A Study in Texts in Connexion with Baal in the Ugaritic Epics* (AOAT 10; Neukirchen-Vluyn: Neukirchener Verlag, 1972) 45.

[219] Wakeman, *God's Battle with the Monster*, 78.

[220] *The Context of Scripture*, 1.271.

other ancient Near Eastern cosmogonies, was three-tiered.[221] Sheol is the realm of the dead. This verse is itself mythopoetic activity. Israel's neighbors saw the netherworld on the model of a city-state, under despotic royal rule. The Book of Ezekiel, rather, sees Sheol under the sovereignty of Yhwh. He determines both the time and the circumstances of one's arrival in Sheol.[222] In Sheol Egypt will lie with the uncircumcised and the polluted (discussed above in chapter three).

Lying alongside Egypt in Sheol are Gog's closest associates, Meshech and Tubal, and all the princes of the north, who do not meet their end until ten chapters later! Again we are cautioned not to judge myth out of twentieth century logical categories. Yet it does raise the question of whether Gog is to be seen as a future projection of Pharaoh. Along with all the other similarities between the two passages, it could be suggested that chapters 38–39 merely constitute round two with Pharaoh. Yet, in fact, it is quite the opposite. Of the seven object lessons for Israel of the future that awaited her if she did not repent, the final form of Ezekiel presented Egypt as the consummate offense to Yhwh, and so was depicted, mythopoetically, as the chaos monster incarnate, a force so under the sway of the forces of un-creation that Egypt's undoing became a foreshadowing of Jerusalem's fall in chapter 33. Egypt is presented as a mirror image of Israel before her restoration. Gog is presented as the archenemy of Israel, leader of a force of cosmic proportions about to destroy Yhwh's people living in seeming political naivete, but trusting in their Creator rather than political alliances. This point will become clear in the discussion of the promised covenant of peace in chapters 34 and 37.

Perhaps the most telling point in the Oracles against the Foreign Nations is made in 32:31. Referring to the pagan princes and armies which have gone down to the Pit in 32:30, the NRSV translates the verse "These the Pharaoh shall see, and he shall be consoled for all his

---

[221] "The ancient Semites, unlike modern scientists, construed their world as a big house with a three-tiered structure. The upper part, heaven, is the realm of the gods; the middle part is our human world, given to us by the gods; the lower part, a great cave situated deep below the surface of the earth, is the nether world" (Bernhard Lang, "Life After Death in the Prophetic Promise," in *Congress Volume, Jerusalem, 1986* [ed. J. A. Emerton; VTSup 40; Leiden: Brill, 1999) 145; see also Nobile, "Beziehung zwischen Ezek. 32, 17–32 und der Gog-Perikope," 258.

[222] Block, *The Book of Ezekiel, Chapters 25–48*, 233–34.

masses. . . ."²²³ As Davis cogently notes,²²⁴ this is a strange form of consolation which, she explains, is better translated. The *niphʿal* verb נחם with the preposition על is translated differently in other uses: Exod 32:12, Isa 57:6, Jer 8:6, 18:8, 10; Amos 7:3, 6; Job 42:6. In these cases נחם על means "to regret, to rue, to repent."²²⁵ It indicates a profound alteration of feeling, understanding, or intention, a change of mind. Such an understanding is a better translation of נחם על in 32:31: that Pharaoh will eventually change his mind and see his wrong. This change of mind, coming as it does at the end of the Oracles against the Foreign Nations, signifies the conversion of a national leader whose predecessors refused to acknowledge Yhwh. His conversion is the definitive testimony of the existence of Yhwh.²²⁶ Again Israel is forewarned, and called to such conversion.

The central image that the Book of Ezekiel confronts in all seven nations is the relationship of the nation-state to the Creator. All seven oracles address the nationalistic absolutism of the foreign nations,²²⁷ and the consequent excision of God from the world order they seek to establish. Through religious myth, the final form of Ezekiel creates and criticizes images that propose to give insight into the relationship between the power possessed by human nations and the sovereignty of the Creator. Martin Buber articulates Ezekiel's message here when he says: "The nations can experience the absolute only because of what they are; Israel can experience the absolute only, when, and because that absolute faces it."²²⁸ It is clear that, while the *Chaoskampf* motif is used in these oracles, their function is not to present the decisive

---

[223] Tanakh, REB, NAB and NJB all have similar translations: "He will be consoled," or "He will be comforted." Cf. *The Complete Parallel Bible Containing the Old and New Testaments with the Apocryphal/Deuterocanonical Books, New Revised Standard Version, Revised English Bible, New American Bible, New Jerusalem Bible* (New York: Oxford University Press, 1993); *Sacred Writings, Judaism: The Tanakh, The New JPS Translation* (New York: Book-of-the-Month-Club, 1992).

[224] Davis, "And Pharaoh Will Change His Mind," 234.

[225] Baumgartner, *The Hebrew Aramaic Dictionary of the Old Testament*, 2.688.

[226] Davis, "And Pharaoh Will Change His Mind," 234–35.

[227] Ellen Davis ("And Pharaoh Will Change His Mind," 226) discusses this nationalistic absolutism of "the other nations" in contrast to absolute covenant fidelity to Yhwh.

[228] Martin Buber, "The Gods of the Nations and God," *Israel and the World, Essays in a Time of Crisis* (New York: Schocken Books, 1948) 198.

battle described in that motif. That battle is yet to come in Ezekiel's cosmogony, in chapters 38–39. In fact, the Oracles against the Nations are a message to Israel, poised poignantly between its final warning and its ultimate loss of nation status, as to what happens to the nation whose wildly inflated self- estimation seeks to reverse the established order of creation and become the center of its own universe. The judgment of Yhwh calls Israel to re-establish its rootedness in the Divine, rather than replacing it with its own pretensions. The author(s) of the final form of Ezekiel draws on the myths of these foreign nations, showing in the critique of them, the corrective needed for a reformulated religious myth that reflects the true religion of the God of Israel. "By engaging the images of the foreign myths and pushing them to their limits, Ezekiel shows how far they fall short of ultimate realities."[229] His skill in manipulating the myths of the foreign nations breaks the absolutizing power of the myths themselves.[230] The cosmic ship and the cosmic tree lay bare the foolish pretensions of petty potentates before the power and majesty of the Creator God of Israel. By the Oracles of the Nations, Israel is called to recognize the true God of their religious myth as the sole Creator and foundation of reality. It is also implied by the theme of regathering in the Oracles against Egypt that the nations are called to do the same.

Ezekiel 34:1–31; 37:1–28

The mythic elements in chapters 33 through 37 center primarily in chapters 34 and 37, yet it will be good for us to comment at least briefly on the function of chapter 33 here and, below, after we have laid the groundwork with discussion of chapter 34, frame chapters 35 and 36 in their context. Chapter 33 serves as a transition chapter from the oracles of judgment to the oracles of salvation by means of (1) a recommissioning of the prophet as watchman and (2) a calling of the people to concede responsibility for the exile, that it is deserved and just, and must be accepted. A key element in this acknowledgment is the reality of Jerusalem's fall which is announced in vv. 21–22.[231] Above we pre-

---

[229] Davis, "And Pharaoh Will Change His Mind," 232.
[230] Davis, "And Pharaoh Will Change His Mind," 233.
[231] Block, *The Book of Ezekiel, Chapters 25–48*, 234–36; Boadt, "The Function of the Salvation Oracles," 7–8.

sented chapters 25–32 as an object lesson for Israel before Jerusalem's fall rather than as a punishment of Israel's enemies. Block notes that the chapter contains no hint that a new era is about to begin, stating that logically the chapter belongs immediately after chapter 24.[232] My research suggests, rather, that chapter 33 is an end to the oracles of judgment. The final form has changed its case at the feet of the guilty party. They must accept responsibility for their failure and the resultant exile. A new beginning will be made.

Chapter 34 begins the oracles of hope and restoration. It focuses on a reorientation of community leadership. To speak of the deleterious affects of human leadership and the blessing that will come from divine leadership, the final form uses the image of the shepherd. This image is very germane not only to the extant literature of ancient Israel but to the entire region of the ancient Near East as well. While the realities of shepherding can sometimes challenge the bucolic images it seems to evoke, the religious literature of the period made very effective and frequent use of it in describing the divine shepherd.

Marduk is referred to as the shepherd of the people or the shepherd of mankind and even the shepherd of the gods: "May he shepherd all the gods like sheep."[233] Shamash, the sun god, is called shepherd of the people and shepherd of both the underworld and the world above.[234] In "The Babylonian Theodicy" the closing line states: "For the shepherd Shamash guides the peoples like a god."[235] Both Marduk and Shamash are praised for their shepherding: "Marduk has fed me," "Shamash is my shepherd." Ishtar, the goddess of war and fertility, is called the shepherdess who accompanies the sheep and the shepherdess of the people in darkness who feeds the black-headed people. She is also referred to as the shepherdess of all countries.[236] Sumer was said to have rested on luxuriant pasture because of the divine shepherd.[237] The text in chapter 34 makes it clear that the true shepherd of

---

[232] Block, *The Book of Ezekiel, Chapters 25–48*, 235.

[233] *ANET*, 72.

[234] *The Context of Scripture*, 1.387.

[235] Wilfred G. Lambert, *Babylonian Wisdom Literature* (Oxford: Clarendon, 1960) 89.

[236] *ANET*, 387–88; Lorenz Dürr, *Ursprung und Ausbau der israelitisch-jüdischen Heilandserwartung* (Berlin: Schwetschke & Sohn, 1925) 121–22; Seibert, *Hirt - Herde - König*, 15–16.

[237] Seibert, *Hirt - Herde - König*, 15.

Israel is Yhwh. He alone will reassert leadership of the flock as its only shepherd.

But the epithet shepherd is also applied to rulers in the ancient Near East. The designation of shepherd for a king is a stock term in the usage of the region and often times synonymous with king: "Ishtar was looking for a shepherd and searching high and low for a king. Inninna was looking for a shepherd and searching high and low for a king.[238] Esarhaddon is described as "the Sun of all peoples, the protecting shadow of . . . the trustworthy shepherd, who shepherds the black-headed race of men."[239] Ur-nammu of Ur, Lipit-Ishtar of Nippur, Hammurabi of Babylon all present themselves as being called from among their people to be shepherd.[240] Shalmaneser I confirms his kingship by referring to himself as the legitimate shepherd.[241] Tiglath-pileser I describes himself as he "who firmly shepherded the hosts of Assyria."[242] One could assemble a litany of kingly titles from ancient Near Eastern literature using the image of shepherd: experienced shepherd, wise shepherd, strongest shepherd, faithful shepherd, zealous shepherd, thoughtful shepherd, pious shepherd, confident shepherd, foreseeing shepherd, favorite shepherd of Enlil, Marduk and Shamash, shepherd who maintains the populations in good order, shepherd who assembles the dispersed, beloved shepherd, shepherd who fears his divinity, shepherd who foresees the needs of the sanctuaries of the great gods, shepherd of all inhabited places, shepherd of the black heads, marvelous shepherd.[243] This is a partial list.

And so in chapter 34 the final form makes effective use of the shepherd image to reorient the leadership of the community. The Hebrew

---

[238] Stephanie Dalley, *Myths from Mesopotamia: Creation, the Flood, Gilgamesh, and Others* (World's Classics; Oxford: Oxford University Press, 1989) 190; Adam Falkenstein and Wolfram von Soden, *Sumerische und akkadische Hymnen und Gebete* (Die Bibliothek der alten Welt, Der alte Orient; Zurich: Artemis, 1953) 29.

[239] *ARAB*, 2.258.

[240] *ANET*, 159, 164; Falkenstein and von Soden, *Sumerische und akkadische Hymnen und Gebete*, 87.

[241] Erich Ebeling, Bruno Meissner, and Ernst F. Weidner, ed., *Die Inschriften der Altassyrischen Könige* (AOBib 1; Leipzig: Quelle & Meyer, 1926) 121.

[242] *ARAB 1: Historical Records of Assyria From the Earliest Times to Sargon* (ed. J. H. Breasted; Ancient Records, 1st series; Chicago: University of Chicago Press, 1927) 88.

[243] Albert Schott, *Die Vergleiche in den akkadischen Königs-inschriften* (MVAG 1925, 2, 30. Jahrg; Leipzig: Hinrichs, 1926) 70–72; Marie-Joseph Seux, *Épithès Royales Akkadiennes et Sumériennes* (Paris: Letouzey et Ané, 1967) 244–50.

verb רעה, (34:2) like its Akkadian cognate *re'û* means to pasture, to tend, to graze, but it also functions as a technical term for "to rule."[244] That leadership, beyond self-interest, must be exercised for the sake of the ruled as servant leadership. This notion was not particular to Israel. "Advice to a Prince," whose dating most probably comes from early first millennium Babylon, speaks just as harshly as vv. 1–10 in chapter 34 in condemning kings and princes who are unjust to their followers. Significant in the document is the reference to chaos in the first line: "If the king does not heed justice, his people will be thrown into chaos, and his land will be devastated."[245] The leadership will be held accountable for its ordering of society and mismanagement of it will be dealt with by the gods.

The theme of the gathering of the dispersed (34:13) also has a long history in the ancient Near East. Hammurabi speaks of having "collected the scattered people of Isin."[246] He also praises himself saying: "The scattered population of Sumer and Akkad I gathered; I offered them bread and drink; with blessing and prosperity I pastured them." When Merodach-baladan was chosen king, Marduk is said to have proclaimed: "This man is indeed the shepherd who once again gathers the dispersed," and the king himself declares that he has gathered and restored the people.[247] Esarhaddon, in his account of the reconstruction of Babylon, portrays himself as one who regathered the Babylonians and restored them to full citizenship: "I regathered those sold into slavery, I broke their bonds and shackles, I redressed all their confiscated property. I clothed them, settled them in dwellings in the city, encouraged them to build orchards, and to dig irrigation channels again. I opened wide to the four winds all their trade routes that they might barter with the nations. I regathered them and made them a people again."[248] Yet in every case the divine shepherd names a human shepherd-king who carries out the actual regathering. What is unique in Ezekiel is that Yhwh the divine patron regathers the sheep himself. This task is not commissioned to a messianic figure.[249] In fact, the

---

[244] J. Alberto Soggin, "רעה," *THAT* 2 (ed. Ernst Jenni; Munich: Chr. Kaiser, 1971) 794.

[245] Lambert, *Babylonian Wisdom Literature*, 110–13.

[246] *ANET*, 164.

[247] Dürr, *Ursprung und Ausbau*, 120.

[248] Borger, *Die Inschriften Asarhaddons*, 25–26.

[249] Geo Widengren, "The Gathering of the Dispersed," *SEÅ* 41/42 (1976–77) 128–29.

chapter lays out very clearly the king's position in relation to Yhwh and in relation to the people.

The chapter plays down the prominence of the Davidic king by placing the mention of it at the end of the chapter (34:23–24). It emphasizes the role of God as the true shepherd of Israel: Yhwh himself holds the office of shepherd over his people. In Ezekiel it is Yhwh who establishes justice between the strong and the weak sheep,[250] which image has parallels with Leviticus 25. The title מלך is avoided in these verses. נשיא is preferred.[251] Engnell's research suggests to him the title "executive king,"[252] who would exercise limited cultic and rulership functions as a subordinate of Yhwh.[253] Yhwh is the divine king over the people; the prince in their midst is his representative. He is subject to Yhwh.

With so many links to themes current in other ancient Near Eastern political and religious literature of the period, it is not surprising that this chapter has a mythic base to it in its structure and content. In 34:25 Yhwh the true shepherd announces "a covenant of peace," ברית שלום. When Yhwh has re-instituted justice and right relationship between himself, human leadership and the community, he will establish a "covenant of peace." This phrase appears three other times in the OT: Isa 54:7–10, Num 25:12 and Gen 9:8–17; and it appears later in Ezek 37:26 as a summary of this text.

Though there are no exact extra-biblical parallels for this phrase,[254]

---

[250] Block, *The Book of Ezekiel, Chapters 25–48*, 291, 300; Boadt, "The Function of the Salvation Oracles," 9; Walter Gross, "Israel's Hope for the Renewal of the State," *JSS* 14 (1988) 124–26.

[251] Erling Hammershaimb ("Ezekiel's View of the Monarchy," in *Some Aspects of Old Testament Prophecy from Isaiah to Malachi* [ed. Erling Hammershaimb; Teologiske Skrifter 4; Copenhagen: Rosenkilde Og Bagger, 1966] 59) argues against this position but his point is that Yhwh is not abolishing the monarchy in favor of theocracy. This is clear from the promise of the re-establishment of the Davidic monarchy in 34:23. Yet the use of the word נשיא in this chapter is not about the abolishment of an institution, but rather about a reformulation of the royal ideology of that institution, understanding the king, in contradistinction to the royal ideology of the ruler's of Tyre and Egypt, as Yhwh's regent.

[252] Engnell, *Studies in the Divine Kingship*, 31.

[253] Werner E. Lemke, "Life in the Present and Hope for the Future," *Int* 38 (1984) 174; Müller, *Ursprünge und Strukturen*, 217.

[254] F. Brent Knutson ("Literary Phrases and Formulae," *RSP* 2 [ed. Loren R. Fisher; AnOr 50; Rome: Institutum Biblicum, 1975] 407–9) notes that the phrase "bond of

along with the themes of this chapter mentioned above, the covenant of peace is not an unknown motif in ancient Near Eastern myth. It appears as part of a pattern attested in two variant forms. The first form is present in the Atrahasis and the Gilgamesh myths. It has three basic elements in its structure in these myths: (1) a deluge as an expression of divine wrath; (2) an oath/covenant never again to destroy all life with a flood; and (3) the identification of a sign guaranteeing the divine oath (the fly-necklace).[255] This ancient Near Eastern mythic theme begins with the revolt of humankind against the gods at creation and ends with the cessation of hostility between them. The flood event was not a capricious act of the gods, but punishment for the violation of right order on the part of humankind, disturbing the divine rest of the gods which is a sign of their superior sovereignty. Disturbance of divine sleep was always resultant of revolt.[256] The divine decision to destroy humankind by flood was just as much a punishment for sin in Atrahasis as it was in the biblical story. The divine regulations for human existence given at the conclusion of the myth re-establish correct order or harmony within the universe. The gods ended their attempt to wipe out humanity by binding themselves under oath to maintain peace and harmony with humankind and even with the whole of creation. This would be guaranteed by a permanent visible sign, symbolic of this new alliance.[257] The result of this covenant of peace will be an era nothing short of the restoration of the idyllic situation comparable to the Garden of Eden, where implicit to the scene is the harmonious relationship between God and his people.

The most obvious OT parallel to this covenant of peace is the account of the great flood in Genesis beginning as it does with humanity's wickedness, followed first by the deluge and then by Yhwh's

---

peace" is used in two Akkadian political treaties between Shuppiluliuma and Niqmadu where the former invites the latter to an alliance against enemies. In these treaties its use is political where the covenant of peace is not.

[255] Block, *The Book of Ezekiel, Chapters 25–34*, 303–4; Benjamin R. Foster, "Atra-Hasis," "Gilgamesh," in *The Context of Scripture I* (ed. William W. Hallo; New York: Brill, 1997) 450–52, 458–60.

[256] Bernard F. Batto ("The Sleeping God: An Ancient Near Eastern Motif of Divine Sovereignty," *Bib* 68 [1987] 153–77) presents evidence for the mythic significance of Divine Sleep in his article.

[257] Bernard F. Batto, "The Covenant of Peace," *CBQ* 49 (1987) 187; Foster, "Atra-Hasis," "Gilgamesh," 452, 460.

covenant with Noah. The testimony to this covenant is the setting of Yhwh's bow in the clouds, but the story line of the covenant of peace is also paralleled by the unfolding of events described in chapter 34. Here the Exile is the expression of divine wrath in response to the infidelity of Yhwh's people. Then Ezek 34: 25–29 describes in detail conditions which are a veritable photocopy picture perfect reproduction of the situation in the Garden of Eden resulting from the covenant of peace. Yet how will Israel no longer be plunder for the nations, or suffer their insults as described in Ezek 34:28, 29? That has yet to be resolved. What is Yhwh's "bow in the clouds" in this context?

The second form of the covenant of peace myth lacks the flood account but tells rather of a single goddess's bloody attempt to slay humankind with her sword. This form contains a motif of a "planting of peace" on earth and the attainment of cosmic harmony achieved in the universe as a result of divine rule. The myth has two extant forms. The first is an Egyptian text known as "Deliverance of Mankind from Destruction," and the second is an Ugaritic text of the Baal Cycle. Both share a common pattern and are actually related.[258] In the Egyptian account Hathor's attack on humankind was commissioned by the creator, Re, in council with the other gods. The ending of the mythic pattern is better preserved in the account from the Baal Cycle. After Anat's bloody rampage against humankind, Baal sends a messenger to Anat with a command to stop the carnage and to "pour peace into the heart of the earth; rain down love in the heart of the fields."[259] Anat accepts Baal's request and stops the slaughter. The story moves on to more familiar themes like the orchestration of the petition to build Baal's palace. But Baal's desire to plant peace and love in the earth is a significant statement. It announces reconciliation with humankind and with the earth itself. This act abolishes hostility between the gods and

---

[258] Batto, "The Covenant of Peace," 196–97; Charles Virolleaud, "La Déesse Anat-Astarté dans les Poèmes de Ras-Shamra," *RES* 1 (1937) 8–9.

[259] Batto, "The Covenant of Peace," 198; Clifford ("Cosmogonies in the Ugaritic Texts," 197) mentions a fertility rite without translation. Dennis Pardee ("The Ba'lu Myth," in *The Context of Scripture I* [ed. William W. Hallo; Leiden: Brill, 1997] 251, 252, 253) renders Batto's translation comparably: "pour well-being into the earth, calmness into the fields." Harold L. Ginsberg ("Poems About Baal and Anat," in *ANET*, 136) translates the text "Pour peace into earth's very bowels, Much amity into earth's bosom."

humans and achieves a new harmony between them, cosmic in nature, ushering in an era of paradisial conditions. As a sign to mark this event, Baal creates lightning and thunder and Anat will plant peace and love on earth. This sign of thunder and lightning is comparable to the fly necklace in Atrahasis.[260] In this account lightning and thunder serve as a sign that the hostility between gods and humans has ceased and that a new era of peace has begun.

This "planting for peace" motif appears as well in Ezek 34:29. Within the context of the "covenant of peace": the removal of every form of hostility from the land and the concomitant advent of paradise-like conditions, there is reference to a planting of peace, as mythopoeic description of Yhwh re-establishing right relationship in the social order. This translation is not without its variants. MT has מטע לשם. Yet both the BDB and Elliger in the critical apparatus in the BHS[261] interpret לשם as a corruption by metathesis of שלם, reminiscent of Lev 26:6, "And I will grant peace in the land."[262] שלם is the translation given in the Greek and Syriac forms and in the Targum. Block would suggest "peaceful plantation,"[263] and Zimmerli has "prosperous plantation."[264] Greenberg, not assuming metathesis, translates the two words as "a planting of renown,"[265] yet interestingly he does not argue against the possibility of שלם rather than לשם, which he presents as an alternative option to his stated preference. NRSV translates it "splendid vegetation."[266] The similarities between Leviticus 26 and Ezekiel 34 and the thematic message of the entire pericope weigh in favor of the translation "planting of peace." Lev 26:4–6 speaks of nature cooperating to produce abundant harvests and the elimination of hostility between man and beast from the land. Ezekiel 34 converts the curses of Leviticus 26 into blessings. The covenant formula of Ezek

---

[260] Batto, "The Covenant of Peace," 199–201; Pardee ("The Baʻlu Myth," 252) gives the translation "lightning"; Ginsberg (ANET, 136) gives the translation "thunderbolt."
[261] BDB, 1028; Elliger and Rudolph, eds., BHS, 961, critical apparatus 29 a-a.
[262] For a discussion of parallels between Ezekiel 34 and Leviticus 26 see Boadt, "The Function of the Salvation Oracles," 9–10; Eichrodt, Ezekiel, 481–84; Zimmerli, Ezekiel 1.51.
[263] Block, The Book of Ezekiel, Chapters 25–48, 295.
[264] Zimmerli, Ezekiel 2.211.
[265] Greenberg, Ezekiel 21–37, 704.
[266] The Harper Collins Study Bible, NRSV, 1278.

34:30 is found in Lev 26:12.[267] The parallels between Lev 26:4–13 and Ezek 34:25–31 give force to the arguments in favor of this translation which has its correlative in the phrase "covenant of peace" in Ezek 34:25.[268]

In reflecting on this covenant as described in Hos 2:18, Tucker notes its extent:[269] this new covenant will establish a new world order which will end violence among all living creatures such as described in Ezek 34:25, 28: "I will make with them a covenant of peace and banish wild animals from the land, so that they may live in the wild and dwell securely. . . .nor shall the animals of the land devour them." He goes on to cite Hans Walter Wolff's commentary on Hosea: this covenant "involves a mediation of peace between Israel and the estranged animal kingdom (cf. Gen 3:15). Yhwh proves his covenant loyalty toward Israel by mediating a covenant between opposing forces within creation (cf. Ezek 34:25–30; Gen 9:8–17)."[270] This covenant will re-establish harmony in all creation.

As Baal commands Anat to "pour peace into the heart of the earth," so Yhwh, the sovereign, will himself sow peace and banish hostility from the face of the earth. This pouring of "peace into the heart of the earth" may be seen not only as a cessation of hostilities. This prevention of war also anticipates and serves as prelude to the emergence of cosmic fertility.[271] That is what is described in Ezek 34:26–29:

> I will make them and the region around my hill a blessing; and I will send down the showers in their season; they shall be showers of blessing. The trees of the field shall yield their fruit, and the earth shall yield its increase. They shall be secure on their soil; . . . They shall no

---

[267] Though interestingly the final form leaves out the text in Lev 26:11 that says "I will set my dwelling among you," Boadt ("The Salvation Oracles in Ezekiel," 10) suggests that perhaps the final form leaves this to be developed in chapters 40–48.

[268] Eichrodt, *Ezekiel*, 483.

[269] Eugene Tucker, "The Peaceable Kingdom and a Covenant with the Wild Animals," in *God Who Creates, Essays in Honor of W. Sibley Towner* (ed. William P. Brown and S. Dean McBride Jr.; Grand Rapids: Eerdmans, 2000) 217.

[270] Hans Walter Wolff, *Hosea: A Commentary on the Book of the Prophet Hosea* (trans Gary Stansell; Hermeneia; Philadelphia: Fortress, 1974) 51; originally published as *Dodeka Propheton 1 Hosea* (BKAT 14/1; Neukirchen-Vluyn: Neukirchener Verlag, 1965); quoted in Tucker, "The Peaceable Kingdom and a Covenant with the Wild Animals," 220.

[271] Smith, *The Ugaritic Baal Cycle*, 207.

more be plunder for the nations, nor shall the animals of the land devour them; they shall live in safety and no one shall make them afraid. I will provide for them a *planting for peace*[272] so that they shall no more be consumed with hunger in the land, and no longer suffer the insults of the nations.

The restoration is in fact part of the final form's cosmogony. Yhwh's act of creation will issue forth in a fruitful and life-sustaining society and Yhwh will be its shepherd, yet, as mentioned above, this covenant of peace is not complete with only the flowering of the earth. Something else is needed so that the events of 597/587 would not happen again.

The next section of the Oracles of Restoration is Ezek 35:1–36:15. Chapter 34 spoke of the restoration of the leadership and the reestablishment of right order through the "planting of peace." This section continues this mythic theme, speaking of the restoration of and establishment of right order in the land through physical recreation and repopulation. Yet before this can happen in Israel, Edom must be dealt with and for all "the planting of peace" which took place in chapter 34, its polar opposite will take place in Edom before the theme of "planting of peace" is continued in the first half of chapter 36. While Israel is to know שלם מסע, Edom will know שממה, "desolation."

While questions have been raised in the past over why such a decisive oracle against Edom stands outside the collection in chapters 25–32,[273] more recent commentaries and studies[274] understand clearly that Edom's encroachment on Israelite territory must be countered before restoration could take place. During the Babylonian invasion, Edom had moved into the territory directly south of Judah. 1 Esdr 4:50 asserts clearly that in the Persian government's decree permitting the Jews to return to Judah "the Idumeans should give up the villages of the Jews that they held." What was mentioned in chapter 25 against Edom was not an obstacle to restoration. By encroaching on the Promised Land, however, Edom knowingly or unknowingly had sought to permanently replace the existing order within Israel. But

---

[272] Emended as explained in the preceding paragraphs.
[273] Wevers, *Ezekiel*, 186–88; Zimmerli, *Ezekiel* 2.234.
[274] Block, *The Book of Ezekiel, Chapters 25–48*, 322; Boadt, "The Function of the Salvation Oracles," 11; Greenberg, *Ezekiel 21–37*, 723.

God does not respect their logic because that logic does not respect his sovereignty or the honor of his name. And so the order must be restored, an order decreed and established by the Creator. They had disturbed the political order, promised in Covenant to a people, Yhwh's people. In opposing God's order as creator, they were guilty of hubris.

This desolation of Edom is a prelude for the reversal of Israel's fortunes: a blessing of the mountains of Israel and the full restoration of the land. The mountains will once again be bountiful with both people and plants. There will be renewed fruitfulness on the land (as described in Lev 26: 4–13.) The new fertility will exceed anything it has experienced in history. As in 34:25–31, it will know paradise-like conditions, like another Garden of Eden. Chapter 36:1–15 is perhaps best described as mythic reprise of a land restored. Both passages are not without mythic parallel. This cosmogony of the Book of Ezekiel is an account of the emergence of a world that is supportive of human life, for the fertility that makes human life possible in the Near East is precarious. Baal's thunder and lightning that come from his palace herald his nourishing rains which will awaken the fertility of the soil. Clifford notes that the ordering of heaven and earth so that a human society can exist is what ancients mean by cosmogony.[275] The cosmogony of the Book of Ezekiel is in process here, with a few more pieces needed to fall into place.

Genesis 1 presents the image of a supreme deity who is above any natural connection with his creation, a deity who creates by fiat.[276] One could liken Ezek 36:26, 27 to creation by fiat, "I will give you a new heart, and a new spirit I will put within you. . . . I will put my spirit within you and make you follow my statutes and be careful to observe my ordinances." The remainder of Ezek 36:16–38 in many ways marks a reversal of the history of Israel's infidelity recounted in chapter 20, and it is done by a deity who creates by fiat. Despite the challenge of the exile to Israelite faith and perhaps even because of that challenge, Ezekiel in its final form is a testimony to the ultimate sovereignty of the Creator over his creation.

This creation by fiat shifts the emphasis presented in 18:31: "Cast away from you all the transgressions that you have committed against

---

[275] Clifford, "Cosmogonies in the Ugaritic Texts and in the Bible," 197.
[276] Levenson, *Creation and the Persistence of Evil*, 3; Long, "Cosmogony," in *EncRel* 4 (ed. Mircea Eliade; London: Collier Macmillan Publishers, 1987) 94–95.

me, and get yourselves a new heart and a new spirit!" The initiative is taken from the people.[277] The restoration is Yhwh's creative act, not the result of human effort, in Ezekiel's mythopoeic re-write of the Israelite Cosmogonic Myth.[278] Even to the point of seemingly sacrificing human freedom, Ezekiel, more than any other book of the OT, preeminently proclaims the sovereignty of the Creator. The bond between Yhwh and his people cannot unilaterally be annulled by Israel. In terms of human freedom, this is problematic.[279] Yet the events of the exile had so challenged the faith of Israel that it provides an understandable context for such an extreme stance. Ezekiel is a word that arises out of a crisis addressed to fallen situations and the victims of these situations.

Mythic references in this section have already been discussed. Ezek 36:24 speaks of Yhwh gathering Israel from among the nations. Verses 30, 33–36 reprise themes discussed in 34:25–31 and 36:1–15. It sums up the ancient Near Eastern perception that the productivity of the land is linked to normalization of relations between the god, the people and the land.[280] Let us move then to the Valley of the Dry Bones in chapter 37.

Of interest in chapter 37 is Ezekiel's Vision of the Dry Bones, which has parallel expressions and ideas in ancient Near Eastern literature

---

[277] Müller, *Ursprünge und Strukturen*, 120, 210–12, 219.

[278] Uffenheimer ("Theodicy and Ethics in the Prophecy of Ezekiel," 214) refers to the irremediable incapacity for reform on the part of Israel as Ezekiel's deterministic pessimism.

[279] Ezek 20:33 tells us: "As I live, says the Lord God, surely with a mighty hand and an outstretched arm, and with wrath poured out, I will be king over you." Greenberg (*Ezekiel 1–20*, 386) notes that there is a midrash on this unique self-assertion in which Israel's forgoing of the reward for obedience to the commandments is considered out of the question. It is recounted in the midrash that elders came to Ezekiel and asked if they passed out of God's jurisdiction when God sold them to the other nations? Ezekiel responded by repeating 20:33 and adding: "After I inflict these three scourges on you one after the other, I will be king over you *whether you like it or not*." The original text for the italicized words is על כרחכם (*Siphre d'be Rab, Corpus Tannaiticum* 3.3.1 [ed. H. Saul Horovitz; Jerusalem: Wahrmann Books, 1966] 128). Neusner (*Sifré to Numbers An American Translation and Explanation 2: Sifré to Numbers 59–115*, 183) translates the same phrase "despite yourselves." The medieval Jewish commentators understood the covenant as final: "We are not entitled to remove ourselves from his jurisdiction." Greenberg, *Ezekiel 1–20*, 386. This does raise issues about the understanding of human freedom in the final form.

[280] Block, *The Book of Ezekiel, Chapters 25–48*, 358.

and myth.[281] Zimmerli sees the vision to be only a dramatic description particular to Ezekiel,[282] yet beliefs about the dead and practices relative to the dead in the ancient Near East frequently coincide with Israel's. Reference to such a grisly array of a plain filled with the bones of unburied corpses is an image found in other ancient Near Eastern literature prior to Ezekiel. The *Annals of Sennacherib* proclaim: "With the bodies of their warriors, I filled the plain."[283] Shalmaneser I boasts "I covered the wide plain with the corpses of their warriors."[284] Religious myth is expressed with one of the treaty curses by which the vassal kings of Esarhaddon were bound. It reads: "May Ninurta, leader of the gods, fell you with his fierce arrow, and fill the plain with your corpses, give your flesh to eagles and vultures to feed upon."[285]

In the ancient Near East, a proper burial for the dead was highly esteemed. Not to be buried was regarded as a curse that bears religious weight. Throwing out the bodies of persons to be eaten by birds and wild animals was practiced for persons whose family had broken the oath of a treaty or a contract. An Assyrian contract agreed upon sometime during the reign of Ashurbanipal in the mid-seventh century contains the curse: "May the dogs tear his corpse which is not buried."[286] In 2 Sam 21:1–14, members of Saul's family were executed to exact pay-

---

[281] Bernhard Lang ("Street Theater, Raising the Dead, and the Zoroastrian Connection in Ezekiel's Prophecy," in *Ezekiel and His Book* [ed. Johan Lust; BETL 74; Leuven: Leuven University Press, 1986]) for one has suggested a Persian influence on the Vision of the Dry Bones. This is an interesting possibility but suspect. In the Persian religion it is not clear that belief in resurrection from the dead became prevalent earlier than it did in Israel. In the literature of that period Greenberg (*Ezekiel 21–37*, 748–49) notes that no explicit reference to such a belief can be found. Otto Kaiser, "Tod, Auferstehung und Unsterblichkeit im Alten Testament und im frühen Judentum in religionsgeschichtlichem Zusammenhang bedacht," in Otto Kaiser and E. Lohse, *Tod und Leben* (Kohlhammer-Taschenbucher 1001: Biblische Konfrontationen; Stuttgart: Kohlhammer, 1977) 80; Franz König, *Zarathustras Jenseitsvorstellungen und das Alte Testament* (Vienna: Herder, 1964) 124–25; Klaas Spronk, *Beatific Afterlife in Ancient Israel and in the Ancient Near East* (AOAT 219; Neukirchen-Vluyn: Neukirchener Verlag, 1986) 57–59.

[282] Zimmerli, *Ezekiel* 2.258.

[283] Luckenbill, *The Annals of Sennacherib*, 46.

[284] Ebeling et al., *Die Inschriften der Altassyrischen Könige*, 121.

[285] *ANET*, 538.

[286] Josef Kohler and A. Ungnad, *Assyrische Rechtsurkunden: in Umschrift und Übersetzung nebst einem Index der Personen-namen und Rechtserlauterungen* (Leipzig: Eduard Pfeiffer, 1913) 16, 19.

ment for Saul's violation of a treaty with the Gibeonites. They were left exposed on a hill to be eaten by the birds and wild animals.

The same images in Ezekiel take on a political dimension. The first half of Ezekiel is the judgment of Israel in its failure to live in right relationship with Yhwh's creation of a life-sustaining society, quintessentially with Yhwh at its center. Israel had, in fact, broken their covenant with the Lord. The text in chapter 37 is using this well-known image of unburied corpses, left out, having been already devoured by the birds and wild animals in redress for Israel's violation of their covenant with the Creator.[287] In the Vision of the Dry Bones the curse is reversed [288] for Israel and the nation is brought to life.[289]

Ezek 37:9 presents a very vivid image of resurrection (re-creation): "Prophesy to the breath, prophesy, mortal, and say to the breath: Thus says the Lord God: Come from the four winds, O breath, and breathe upon these slain, that they may live." A similar image appears in the Babylonian Creation Epic where the four winds are called up in the slaying of Tiamat from whose body the earth was created: "He (Marduk) then made a net to enfold Tiamat therein. The four winds he stationed that nothing of her might escape."[290] Greenberg, Gressmann and Zimmerli[291] all note this correspondence between Ezek 37:9 and the Babylonian Creation Epic. As Chester observed in an even more recent article,[292] these four winds denoting the four corners of the earth give a specific and deliberate cosmic meaning to the reference.

Greenspoon posits a significant connection of the Vision of the Dry

---

[287] Block, *The Book of Ezekiel, Chapters 25–48*, 377; Frank C. Fensham, "The Curse of the Dry Bones in Ezekiel 37:1–14 Changed to a Blessing of Resurrection," *JNSL* 13 (1987) 59–60.

[288] Spronk (*Beatific Afterlife in Ancient Israel*, 230) notes that this reversal of the curse through resurrection has its negative counterpart, re-enforcing the image here. In Ezek 39:11–16, instead of revivification, the bones of Gog and his horde are forever buried in order to purify the land.

[289] Block, *The Book of Ezekiel, Chapters 25–48*, 410; Boadt, "The Function of the Salvation Oracles," 15–16; Gross, "Israel's Hope for the Renewal of the State," 127–30.

[290] *The Context of Scripture*, 1.397.

[291] Greenberg, *Ezekiel 1–20*, 58; Hugo Gressmann, *Altorientalische Texten zum Alten Testament* (2d ed.; Berlin: de Gruyter, 1926) 117; Zimmerli, *Ezekiel*, 2.261.

[292] Andrew Chester, "Resurrection and Transformation," in *Auferstehung - Resurrection* (ed. Friedrich Avemarie and Hermann Lichtenberger; Tübingen: Mohr-Siebeck, 2001) 49.

Bones with the theme of the Divine Warrior whose return leads to fertility and productive activity throughout nature.[293] Spronk would challenge that view. He cites as support the Ugaritic cult of the dead, which presents El as giving life: "There, shoulder to shoulder were the brothers, whom El made to stand up in haste. There the name of El revivified the dead, the blessings of the name of El revivified the heroes."[294] In this passage, the invocation of the name of El has creative or life-giving power, since it brings the spirits of the dead back to life. While Baal contributes in his own way to the revivification process in the Ugaritic myths, it is El who gives life because he was believed to be the creator.[295] Baal does not possess the same creative power. This is an important distinction to make in order to understand the significance of the scene of resurrection depicted in Chapter 37.

The final form in the Vision of the Dry Bones does not depict a cycle of nature's rejuvenation. The vision of Yhwh in Ezek 37:1–14 describes Yhwh as the Creator God, not as a god of nature overcoming seasonal rest. The description of the revivification by Yhwh is not connected with the revival of nature but with creation. The point is that this national restoration will be nothing less than an act of creation. The revivification of nature concerns the arrival of the right conditions to bring to flower all which is in hope in the plants. In Ezek 37:1–14, the resources of the people exist no longer; their "bones are dried up"[296] and their "hope has perished" (v. 11). They have nothing in hope within

---

[293] Leonard J. Greenspoon, "The Origin of the Idea of Resurrection," in *Traditions in Transformation, Turning Points in Biblical Faith, Festschrift Honoring Frank Moore Cross* (ed. Baruch Halpern and Jon D. Levenson; Winona Lake, IN: Eisenbrauns, 1981) 292.

[294] Johannes C. De Moor, "El, the Creator," in *The Bible World, Essays in Honor of Cyrus H. Gordon* (ed. Gary Rendsburg, Ruth Adler, Milton Arfa, Nathan H. Winter; New York: KTAV, 1980) 179.

[295] Spronk, *Beatific Afterlife in Ancient Israel*, 173. Both Clifford (*Creation Accounts in the Ancient Near East and in the Bible*, 118–26) and Oswald Loretz (*Ugarit und die Bibel*, 153–60) discuss the differing roles of El and Baal in the Ugaritic Myths.

[296] The notion that "our bones are dried up" is based in the sense that the bones are the seat of perceptions, representative of the whole man (Zimmerli, *Ezekiel*, 2.262). Ps 6:3 (Heb. text) cries: "O Lord, heal me, for my bones are shaking with terror." Ps 35:10 says: "All my bones say: Yhwh who is like you." Prov 17:22 touches the heart of the Ezekiel 37 imagery when it says: "A cheerful heart enlivens the body, but a downcast spirit dries up the bones."

themselves. If the weather and rain are good at the time of the funeral, the corpse does not come back to life.[297] Greenspoon's theory concerning the Divine Warrior providing fertility and productive activity throughout nature misses the point of the dire straits in which the people are depicted in Ezekiel 37. Rather Zimmerli and Gressmann's intuitions are more suasive. The mythic roots of the Vision of the Dry Bones coming to life are grounded in the creation accounts of the ancient Near East. The mythopoeic development here relates to the Creator, not to the god who generates the change of seasons.

Some mythic themes mentioned earlier recur in chapter 37: the gathering of the dispersed and the "covenant of peace." Both of these are reprised in Ezek 37:15–28.[298] 37:21 speaks of the gathering of the dispersed, and 37:26 speaks of the "covenant of peace." This section touches on the elements of national restoration of Israel among the nations through the creation of a stable life-sustaining environment among the community of nations. Within the ancient Near Eastern cultural context, the achievement of this status involved a combination of ethnic, political, territorial, religious and linguistic factors which is discussed in Ezek 37:15–28.[299] Significant for our discussion is the mention of the "covenant of peace" in 37:26.

Eichrodt, Hossfeld, Hanson and Lang, in particular, see chapters 38–39 as an unusual interruption of the natural connection existing between chapters 37 and 40.[300] Yet I propose that, like chapters 40–48, chapters 38–39 are prepared for in chapter 37. Ezek 37:26 in fact issues a double promise: "I will make a covenant of peace with them; it shall be an everlasting covenant with them; and I will bless them and multiply them, and will set my sanctuary among them forever more." The verse promises both a covenant of peace and the setting up of Yhwh's sanctuary among them forever. The setting up of the sanctuary is clearly played out in chapters 40–48.

I suggest that the covenant of peace is established in chapters 38–39. As it is described in chapter 34 something is missing which needs to be

---

[297] Spronk, *Beatific Afterlife in Ancient Israel*, 173.
[298] Müller, *Ursprünge und Strukturen*, 218.
[299] Daniel I. Block, "Nations," in *ISBE* 3 (ed. Geoffrey W. Bromiley; 2d ed.; Grand Rapids: Eerdmans, 1986) 492–94.
[300] Eichrodt, *Ezekiel*, 519–20; Hossfeld, "Das Buch Ezechiel," in *Einleitung in das Alte Testament*, 453; Hanson, *The People Called*, 269; Lang, *Ezechiel*, 111–12.

factored into the equation. How will these newly restored chosen people described in chapters 38–39 as living out this covenant of peace securely and without walls no longer be "plunder for the nations," Ezek 34:28? How will Yhwh close forever the possibility of the losing of his anger against his people through the devastation of the exile or its like ever happening again? If the act of creation is to come to full term, one more thing is necessary. It is here that the final form of Ezekiel introduces into Israel's new cosmogonic myth the myth of the decisive battle where Yhwh gathers all possible future enemies of Israel under the leadership of Gog, leads them against Israel and destroys them. Yhwh, we must remember, is "in charge" of the entire battle from start to finish as was mentioned above. At first it would seem strange that Yhwh would bring such a consummately evil force against his own people living at peace; yet knowing that he will destroy Gog and his hordes he is not only eliminating any potential future enemies of Israel. In this way, Yhwh is, in effect, "disarming" himself so that he will never again be able to loose his anger on them (Ezek 39:29) as he did in the devastating events of 597/587. This decisive battle then becomes the final stroke by which Yhwh establishes his covenant of peace forever. Never again will he unleash his anger against his people. In Ezekiel's telling of the final battle, the Divine Warrior himself effectively lays down his arms! With the decisive battle of chapters 38–39 accomplished the Temple of the victorious God of Israel can be erected in fitting celebration.

Ezekiel 40–48

Much has been written about chapters 40–48, their structure and design and other aspects within them which do not share the focus[301] here: the role of myth in Israelite religion and its influence on the final form's theology of the Temple in the context of cosmogony. The ordering of the temple resembles the creation of the cosmos.[302] In the midst

---

[301] For example: George Cooke, "Some Considerations on the Text and Teaching of Ezekiel, 40–48," *ZAW* 42 (1924) 105–15; Hartmut Gese, *Der Verfassungsentwurf des Ezechiel, (Kap 40–48) Traditionsgeschichtlich Untersucht* (BHT 25; Tübingen: Mohr, 1957); Greenberg, "The Design and Themes of Ezekiel's Program of Restoration," 181–208.

[302] Fisher, "Creation at Ugarit and in the Old Testament," 319.

of what some might mistakenly consider pedantry [303] are mythic referents which helped to form the author's vision of the restored Temple in a fully realized creation.

While in titling other sections I have isolated those areas of the section which deal with myth, and although this section has several such clearly mythopoeic accounts (e.g. 40:2–4; 43:1–12; 47:1–12), I include the whole section here because, in fact, the various elements and dimensions of the building of the Temple are so rooted in the myth of Israel and the ancient Near East that it is the entire section, this building of the "palace" for Yhwh, which expresses the mythopoeic vision of the final author. After the decisive victory finally completing cosmogony, in the ancient Near Eastern understanding of the world of the gods, a palace must be built for the victorious god.[304] A temple is constructed to honor the divine victor. Such a pattern appears twice in the *Enuma Elish*. When Ea killed Apsu, he built his palace upon the slain god and rested in the sanctuary which he established there; when Marduk slew Tiamat, he built Esharra.[305] We read further on that after the creation was completed, the temple Esagila was built for Marduk so that he could rest in it together with his retinue: "We will make a shrine . . . your chamber that shall be our stopping place, we shall find rest therein . . . we shall lay out the shrine, when we come, we shall find rest therein."[306] Such a pattern also appears in the Mesopotamian

---

[303] Levenson (*Theology of the Program of Restoration of Ezekiel 40–48*, 16–17, 23) cautions too quick a dismissal of the detailed description of the restoration of the Temple: "Like the heavens, like day and night (Ps 19:1–4), the structures on Mt. Zion tell the glory of God without words. Were they only human artifacts, such detailed description as the restoration vision gives them would surely be the pedantry some see therein. Since they are designed by God himself, the work of his hands and a non-verbal expression of some truth about him it is essential that they be described with rigorous precision. . . . How much detail is necessary in any endeavor and how much is excessive depends upon the underlying presuppositions about the endeavor and cannot be determined by a surface description of the attention to detail. . . . Intelligent conversation between . . . a past community and one of the present, is possible only where there is *a priori* a commitment to empathy rather than to antipathy."

[304] Victor (Avigdor) Hurowitz, *I Have Built You an Exalted House* (JSOTSup 115; Sheffield: JSOT, 1992) 94; Loretz, *Ugarit und die Bibel*, 159; Weinfeld, "Sabbath, Temple, and the Enthronement of the Lord," 501–2.

[305] *The Context of Scripture*, 1.391–92, 401; Weinfeld, "Sabbath, Temple and the Enthronement of the Lord," 501.

[306] *The Context of Scripture*, 1.271, 398–99, 401.

Myth of Inanna and Ebih.[307] In the Baal Cycle of Ugarit, when Baal is victorious over his rival Mot, after much maneuvering and female persuasion, a palace is built in his honor.[308] Baal's temple is, in fact, a microcosm of creation.[309]

This pattern echoes in Exod 31:12–17. With the completion of the instructions for building the Tabernacle, the commandment concerning the Sabbath appears. The phrasing of the text reflects the connection that existed between creation and the building of the Temple. The erection of the Temple was the completion of creation.[310] The Midrashim also see a connection between the completion of creation and the completion of the building of the Temple: "On the day the work on the Temple was finished, God declared the work of the six days of creation as finished, ... Only when Solomon came and built the Temple would the Holy One, blessed be He, say: Now the work of creating heaven and earth is completed."[311] In Israel there is a relation between the Temple and creation on the one hand, and between Temple and God's victory over his enemies, on the other.[312]

The Gudea cylinders introduce another aspect of temple restoration which highlights the uniqueness of Israel's covenant with Yhwh. After the description of the building of the temple and the opulence of its decoration and furnishing, Gudea prays to the returning deity: "Ningirsu, my master, lord, semen reddened in the deflowering, lord, whose word takes precedence, heir of Enlil, warrior! You commanded me and I have set hand to it for your right. Ningirsu I have built here

---

[307] Henri Limet, "Le poème épique 'Innina et Ebih,' une version des lignes 123 à 182," *Or* 40 (1971) 27.

[308] *The Context of Scripture*, 1.252, 261.

[309] Tsevi Fenton, "Differing Approaches to the Theomachy Myth in Old Testament Writers," in *Studies in Bible and the Ancient Near East, Presented to Samuel E. Lowenstamm on His Seventieth Birthday* (ed. Yitschak Avishur and Joshua Blau; Jerusalem: E. Rubenstein's Publishing House, 1978) 345–46; Fisher, "Creation at Ugarit and in the Old Testament," 318–20.

[310] Hurowitz, *I Have Built You an Exalted House*, 95; Weinfeld, "Sabbath, Temple and the Enthronement of the Lord," 502; Peter Weimar, "Sinai und Schöpfung, Komposition und Theologie der Priesterschriftlichen Sinaigeschichte," *RB* 95 (1988) 371.

[311] Rivka Ulmer, *Pesiqta Rabbati, A Synoptic Edition of Pesiqta Rabbati Based upon All Extant Manuscripts and the Editio Princeps* 1 (South Florida Studies in the History of Judaism 155; Atlanta: Scholars Press, 1997) 84–85.

[312] Weinfeld, "Sabbath, Temple and the Enthronement of the Lord," 508.

your house for you, may you enter it in joy!"[313] The precision and devotion with which the restoration of the Temple was carried out is also not without its ancient Near Eastern parallels. Esarhaddon was not bashful about proclaiming his aggressive practice of piety toward the gods:

> The images of the great divinities I made more beautiful than they were before. I made them exceedingly splendid, I made their magnificence awe-inspiring . . . (The image) of Ile-Amurru, . . . I restored. (The images) of Abshshu and Abtagigi, . . . I restored and returned to their places. Aia, queen of Der . . . I returned to the temple, to Der, their city. . . . Shamash of Larsa . . . I returned. . . . Energalanna, the shrine of Ishtar, my lady, . . . I carefully sought out its location, with handsome bricks from the kiln I repaired its damage. . . . Esarhaddon, king of the universe, . . . completely renews the shrines of (every) metropolis, who establishes therein traditional cults.[314]

When Esarhaddon completed rebuilding Esagila, the Temple of Marduk in Babylon he heralded his largesse: "The gods and the goddesses who had lived there, who had caused the thunderstorm and flood, whose gaze had become saddened, I lifted them from their decaying surroundings. I polished their dusty trains. I cleaned their soiled garments and caused them to live in their sanctuaries forever."[315]

Ashurbanipal asserts with pride: "At that time Ehulhul, the temple of Sin in Harran . . . I restored its ruins and laid its foundation platform. . . . I grasped the hands of Sin (?) and caused him to enter amid rejoicing and caused him to take up his abode."[316] Nabonidus of Babylon records his own meticulous devotion to detail: "Thereupon I carefully executed the command of his (Sin's) great godhead, I was not careless nor negligent but set in motion people . . . whom Sin, the king of gods, had entrusted to me, I built anew the Ehulhul, the temple of Sin, and completed this work. I led in procession Sin, Ningal, Nusky and Sadarnunna from Shuanna, my royal city, and brought (them) in joy and happiness (into the temple), installing them on a permanent dais."[317]

---

[313] Jacobsen, *The Harps That Once* . . . , 427.
[314] *ARAB*, 2.262, 282, 284.
[315] Borger, *Die Inschriften Asarhaddons*, 23.
[316] *ARAB*, 2.253, 254.
[317] *ANET*, 563.

In Ezekiel, the restored Temple is described from 40:5 to 42:20. To what extent was this description influenced by other ancient Near Eastern temples constructed as dwelling places for their gods? The answer is both greatly and indirectly. The book's description is based on the structure of Solomon's Temple.[318] At present there are at least two dozen excavated Temples that may be compared to Solomon's Temple. Its plan is rooted in the religious architecture of the second millennium B.C.E. in Canaan and northern Syria. The temples at Ebla, Megiddo, Hazor, Emar, Tell Munbaqa and Shechem are prototypes. Later examples are those of the eighth-century temples at Tell Tainat and 'Ain Dara in northern Syria.[319] This "long-room" plan was a basic three-room structure with a portico, a main hall and a small shrine area at the back of the main hall.[320] In cooperation with Hiram of Tyre, Solomon contracted Phoenician builders to construct his Temple. They used the plan familiar to them.[321] Examples of parallel stylistic architectural features described in Ezekiel's Temple and discussed in other ancient Near Eastern temples are the palmettes (40:16) on the column capitals,[322] the construction of the wall separating the inner sanctuary from the main hall (41:3),[323] the ambulatory chambers (42:10).[324]

In 40:2–4, the prophet is brought to Israel and set down upon a very high mountain with a city to the south. The Temple Mount and its Temple are not named, but presented in mythic dimension. They cannot be seen in purely historical and geographical terms, but at least

---

[318] Thomas A. Busink, *Der Tempel von Jerusalem von Salomo bis Herodes* (Leiden: Brill, 1970) 58–61; Amihai Mazar, *Archaeology of the Land of the Bible* (AB Reference Library; New York: Doubleday, 1990) 376; George R. H. Wright, *Ancient Building in South Syria and Palestine* I (HO 70; Leiden: Brill, 1985) 254, 260, 465–66.

[319] Volkmar Fritz, "What Can Archaeology Tell Us About Solomon's Temple?" *BAR* 13.4 (1987) 40, 43, 46; Mazar, *Archaeology of the Land of the Bible*, 377; Monson, "The New 'Ain Dara Temple," 22.

[320] Fritz, "What Can Archaeology Tell Us About Solomon's Temple?" 43; Monson, "The New 'Ain Dara Temple," 31.

[321] Fritz, "What Can Archaeology Tell Us About Solomon's Temple?" 44–45; Monson, "The New 'Ain Dara Temple," 35.

[322] *ANEP*, 214; Mazar, *Archaeology of the Land of the Bible*, 475.

[323] Wright, *Ancient Building in South Syria and Palestine* I, 256; Monson, "The New 'Ain Dara Temple," 23–24.

[324] Wright, *Ancient Building in South Syria and Palestine* I, 260; Monson, "The New 'Ain Dara Temple," 28, 30.

in part, must be understood in the light of mystic concepts of a cosmic mountain to grasp their significance for the final form. They are a mythopoeic realization of heaven on earth, Paradise, the Garden of Eden. Here, order was established at creation and was renewed and maintained through rituals and ceremonies. It was the sacred center where Yhwh established his dwelling, where the three foundational elements of creation, kingship and Temple come together.[325] Here there is security, inviolability and a peace which no event in history can thwart. Only allusion to this mythic realm can make sense of the description. It is a symbol of "divine promise, of assurance of things humanly impossible and yet hoped for, of a grace which works a change in the very structure of human character."[326] As mentioned above in the discussion on chapter 28, Solomon's Temple was located where it was, not only for political but also for religious reasons.

Following the description of the Temple itself is, at the beginning of chapter 43, the entrance of the divine כבוד into his dwelling and the description of the altar. The throne of Baal is referred to as his resting place. The entrance of Yhwh into his sanctuary was interpreted in Israel as "rest," similar to the rest of God on the seventh day of creation.[327] The glory of Yhwh filling his dwelling is the guarantee that the continuance of Israel as a people can be put to question no longer.[328] Ps 132:14 puts on the lips of Yhwh: "This is my resting place forever; here I will reside, for I have desired it."

The following verses speak in mythic terms of the reaffirmation of the Creator God to the land and to his people. Verse 3 talks about the God of Israel coming like the sound of mighty waters, evocative of the image of the powerful waters of chaos,[329] but here used to describe him whose power is greater than the waters of chaos, which were imaged only a few chapters before by the flood of Gog and his vast hordes. The Gudea cylinder speaks of the entrance of Ningirsu into his temple with a similar image: "The warrior Ningirsu entered the

---

[325] Levenson, *The Theology of the Program of Restoration*, 8; Stager, "Jerusalem as Eden," 37, 39.

[326] Levenson, *Theology of the Program of Restoration*, 161.

[327] *The Context of Scripture*, 1.252, 271.

[328] Cohn, *Cosmos, Chaos, and the World to Come*, 154; Weimar, "Sinai und Schöpfung," 372.

[329] May, "Some Cosmic Connotations of *Mayim Rabbim*, Many Waters," 17, 20.

house, the owner of the house had come, . . . The warrior's entering his house was a storm roaring into battle."[330] Pss 29:4–11 and 93:4, psalms of enthronement, speak of the glory and power of God thundering over mighty waters. In Ezekiel 43 we have the coming of the mighty throne-chariot of God to be enthroned in his restored sanctuary.

In v. 7 Yhwh affirms: "This is the place of my throne and the place for the soles of my feet, where I will reside among my people forever." The image is one of Yhwh entering the holy of holies and resting his feet on his footstool. In his mourning for Baal, El's footstool is mentioned: "Thereupon the gracious one, the kindly god, descends from the throne, sits on the footstool, (descends) from the footstool and sits on the earth."[331] During the period of Baal's captivity in the netherworld, Lady Asherah chooses Ashtar the Tyrant as a substitute to sit on Baal's empty throne, but his feet don't reach to the footstool.[332] The ark of the covenant was considered to be the place for the soles of Yhwh's feet (כפות).[333] Esarhaddon in his own efforts at temple restoration mentions "a footstool, covered with ruddy gold, for Tashmetu, the great goddess, who dwells in Ekua, the holy of holies of Marduk, in Babylon, I built anew."[334] The fact that Yhwh is barefoot also has interesting ancient Near Eastern resonance. The temple at 'Ain Dara in northern Syria contains two sets of footprints on the floor slabs. Each footprint is more than three feet long. Two footprints appear on the first slab in the portico area and a left footprint is on the second slab there. The right footprint appears thirty feet away at the entrance to the main hall. A stride of thirty feet would belong to a person (or a god) about sixty-five feet tall.[335] Ezek 43:7 suggests that Yhwh was barefoot as was the deity at 'Ain Dara.[336] The supra-human height of the god gives a spatial image to Yhwh's glory filling the Temple.

Verses 7 and 9 also speak of the defiling of Yhwh's Holy Name by funeral sacrifices in the Temple area with the corpse of the dead king

---

[330] Jacobsen, *The Harps That Once* . . . , 429.
[331] *The Context of Scripture*, 1.167.
[332] *The Context of Scripture*, 1.269.
[333] Martin Metzger, *Königsthron und Gottesthron* (AOAT 15; Neukirchen-Vluyn: Neukirchener Verlag, 1985) 358–59.
[334] *ARAB*, 2.252.
[335] Monson, "The New 'Ain Dara Temple," 28; Stager, "Jerusalem as Eden," 46.
[336] Stager, "Jerusalem as Eden," 46.

present. Such sacrifices were also known in Ugarit and Mari. Loretz[337] suggests here that the final form is denouncing this Canaanite heritage which, from the witness of these verses, existed at least until the time of the prophet.

Verses 13–17 deal with the description of the altar. Block in his commentary notes: "In the past it has been fashionable to find inspiration for this altar design in the Babylonian ziggurat (terraced temple towers). . . . the resemblances with the Solomonic altar are more striking."[338] While I accept that the final form's description of the altar could as easily come from the Temple in Jerusalem as from the Babylonian ziggurat to which it is often compared,[339] I also ask from the research presented above where the design of the Solomonic altar came from. As noted above, in answer to the question of the extent of influence of the ancient Near East on the design of the altar in Ezekiel, it was more than likely influenced greatly, but indirectly.

Verses 14 and 15 each contain Hebrew words (v. 14: חֵיק הָאָרֶץ; v. 15: הַרְאֵל) which can be understood in more than one sense. The first, חֵיק הָאָרֶץ, describes the base platform of the altar of the envisaged Temple and is translated "the base on the ground." In Akkadian there is an equivalent phrase, "bosom/chest of the earth" (*irat erṣetim*)[340] denoting the upper surface of the netherworld in the sense of foundation and in New Babylonian building descriptions of the temple of Babylon it is used to indicate the foundation site of the temple tower. Both Nabopolassar and Nebuchadnezzar refer to establishing the temple tower on the breast of the underworld.[341] The second, הַרְאֵל, denotes the summit of the altar with its four horns and is translated "mountain of God." The purpose of the altar is not to appease an angry God, but to restore rupture in the community and the cosmos:

---

[337] Loretz, *Ugarit und die Bibel*, 127.

[338] Block, *The Book of Ezekiel, Chapters 25–48*, 596.

[339] W. F. Albright, "The Babylonian Temple-Tower and the Altar of Burnt-Offering," *JBL* 39 (1920) 139; Fohrer, *Ezechiel*, 238; Roland de Vaux, *Ancient Israel, Its Life and Institutions* (trans. John McHugh; McGraw-Hill paperbacks; New York: McGraw-Hill, 1965) 412; originally published as *Les Institutions de L'Ancien Testament* (Paris: Les Editions du Cerf, 1958–60).

[340] Garfinkel, "Studies in Akkadian Influences in the Book of Ezekiel," 76–77.

[341] Fohrer, *Ezechiel*, 238; Stephen Langdon, *Die neubabylonische Königsinschriften* (VAB 4; Leipzig: Hinrichs, 1912) 61, 73.

the altar cleanses the House of the effects of chaos.[342] Nabopolassar and Nebuchadnezzar not only establish the foundation of the temple tower on the bosom of the earth, but they also construct it high enough to reach the mountain of god.[343] The temple tower was considered in Babylonian theology the link of heaven and earth, founded in the underworld and reaching to heaven. These phrases in Ezek 43:14,15 are not only building instructions. They are also cosmic references deliberately placed in the description of the altar of burnt offering. The Jerusalem Temple was understood as a cosmic institution. The appointments within the Temple itself were conceived as symbolic of the cosmos and reminiscent of the great cosmogonic acts of Yhwh.[344] The Temple played a very significant role in the book's cosmogony.

The last mythic reference that needs to be looked at in this section is 44:1–3 which speaks of the closed gate. 43:18–26 describe the seven day ritual for purification of the holy space. It parallels the *akitu*, the cleansing of the temple in the Babylonian New Year ceremony which occurs after the god Marduk has taken possession of his house. 44:1–3 also parallels, but in a contrastive way, the Babylonian New Year festival. The thematic of the festival was the celebration of the eternally reappearing first creation, when the sun-god conquered the dragon of chaos and darkness. This is seen in the reading of the Epic of Creation of Marduk at Babylon. This same association of the New Year with the creation of the world survived in the rabbinic interpretation of the Jewish New Year festival.[345] The Babylonian festival contained the ritual of the "opening of the gate."[346] This sacred gate apparently

---

[342] Gorman, *The Ideology of Ritual*, 37; Stevenson, *The Vision of Transformation*, 142.

[343] Michael Fishbane, *Biblical Interpretation in Ancient Israel* (Oxford: Clarendon, 1985) 370; Langdon, *Die neubabylonische Königsinschriften*, 61, 73; de Vaux, *Ancient Israel, Its Life and Institutions*, 412.

[344] Albright, "The Babylonian Temple Tower and the Altar of Burnt-Offering," 140; Jon D. Levenson, "The Jerusalem Temple in Devotional and Visionary Experience," *Jewish Spirituality from the Bible through the Middle Ages* (ed. Arthur Green; World Spirituality: An Encyclopedic History of the Religious Quest 13; London: Routledge & Kegan Paul, 1986) 51–52.

[345] Jacob Klein, "Akitu," *ABD* 1 (New York: Doubleday, 1992) 139; Herbert G. May, "Some Aspects of Solar Worship at Jerusalem," *ZAW* 55 (1937) 278–79; Stevenson, *The Vision of Transformation*, 139.

[346] *ANET*, 334.

remained closed to all except on the day of the festival when Marduk would exit and return through it in procession. Verse 2 provides one reason why the gate is to remain closed. Yhwh is described here for the first and only time in the book with the full title, "Yhwh, the God of Israel." Because he has entered by this gate, the gate must be closed and remain closed. The closed gate proclaims the majesty of the one who has entered there. Another reason the gate is to remain closed is mentioned in 43:7, 9. Yhwh has entered his sanctuary for all time. There will be no need to open it for a new departure.[347] Yhwh has taken possession of his sanctuary.

The contrastive parallel continues. The prince (נשיא) occupies the gate through which Yhwh has taken possession of his Temple. Whereas in Babylon the king was responsible for significant parts of the New Year's Festival, here he must be content with eating a meal in a permanently closed doorway. His status is diminished. He no longer takes the god by the hand and leads him into the house. Yhwh comes alone. Yhwh is power holder of the territory.[348] He is king.

Ezek 47:1–48:35 reflects two influences of religious myths of Israel as well as the surrounding cultures of the ancient Near East. The first is the vision of the water flowing from the Temple (47:1–12). Cosmic mountains were traditionally situated above the primordial waters whose fertility provided luxuriant growth. In the ancient Near Eastern understanding, the earth is an island floating on cosmic waters that rise to the surface where they benefit humankind. In Jacob's last words to his sons, the phrase "blessings of the deep that lies beneath" (Gen 49:25) reflects a similar understanding. In an orderly cosmos, the blessing of these cosmic waters flowing up from the deep became the source of the sacred rivers that watered the four quarters of the earth. They signified the orderliness and tranquility of God's creation, on which humans could rely, and so the abode of God in Jerusalem is depicted as having water flowing from it. Yhwh has subdued the waters of chaos so that they provide life-giving nourishment for plant, animal and

---

[347] Block, *The Book of Ezekiel, Chapters 25–48*, 615; Eckhard Unger, *Babylon, Die Heilige Stadt nach der Beschreibung der Babylonier* (Berlin: de Gruyter, 1931) 204; Zimmerli, *Ezekiel* 2.440.

[348] Block, *The Book of Ezekiel, Chapters 24–48*, 615–16; Stevenson, *The Vision of Transformation*, 53.

human life. Turning the desert into an orderly and fertile place is a way of turning chaos into cosmos.[349] In the mythic literature of Ugarit, El's home is at the source of the waters.[350] These springs were "perpetually recurring streams of living water productive of fruitfulness and abundance bestowed by divine munificence."[351] In the *Enuma Elish* after Marduk slays Tiamat, he founded the Great Sanctuary in her remains and from her eyes he caused the Euphrates and Tigris to flow forth.[352] Cylinder B of Gudea from the late third millennium speaks of the introduction of Ningirsu and his consort, Baba, to their new temple home whose goblets in the dining hall were compared to the Tigris and Euphrates because of their continually overflowing abundance.[353] There was a resultant prosperity to the land similar to that described in Ezek 47:1–12 because of the presence of the god in his temple. The abundant fish, heavy laden fruit trees, medicinal leaves are all reminiscent of the arrival of Ningirsu in his temple and the effect his presence had.[354]

In the palace at Mari, built in the early second millennium, amidst other wall paintings, is one of two goddesses with vases from which four streams of water flow and vegetation sprouts. A thirteenth century B.C.E. ivory inlay from the Assyrian capital of Ashur depicts water flowing from a mountain god in all directions.[355] In both these cases, the gods not only pour the water. In fact, they are the vital power of water itself. The text distinguishes between the water and the source, Yhwh's dwelling, but the parallels are otherwise evident. The symbolism here is cosmic. The stream heals the land from the effects of chaos

---

[349] Cohn, *Cosmos, Chaos, and the World to Come*, 154; Loretz, *Ugarit und die Bibel*, 160; May, "Cosmic Connotations of *Mayim Rabbim*, Many Waters," 21; Seow, "The Deep," *ABD* 2 (New York: Doubleday, 1992) 125; Stager, "Jerusalem as Eden," 37, 39, 41.

[350] *The Context of Scripture*, 1.247; Seow, "The Deep," *ABD* 2 (New York: Doubleday, 1992) 125.

[351] Elizabeth Douglas van Buren, *Symbols of the Gods in Mesopotamian Art* (AnOr 23; Rome: Pontifical Biblical Institute, 1945) 124–25.

[352] *The Context of Scripture*, 1.398–99.

[353] Jacobsen, *The Harps That Once . . .* , 386–87, 439–40.

[354] Jacobsen, *The Harps That Once . . .* , 438; Steven Tuell, "The Rivers of Paradise," in *The God Who Creates, Essays in Honor of W. Sibley Towner* (ed. Willaim P. Brown and S. Dean McBride Jr.; Grand Rapids: Eerdmans , 2000) 182–83.

[355] Buren, *Symbols of the Gods in Mesopotamian Art*, 128; Stager, "Jerusalem as Eden," 39, 41.

which was symbolized in the desert.[356] It perpetually restores and regenerates Yhwh's creation.

The second influence is evident in 48:30–35 which speaks of the exits of the city. Block notes that it is strikingly unconventional to depict a city with twelve gates. Though the Jerusalem of Ezekiel's time had six gates, city walls were usually designed with only one. There is, however, a notable exception to this pattern.[357] Not surprisingly, the Babylonian temple tower of Marduk, Etemenanki, was accessible through twelve gates. These were not distributed equally as in Ezekiel, but rather three on the north wall, two on the east wall, four on the south wall, and three on the west wall.[358] The naming of the Temple gates after the twelve tribes of Israel in the final form parallels in several ways the practice of naming the nine gates of the city of Babylon after the Babylonian deities: Marduk, Zababa (Ninurta), Enlil, Urash, Shamash, Adad, Lugalgirra (Nergal), Ishtar, and Sin.[359] Gates were named after the patron deity of the city in Babylonia to which the road exiting from them led and were the processional entrance points of each god at the New Year's *akitu* festival in honor of Marduk.[360] The image is comparable to that evoked by Ps 122:1–4, "I was glad when they said to me, 'Let us go to the house of the Lord!' Our feet are standing within your gates, O Jerusalem. . . . To it the tribes go up, the tribes of the Lord, as was decreed for Israel, to give thanks to the name of the Lord." The name Babylon itself was interpreted as meaning the "gate of the gods" and signifies it as a holy city.[361] In like manner, Jerusalem will receive Yhwh's chosen people through its twelve gates where they will meet Yhwh, for Jerusalem's name is יהוה־שמה, Yhwh is there.

---

[356] Marco Nobile, *Ecclesiologia Biblica: traiettorie storico-culturali e teologiche* (Collana Studi biblici 30; Bologna: Edizioni Dehoniane, 1996) 131; Stevenson, *The Vision of Transformation*, 142.

[357] Block, *The Book of Ezekiel, Chapters 25–48*, 736.

[358] Unger, *Babylon, die Heilige Stadt*, 200.

[359] Block, *The Book of Ezekiel, Chapters 25–48*, 738; Donald J. Wiseman, *Nebuchadrezzar and Babylon* (Schweich Lectures of the British Academy 1983; Oxford: Oxford University Press, 1985) 46.

[360] Unger, *Babylon, die Heilige Stadt*, 65–67, and plate 57.

[361] Römer, *Sumerische Königshymnen*, 51; Unger, *Babylon, die Heilige Stadt*, 201.

CHAPTER 6

Summary and Conclusions

For millennia, the religious imagination of humankind has struggled to understand and explain the world of powers and forces beyond their own whose effects had impact on their lives even as the presence of these forces were often unseen. The role of myth in the ancient Near East to understand the phenomena of nature and the workings of the human body had far reaching effects. The religious myths of the people were not static but alive and active, constantly integrating new data and describing new divine activity.

In this work we have studied the influence of a mythic frame of reference on the final form of Ezekiel by forming a hermeneutic, in the broad sense of the term, which considers the role of myth in Israel and the ancient Near East. Fundamental in humankind's grasping to understand was the quest to know how we and our world came into being. Out of the answer to that question the creation myths of the various ancient civilizations were formed. These cosmogonic myths of the ancient Near East differed between one another and in comparison to the modern understanding of creation which is limited to the origins of our physical world. The ancient Near Eastern understanding of creation included the creation of a stable, life-sustaining society. It was these religious myths that formed the religious consciousness of the people, the hopes and expectations of their belief system. After the fall of Jerusalem and the destruction of the Temple, Israel's own creation myth was in tatters and was looking for an alternative explanation: either Yhwh had been defeated by Marduk, having ruthlessly abandoned his promises and his people or. . . . In the context of this cognitive dissonance between traditional theology and the experience of the exile, the Book of Ezekiel struggled to resignify its creation myth, which included an ending that had yet to be realized.

Parallels do not prove Ezekiel's dependence on any particular myth. The hermeneutic developed allows us to put the future events foretold in Ezekiel in a context of the religious search of the region at that time. Understanding the myths of the region is a precondition for understanding the intention of the final form. It is important for understanding how the believing community who received it found life in the story.

The placement and function of chapters 38–39 in the final form have long been a source of discussion. I have proposed here that in the final form the book is presenting a new ending to the Israelite cosmogonic myth, and that in this cosmogonic myth, understandable and yet distinct in the context of the religious myths of the ancient Near East, chapters 38–39, the decisive battle and defeat of Gog and his hordes, must take place if the covenant of peace promised in chapters 34–37 is to be realized and the Temple is to be re-established (chapters 40–48) whose function is both symbol and fulfillment of cosmogony's completion in the Israelite creation myth.

Getting a sense of the significance of myth in the ancient Near East gave us entry into the hermeneutic for understanding the role of myth in Ezekiel. The central religious myths of a people reveal what they consider essential in the supernatural experience. The *Chaoskampf* myth is one of these central myths which also has particular relevance to chapters 38–39. It is a myth concerned with the maintenance of the cosmos; it is a part of the myth of creation. It is in the context of cosmogony that the *Chaoskampf* myth finds its fullest meaning. Throughout the ancient Near East the point of creation and the truth to which the creation myth testifies is not the ordering of physical creation but the power of a god to effect the emergence of a stable community in a benevolent and life-sustaining order. This is the end goal of creation myths. Cosmogonic myths of the ancient Near East give concrete expression to the belief that the universe is a purposeful and meaningful creation fashioned by divine intelligence with order, peace and prosperity. The final form of Ezekiel presents a new mythic conclusion to the Israelite creation account that would give the exiles hope.

Myth for the authors of the OT was a reservoir of symbols which expressed the hopes and fears of the faith of Israel. All myths have histories and no one version is any more true or more original than any other version. They reflect and endure the social order and so are changing even as they are felt as the same myth. The *Chaoskampf* myth in the context of the ancient Near East was significant in the formation of royal theology, and in the raising of a political theme to a supernatural level. When played out in human history, the conflict represents a realization of what the gods had already created in their own world. Royal theology was significant, as royalty helped to bring about the ultimate goal of the creation myth: the benign and successful working together of the elements that promote human life.

Gog and Magog had a significant impact on non-canonical literature after the exile. They had, so to speak, "a shelf life," which lasted over a thousand years. The similarities and dissimilarities with other uses of the *Chaoskampf* myths in Israel and the ancient Near East mark out clearly this reformulation of the old myth in the distinctive style of Ezekiel in response to a time of crisis. To what are all these references in chapters 38–39 leading? In what context would they be more comprehensible? Why would Yhwh call this quintessential enemy to attack his people living securely in peace under his covenant? What was the significance of the magnitude and scope of the enemy force gathered against Israel for this decisive battle? If the covenant of peace promised in chapters 34–37 is to come about such a decisive battle must take place that Yhwh would put an end to the possibility of unloosing his anger in the destruction of his people, Israel, ever again.

The influences of myth in Ezekiel are many and can be seen at various points in the book from its very beginnings to its final chapters: (1) 1:4–28, the throne chariot vision; (2) 8–11, Yhwh's departure from the Temple; (3) 25–32, the Oracles against the Foreign Nations; (4) 33–37, the restoration of Israel; and (5) 40–48, the restoration of the Temple and the Land. Each in its own way makes a contribution to constructing a new Israelite cosmogonic myth.

In the prophet's vision of Yhwh in the throne chariot, we are introduced to a mythic portrayal of the power of God himself in the two constituent elements of creator and judge who will pronounce a verdict against his unfaithful people. Chapters 8–11 speak of Yhwh's departure from his Temple. It is precisely the differences between the mythic departures of other gods of the region from their dwellings and the departure of Yhwh from his, that makes it clear that his sovereignty as Creator is not put into question by this divine abandonment. In Yhwh's withdrawal, he suffered no diminishment in power or status by removing himself from his sanctuary. It was judgment that would lead to restored creation. It is Israel's sin that caused his departure, not a threatening enemy attack.

The Oracles against the Nations, chapters 25–32, serve a particular function. This is key to their understanding. These oracles are not an earlier part of the decisive battle, brought to conclusion in 38–39; rather, they serve a different purpose, suggesting metaphorically the nature of Israel's failing and the reason for the fall of Jerusalem in chapter 33. They reinforce Israel's judgment. In the Oracles against the Nations the central image confronted is their relationship to the Creator. These nations are judged by Yhwh for disrupting the right order of creation and the proper development of a stable, life-sustaining community, as a result. They are presented as object lesson to instruct Israel about its future because of its impotence in initiating the needed moral reform.

Chapter 34 begins the oracles of hope and restoration. It focuses on a reorientation of community leadership, using the image of shepherd which has its own ancient Near Eastern mythic underpinnings. The text of Ezekiel makes it clear in this chapter that Yhwh is the only true shepherd. This is meant not only to exclude foreign gods but also to clarify the royal theology of Israel. Here, for the first time the covenant of peace is promised. When the structure of the myth is reviewed in its Egyptian, Canaanite and Mesopotamian counterparts, the infidelities of Israel and the resultant exile show clear parallels with the Atra-Hasis and Gilgamesh myths, and with the avenging wrath of Hathor and Anat. The closing verses of chapter 34 clearly described a pouring of peace into the earth. This was amplified in the verdant fertility and abundant yield presented in chapter 36. Yet there was no demonstration of the promise that Israel would no longer be prey to the nations and forced to endure their insults.

The emphasis in this chapter is no longer on judgment. Chapter 37, the Vision of the Dry Bones, speaks of the reconstitution of the nation. The national restoration will be nothing less than an act of new creation. How will this newly restored nation, described in chapters 38–39 as living out this covenant of peace securely and without walls, no longer be "plunder for the nations" (Ezek 34:28)? If Yhwh's act of creation is to come to full term, with a community of benevolent and life-sustaining order, forever unthreatened by destruction, one more thing is necessary.

At the end of chapter 37, the text again mentions the covenant of peace in the context of a double promise: the covenant of peace and the re-establishment of Yhwh's dwelling place among his people. Both elements of the promise will last forever. In chapters 38–39 the promised covenant of peace, put in place and assured by the decisive battle, is established. Any possible hostile enemy threat to Israel in the future was destroyed and Yhwh, victorious in battle, established his covenant of peace with his people, Israel, forever. The decisive battle, which in this case would be the final battle because its effects would last forever, parallels the flowering of the earth in chapter 36 as the second part of the fulfillment of the covenant of peace promised in chapter 34. And the author(s) of the final form and its readers could understand this thanks to prior Israelite myths often paralleled in the ancient Near East. Here Yhwh destroys any future weapons he could ever use against Israel as he used Babylon at the time of the exile.

This context, the destruction of any possible future enemy of Israel, was the only suitable setting for the return of the Creator to his dwelling in chapter 43. Such a victory must be celebrated in mythic proportions with the building of a new palace. The Restoration of the Temple (Ezek 40–48), the building of the palace for the victorious god at the conclusion of cosmogony, celebrates the completion of the creation of a stable, life-sustaining society. What is the final form's theology of the Temple in the context of cosmogony? The ordering of the Temple resembles the creation of the cosmos. In the theology of Israel, the Temple and its function are symbol and fulfillment of the benevolent and life-sustaining order of the stable community which completes cosmogony.

The final form was not about setting up a myth that would endorse the claims of a ruling family. Its religious myth would bring about the replication of the heavenly realm through the direct involvement of the heavenly king, the God of Israel. In the course of developing this myth, the Book of Ezekiel challenges the veracity of a commonly accepted set of Israelite and ancient Near Eastern mythic beliefs about monarchy.

In it, the author re-establishes the centrality of Yhwh, the Creator, and establishes a firm basis in religious myth for the sure hope that the Creator God will bring his act of creation to completion. It is in that context that we have looked at the religious myths of Israel and the ancient Near East and their parallels in Ezekiel.

This decisive battle, Yhwh's final redemptive act to insure the perduring generativity of his creation, was fought so that those dwelling securely without walls could enjoy the divine rest of Yhwh, sovereign Creator. They could continue to dwell in praise of their Creator, in unabated tranquility, and in the good order that would insure the perpetuity of creation rather than its annihilation. The destruction of Gog and his hordes in chapters 38–39 is of its very nature a cosmogonic combat.

This restored social context accounts for the disappearance of all occurrences of the recognition formula after chapter 39. There will exist, after the decisive battle, universally among the nations only those who recognize Yhwh, their Creator. There would be no need to distinguish between those who did and those who did not. In the latter years, recognition of Yhwh the Creator by each and every one of his creatures would be inherent, and calling for recognition would seem strangely anachronistic.

The Gog-Magog passage is not an unconnected insertion into an Ezekiel anthology. It belongs to the final chapter of the Ezekiel cosmogony after which a regal dwelling place is built for the Creator God Yhwh to celebrate his victory. Not only does its inner content reflect the mythic elements of Israel and the ancient Near East, its placement in the overall structure of the book also reflects their mythic patterns. While Yhwh was portrayed more fully sovereign than other gods, the religious myth of this final form was not discontinuous or independent from the religious myths of the region and was played out in this way because of its rootedness in these very myths. The final form mythopoeically reshaped the truths these myths struggled to articulate in order to renew Israelite faith in their sovereign Creator God and to give hope to the people of its time. Yhwh's creation will come to completion: they as a people will be transformed, they will live at peace among the nations and Yhwh will dwell with them forever in his temple: "The Lord is there," יהוה־שמה.

Bibliography

Primary Sources

Elliger, Karl, and Wilhelm Rudolph, eds. *Biblia Hebraica Stuttgartensia*. 3d ed. Stuttgart: Deutsche Bibelgesellschaft, 1987.

Ziegler, Joseph, ed. *Septuaginta, Vetus Testamentum Graecum, 16.1 Ezechiel*. 2d ed. Göttingen: Vandenhoeck & Ruprecht, 1977.

Secondary Sources:

Ackerman, Susan. "A Marzēaḥ in Ezekiel 8:7–13?" *HTR* 82 (1989) 267–81.

———. *Under Every Green Tree: Popular Religion in Sixth-Century Judah*. HSM 46. Atlanta: Scholars Press, 1992.

Ahlström, Gösta. *Royal Administration and National Religion in Ancient Palestine*. Studies in the History of the Ancient Near East 1. Leiden: Brill, 1982.

Ahroni, Reuben. "The Gog Prophecy and the Book of Ezekiel." *HAR* 1 (1977) 1–27.

Albrektson, Bertil. *History and the Gods: An Essay on the Idea of Historical Events as Divine Manifestations in the Ancient Near East and in Israel*. ConBOT 1. Lund: CWK Gleerup, 1967.

Albright, William F. "The Babylonian Temple-Tower and the Altar of Burnt-Offering." *JBL* 39 (1920) 137–42.

———. "Gog and Magog." *JBL* 43 (1924) 378–85.

———. "The Place of the Old Testament in the History of Thought." In *History, Archaeology and Christian Humanism*, 83–100. New York: McGraw-Hill, 1964.

Allen, Leslie C. "The Structure and Intention of Ezekiel I." *VT* 43 (1993) 145–61.

———. *Ezekiel 1–19*. Word Biblical Commentary 28a. Dallas: Word Books, 1994.

———. *Ezekiel 20–48*. Word Biblical Commentary 29. Dallas: Word Books, 1990.

Astour, Michael C. "Ezekiel's Prophecy of Gog and the Cuthean Legend of Naram-Sin." *JBL* 95 (1976) 567–79.

Bartelmus, Rüdiger. "Die Tierwelt in der Bibel II." In *Gefährten und Feinde des Menschen*. Edited by Bernd Janowski, Ute Neumann-Gorsolke, and Uwe Gleßmer, 283–306. Neukirchen-Vluyn: Neukirchener Verlag, 1993.

Barthélemy, Dominique. *Critique Textuelle de l'Ancien Testament 3*. OBO 50. Göttingen: Vandenhoeck & Ruprecht, 1992.

Batto, Bernard F. "The Covenant of Peace." *CBQ* 49 (1987) 187–211.

———. "The Reed Sea: *Requiescat in Pace*." *JBL* 102 (1983) 27–35.

———. *Slaying the Dragon: Mythmaking in the Biblical Tradition*. Louisville: Westminster/John Knox, 1992.

———. "The Sleeping God: An Ancient Near Eastern Motif of Divine Sovereignty." *Bib* 68 (1987) 153–77.

Baumgartner, Walter et al., eds. *The Hebrew and Aramaic Dictionary of the Old Testament*, 1–5. Translated and edited by Mervyn E. J. Richardson. Leiden: Brill, 1994–2000. Originally published as *Hebräisches und aramäisches Lexikon zum Alten Testament*, 1–6 (Leiden: Brill, 1967–96).

Becker, Joachim. "Erwängungen zur ezechielischen Frage." In *Künder des Wortes: Beitrage zur Theologie der Propheten*. Edited by Lothar Ruppert, Peter Weimar, Erich Zenger, 137–150. Wurzburg: Echter, 1982.

———. *Ezechiele-Daniele*. Translated by Gianni Poletti. Assisi: Cittadella Editrice, 1989. Originally published as *Der priesterliche Prophet, Das Buch Ezechiel* (SKKAT 12; Stuttgart: Katholisches Bibelwerk, 1971).

Berry, George R. "The Date of Ezekiel 38:1 – 39:20." *JBL* 41 (1922) 224–32.

Bertholet, Alfred. *Das Buch Hesekiel*. KHC 12. Leipzig/Tübingen: Mohr, 1897.

———, and Kurt Galling. *Hesekiel*. HAT 13. Tübingen: Mohr, 1936.

Biran, Avraham. "Two Bronze Plaques and the Ḥuṣṣot of Dan." *IEJ* 49/1–2 (1999) 43–54.

Blenkinsopp, Joseph. *Ezekiel*. Interpretation. Louisville: John Knox, 1990.

———. *A History of Prophecy in Israel*. Rev. and enl. ed. Louisville: Westminster John Knox, 1996.

Block, Daniel I. *The Book of Ezekiel, Chapters 1–24*. NICOT. Grand Rapids: Eerdmans, 1997.

———. *The Book of Ezekiel, Chapter 25–48*. NICOT. Grand Rapids: Eerdmans, 1998.

———. *The Gods of the Nations: Studies in Ancient Near Eastern National Theology*. Evangelical Theological Society Monograph Series 2. Jackson, MS: Evangelical Theological Society, 1988.

———. "Gog and the Pouring Out of the Spirit, Reflections on Ezekiel xxxix 21–9." *VT* 37 (1987) 257–70.

———. "Gog in Prophetic Tradition: A New Look at Ezekiel XXXVIII:17." *VT* 42 (1992) 154–72.

———. "Israel's House: Reflections on the Use of בית ישראל in the Old Testament in the Light of Its Ancient Near Eastern Environment." *JETS* 28 (1985) 257–75.

———. "Nations." *ISBE*. Vol. 3, 2d ed. Edited by Geoffrey W. Bromiley, 492–96. Grand Rapids: Eerdmans, 1986.

Boadt, Lawrence. *Ezekiel's Oracles Against Egypt, A Literary and Philological Study of Ezekiel 29–32*. BibOr 37. Rome: Biblical Institute Press, 1980.

———. "The Function of the Salvation Oracles in Ezekiel 33–37." *HAR* 12 (1990) 1–21.

———. "Mythological Themes and the Unity of Ezekiel." In *Literary Structure and Rhetorical Strategies in the Hebrew Bible*. Edited by L. J. de Regt, J. de Waard, and J. P. Fokkelman, 211–31. Assen: Van Gorcum, 1996.

———. "Rhetorical Strategies in Ezekiel's Oracles of Judgment." In *Ezekiel and His Book*. Edited by Johan Lust, 182–200. BETL 74. Leuven: Leuven University Press, 1986.

Bolle, Kees. "Myth, An Overview." *EncRel* 10. Edited by Mircea Eliade, 261–73. London: Collier Macmillan, 1987.

Borger, Riekele. "Gott Marduk und Gott-König Šulgi als Propheten. Zwei prophetische Texte." *BO* 28 (1971) 3–24.

———. *Die Inschriften Asarhaddons Königs von Assyrien, AfO* 9. Graz: Ernst Weidner, 1956.

Bracke, John M. "*šûb šebût*: A Reappraisal." *ZAW* 97 (1985) 233–44.

Braude, William G., trans. *Pesikta Rabbati: Discourses for Feasts, Fasts, & Special Sabbaths*. YJS 18. New Haven: Yale University Press, 1968.

———, and Israel J. Kapstein, trans. *Pěsikta dě-Rab Kahana: Compilation of Discourses for Sabbaths & Festal Days*. London: Routledge & Kegan Paul, 1975.

Brown, Francis, S. R. Driver, and Charles A. Briggs, eds. *A Hebrew and English Lexicon of the Old Testament*. Oxford: Clarendon, 1906.

Brownlee, William H. *Ezekiel 1–19*. Word Bible Commentary 28. Waco: Word Books, 1986.

Buber, Martin. "The Gods of the Nations and God." In *Israel and the World, Essays in a Time of Crisis*, 197–213. New York: Schocken Books, 1948.

Buber, Martin, and Franz Rosenzweig. *Scripture and Translation*. Translated by Lawrence Rosenwald. Indiana Studies in Biblical Literature. Bloomington: Indiana University Press, 1994. Originally published as *Die Schrift und ihre Verdeutschung* (Berlin: Schocken, 1936).

Bultmann, Rudolf. *Jesus Christ and Mythology*. New York: Scribner, 1958.

Buren, Elizabeth Douglas van. *Symbols of the Gods in Mesopotamian Art*. AnOr 23. Rome: Pontificium Institutum Biblicum, 1945.

Busink, Thomas A. *Der Tempel von Jerusalem von Salomo bis Herodes*. Vol. 1. Leiden: Brill, 1970.

Cagni, Luigi. *The Poem of Erra*. SANE 1.3. Malibu: Undena, 1977.

Cassuto, Umberto. "The Arrangement of the Book of Ezekiel." In *Biblical and Oriental Studies 1: Bible*, 227–240. Translated by Israel Abrahams. Jerusalem: Magnes, 1973.

———. *A Commentary on the Book of Genesis, Part I: From Adam to Noah*. Jerusalem: Magnes, 1944. Translated by Israel Abrahams. Publications of the Perry Foundation for Biblical Research in the Hebrew University of Jerusalem. Jerusalem: Magnes, 1961.

———. *The Goddess Anath: Canaanite Epics of the Patriarchal Age.*

Translated by Israel Abrahams. Jerusalem: Magnes, 1971. Originally published in Hebrew (Jerusalem: Magnes, 1953).
Chester, Andrew. "Resurrection and Transformation." In *Auferstehung—Resurrection*. Edited by Friedrich Avemarie and Hermann Lichtenberger, 47–77. Tübingen: Mohr Siebeck, 2001.
Childs, Brevard S. "The Enemy from the North and the Chaos Tradition." *JBL* 78 (1959) 187–98.
———. *Introduction to the Old Testament as Scripture*. Philadelphia: Fortress, 1979.
———. *Myth and Reality in the Old Testament*. SBT 27. London: SCM, 1960.
Clapham, Lynn. "Mythopoeic Antecedants of the Biblical World-View and Their Transformation in Early Israelite Thought." In *Magnalia Dei, The Mighty Acts of God: Essays on the Bible and Archaeology in Memory of G. Ernest Wright*. Edited by F. M. Cross, Werner E. Lemke, and Patrick D. Miller, Jr., 108–19. Garden City: Doubleday, 1976.
Clements, Ronald E. *Ezekiel*. Westminster Bible Companion. Louisville: Westminster John Knox, 1996.
Clifford, Richard J. *The Cosmic Mountain in Canaan and in the Old Testament*. HSM 4. Cambridge, MA: Harvard University, 1972.
———. "Cosmogonies in the Ugaritic Texts and in the Bible." *Or* 53 (1984) 183–201.
———. *Creation Accounts in the Ancient Near East and in the Bible*. CBQMS 26. Washington, D.C.: The Catholic Biblical Association of America, 1994.
———. "The Hebrew Scriptures and the Theology of Creation." *TS* 46 (1985) 507–23.
———. "The Roots of Apocalypticism in Near Eastern Myth." In *The Encyclopedia of Apocalypticism*, 1. Edited by John J. Collins, 3–38. New York: Continuum, 1998.
———. "The Unity of the Book of Isaiah and Its Cosmogonic Language," *CBQ* 55 (1993) 1–17.
Cody, Aelred. *Ezekiel, with an Excursus on Old Testament Priesthood*. OTM 11. Wilmington, DE: Glazier, 1984.
Cogan, Morton. *Imperialism and Religion: Assyria, Judah and Israel in the Eighth and Seventh Centuries, B.C.E.* SBLMS 19. Atlanta: Scholars Press, 1974.
Cohn, Norman. *Cosmos, Chaos, and the World to Come, The Ancient*

Roots of Apocalyptic Faith. New Haven: Yale University Press, 1993.

Collins, Adela Yarbro. *Cosmology and Eschatology in Jewish and Christian Apocalypticism.* JSJSup 50. Leiden: Brill, 1996.

———. *The Combat Myth in the Book of Revelation.* HDR 9. Missoula, MT: Scholars Press, 1976.

The Complete Parallel Bible: Containing the Old and New Testaments with the Aprocryphal/Deuterocanonical Books, New Revised Standard Version, Revised English Bible, New American Bible, New Jerusalem Bible. New York: Oxford University Press, 1993.

Conroy, Charles. "Hebrew Epic: Historical Notes and Critical Reflections." *Bib* 61 (1980) 1–30.

Coogan, Michael D. *Stories from Ancient Canaan.* Philadelphia: The Westminster Press, 1978.

Cook, Stephen L. *Prophecy & Apocalypticism: The Postexilic Social Setting.* Minneapolis: Fortress, 1995.

Cooke, George A. *A Critical and Exegetical Commentary on the Book of Ezekiel.* ICC. Edinburgh: T. & T. Clark, 1936.

———. "Some Considerations on the Text and Teaching of Ezekiel, 40–48." *ZAW* 42 (1924) 105–15.

Cornill, Carl. *Das Buch des Propheten Ezechiel.* Leipzig: Hinrichs, 1886.

———. "Ezekiel, Book of." In *JEnc* 5. Edited by Isidore Singer, 316–18. New York: Funk and Wagnells, 1907.

Cross, Frank M. *Canaanite Myth and Hebrew Epic: Essays in the History of the Religion of Israel.* Cambridge, MA: Harvard University Press, 1973.

———. "The Development of Israelite Religion." *Bible Review* 8.5 (1992) 18–29, 50.

———. *From Epic to Canon: History and Literature in Ancient Israel.* Baltimore: The Johns Hopkins Press, 1998.

———. "Israelite Origins." *Bible Review* 8.4 (1992) 23–32, 61–62.

Dahl, George. "Crisis in Ezekiel Research." In *Quantulacumque. Studies Presented to Kirsopp Lake by Pupils, Colleagues and Friends.* Edited by Robert P. Casey, Silva Lake, and Agnes K. Lake, 265–84. London: Christophers, 1937.

Dahood, Mitchell J. "Ugaritic Lexicography." In *Mélanges Eugène Tisserant* 1: *Écriture sainte — Ancien Orient*, 81–104. Studi e testi 231. Città del Vaticano: Biblioteca apostolica vaticana, 1964.

Dalley, Stephanie. *Myths from Mesopotamia: Creation, the Flood, Gilgamesh, and Others.* World's Classics. Oxford: Oxford University Press, 1989.
Danby, Hubert, trans. *The Mishnah.* London: Oxford University Press, 1958.
Darr, Katheryn Pfisterer. "Ezekiel Among the Critics." *Currents in Research: Biblical Studies* 2 (1994) 9–24.
Davidson, Andrew B. *The Book of the Prophet Ezekiel.* CBSC. Cambridge: University Press, 1892.
Davies, G. Henton. "An Approach to the Problem of Old Testament Mythology." *PEQ* 88 (1956) 83–91.
Davis, Ellen F. "And Pharaoh Will Change His Mind . . . (Ezek. 32:31): Dismantling Mythical Discourse." In *Theological Exegesis, Essays in Honor of Brevard S. Childs.* Edited by Christopher Seitz and Kathryn Greene-McCreight, 224–39. Grand Rapids: Eerdmans, 1999.
———. "Psalm 98, Rejoicing in Judgment." *Int* 46 (1992) 171–75.
———. *Swallowing the Scroll: Textuality and the Dynamics of Discourse in Ezekiel's Prophecy.* JSOTSup 78. Bible and Literature Series 21. Sheffield: Almond, 1989.
Day, John. *God's Conflict with the Dragon and the Sea: Echoes of a Canaanite Myth in the Old Testament.* University of Cambridge Oriental Publications 35. Cambridge: Cambridge University Press, 1985.
De Moor, Johannes C. "El, the Creator." In *The Bible World, Essays in Honor of Cyrus H. Gordon.* Edited by Gary Rendsburg, Ruth Adler, Milton Arfa, Nathan H. Winter, 171–87. New York: KTAV, 1980.
Dietrich, Manfried, and Oswald Loretz, "Ugaritisch ṣrrt ṣpn, ṣrry und hebräisch jrktj ṣpwn," *UF* 22 (1990) 79–86.
Dijk, H. J. van. *Ezekiel's Prophecy on Tyre (Ez. 26:1 – 28:19), A New Approach.* BibOr 20. Rome: Pontifical Biblical Institute, 1968.
Driver, Samuel R. *An Introduction to the Literature of the Old Testament*, 9th ed. International Theological Library. Edinburgh: T. & T. Clark, 1913.
Dupont-Sommer, André, and Marc Philonenko, eds. *La Bible. Écrits Intertestamentaires.* Bibliothèque de la Pleiade 337. Paris: Gallimard, 1987.

Dürr, Lorenz. *Ursprung und Ausbau der israelitisch-jüdischen Heilandserwartung*. Berlin: Schwetschke & Sohn, 1925.

Ebeling, Erich, Bruno Meissner, and Ernst F. Weidner, eds. *Die Inschriften der Altassyrischen Könige*. AOBib 1. Leipzig: Quelle & Meyer, 1926.

Eichrodt, Walther. *Der Prophet Hesekiel: übersetzt und erklärt*. ATD 22. Göttingen: Vandenhoeck & Ruprecht, 1965–1966. Trans. C. Quin. *Ezekiel, A Commentary*. OTL. Philadelphia: Westminster, 1970.

Eißfeldt, Otto. *Baal Zaphon, Zeus Kasios und der Durchzug der Israeliten durchs Meer*. BRA 1. Halle: Max Niemeyer, 1932.

———. *The Old Testament, An Introduction*. Translated by Peter R. Ackroyd. Oxford: Basil Blackwell, 1965. Originally published as *Einleitung in das Alte Testament* (3rd ed.; Neue theologische Grundrisse; Tübingen: Mohr, 1964).

———. "El and Yahweh," *JSS* 1 (1956) 25–37.

Eliade, Mircea. *Cosmos and History, The Myth of the Eternal Return*. Bollingen Series 46. New York: Harper, 1954.

———. "Lebensbaum." *RGG* 4. Edited by Kurt Galling, 250–51. Tübingen: Mohr, 1960.

Engnell, Ivan. *Studies in Divine Kingship in the Ancient Near East*. Uppsala: Almqvist & Wiksells, 1943.

Epstein, Isidore, ed. *The Babylonian Talmud, Seder Nezikin*. London: Soncino Press, 1935.

Ewald, Georg Heinrich. *Die Propheten des Alten Bundes erklärt 2*. Stuttgart: Adolph Krabbe, 1841.

Falkenstein, Adam, and Wolfram von Soden. *Sumerische und akkadische Hymnen und Gebete* Die Bibliothek der alten Welt. Der alte Orient. Zürich: Artemis, 1953.

Fechter, Friedrich. *Bewältigung der Katastrophe: Untersuchungen zu ausgewählten Fremdvölkersprüchen im Ezechielbuch*. BZAW 208. Berlin: de Gruyter, 1992.

Feist, Udo. *Ezechiel: Das literarische Problem des Buches forschungsgeschichtlich betrachtet*. BWANT 138. Stuttgart: Kohlhammer, 1995.

Fensham, Frank C. "The Curse of the Dry Bones in Ezekiel 37:1–14 Changed to a Blessing of Resurrection." *JNSL* 13 (1987) 59–60.

Fenton, Tsevi. "Differing Approaches to the Theomachy Myth in Old

Testament Writers." In *Studies in Bible and the Ancient Near East, Presented to Samuel E. Lowenstamm on His Seventieth Birthday*. Edited by Yitschak Avishur and Joshua Blau, 337–81. Jerusalem: E. Rubenstein, 1978.

Fisch, Harold, ed. *The Jerusalem Bible*. Jerusalem: Koren Publishers, 1983.

Fishbane, Michael. *Biblical Interpretation in Ancient Israel*. Oxford: Clarendon, 1985.

———. "Sin and Judgement in the Prophecies of Ezekiel." *Int* 38 (1984) 131–50.

Fisher, Loren. "Creation at Ugarit and in the Old Testament." *VT* 15 (1965) 313–24.

Fitzgerald, Aloysius. *The Lord of the East Wind*. CBQMS 34. Washington, DC: Catholic Biblical Association of America, 2002.

Fohrer, Georg. *Einleitung in das Alte Testament*. Heidelberg: Quelle & Meyer, 1969.

———. *Die Hauptprobleme des Buches Ezechiel*. BZAW 72. Berlin: Alfred Töpelman, 1952.

———. "Neue Literatur zur alttestamentlichen Prophetie (1961–70): VIII. Ezechiel." *TRu* n.F. 45 (1980) 121–29.

Fohrer, Georg, and Kurt Galling. *Ezechiel*. HAT 13. Tübingen: Mohr, 1955.

Fontenrose, Joseph E. *Python: A Study of Delphic Myth and Its Origins*. Berkeley: University of California Press, 1959.

Forsyth, Neil. *The Old Enemy: Satan and the Combat Myth*. Princeton: Princeton University Press, 1987.

Foster, Benjamin R. "Atra-Hasis." *The Context of Scripture 1*. Edited by William W. Hallo, 450–52. New York: Brill, 1997.

———. *Before the Muses: An Anthology of Akkadian Literature 1: Archaic, Classical, Mature*. Bethesda, MD: CDL Press, 1993.

———. "Gilgamesh." *The Context of Scripture 1*. Edited by William W. Hallo, 458–60. New York: Brill, 1997.

Freedman, David N., and B. E. Willoughby. "ענן." *TWAT* 6.270–74. Stuttgart: Kohlhammer, 1989.

Freedman, David N., and Michael Patrick O'Connor. "כרוב." *TWAT* 4.322–34. Stuttgart: Kohlhammer, 1984.

Freedman, Harry, trans. *The Babylonian Talmud, 3: Shabbath*. London: Soncino Press, 1987.

———, trans. *Midrash Rabbah, Genesis I*. London: Soncino Press, 1983.
Freedman, Harry, and Maurice Simon, trans. *Midrash Rabbah, Esther, Song of Songs*. London: Soncino Press, 1961.
Frese, Pamela R., and S. J. M Gray. "Trees." *EncRel* 15. Edited by Mircea Eliade, 26–33. New York: MacMillan, 1987.
Fritz, Volkmar. "What Can Archaeology Tell Us About Solomon's Temple?" *BAR* 13.4 (1987) 38–49.
Garcia Martìnez, Florentino. *The Dead Sea Scrolls Translated: the Qumran Texts in English*. New York: Brill, 1994.
Garfinkel, Stephen P. "Studies in Akkadian Influences in the Book of Ezekiel." Ph.D. diss., Columbia University, 1983.
Garscha, Jörg. *Studien zum Ezechielbuch: Eine redaktionskritische Untersuchung von 1–39*. EHS 23.23. Bern: Herbert Lang, 1974.
Gawaltney Jr., W. C. "The Biblical Book of Lamentations in the Context of Near Eastern Lament Literature." In *More Essays on the Comparative Method*. The Context of Scripture 2. Edited by William W. Hallo, James C. Moyer, Leo G. Perdue, 191–211. Winona Lake, IN: Eisenbrauns, 1983.
Gese, Hartmut. *Der Verfassungsentwurf des Ezechiel (Kap 40–48) Traditionsgeschichtlich Untersucht*. BHT 25. Tübingen: Mohr, 1957.
Gesenius, Wilhelm. *Gesenius' Hebrew Grammar*. Edited by E. Kautsch. 2nd English ed. Translated by A. E. Cowley. Oxford: Clarendon, 1910.
Geyer, John B. "Ezekiel 27 and the Cosmic Ship." In *Among the Prophets, Language, Image and Structure in the Prophetic Writing*. Edited by Philip R. Davies and David J. A. Clines, 107–26. JSOTSup 144. Sheffield: JSOT, 1993.
Ginzberg, Louis. *The Legends of the Jews, Vol. 1*. Philadelphia: Jewish Publication Society of America, 1961.
———. *The Legends of the Jews, Vol. 2, 3 & 4*. Philadelphia: Jewish Publication Society of America, 1954.
———. *The Legends of the Jews, Vol. 6*. Philadelphia: Jewish Publication Society of America, 1959.
Ginsberg, Harold L. "Poems About Baal and Anat." *ANET*. Edited by James Pritchard, 129–42. Princeton: Princeton University Press, 1969.
Girardot, Norman. "Chaos." *EncRel* 3. Edited by Mircea Eliade, 213–18. London: Collier Macmillan, 1987.

Goldin, Judah, trans. *The Fathers According to Rabbi Nathan*. YJS 10. New Haven: Yale University Press, 1955.

Gorman, Jr., Frank H. *The Ideology of Ritual*. JSOTSup 91. Sheffield: Sheffield Academic Press, 1990.

Gosse, Bernard. "Le recueil d'oracles contre les nations d'Ezéchiel XXV-XXXII dans la rédaction du livre d'Ézéchiel." *RB* 93 (1986) 535–62.

Grayson, Albert K. *Assyrian Royal Inscriptions* 2. RANE. Weisbaden: Otto Harrassowitz, 1972.

Green, Margaret. "The Eridu Lament." *JCS* 30 (1978) 127–67.

Greenberg, Moshe "The Design and Themes of Ezekiel's Program of Restoration." *Int* 38 (1984) 181–208.

———. *Ezekiel 1–20*. AB 22. New York: Doubleday, 1983.

———. *Ezekiel 21–37*. AB 22A. New York: Doubleday, 1997.

———. "Ezekiel's Vision: Literary and Iconographic Aspects." In *History, Historiography and Intepretation: Studies in Biblical and Cuneiform Literatures*. Edited by Hayim Tadmor and Moshe Weinfeld, 159–68. Jerusalem: Magnes, 1983.

———. "Prolegomenon." In Charles C. Torrey, *Pseudo-Ezekiel and the Original Prophecy*, XI-XXIV. LBS. New York: Ktav, 1970.

———. "The Vision of Jerusalem of Ezekiel 8–11: A Holistic Interpretation." In *The Divine Helmsman*. Edited by J. L. Crenshaw and S. Sandmel, 143–64. New York: Ktav, 1980.

———. "What are Valid Criteria for Determining Inauthentic Matter in Ezekiel?" *Ezekiel and His Book*. Edited by Johan Lust, 123–35. BETL 74. Leuven: Leuven University Press, 1986.

Greenspoon, Leonard J. "The Origin of the Idea of Resurrection." In *Traditions in Transformation, Turning Points in Biblical Faith. Festschrift Honoring Frank Moore Cross*. Edited by Baruch Halpern and Jon D. Levenson, 247–321. Winona Lake, IN: Eisenbrauns, 1981.

Gressmann, Hugo. *Altorientalische Texte und Bilder zum Alten Testament*, 2d ed. Berlin: de Gruyter, 1926.

———. *Der Messias*. Göttingen: Vandenhoeck & Ruprecht, 1929.

———. *Der Ursprung der Israelitisch-jüdischen Eschatologie*. FRLANT 6. Göttingen: Vandenhoeck & Ruprecht, 1905.

Gross, Walter. "Israel's Hope for the Renewal of the State." *JSS* 14 (1988) 121–33.

Gunkel, Hermann. *Genesis übersetzt und erklärt.* HAT 1. Göttingen: Vandenhoeck & Ruprecht, 1901.

———. *Schöpfung und Chaos in Urzeit und Endzeit: Eine religionsgeschichtliche Untersuchung über Gen 1 und Ap Joh 12.* Göttingen: Vandenhoeck & Ruprecht, 1895.

Hallo, William W., ed. *The Context of Scripture, 1: Canonical Compositions from the Biblical World.* New York: Brill, 1997.

Hals, Ronald M. *Ezekiel.* FOTL 19. Grand Rapids: Eerdmans, 1989.

Hammer, Reuven, trans. *Sifre, A Tannaitic Commentary on the Book of Deuteronomy.* YJS 24. New Haven: Yale University Press, 1986.

Hammershaimb, Erling. "Ezekiel's View of the Monarchy." In *Some Aspects of Old Testament Prophecy from Isaiah to Malachi.* Edited by Erling Hammershaimb, 51–62. Teologiske Skrifter 4. Copenhagen: Rosenkilde Og Bagger, 1966.

Hamp, Vincenz. "אש, IV. Feuer in Verbindung mit Gott." *TWAT* 1.459–63. Stuttgart: Kohlhammer, 1973.

Hanson, Paul D. *The Dawn of Apocalyptic, the Historical and Sociological Roots of Jewish Apocalyptic Eschatology,* rev. ed. Philadelphia: Fortress, 1979.

———. *Old Testament Apocalyptic.* Interpreting Biblical Texts. Nashville: Abingdon, 1987.

———. *The People Called: the Growth of Community in the Bible.* San Francisco: Harper & Row, 1986.

Harford, John Battersby. *Studies in the Book of Ezekiel.* Cambridge: Cambridge University Press, 1935.

The Harper Collins Study Bible. NRSV. Edited by Wayne A. Meeks. London: Harper Collins, 1993.

Harrelson, Walter. "Myth and Ritual School." *EncRel* 10. Edited by Mircea Eliade, 282–85. London: Collier Macmillan, 1987.

Heinisch, Paul. *Das Buch Ezechiel übersetzt und erklärt.* HSAT 8.1. Bonn: Peter Hanstein, 1923.

Hengstenberg, Ernst W. *The Prophecies of Ezekiel Elucidated.* Translated by A. C. Murphy and J. G. Murphy. Edinburgh: T. & T. Clark, 1869. Originally published as *Die Weissagungen des Prophet Ezechiel erklärt* (Leipzig: Hinrichs, 1867/68).

Herntrich, Volkmar. *Ezechielprobleme.* BZAW 61. Giessen: Alfred Töpelmann, 1932.

Herodotus. *The Histories.* Oxford World's Classics. Translated by Robin Waterfield. Oxford: Oxford University Press, 1998.

Herrmann, Johannes. *Ezechielstudien.* BWAT 2. Leipzig: Hinrichs, 1908.

———. *Ezechiel übersetzt und erklärt.* KAT 11. Leipzig: A. Deichertsche, 1924.

Herrmann, Wolfgang. "Baal." In *Dictionary of Deities and Demons in the Bible,* 2d ed. Edited by Karel van der Toorn, Bob Becking, and Pieter W. van der Horst, 132–39. Leiden: Brill, 1999.

———. "El." In *Dictionary of Deities and Demons in the Bible,* 2d ed. Edited by Karel van der Toorn, Bob Becking, and Pieter W. van der Horst, 274–80. Leiden: Brill, 1999.

———. "Rider Upon the Clouds." In *Dictionary of Deities and Demons in the Bible,* 2d ed. Edited by Karel van der Toorn, Bob Becking, and Pieter W. van der Horst, 703–5. Leiden: Brill, 1999.

S. Hieronymi Presbyteri Opera 1: Opera exegetica 4: Commentarium in Hezechielem libri 14. Corpus Christianorum, Series Latina 75. Turnholti: Brepols Editores Pontificii, 1964.

Hitzig, Ferdinand. *Der Prophet Ezechiel erklärt.* KHAT 8. Leipzig: Weidmannsche, 1847.

Holladay, John S. "Religion in Israel and Judah Under the Monarchy: An Explicitly Archaeological Approach." In *Ancient Israelite Religion, Essays in Honor of Frank Moore Cross.* Edited by Patrick D. Miller, Jr., Paul D. Hanson, S. Dean McBride, 249–99. Philadelphia: Fortress, 1987.

Hölscher, Gustav. *Geschichte der israelitischen und jüdischen Religion.* Giessen: Alfred Töpelmann, 1922.

———. *Hesekiel, der Dichter und das Buch eine literarkritische Untersuchung.* BZAW 39. Giessen: Alfred Töpelmann, 1924.

———. *Die Propheten, Untersuchungen zur Religionsgeschichte Israels.* Leipzig: Hinrichs, 1914.

Hoonacker, Alban van. "Eléments sumériens dans le livre d'Ezekiel?" ZA 28 (1914) 333–36.

Horovitz, H. Saul, ed. *Siphre d'be Rab.* Corpus Tannaiticum 3.3.1. Jerusalem: Wahrmann Books, 1966.

Horowitz, Wayne, and Victor Hurowitz. "Urim and Thummim in Light of a Psephomancy Ritual from Assur (LKA 137)." *JANES* 21 (1992) 95–115.

Hossfeld, Frank. *Untersuchungen zu Komposition und Theologie des Ezechielbuches.* FB 20. Würzburg: Echter, 1977.

———. "Das Buch Ezechiel." In *Einleitung in das Alte Testament,* 3d ed. Edited by Erich Zenger, 440–57. Kohlhammer-Studienbücher Theologie 1. Stuttgart: Kohlhammer, 1998.

Howie, Carl G. *The Date and Composition of Ezekiel*. SBLMS 4. Philadelphia: SBL, 1950.

Hurowitz, Victor (Avigdor). *I Have Built You an Exalted House*. JSOTSup 115. Sheffield: JSOT, 1992.

Irwin, William A. "Harford, John Battersby, Studies in the Book of Ezekiel." *JR* 16 (1936) 208–10.

———. *The Problem of Ezekiel: An Inductive Study*. Chicago: University of Chicago Press, 1943.

Israelstam, J., and Judah Slotki, trans. *Midrash Rabbah, Leviticus*. London: Soncino Press, 1961.

Jacobsen, Thorkild. *The Harps That Once . . . Sumerian Poetry in Translation*. New Haven: Yale University Press, 1987.

———. *The Treasures of Darkness, A History of Mesopotamian Religion*. New Haven: Yale University Press, 1976.

Jeremias, Jörg. *Theophanie: die Geschichte einer alttestamentlichen Gattung*, rev. and enl. 2d ed. WMANT 10. Neukirchen-Vluyn: Neukirchener Verlag, 1977.

Joüon, Paul. *A Grammar of Biblical Hebrew*. Translated and revised by Takamitsu Muraoka. 2 vols. Subsidia Biblica 14. Rome: Pontifical Biblical Institute, 1991.

———. "Notes philologiques sur le texte hébreu d'Ézéchiel." *Bib* 10 (1929) 304–12.

Joyce, Paul M. *Divine Initiative and Human Response in Ezekiel*. JSOTSup 51. Sheffield: Sheffield Academic Press, 1989.

———. "Synchronic and Diachronic Perspectives on Ezekiel." In *Synchronic or Diachronic?: A Debate on Method in Old Testament Exegesis*. OTS 34. Edited by Johannes C. de Moor, 115–28. Leiden: Brill, 1995.

Kaiser, Otto. *Introduction to the Old Testament: A Presentation of its Results and Problems*. Translated by John Sturdy. Oxford: Basil Blackwell, 1975. Reprint, 1984. Originally published as *Einleitung in das Alte Testament; eine Einführung in ihre Ergebnisse und Probleme*, rev. 2d ed. Gütersloh: Gütersloher Verlagshaus Gerd Mohn, 1970.

———. "Tod, Auferstehung und Unsterblichkeit im Alten Testament und im frühen Judentum in religionsgeschichtlichem Zusammenhang bedacht." In *Tod und Leben*, 7–80. Kohlhammer-Taschenbucher 1001: Biblische Konfrontationen. Stuttgart: Kohlhammer, 1977.

Kaltner, John. "The Gog/Magog Tradition in the Hebrew Bible and the Qur'an, Points of Similarity and Dissimilarity." *USQR* 49 (1995) 35–48.

Keel, Othmar, and Christoph Uehlinger. *Gods, Goddesses, and Images of God in Ancient Israel*. Translated by Thomas H. Trapp. Minneapolis: Augsburg Fortress, 1998. Originally published as *Göttinnen, Götter und Gottessymbole*. Quaestiones disputatae 134 (Fribourg: Herder, 1992).

Keel, Othmar. *Jahwe-Visionen und Siegelkunst*. SBS 84/85. Stuttgart: Verlag Katholisches Bibelwerk, 1977.

———. *The Symbolism of the Biblical World: Ancient Near Eastern Iconography and the Book of Psalms*. Translated by Timothy J. Hallet. New York: The Seabury Press, 1978. Originally published as *Die Welt der altorientalischen Bildsymbolik und das Alte Testament: Am Beispiel der Psalmen* (Neukirchen: Neukirchener Verlag, 1972).

Keller, B. "La terre dans le livre d'Ézéchiel." *RHPR* 55 (1975) 481–90.

Kingsley, Peter. "Exile by the Grand Canal: between Jewish and Babylonian Tradition." *JRAS*, 3d Series, 2 (1992) 339–46.

Klein, Jackob. "Akitu." In *Anchor Bible Dictionary*, vol 1. Edited by David N. Freedman, et al., 138–40. New York: Doubleday, 1992.

Klein, Ralph W. *Israel In Exile*. Overtures to Biblical Theology 6. Philadelphia: Fortress, 1979.

Knutson, F. Brent. "Literary Phrases and Formulae." *RSP*. AnOr 50. Edited by Loren R. Fisher, 401–22. Rome: Institutum Biblicum, 1975.

Kohler, Josef, and A. Ungnad. *Assyrische Rechtsurkunden: in Umschrift und Übersetzung nebst einem Index der Personennamen und Rechtserlauterungen* . Leipzig: Eduard Pfeiffer, 1913.

König, Franz. *Zarathustras Jenseitsvorstellungen und das Alte Testament*. Wien: Herder, 1964.

Korpel, Marjo. "Creator of All." In *Dictionary of Deities and Demons in the Bible*, 2d ed. Edited by Karel van der Toorn, Bob Becking, Pieter W. van der Horst, 208–11. Leiden: Brill, 1999.

———. *A Rift in the Clouds, Ugaritic and Hebrew Descriptions of the Divine*. UBL 8. Münster: Ugarit Verlag, 1990.

Korpel, Marjo, and Johannes C. de Moor. Review of *Conflict with the Dragon and the Sea* by John Day. *JSS* 31 (1986) 243–45.
Kraetzschmar, Richard. *Das Buch Ezechiel*. HKAT 3. Göttingen: Vandenhoeck & Ruprecht, 1900.
Kramer, Samuel N. *History Begins at Sumer*. 3d rev. ed. Philadelphia: University of Pennsylvania Press, 1981. Originally published as *From the Tablets of Sumer* (Indian Hills, CO: Falcon's Wing, 1956).
———. "Lamentation Over the Destruction of Nippur." *EI* 9 (1969) 89–93.
———. "Sumerian Literature and the Bible." *AnBib* 12 (1959) 185–204.
———. *Sumerian Mythology*. Memoirs of the American Philosophical Society 21. Philadelphia: American Philosophical Society, 1944. Reprint, Westport, CT: Greenwood, 1988.
Kraus, Hans-Joachim. *The Theology of the Psalms*. Translated by Keith Crim. Minneapolis: Augsburg Publishing House, 1986. Originally published as *Theologie der Psalmen*. (BKAT 15/3; Neukirchen-Vluyn: Neukirchener Verlag, 1979).
Krüger, Thomas. *Geschichtskonzepte im Ezechielbuch*. BZAW 180. Berlin: de Gruyter, 1989.
Kuhl, Kurt. "Neuere Hesekiel-Literature." *TRu* NF 20 (1952) 13–14.
———. "Zum Stand der Hesekiel-Forschung." *TRu* NF 24 (1957–58) 128–31.
Kutsko, John F. *Between Heaven and Earth, Divine Presence and Absence in the Book of Ezekiel*. Biblical and Judaic Studies from the University of California, San Diego 7. Winona Lake, IN: Eisenbrauns, 2000.
Lambert, Wilfred G. *Babylonian Wisdom Literature*. Oxford: Clarendon, 1960.
———. "Enmeduranki and Related Matters." *JCS* 21 (1967) 126–33.
———. "Trees, Snakes and Gods in Ancient Syria and Anatolia." *BSOAS* 48 (1985) 435–51.
Lang, Bernhard. *Ezechiel: Der Prophet und das Buch*. ErFor 153. Darmstadt: Wissenschaftliche Buchgesellschaft, 1981.
———. *Kein Aufstand in Jerusalem: Die Politik des Propheten Ezechiel*. 2nd ed. SBB. Stuttgart: Verlag Katholisches Bibelwerk, 1978.
———. "Life After Death in the Prophetic Promise." In *Congress Volume, Jerusalem, 1986*. Edited by J. A. Emerton, 144–56. VTSup 40. Leiden: Brill, 1988.

———. "Street Theatre, Raising the Dead, and the Zoroastrian Connection in Ezekiel's Prophecy." In *Ezekiel and His Book*. Edited by Johan Lust, 307–14. BETL 74. Leuven: Leuven University Press, 1986.

Langdon, Stephen. *Die neubabylonische Königsinschriften*. VAB 4. Leipzig: Hinrichs, 1912.

Lauha, Aarre. *Zaphon, der Norden und die Nordvölker im Alten Testament*. AASF B49. Helsinki: Der Finnischen Literaturgesellschaft, 1943.

Layton, Scott. "Biblical Hebrew 'to set the face' in the Light of Akkadian and Ugaritic." *UF* 17 (1986) 169–81.

Le Déaut, Roger, trans. *Targum du Pentateuque 3: Nombres*. Sources chrétiennes 261. Paris: Editions du Cerf, 1979.

———, trans. *Targum du Pentateuque II: Exodus et Lévitique*. Sources chrétiennes 256. Paris: Editions du Cerf, 1979.

Lehrman, Simon M. trans. *Midrash Rabbah, Exodus*. London: Soncino Press, 1983.

Lemke, Werner E. "Life in the Present and Hope for the Future." *Int* 38 (1984) 165–80.

Levenson, Jon D. "The Jerusalem Temple in Devotional and Visionary Experience." In *Jewish Spirituality From the Bible through the Middle Ages*. Edited by Arthur Green, 32–61. World Spirituality: An Encyclopedic History of the Religious Quest 13. London: Routledge & Kegan Paul, 1986.

———. *Creation and the Persistence of Evil*. San Francisco: Harper & Row, 1988.

———. *Theology of the Program of Restoration of Ezekiel 40–48*. HSM 10. Atlanta: Scholars Press, 1986.

Levey, Samson H. trans. *The Targum of Ezekiel*. Aramaic Bible 13. Edinburgh: T. & T. Clark, 1987.

Lewy, Hans. *Chaldean Oracles and Theurgy*. Paris: Études Augustiniennes, 1978.

Limet, Henri. "Le poème épique 'Innina et Ebih,' une version des lignes 123 à 182." *Or* 40 (1971) 11–28.

Lipiński, Eduard. "Gyges et Lygdamis d'après les sources neo-assyriennes et hebraïques." In *XXXIV International Assyriology Congress*, 159–65. Turk Tarih Kurumu yayinlari. XXVI dizi 3. Ankara: Türk Tarih Kurumu Basimevi, 1998.

———. "צפן." *TWAT* 6. Edited by Helmer Ringgren and Heinz-Josef Fabry, 1093–1102. Stuttgart: Kohlhammer, 1989.

———. "Shemesh." In *Dictionary of Deities and Demons in the Bible.* 2d ed. Edited by Karel van der Toorn, Bob Becking, and Pieter W. van der Horst, 764–67. Leiden: Brill, 1999.

Livingstone, Alasdair. *Mystical and Mythological Explanatory Works of Assyrian and Babylonian Scholars.* Oxford: Clarendon, 1986.

———. "Nergal." In *Dictionary of Deities and Demons in the Bible,* 2d ed. Edited by Karel van der Toorn, Bob Becking, Pieter W. van der Horst, 621–22. Leiden: Brill, 1999.

Long, Charles H. "Cosmogony." *EncRel* 4. Edited by Mircea Eliade, 94–100. London: Collier Macmillan, 1987.

Longman III, Tremper. *Fictional Akkadian Autobiography: A Generic and Comparative Study.* Winona Lake, IN: Eisenbrauns, 1991.

Loretz, Oswald. "A Hurrian Word for the Chariot of the Cloud Rider?" In *Ugarit, religion and culture, Proceedings of the International Colloquium on Ugarit, religion and culture,* 167–78. UBL 12. Münster: Ugarit-Verlag, 1996.

———. "Der Sturz des Fürsten von Tyrus (Ez 28,1–19)." *UF* 8 (1976) 455–58.

———. *Ugarit und die Bibel.* Darmstadt: Wissenschaftliche Buchgesellschaft, 1990.

———. *Ugarit-Texte und Thronbesteigungspsalmen, Die Metamorphose des Regenspenders Baal-Jahwe.* UBL 7. Münster: Ugarit-Verlag, 1988.

———. "Der Wohnort Els nach ugaritischen Texten und Ez 28, 1–2.6–10." *UF* 21 (1989) 259–67.

Luckenbill, Daniel D. *Ancient Records of Assyria and Babylonia 1: Historical Records of Assyria From the Earliest Times to Sargon.* Ancient records, 1st series. Edited by J. H. Breasted. Chicago: University of Chicago Press, 1926.

———. *Ancient Records of Assyria and Babylonia 2: Historical Records of Assyria From Sargon to the End.* Ancient records, 1st series. Edited by J. H. Breasted. Chicago: University of Chicago Press, 1927.

———. *The Annals of Sennacherib.* Oriental Institute Publications 2. Chicago: Chicago University Press, 1924.

Machinist, Peter B. "Literature as Politics: The Tukulti-Ninurta Epic and the Bible." *CBQ* 38 (1976) 455–82.

Mafico, Temba L. J. "Judge, Judging." In *Anchor Bible Dictionary,* vol. 3. Edited by David N. Freedman, et al., 1194–96. New York: Doubleday, 1992.

Malamat, Abraham. "New Light from Mari (ARM XXVI) on Biblical Prophecy (III – IV)." In *Storia e tradizioni di Israele: scritti in onore di J. Alberto Soggin*. Edited by Daniele Garrone and Felice Israel, 185–90. Brescia: Paideia Editrice, 1991.

May, Herbert G. "Some Aspects of Solar Worship at Jerusalem." *ZAW* 55 (1937) 269–81.

———. "Some Cosmic Connotations of *Mayim Rabbîm*, Many Waters." *JBL* 47 (1955) 9–22.

Mazar, Amihai. *Archaeology of the Land of the Bible*. AB Reference Library. New York: Doubleday, 1990.

McCarter, P. Kyle. "The River Ordeal in Israelite Literature." *HTR* 66 (1973) 403–12.

McKeating, Henry. *Ezekiel*. OTG. Sheffield: JSOT, 1993.

Mettinger, Tryggve N. D. "Cherubim." In *Dictionary of Deities and Demons in the Bible*, 2d ed. Edited by Karel van der Toorn, Bob Becking, and Pieter W. van der Horst, 189–92. Leiden: Brill, 1999.

———. "Fighting the Powers of Chaos and Hell — Towards the Biblical Portrait of God." *ST* 39 (1985) 21–38.

———. *The Dethronement of the Sabaoth*. ConBOT 18. Lund: Wallin & Dalholm, 1982.

———. "The Name and the Glory: The Zion-Sabaoth Theology and Its Exilic Successors." *JNSL* 24 (1998) 1–24.

———. *No Graven Image? Israelite Aniconism in Its Ancient Near Eastern Context*. ConBOT 42. Stockholm: Almqvist & Wiksell International, 1995.

Metzger, Martin. *Königsthron und Gottesthron*. AOAT 15. Neukirchen-Vluyn: Neukirchener Verlag, 1985.

———. "Zeder, Weinstock und Weltenbaum." In *Ernten, was man sät, Festschrift für Klaus Koch zu seinem 65. Geburtstag*. Edited by Dwight R. Daniels, Uwe Glessmer und Martin Rösel, 197–229. Neukirchen-Vluyn: Neukirchener Verlag, 1991.

Meyer, Jan-Waalke. "Lebermodelle." In *Reallexikon der Assyriologie und Vorderasiatischen Archäologie* 6, 518–27. Berlin: de Gruyter, 1982.

Milgrom, Jacob. *The JPS Torah Commentary, Numbers*. Philadelphia: Jewish Publication Society, 1990.

Millard, Alan R. "The Etymology of Eden." *VT* 34 (1984) 103–6.
Miller, Jr., Patrick D. "Animal Names as Designations in Ugaritic and Hebrew." *UF* 2 (1970) 177–86.
———. "Fire in the Mythology of Canaan and Israel." *CBQ* 27 (1965) 256–61.
Mishcon, A., and A. Cohen, trans. *The Babylonian Talmud, 21: Abodah Zarah*. London: Soncino Press, 1988.
Monson, John. "The New 'Ain Dara Temple, Closest Solomonic Parallel." *BAR* 26.2 (2000) 20–35, 67.
Müller, Hans-Peter. *Jenseits der Entmythologisierung*. 2d ed. Neukirchen-Vluyn: Neukirchener Verlag, 1979.
———. "Mythische Elemente in der Jahwistischen Schöpfungserzählung." In *Babylonien und Israel, Historische, religiöse und sprachliche Beziehungen*. WF 633. Edited by Hans-Peter Müller, 114–153. Darmstadt: Wissenschaftliche Buchgesellschaft, 1991.
———. "Parallelen zu Gen 2f. und Ez 28 aus dem Gilgamesch-Epos." *ZAH* 3 (1990) 167–78.
———. *Ursprünge und Strukturen alttestamentlicher Eschatologie*. BZAW 109. Berlin: Alfred Töplemann, 1969.
———. *Vergleich und Metapher im Hohenlied*. OBO 56. Freiburg, Switzerland: Universitätsverlag; Göttingen: Vandenhoeck & Ruprecht, 1984.
Munz, Peter. *When the Golden Bough Breaks; Structuralism or Typology?* London: Routledge & Kegan Paul, 1973.
Neusner, Jacob, trans. *Sifré to Numbers, An American Translation and Explanation 2: Sifré to Numbers 59–115*. Atlanta: Scholars Press, 1986.
Newsom, Carol A. "A Maker of Metaphors — Ezekiel's Oracles Against Tyre." *Int* 38 (1984) 151–64.
———. *Songs of the Sabbath Sacrifice: A Critical Edition*. HSS 27. Atlanta: Scholars Press, 1985.
Niditch, Susan. "Ezekiel 40–48 in a Visionary Context." *CBQ* 48 (1986) 208–24.
Nobile, Marco. "Beziehung zwischen Ezek. 32, 17–32 und der Gog-Perikope (Ezek. 38–39) im Lichte der Endredaktion." In *Ezekiel and His Book*. Edited by Johan Lust, 255–59. BETL 74. Leuven: Leuven University Press, 1986.
———. *Ecclesiologia Biblica: traiettorie storico-culturali e teologiche*. Collana Studi biblici 30. Bologna: Edizioni Dehoniane, 1996.

———. "Ez 37, 1–14 come costitutivo di uno schema cultuale." *Bib* 65 (1984) 476–89.

———. "Ez 38–39 ed Ez 40–48: i due aspetti complementari del culmine di uno schema cultuale di fondazione." *Anton* 62 (1987) 141–71.

———. *Una lettura simbolico-strutturalistica di Ezechiele*, extract. Rome: Pontificio Istituto Biblico, 1982.

———. *Introduzione all'Antico Testamento*. Epifania della Parola. Ns 5. Bologna: Edizioni Dehoniane, 1995.

———. *Teologia dell'Antico Testamento*. LOGOS, Corso di Studi Biblici 8/1. Torino: Editrice Elle Di Ci, 1998.

Odell, Margaret S. "Are You He of Whom I Spoke By My Servants the Prophets? Ezekiel 38–39 and the Problem of History in the Neo-Babylonian Context." Ph.D. diss., University of Pittsburgh, 1988.

———. "The City of Hamonah in Ezekiel 39:11–16: The Tumultuous City of Jerusalem." *CBQ* 56 (1994) 479–89.

Oden, Jr., Robert A. *The Bible Without Theology*. New Voices in Biblical Studies. San Francisco: Harper & Row, 1987.

Oesterley, William O. E. "The Book of Ezekiel: A Survey of Recent Literature." *CQR* 116 (1933) 187–200.

Ohler, Annmarie. "Die Gegenwart Gottes in der Gottesferne." *BibLeb* 11 (1970) 79–89.

Olmo Lete, Gregorio del. *Mitos, leyendas y rituales de los semitas occidentales*. Pliegos de Oriente. Serie Proximo Oriente. Madrid: Editorial Trotta, 1998.

Oppenheim, A. Leo. "Mesopotamian Mythology II." *Or* 17 (1948) 17–58.

Page, Hugh R. *The Myth of Cosmic Rebellion: A Study of Its Reflexes in Ugaritic and Biblical Literature*. VTSup 65. New York: Brill, 1996.

Pardee, Dennis. "The Baʻlu Myth." In *The Context of Scripture I*. Edited by William W. Hallo, 241–73. Leiden: Brill, 1997.

Parrot, André. *Babylone et l'Ancien Testament*. Cahiers d'Archéologie Biblique 8. Paris: Neuchatel, 1956.

Parunak, Henry van Dyke. *Structural Studies in Ezekiel*. Ph.D. diss., Harvard University, 1978.

Philostratus, Flavius. *Das Leben des Apollonios von Tyana*. Translated by Vroni Mumprecht. München: Artemis, 1983.

Piatelli, Abramo Alberto, trans. *Targum Shir Ha-Shirim*. Textus biblici 1 001. Rome: Barulli, 1975.

Plato, *The Republic* in *The Collected Dialogs of Plato*. Bollingen Series 71. Edited by Edith Hamilton and Huntington Cairns. Princeton: Princeton University Press, 1963.

Podella, Thomas. *Das Lichtkleid JHWH's, Untersuchungen zur Gestalthaftigkeit Gottes im Alten Testament und seiner altorientalischen Umwelt*. FAT 15. Tübingen: Mohr, 1996.

Pohlmann, Karl-Friedrich. "Ezechiel oder das Buch von der Zukunft der Gola und der Heimkehr der Diaspora." In Otto Kaiser. *Grundriß der Einleitung in die kanonischen und deutero-kanonischen Schriften des Alten Testments 2: Die prophetischen Werke*, 82–102. Mohn: Gütersloher Verlagshaus, 1994.

———. *Ezechielstudien: Zur Redaktionsgeschichte des Buches und zur Frage nach den ältesten Texten*. BZAW 202. Berlin: de Gruyter, 1992.

———. *Der Prophet Hesekiel/Ezechiel 1–19*. ATD 22.1 Göttingen: Vandenhoeck & Ruprecht, 1996.

Pope, Marvin H. *El in the Ugaritic Texts*. VTSup 2. Leiden: Brill, 1955.

———. *Probative Pontificating in Ugaritic and Biblical Literature*. Edited by Mark S. Smith. UBL 10. Münster: Ugarit-Verlag, 1994.

Preuss, Horst Dietrich. "דמה." *TWAT* 2.266–77. Stuttgart: Kohlhammer, 1977.

———. "גלולים." *TWAT* 2.1–5 Stuttgart: Kohlhammer, 1977.

———. *Old Testament Theology* 1. Translated by Leo G. Perdue. OTL. Louisville: Westminster John Knox, 1995. Originally published as *Theologie des Alten Testaments* 1. Stuttgart: Kohlhammer, 1991.

———. *Old Testament Theology* 2. Translated by Leo G. Perdue. OTL. Louisville: Westminster John Knox, 1996. *Theologie des Alten Testaments* 2. Stuttgart: Kohlhammer, 1992.

Price, James D. "Rosh: An Ancient Land Known to Ezekiel." *GTJ* 6.1 (1985) 67–89.

Pritchard, James B., ed. *ANEP*. Princeton: Princeton University Press, 1969.

———, ed. *ANET*. 3d ed. with suppl. Princeton: Princeton University Press, 1969.

Rabenau, Konrad von. "Die Entstehung des Buches Ezechiel in formgeschichtlicher Sicht." *WZ* 4 (1955–56) 659–94.

Rad, Gerhard von. *Genesis, A Commentary*. Translated by John H. Marks. OTL. London: SCM, 1966. Originally published as *Das erste Buch Moses, Genesis*. ATD 2. Göttingen: Vandenhoeck & Ruprecht, 1956.

———. *Old Testament Theology, Volume One: The Theology of Israel's Traditions*. Translated by D. M. G. Stalker. New York: Harper & Row, 1962. Originally published as *Theologie des Alten Testaments, BD 1: Die Theologie der geschlichtlichen Überlieferungen Israels*. Munich: Chr. Kaiser, 1957.

Rendtorff, Rolf. "The Concept of Revelation in Ancient Israel." In *Revelation as History*. Translated by David Granskou. Edited by Wolfhart Pannenberg, 25–52. New York: Macmillan, 1968. Originally published as "Die Offenbarungsvorstellungen im Alten Israel," In *Offenbarung als Geschichte*. Edited by Wolfhart Pannenberg, 21–42. KD 1. Göttingen: Vandenhoeck & Ruprecht, 1961.

———. "El, Ba'al und Jahwe." *ZAW* 78 (1966) 277–91.

Renz, Thomas. *The Rhetorical Function of the Book of Ezekiel*. VTSup 76. Leiden: Brill, 1999.

Ricoeur, Paul. "Myth: Myth and History." In *EncRel* 10. Edited by Mircea Eliade, 273–82. London: Collier Macmillan, 1987.

Rogerson, John W. "Ewald, Georg Heinrich August." In *Dictionary of Biblical Interpretation*. Edited by John H. Hayes, 363–64. Nashville: Abingdon, 1999.

———. *Myth in Old Testament Interpretation*. BZAW 134. Berlin: de Gruyter, 1974.

Römer, Thomas. "La redécouverte d'un mythe dans l'ancien testament: la création comme combat." *ETR* 64 (1989) 561–73.

Römer, Willem H. *Sumerische Königshymnen der Isin-Zeit*. DMOA 13. Leiden: Brill, 1965.

Rosenberg, Abraham J. *Ezekiel* 2. New York: Judaica Press, 1991.

Rowley, Harold H. "The Book of Ezekiel in Modern Study." *BJRL* 36 (1953–54) 146–90.

Ruwe, Andreas. "Die Veränderung tempeltheologischer Konzepte in Ezechiel 8–11." In *Gemeinde ohne Tempel, Community without Temple*. Edited by Beate Ego, Armin Lange, Peter Pilhofer, 3–18. WUNT 118. Tübingen: Mohr Siebeck, 1999.

Sacred Writings, Judaism: The Tanakh, The New JPS Translation. New York: Book-of-the-Month-Club, 1992.

Saggs, Henry W. F. *The Encounter with the Divine in Mesopotamia and Israel*. Jordan Lectures in Comparative Religion 12. London: Athlone Press, 1978.

Sarna, Nahum. "The Psalm for the Sabbath Day (Ps 92)." *JBL* 81 (1962) 155–68.

Shachter, Jacob, and Harry Freedman, trans. *The Babylonian Talmud, 19: Sanhedrin*. London: Soncino Press, 1987.

Schmidt, Johann Michael. *Die jüdische Apokalyptik: Die Geschichte ihrer Erforschung von den Anfängen bis zu den Textfunden von Qumran*. Neukirchen-Vluyn: Neukirchener Verlag, 1969.

Schmökel, Hartmut. *Geschichte des alten Vorderasien*. HO 2.3. Leiden: Brill, 1957.

Schott, Albert. *Die Vergleiche in den akkadischen Königsinschriften*. MVAG 1925, 2, 30. Jahrg Leipzig: Hinrichs, 1926.

Seters, John van. "The Creation of Man and the Creation of the King." *ZAW* 101 (1989) 333–41.

Seibert, Ilse. *Hirt – Herde – König; zur Herausbildung des Konigtums in Mesopotamien*. Deutsche Akademie der Wissenschaften zu Berlin. Schriften der Sektion fur Altertumswissenschaft, 53. Berlin: Akademie-Verlag, 1969.

Seinecke, Ludwig Chr. *Geschichte des Volkes Israel* 2. Göttingen: Vandenhoeck & Ruprecht, 1884.

Seow, Choon L. "The Deep." In *Anchor Bible Dictionary*, vol. 2. Edited by David N. Freedman, et al., 125–26. New York: Doubleday, 1992.

Seux, Marie-Joseph. *Épithès Royales Akkadiennes et Sumériennes*. Paris: Letouzey et Ané, 1967.

Sheppard, Gerald T. "The Book of Isaiah: Competing Structures according to a Late Modern Description of Its Shape and Scope." In *SBL 1992 Seminar Papers*. Edited by Eugene H. Lovering, Jr., 549–82. Atlanta: Scholars Press, 1992.

Simons, Jan. *The Geographical and Topological Texts of the Old Testament*. Studia Francisci Scholten memoriae dicata, 2. Leiden: Brill, 1959.

Singer, Itamar. *Muwatalli's Prayer to the Assembly of Gods Through the Storm-god of Lightning (CTH 381)*. Atlanta: Scholars Press, 1996.

Slotki, Judah, trans. *Midrash Rabbah, Numbers II*. London: Soncino Press, 1961.

Smend, Rudolf. *Der Prophet Ezekiel.* 2d ed. KEHAT 8. Leipzig: S. Hirzel, 1880.

Smith, James. *The Book of the Prophet Ezekiel, A New Interpretation.* New York: Macmillan, 1931.

Smith, Mark S. "Mythology and Myth Making in Ugaritic and Israelite Literature." In *Ugarit and the Bible: Proceedings of the International Symposium on Ugarit and the Bible, Manchester, September 1992.* Edited by George J. Brooke, Adrian H. W. Curtis, and John F. Healey, 293–341. UBL 11. Munster : Ugarit-Verlag, 1994.

———. "The Near Eastern Background of Solar Language for Yhwh," *JBL* 109 (1990) 29–39.

———. *The Ugaritic Baal Cycle, Volume I: Introduction with Text , Translations and Commentary of KTU 1.1–1.2* VTSup 55. Leiden: Brill, 1994.

———. "Ugaritic Studies and the Hebrew Bible, 1968–1998 (With Excursus on Judean Monotheism and the Ugaritic Texts)." *Congress Volume, Oslo 1998.* Edited by André Lemaire and M. Sæbø, 327–52. VTSup 80. Leiden: Brill, 2000.

Soden, Wolfram von. "Trunkenheit im babylonisch-assyrischen Schrifttum." In *Bibel und Alter Orient.* Edited by Hans-Peter Müller, 187–94. ZAW 162. Berlin: de Gruyter, 1985.

Soggin, J. Alberto. "רעה." *THAT* 2. Edited by Ernst Jenni and Claus Westermann, 791–94. München: Chr. Kaiser, 1971.

Spronk, Klaas. *Beatific Afterlife in Ancient Israel and in the Ancient Near East.* AOAT 219. Neukirchen-Vluyn: Neukirchener Verlag, 1986.

Stager, Lawrence. "Jerusalem as Eden." *BAR* 26.3 (2000) 36–47, 66.

Steck, Odil H. "Bermerkungen zu Jesaja 6." *BZ*, NF 16 (1972) 188–206.

Steiner, Richard C., and Charles F. Nims. "You Can't Offer Your Sacrifice and Eat It Too: A Polemical Poem from the Aramaic Text in Demotic Script." *JNES* 43 (1984) 89–114.

Stevenson, Kalinda Rose. *The Vision of Transformation: The Territorial Rhetoric of Ezekiel 40–48.* SBLDS 154. Atlanta: Scholars Press, 1996.

Strange, John. "The Idea of Afterlife in Ancient Israel: Some Remarks on the Iconography in Solomon's Temple." *PEQ* 117 (1985) 35–40.

Torrey, Charles C. *Pseudo-Ezekiel and the Original Prophecy.* YOS Researches 18. New Haven: Yale University Press, 1930. Repub-

lished with critical articles by S. Spiegel, C. C. Torrey, and a Prolegomenon by M. Greenberg. LBS. New York: KTAV, 1970.
Toy, Crawford H. *The Book of the Prophet Ezekiel.* The Sacred Books of the Old and New Testaments 12. London: James H. Clarke, 1899.
Tucker, Eugene. "The Peaceable Kingdom and a Covenant with the Wild Animals." In *God Who Creates, Essays in Honor of W. Sibley Towner.* Edited by William P. Brown and S. Dean McBride Jr., 215–25. Grand Rapids: Eerdmans, 2000.
Tuell, Steven. "The Rivers of Paradise." In *The God Who Creates, Essays in Honor of W. Sibley Towner.* Edited by William P. Brown and S. Dean McBride Jr., 171–89. Grand Rapids: Eerdmans, 2000.
Uffenheimer, Benjamin. "Theodicy and Ethics in the Prophecy of Ezekiel." In *Justice and Righteousness: Biblical Themes and Their Influence.* Edited by Henning G. Reventlow and Yair Hoffman, 200–227. JSOTSup 137. Sheffield: JSOT, 1992.
Ulmer, Rivka. *Pesiqta Rabbati, A Synoptic Edition of Pesiqta Rabbati Based upon All Extant Manuscripts and the Editio Princeps 1.* South Florida Studies in the History of Judaism 155. Atlanta: Scholars Press, 1997.
Unger, Eckhard. *Babylon, die Heilige Stadt nach der Beschreibung der Babylonier.* Berlin: de Gruyter, 1931.
Vaux, Roland de. *Ancient Israel, Its Life and Institutions.* Translated by John McHugh McGraw-Hill paperbacks. New York: McGraw-Hill, 1965. Originally published as *Les Institutions de L'Ancien Testament.* Paris: Les Editions du Cerf, 1958–60.
Virolleaud, Charles. "La Déesse Ant-Astarté dans les Poèmes de Ras-Shamra." *RES* 1 (1937) 4–22.
Vogel, Walter. "Restauration de l'Egypte et universalisme en Ezek 29, 13–16." *Bib* 53 (1972) 473–94.
Vriezen, Theodore C. "Prophecy and Eschatology." In *Congress Volume, Copenhagen 1953.* Edited by G. W. Anderson, et al., 199–229. VTSup 1. Leiden: Brill, 1953.
Wakeman, Mary K. *God's Battle With the Monster.* Leiden: Brill, 1973.
Weimar, Peter. "Sinai und Schöpfung, Komposition und Theologie der Priesterschriftlichen Sinaigeschichte." *RB* 95 (1988) 337–85.
Weinfeld, Moshe. "כבוד." *TWAT* 4.23–40. Stuttgart: Kohlhammer, 1984.
———. "Sabbath, Temple, and the Enthronement of the Lord — The Problem of the *Sitz im Leben* of Genesis 1:1 – 2:3." In *Mélanges*

bibliques et orientaux en l'honneur de M. Henri Cazelles. Edited by A. Caquot et M. Delcor, 501–12. AOAT 212. Neukirchen-Vluyn: Neukirchener Verlag, 1981.

Westermann, Claus. *Genesis 1*, BKAT 1.1 Neukirchen-Vluyn: Neukirchener Verlag, 1974.

Wevers, John W. *Ezekiel.* NCBC. London: Nelson & Sons, 1969.

Wharton, J. A. "Redaction Criticism, OT." In *IDBSup.*, 721–32. Nashville: Abingdon, 1976.

Widengren, Geo. *The Ascension of the Apostle and the Heavenly Book.* UUÅ 1950:7. Uppsala: A. B Lundequistska, 1950.

———. "The Gathering of the Dispersed." *SEÅ* 41/42 (1976–77) 124–34.

———. *The King and the Tree of Life in Ancient Near Eastern Religion.* UUÅ 1951:4. Uppsala: A. B. Lundequistska, 1951.

Williams, Anthony J. "The Mythological Background of Ezekiel 28:12–19." *BTB* 6 (1976) 49–61.

Williamson, Hugh Godfrey M. "Synchronic and Diachronic in Isaian Perspective." In *Synchronic or Diachronic?: A Debate on Method in Old Testament Exegesis.* Edited by Johannes C. de Moor, 211–26. OTS 34. Leiden: Brill, 1995.

Wilson, Robert R. "The Death of the King of Tyre: The Editorial History of Ezekiel 28." In *Love & Death in the Ancient Near East: Essays in Honor of Marvin H. Pope.* Edited by John H. Marks and Robert M. Good, 211–18. Guilford, CT: Four Quarters, 1987.

———. "Ezekiel." In *The Harper Collins Bible Commentary.* Edited by J. L. Mays: 583–622. San Francisco: Harper San Francisco, 2000.

———. "Prophecy in Crisis: The Call of Ezekiel." *Int* 38 (1984) 117–30.

Winckler, Hugo. *Altorientalische Forschungen 2.* Leipzig: Eduard Pfeiffer, 1901.

Wiseman, Donald J. *Nebuchadrezzar and Babylon.* Schweich Lectures of the British Academy 1983. Oxford: Oxford University Press, 1985.

Wolff, Hans Walter. *Hosea: A Commentary on the Book of the Prophet Hosea.* Translated by Gary Stansell. Hermeneia. Philadelphia: Fortress, 1974. Originally published as *Dodeka Propheton 1 Hosea.* BKAT 14/1. Neukirchen-Vluyn: Neukirchener Verlag, 1965.

Wright, George R. H. *Ancient Building in South Syria and Palestine* I. HO 70. Leiden: Brill, 1985.

Wyatt, Nick. "The Hollow Crown: Ambivalent Elements in West Semitic Royal Ideology," *UF* 18 (1986) 421–36.

———. *Myths of Power.* UBL 13. Münster: Ugarit-Verlag, 1996.
Yadin, Yigal. "Explorations at Hazor, 1958, Preliminary Communiqué." *IEJ* 9 (1959) 74–88.
Zijl, Peter J. van. *Baal, A Study in Texts in Connexion with Baal in the Ugaritic Epics.* AOAT 10. Neukirchen-Vluyn: Neukirchener Verlag des Erziehungsvereins, 1972.
Zimmerli, Walther. *Ezekiel I: A Commentary on the Book of the Prophet Ezekiel, Chapters 1–24.* Translated by R. E. Clements. Hermeneia. Philadelphia: Fortress, 1979. Originally published as *Ezechiel I.* BKAT 13/1. Neukirchen-Vluyn: Neukirchener Verlag, 1969.
———. *Ezekiel II: A Commentary on the Book of the Prophet Ezekiel, Chapters 25 – 48.* Translated by James D. Martin. Hermeneia. Philadelphia: Fortress, 1983. Originally published as *Ezechiel II.* BKAT 13/2; Neukirchen-Vluyn: Neukirchener Verlag, 1969.
———. *I Am Yahweh.* Translated by Douglas W. Stott. Edited and with an Introduction by Walter Brueggemann. Atlanta: John Knox, 1982.
———. "The Special Form- and Traditio-Historical Character of Ezekiel's Prophecy." *VT* 15 (1965) 515–27.
Zorell, Franciscus, ed. *Lexicon Hebraicum et Aramaicum Veteris Testamenti.* Rome: Pontificium Institutum Biblicum, 1984.
Zunz, Leopold. *Die gottesdienstlichen Vorträge der Juden, historisch entwickelt.* Berlin: A. Asher, 1832.
———. "Bibelkritisches." *ZDMG* 27 (1873) 676–81, 688.

Index of Passages

Genesis		24:10	119	Joshua	
2–3	146	24:16f.	121	3:16-17	104
2:4b–3:24	141, 150	24:17	126	8:14ff.	95
2:5	104	31:12-17	183		
3:15	173	32:12	164	Judges	
6:1-4	141	40:34f.	121	4:14ff.	95
9:1-6	99			5:4	95
9:4	99	Leviticus		5:4-5	114
9:8-17	169, 173	3:16-17	99, 112	13:11	91
10:3	75	25	169	20	95
27:21	91	26	172		
49:25	190	26:4-13	173, 175	1 Samuel	
		26:4-6	172	7:7ff.	95
Exodus		26:6	172	8:5	136, 151
13:21	104	26:12	173	14:15ff.	95
14:21	65, 104, 140			14:41	67
15:1-18, 21	62	Numbers		28:6	67
15:13	62	14:10	115		
15:16	62	16:19	115	2 Samuel	
16:7	121	19	98	2:20	91
16:10	115	25:12	169	5:20ff.	95
19–20	123	27:21	67	7:5	92
19:16ff.	121			9:12	91
19:16-19	104	Deuteronomy		20:17	91
19:16-20	114	4:17	77	21:1-14	177
20:2-6	113	5:6-10	113		
20:18	104	5:25	126	1 Kings	
				6:24	117

1 Kings (cont.)

7:29	117
7:36	117
9:9	92
13:14	91
17–21	138
17	104
18:7	91
18:17	91
18:38	104
21:21	92
21:29	92

2 Kings

21:12	92
22:16	92
22:20	92
23:32	127
23:37	127
24:9	127
24:19	127

1 Chronicles

1:6	75

Job

26:12	138
38	141
38:1	115
40:6	115
42:6	164

Psalms

3:4	126
6:3 (MT)	179
18:7	118
18:14	115
18:16	118, 138
19:1-4	182
29:1	126
29:4-11	187
30:16	77
35:10	179
45:7	145
46:3-4	118
48:3	105
63:3	126
69:15	138
74	59
74:12-17	62
74:14	100
77:19	119
82	141
88:4	77
93:4	187
98:8-9	122
104:1-4	120
104:3	119
104:4	118
122:1-4	192
123:4	77
132:14	186
144:6	115
145:11	126

Proverbs

8:22-29	62
17:22	179

Isaiah

6	114, 122
6:1	120
14	141
14:4-21	150
14:13	105
14:24-25	92
19:6	115
19:23	157
25:6-8	110
27:1	59, 152
34:5-8	110
51:9	62, 152
51:15	138
54:7-10	169
56:11	77
57:6	164
59:15-20	122

Jeremiah

4-6	92
4:6	92
5:15	92
6:19	92
7:16–8:3	127
8:6	164
11:11	92
13:27	127
17:1-4, 19-27	127
18:8	164
18:10	164
19:1-13	127
19:3	92
23:19	115
30:23	115
31:8	92
31:35	138
32:34-35	127
32:42	92
35:17	92
48:8	92
49:5	92
51:64	92

Ezekiel

1–24	134, 154
1–32	24
1–37	32, 33, 112
1:1–3:1	26
1	126
1:	30
1:3	30
1:4–2:2	20
1:4-28	120, 128, 195

1:4	123	7:27	80	14:9	155		
1:13	123	8-11	26, 125–33, 195	14:13	154, 155		
1:26-27	119			14:17	154		
1:27	123	8	132	14:19	154		
1:28	76, 126	8:4	76, 126	14:21	154		
2:3-3:9	20	8:10	72	14:23	80		
2:4	123	9	132	15:1-5	22		
2:5	80, 123	9:3	76, 126, 132	15:4	77		
2:16-21	123	10:4	76, 126, 132	15:6-8	22		
3:6	81, 154	10:18	76, 126, 132	15:6	77		
3:12	76, 126	10:19	76, 126, 132	15:7	80		
3:16a + 4-5	26	11	125	16:1-43	39		
3:23	76, 126	11:9	155	16:27	155		
4–24	13	11:10	80	16:28	77		
4–32	37	11:12	80	16:36	72		
5:5-17	39	11:16-17	75	16:41	155		
5:7	98	11:17-20	154	16:49	77		
5:10	155	11:17	76, 131	16:59-63	153		
5:12	154	11:22	76, 126	16:62	80		
5:13	76, 79, 80	11:23	76, 126, 132	16:63	154		
5:14	75, 154–55	12:14	75	17	157		
5:15	79	12:15	80	17:1-10	30		
5:17	79	12:16	80	17:3	157		
6	101	12:19	76, 131	17:6	157		
6:2	75, 154	12:20	80	17:7	157		
6:3	75, 92, 155	12:22	76, 131	17:17	76		
6:4	72	13	101	17:21	75, 79, 80		
6:5	72	13:4	75	17:22	157		
6:6	72	13:9	76, 80, 131	17:23	77, 157		
6:7	80	13:11	77	17:24	79, 80, 157		
6:9	72	13:13	77	18	101		
6:10	80	13:14	80	18:2	76, 131		
6:13	72, 80	13:17	154	18:6	72		
6:14	80, 155	13:21	80	18:12	72		
7	14, 101	13:23	80	18:15	72		
7:2	76, 131	14:3	72	18:31	175		
7:4	80	14:4	72	19	6, 150		
7:9	80	14:5	72	19:9	75		
7:12-14	98	14:6	72	19:11	155		
7:20	154	14:7	72	20	26, 101, 175		
7:24	154	14:8	80	20:1-44	39		

Ezekiel (cont.)		23:39	72	27:13	75
20:7	72	23:40-42	98	27:14	75
20:8	72	23:49	72, 80	27:20	89
20:12	80	24	26, 137, 166	27:22	89
20:16	72	24:7	137	27:26	140
20:18	72	24:8	137	27:33	81, 154
20:26	80	24:14	79	28	137, 140,
20:24	72	24:21	154		141, 142,
20:31	72	24:24	80		146, 150,
20:32	136	24:27	80		186
20:33	176	25-32	35, 38,	28:1-19	137
20:34	75		39, 133, 134,	28:1-10	137, 140,
20:38	76, 80, 131		135, 166, 174,		143
20:39-44	154		195-96	28:2-10	150
20:39	72	25	136	28:2	142, 143,
20:41	75, 76	25:3	76, 131, 137		145
20:42	76, 80, 131	25:5	80, 135	28:3-4	142
20:44	80	25:6	76, 131	28:6	142
21:2	154	25:7	80, 135	28:7	92
21:5	80	25:8	136	28:8	143
21:7	76, 131, 154	25:9	80, 135	28:9	143
21:8	76, 131	25:11	80, 135	28:10	79
21:10	76	25:13	75	28:11-19	137, 140,
21:22	79	25:14	80, 135		143, 146,
21:26 (MT)	66	25:15-27	134		148-51
21:36	76	25:17	80, 135	28:12-19	150
21:37	79	26-32	27	28:13-14	147
22:3	72	26	26, 137, 156	28:13	142, 146,
22:4	72	26:1-21	137		147
22:14	79	26:4	137	28:14	141, 146
22:16	80	26:6	76, 80, 135	28:14b	148
22:21	76	26:7	75, 92	28:15-17	146
22:22	80	26:14	79, 137	28:16	143
22:31	76	26:19	138	28:18	151
23:1-30	39	26:20	75	28:20-24	136
23:2-25	30	27	76, 89,	28:22	76, 80,
23:7	72		137, 139		126, 135
23:10	155	27-32	42	28:23	80, 135
23:12	75	27:1-36	137	28:24-26	154
23:30	72	27:10	75	28:24	80, 135
23:37	72	27:12	89	28:25-26	75

Index of Passages

28:25	76	31	157–58		165, 195
28:26	76, 80, 135	31:1-18	27, 155	33–39	4, 8,
28:27	140	31:2	156		13, 45
29	14, 152,	31:3	155–57	33–48	15, 16,
	154, 161	31:4	157–58		17, 134
29:1-16	26, 152	31:5	157	33	4, 13, 135,
29:2	154	31:6	155, 157		163, 165–66
29:3	152	31:7	155, 157	33:2	160
29:4	81, 154	31:8	155	33:18	160
29:4f.	81,154	31:9	155, 157	33:21-22	134, 165
29:5	77, 99, 153	31:10	156	33:21-23	19
29:6	76, 80, 135	31:11-12	157	33:24	75, 76,
29:8	92, 154	31:11	81, 154–55		131
29:9	75, 80, 135	31:12	155–57	33:25	72
29:10-12	153	31:13	156	33:27	75, 77,
29:10	75, 81	31:14	155		99, 153
29:11	154	31:18	76, 126	33:28	75
29:13-16	153	32	99, 156,	33:29	80
29:13	81, 154		161	33:33	80
29:14	81	32:1-10	44	34–37	28, 30,
29:16	80, 135	32:1-16	27		35, 38, 39,
29:21	80, 135,	32:2	75, 161		41, 194–95
	154	32:3	75, 161	34–48	24, 35,
29:17	5	32:4-5	162		44, 73
29:17-20	5	32:4	77, 99,	34	9, 88, 93,
29:17-21	26		153, 161		102, 149,
29:19	81, 154	32:5	77, 155, 161		151, 163,
30:6	76	32:6	161		165–67,
30:8	80, 135	32:7-8	162		171–72,
30:10	81, 154	32:7	76		174, 180,
30:11	154	32:13	154		197
30:12	79, 81, 154	32:14	162	34:1-10	168
30:13	72	32:15	80, 135	34:2	168
30:14	155	32:16	75	34:5	77
30:18	76, 154	32:17-32	27, 162	34:8	77
30:19	80, 135, 155	32:30	163	34:11ff.	154
30:20-26	27	32:31	163, 164	34:13	75, 155, 168
30:22	81, 154	33-36	3	34:23-24	169
30:25	80, 81,	33-37	7, 8, 14,	34:23	169
	135, 154–55		16, 20, 38,	34:24	79
30:26	80, 135		39, 43,		

Ezekiel (cont.)		36:30	176	38:3	78, 79, 81, 84, 154
34:25-31	173, 175–76	36:33-36	176	38:4	30, 75, 81, 93, 154
34:25-30	173	36:33	77		
34:25-29	171	36:35	75	38:5	75, 78, 79
34:25-28	42, 43, 45	36:36	76, 79, 80	38:6	75, 87, 106, 107
34:25	76, 169, 173	36:38	75, 80		
		37-39	3	38:7-9	93
34:26-29	173	37	3, 6, 8-10, 25, 28, 33, 35, 40, 41-42, 88, 93, 102, 155, 162, 165, 176, 178–80, 197	38:8	8, 12, 24, 35, 59, 75, 76, 81, 90, 94, 102, 154
34:27	76, 80				
34:28	76, 171, 173, 181, 197				
				38:9	75, 76
34:29	171, 172	37:1-14	179	38:10-16	13
34:30	80, 173	37:6	80	38:10	78, 79, 84, 88, 102, 106, 135
35:1–36:15	174	37:9	178		
35	35, 39, 165	37:11ff.	154		
35:4	75, 80	37:12	76, 131	38:11	76, 94, 105
35:9	80	37:13	80	38:12	12, 75, 81, 89, 154
35:12	75, 77, 80	37:14	79, 80		
35:15	80	37:15-28	180	38:13	76, 89
36-48	38	37:21	24, 75, 180	38:14-16	93, 104
36	5, 165, 174, 197	37:22	75	38:14	76, 78, 84, 94, 135
		37:23	72, 77		
36:1-15	175–76	37:25-28	42, 43, 45		
36:1	75	37:26	28, 169, 180	38:15	75, 76, 106
36:4	75, 155				
36:5	76	37:26-28	28	38:16	76, 80, 84, 90, 93, 102
36:6	76, 131, 155	37:26b-28	14		
		37:28	28, 76, 80	38:17	10, 13, 78, 79, 84, 90-94
36:8	75	38-48	19, 35		
36:11	80	38:1	78		
36:16-38	175	38:1-3a	32	38:18–39:8	85, 94, 105
36:16-23a	41-42	38:1-4a	22-23		
36:18	72	38:1-9	13, 30	38:18-23	12, 13, 84, 93, 107, 108
36:22ff.	154	38:1-9a	31		
36:23	76, 80	38:2-17	85, 96, 105	38:18	76, 78, 79, 84, 95, 102, 131, 135
36:24	75, 176				
36:25	72, 77	38:2	78, 79, 84, 105		
36:26	175				
36:27	175	38:3-6	111	38:19	76, 95,

	102, 131, 135	39:14-16 39:14	13 77	39:28	75, 80, 84, 102
38:21	78, 79, 84	39:15	99	39:29	78, 79, 84, 101, 102, 181
38:22	75, 77, 95	39:16	77, 80, 89		
38:23	76, 80, 84, 96	39:17	75, 77, 78, 79, 84, 90, 100, 112	40ff. 40-48	28 3, 8, 19, 22, 24, 27, 30, 32, 33, 35- 38, 39, 41- 42, 45- 46, 48, 112, 154, 180–81, 194–95, 197
39	12, 80, 101, 107		
39:1-8	28, 94-96, 108	39:17-20	13, 30-31, 83, 109, 110
39:1-5	13, 26, 31	39:19	77, 81, 112, 154
39:1b-5	32		
39:1	75, 78, 79, 81, 84, 94, 154	39:20	77, 78, 79, 84, 112
		39:21-29	85, 100-102	40	36, 40, 180
39:2-5	30			40:1	5, 6, 101
39:2	75, 87, 90, 96, 106	39:21-24	102	40:2-4	182, 185
		39:21-22	101, 102	40:5	185
		39:21	80, 100, 101, 135	40:16	185
39:3	81			41:3	185
39:4	75, 77, 81, 90, 97, 154	39:21a	102	42:10	185
		39:21b	102	42:20	185
39:5	81, 84, 153–54	39:22	78, 80, 84, 101, 102	43	133, 186–87, 197
39:6	76, 80, 84, 97	39:23-29	33	43:1-12	182
		39:23-24	84, 101, 102	43:2	76, 126
39:7	76, 80, 84, 97, 102			43:3	186
		39:25-29	14, 32, 36, 40, 84, 154	43:4	76, 126
39:6-8	13			43:5	76, 126
39:8	10, 78, 79, 84, 96, 97	39:23	76, 78, 80, 81, 84, 100, 102	43:7	187, 190
				43:9	187, 190
39:9	96			43:13-17	188
39:9-20	85, 97, 105, 109	39:24	102	43:14	188–89
		39:25	78, 79, 81, 84, 100-102	43:15	188–89
39:9-10	13			43:18-26	189
39:10	78, 79, 84			43:26	77
39:11-13	13	39-25-29	102	44:1-3	189
39:11-16	99, 178	39:26-27	102	44:2	190
39:11	102	39:26	76, 94	44:4	76, 126
39:12	77, 78, 154	39:27	75, 76, 81, 154	44:10	72
39:13	76, 78, 79, 84, 102, 126			44:12	72

Ezekiel (cont.)		Amos		Zechariah	
44:16	77, 112	1:2	122	4	114
47:1-48:35	190	7:3	164	9:14	115
47:1-12	60, 182, 190–91	7:6	164	10:11	157
				14:1-5	58
48:30-35	192	Micah			
		1:2-7	122	Malachi	
Daniel				3:1-5	122
8:17	78	Nahum			
11-12	141	1:3-8	115	Revelation	
11:40-45	58			19:17-21	83
		Habakkuk		20:7-10	83
Hosea		3:8-15	115		
2:18	173				
6:3	117	Zephaniah			
7:11	157	1:7	110		

Index of Authors

Ackerman, S., 127
Ahlström, G., 70
Ahroni, R., 31-32, 45-46, 91, 92
Albrektson, B., 64, 65, 67
Albright, W. F., 86, 109, 188, 189
Allen, L., 42-43, 45, 84, 99, 123
Astour, M., 31, 45-46, 86

Bartelmus, R., 118, 121
Barthélemy, D., 93
Batto, B., 51, 55, 56, 60, 87, 99, 134, 138, 151, 152, 153, 154, 161, 170, 171, 172
Baumgartner, W., 96, 156, 164
Becker, J., 35, 45
Berry, G., 14-15, 23
Bertholet, A., 6-7, 20, 23, 24, 122, 140
Biran, A., 72
Blenkinsopp, J., 34, 40-41, 45, 84, 91, 92, 96, 110.
Block, D., 44, 46, 77, 78, 79, 80, 84, 88, 90, 92, 94, 98, 99, 100, 101, 103, 110, 116, 127, 128, 132, 138, 140, 148, 152, 158, 161, 163, 165, 166, 169, 170, 172, 174, 176, 178, 180, 188, 190, 192.
Boadt, L., 43, 46, 55-56, 58, 69, 81, 90, 95, 97, 135, 136, 138, 146, 151, 153, 154, 155, 156, 157158, 159, 161, 165, 169, 172, 173, 174, 178
Bolle, K., 51, 55, 60, 64
Borger, R., 65, 130, 168, 184
Bracke, J., 102
Braude, W., 83
Briggs, C., 172
Brown, F., 172
Brownlee, W., 122
Buber, M., 47, 164
Bultmann, R., 57
Buren, E. D. van, 191
Busink, T., 185

Cagni, L., 159
Cassuto, U., 23-24, 45, 61, 112, 144
Chester, A., 178
Childs, B., 34, 45-46, 57, 69, 87, 95
Clapham, L., 64, 66
Clements, R., 29, 43, 45-46
Clifford, R., 53, 56, 61, 63, 64, 90, 95, 107, 124, 144, 145, 171, 175, 179
Cody, A., 36-37, 45-46
Cogan, M., 128
Cohn, N., 50, 62, 72, 88, 186, 191
Collins, A. Y., 105

Conroy, C., 64
Coogan, M. D., 110, 111, 153
Cooke, G., 20-21, 23, 100, 146, 181
Cornill, K., 6
Cross, F. M., 50, 54, 64, 69, 104, 106, 108, 119, 143

Dahood, M. J., 147
Dalley, S., 167
Danby, H., 82
Davidson, A., 7-8, 122
Davies, G. H., 57
Davis, E., 40, 46, 122, 124, 133, 134, 135, 136, 137, 151, 164, 165
Day, J., 108, 109, 152
DeMoor, J. C., 109, 179
Dietrich, M., 106
Dijk, H. J., 138, 140, 143, 145
Driver, S., 8-9, 21, 28
Dupont-Sommer, A., 100
Dürr, L., 166, 168

Ebeling, E., 167, 177
Eichrodt, W., 27-28, 45, 78, 91, 92, 95, 100, 117, 122, 127, 134, 146, 172, 173, 180
Eissfeldt, O., 26-27, 45, 144
Eliade, M., 53, 158, 159
Elliger, K., 91, 156, 172
Egnell, I., 141, 160, 169
Epstein, I., 100
Ewald, G. H., 4

Falkenstein, A., 167
Fechter, F., 42, 45, 46, 143, 144, 147, 150
Fensham, F. C., 178
Fenton, T., 183
Fishbane, M., 189
Fisher, L., 61, 181, 183
Fitzgerald, A., 140
Fohrer, G., 24-25, 45, 100, 122, 127, 152, 188

Fontenrose, J. E., 51
Forsyth, N., 52, 104, 104
Foster, B. R., 130, 170
Freedman, D. N., 87, 123, 148
Freedman, H., 82
Frese, P., 158
Fritz, V., 185

Garcia Martínez, F., 58
Garfinkel, S., 116, 188
Garscha, J., 30-31, 33, 36, 45, 84
Gawaltney, Jr., W., 129, 131
Gesenius, W., 143, 147
Gese, H., 181
Geyer, J., 139
Ginsberg, H., 171, 172
Ginzberg, L., 83
Girardot, N., 58
Goldin, J., 82
Gorman, Jr., F., 153, 189
Gosse, B., 134
Gray, S., 158
Grayson, A., 162
Green, M., 130
Greenberg, M., 17, 35-36, 43, 46, 101, 116, 119, 121, 123, 125, 127, 139, 152, 156, 160, 172, 174, 176, 177, 178, 181
Greenspoon, L., 179
Gressmann, H., 4, 11-13, 23, 110, 111-12, 178–80
Gross, W., 169, 178
Gunkel, H., 4, 10-11, 59, 68, 146, 152, 161

Hallo, W., 51, 52, 60, 104, 105, 108, 109, 110, 111, 112, 119, 129, 137, 145, 150, 153, 161, 162, 166, 171, 178, 182, 186, 187, 191
Hals, R., 77, 79
Hammer, R., 83
Hammershaimb, E., 169
Hamp, V., 123

Hanson, P., 33, 45-46, 70, 180
Harford, J. B., 21
Harrelson, W., 68, 69
Heinisch, P., 86
Hengstenberg, E., 4-5
Herntrich, V., 19-20, 21, 23
Herrmann, J., 13-14, 23, 33, 100
Herrmann, W., 116, 117, 144
Hitzig, F., 4, 5, 7
Holladay, J., 70, 71, 72
Hölscher, G., 15-17, 22-23, 100
Hoonacker, A. van, 86
Horovitz, H., 176
Horowitz, W., 67
Hossfeld, F., 32-33, 36, 45, 84, 100, 101, 180
Howie, C., 24, 45
Hurowitz, V., 67, 182, 183

Irwin, W., 10, 21-22, 23, 156
Israelstam, J., 82

Jacobsen, T., 50, 54, 61, 108, 139, 184, 187, 191
Jeremias, J., 106, 122
Joüon, P., 147, 156
Joyce, P., 48

Kaiser, O., 177
Kaltner, J., 83
Kapstein, I., 83
Keel, O., 114, 118, 120, 121
Keller, B., 132
Kingsley, P., 115, 116
Klein, J., 189
Klein, R., 122
Knutson, F. B., 169
Kohler, J., 177
König, F., 177
Korpel, M., 62, 109, 119
Kraetzschmar, R., 9-10, 11, 13, 20, 22-23, 122

Kramer, S., 52, 105, 108, 129, 131
Kraus, H.-J., 69
Krüger, T., 39-40, 45-46
Kutsko, J. F., 132

Lambert, W., 124, 131, 159, 166, 168
Lang, B., 34-35, 37, 43, 46, 177, 180
Langdon, S., 188, 189
Lauha, A., 69, 87, 89
Layton, S., 79
Le Déaut, R., 82
Lehrman, S., 82
Lemke, W., 169
Levenson, J., 58, 59, 63, 83, 133, 175, 182, 186, 189
Levey, S., 82, 111
Lewy, H., 115
Limet, H., 183
Lipiński, E., 85, 107
Livingstone, A., 115
Lohse, E., 177
Long, C., 175
Longman III, T., 130
Loretz, O., 61, 63, 106, 107, 115, 117, 132, 143, 179, 182, 188, 191
Luckenbill, D., 66, 85, 167, 177, 184, 187

Machinist, P., 124, 128
Mafico, T., 124
Malamat, A., 66
May, H., 119, 138, 152, 158, 161, 186, 189, 191
Mazar, A., 185
McCarter, P. K., 138
Meissner, B., 167
Mettinger, T. N. D., 69, 71, 72, 118, 119, 125, 128, 132, 141
Metzger, M., 156, 158, 187
Meyer, J.-W., 66
Milgrom, J., 67
Millard, A. R., 147
Miller, Jr., P., 111, 119

Mischon, A., 82
Monson, J., 142, 185, 187
Müller, H.-P., 49, 50, 51, 55, 69, 70, 122, 148, 176, 180
Munz, P., 55

Neusner, J., 83, 176
Newsom, C., 56, 117, 134, 137, 139, 140, 144, 145, 146
Niditch, S., 46
Nobile, M., 37-39, 43, 46, 88, 107, 114, 117, 119, 122, 124, 132, 135, 163, 192

O'Connor, M., 148
Odell, M., 80, 89, 90, 91, 92, 97, 98, 101, 103
Oden, Jr., R., 69
Ohler, A., 69, 116
Olmo Lete, G. del, 63
Oppenheim, A., 148

Page, H., 140, 141, 142, 143, 144, 145, 146
Pardee, D., 106, 172
Parrot, A., 67
Parunak, H. van D., 84
Philonenko, M., 100
Philostratus, F., 115
Piatelli, A., 82
Plato, 86
Podella, T., 58, 114, 131, 132
Pohlmann, K.-F., 41-42, 45, 118, 119, 125, 116, 117, 120
Pope, M., 64, 116, 143, 144, 149
Preuss, H. D., 62, 63, 64, 68, 69, 72, 160
Price, J. D., 105
Pritchard, J. B., 52, 66, 105, 106, 108, 109, 121, 128, 129, 158, 166, 167, 168, 177, 184, 185, 189

Rabenau, K. von, 26, 45
Rad, G. van, 47, 62
Rendtorff, R., 69, 126
Renz, T., 44-45, 46
Richardson, M., 96, 156, 164
Ricoeur, P., 67, 68
Rogerson, J. W., 50
Römer, T., 61, 63, 64
Römer, W., 159, 192
Rosenberg, A., 96
Rosenzweig, F., 47
Rudolph, W., 91, 156, 172
Ruwe, A., 132

Saggs, H. W. F., 66
Sarna, N., 61, 138
Schmidt, J., 4
Schmökel, H., 85
Schott, A., 167
Seibert, I., 159, 160, 166
Seinecke, L., 5-6, 10, 15
Seow, C. L., 138, 158, 191
Seters, J. van, 146, 149
Seux, M.-J., 167
Shachter, J., 82
Sheppard, G. T., 47
Simon, M., 83
Simons, J., 105
Singer, I., 65
Slotki, J., 83
Smend, Sr., R., 5, 100, 122
Smend III, R., 34
Smith, J., 18-19
Smith, M. S., 49, 50, 54, 58, 64, 119, 127, 173
Soden, W. von, 112, 167
Soggin, J. A., 168
Spronk, K., 177, 178, 179, 180
Stager, L., 142, 145, 186, 187, 191
Steck, O. H., 123
Stevenson, K., 46, 48, 189, 190, 192

Strange, J., 158, 159

Torrey, C., 10, 17-18, 19, 22
Toy, C., 8, 16, 122
Tucker, E., 173
Tuell, S., 191

Uehlinger, C., 114, 120, 121
Uffenheimer, B., 73, 176
Ulmer, R., 183
Unger, E., 190, 192
Ungnad, A., 177

Vaux, R. de, 188, 189
Virolleaud, C., 171
Vogel, W., 154
Vriezen, T., 25-26, 45

Wakeman, M., 55, 83, 87, 88, 124, 138, 153, 161, 162
Weidner, E., 167
Weimar, P., 183, 186
Weinfeld, M., 61, 126, 182, 183
Westermann, C., 60, 63

Wevers, J., 28-29, 45, 84, 100, 174
Widengren, G., 141, 142, 145, 159, 168
Williams, A., 146
Williamson, H. G. M., 48
Willoughby, B., 87, 123
Wilson, R., 84, 149
Winckler, H., 10-11, 23
Wiseman, D. J., 192
Wolff, H. W., 173
Wright, G. R., 185
Wyatt, N., 51, 53, 54, 58, 63, 109, 140, 141, 142, 144, 150, 152, 161

Yadin, Y., 67

Zijl, P. J., 162
Zimmerli, W., 29-30, 31, 34, 35, 36, 45, 79-80, 84, 85, 87, 90, 91, 96, 99, 100, 118, 119, 121, 122, 127, 134, 138, 139, 143, 146, 152, 156, 172, 174, 177, 178, 179, 180, 190
Zorell, F., 106
Zunz, L., 2-3, 5, 10, 15

Index of Subjects

Abshshu, 184
Abtagigi, 184
Adad, 192
Aia, 184
akitu, 189, 192
amber, 115–16, 120
Ammon, 136–37
An, 129
Anat, 60, 65, 108–10, 153, 171–73, 196
aniconic (aniconism), 71-72, 131
anthology, 21, 23, 198
Anu, 149, 159
Anzag-Demon, 105
Anzu-Bird, 104–6, 109
Apsu, 182
Aqhat, 65
Aruru, 130
Ashananna, 130
Asherah, 111, 150, 187
Ashimbabar, 130
Ashtar, 150, 187
Ashur, 121, 191
Ashurbanipal, 85, 177, 184
Ashurnasirpal II, 162
Assyria, 126, 130, 156–57, 160, 167
Astarte, 141
Atrahasis, 170, 172, 196

Baal, 51, 52, 54, 58, 63, 65, 103, 106–9, 111, 112, 115–17, 120, 138, 149–51, 153, 159, 161–62, 171–73, 179, 183, 186–87
Baba, 191
Babylon, 5, 7, 12, 13, 19, 21, 24, 29, 35, 41, 46, 50, 54, 66, 115, 118, 125, 127, 130, 134, 167–68, 187–90, 192
Behemoth, 100, 109, 111
Belet-ili, 149
Belial, 58

cedar, 155–58, 160
Challenge to a Duel Formula, 79, 81, 154
chaos monster, 152–53, 160–63
cherub (cherubim), 117–19, 146–47
cognitive dissonance, 59, 125, 194
Combat (*Chaoskampf*) Myth, 52-54, 56-63, 73, 83–84, 103–5, 108–9, 113, 138, 140, 164, 194–95
Commissioning Formula, 79, 84
Conclusion Formula, 79
cosmic mountain, 186, 190
cosmic ship, 139, 165
cosmic tree, 157–60, 165
cosmic waters, 190
cosmogony (cosmogonic), 57, 60-63, 70, 73, 90, 95, 97, 103, 107, 113–14,

240

121–22, 124–25, 127, 132, 147, 152, 165, 174–76, 181–82, 189, 193–98
Covenant of peace, 28, 43, 60, 88, 90, 93, 103, 163, 169–74, 180–81, 194–97
creation myth, 11, 50, 61, 103, 124, 194–95
cult and myth, 68-70
Cuthean Legend of Naram-Sin, 31

Damgalnunna, 130
Daniel, 18
decisive battle, 32, 51, 95, 164–65, 181, 195–98
(the) deep, 138, 155, 158, 160, 190
divine abandonment, 125–26, 131, 196
divine warrior, 57, 65, 94, 104, 106, 112, 115, 119, 179–81
Deuteronomistic History, 91
Deuteronomy, 16
direct speech markers, 78

Ea, 63, 105, 149, 182
Eanna
Ebih, 183
Eden, 142, 146–47, 155, 160, 170–71, 175, 186
Edom, 6, 39, 136, 174
Egypt, 14, 99, 121–22, 126, 134, 136, 151–53, 156–57, 160, 162–63, 169
El, 61, 63, 65, 103, 106, 138, 141, 144–46, 149–51, 153, 179, 187, 191
enemy (foe) from the north, 4, 12, 33, 87, 107
Enki, 130, 139
Enlil, 106, 128–29, 149, 167, 183, 192
Enmeduranki, 130, 159
Enuma Elish, 60-61, 182, 191
epic, 64, 66
Erra, 159
Esarhaddon, 65, 116, 159, 165, 168, 177, 184, 187
Ezekiel (the prophet), 15, 16, 24, 29, 125

final form, 47-48
forms of address, 78

Genesis, 170
Gilgamesh, 66, 148–49, 170, 196
glory (chabod), 76, 114, 121–23, 125–27, 131–32, 147, 186–87
Gog, 3, 5–10, 14, 16, 17, 39, 81, 83, 85–89, 91–93, 96-99, 102–8, 110, 154, 181, 194–95, 198
Grimm, 57
Gyges of Lydia, 5, 85-86

"halving pattern," 101
Hammurabi, 167–68
Hamonah, 98
Hathor, 171, 196
history and myth, 64-67
Holiness Code, 16
Hostile Orientation Formula, 79

Ile-Amurru, 184
Inaugural Vision, 121
Isaiah, 13, 91, 106
Ishmadagan of Isin, 159
Ishtar (Inanna, Ininna), 116, 128, 145, 166–67, 183–84, 192

Jeremiah, 3, 13, 87, 91, 92, 127, 134
Jerusalem, 5, 19, 20, 27, 50, 73, 89, 93, 98, 125–27, 132, 134, 137, 160, 163, 165–66, 188–90, 192, 196
Joel, 18
judgment, 95, 102, 114, 123–27, 133–34, 138–40, 147, 149, 160, 165–66, 196

Keret, 65, 110, 142, 150
king (kingship, monarchy), 53, 54, 57-58, 61, 120, 129, 132–33, 139–43, 145–51, 158–60, 162, 167, 169, 186, 197
(1-2) Kings, 92

(the) land, 28, 33, 97, 176, 195
Lebanon, 156
Leviathan, 51, 59, 100, 109–11
Lipit-Ishtar, 165
liver divination, 66

Magog, 10, 83, 86-87, 195, 198
"many (mighty, great) waters," 114, 117–19, 140, 155, 186–87
Marduk, 52, 54, 60-61, 63, 65, 108–9, 115, 124, 130, 158, 161–62, 166–68, 178, 182, 184, 187, 189–93
Melqart, 141
Merodach-baladan, 168
Meshech, 75, 89, 105, 163
Messenger Formula, 78, 84, 123
Moab, 136–37
Mot, 52, 60, 65, 109–10, 138, 150, 153
mountain of God, 147–48, 189
mountains of Israel, 75, 87, 89, 90, 96, 99, 104, 107, 175
Mullil, 130
myth (defined), 50-51
mythopoeic (mythopoeism, mythopoeically), 55–56, 58, 59, 61, 73, 94, 103, 108, 114, 125, 131, 133, 135, 172, 176, 186, 198
mythopoetic, 55-56, 135, 146, 151–52, 157–58, 163, 182

Nabonidus, 184
Nabopolassar, 188–89
Nanna, 129, 130
Naram-Sin, 128
navel of the earth, 12, 107
Nebuchadnezzar, 7, 31, 66, 92, 131, 134, 137, 188–89
Nergal (Lugalgirra), 116, 149 192
Ningal, 129, 184
Ningirsu, 183, 186, 191
Ninhursaga, 139

Ninlil, 129
Ninurta (Zababa), 105, 108, 109, 149, 177, 192
Nippur, 128–29
Niqmadu, 170
Nusku (Nusky), 149, 184

Oracles against Egypt, 14, 75, 80, 151, 154, 165
Oracles against the (Foreign) Nations, 33-35, 39, 46, 56, 81, 113, 133–37, 154, 160, 163–65, 195–96
Oracle against Tyre, 75, 137, 154
Oracles of Judgment, 123, 154, 165–66
Oracles of Salvation, 135, 165
Osiris, 153

Pharaoh, 44, 152–57, 160, 163–64
Philistia, 136
planting of peace, 171–72, 174
Primal Man, 146, 148
prophetic commands, 78
Prophetic Word Formula, 78, 85
Prophetic Utterance Formula, 79, 84
pseudepigraph (pseudepigraphon), 6, 15, 17, 35

Qur'an, 83

Rahab, 62
Re, 139, 171
Recognition Formula, 30, 76, 80, 84, 198

Samaritan, 18
Samaritan priesthood, 18
Sadarnunna, 184
Sargon II, 128
Saul, 178
Scythian advance, 8, 10
Sennacherib, 141, 177
Shalmaneser I, 167, 177

Index of Subjects · 243

Shamash, 66, 108, 124, 166–67, 184, 192
Sheol, 163
shepherd, 166–69, 174, 196
Shulgi, 159
Shuppiluliuma, 170
Sibylline Oracles, 82
Sidon, 136–37
Sin, 184, 192
Solomon, 142, 183–86

Tablets of Destiny, 106, 145, 148
Tashmetu, 187
Temple (sanctuary), 3, 19, 28, 37, 50, 57, 61, 64, 93, 112–13, 117, 120–21, 125–29, 131–33, 142, 181–90, 193–95, 197
theomachy, 149–50
theophany, 114–19, 122–24
Throne Chariot, 2, 20, 114, 119, 121, 127, 187
Tiamat, 52, 61, 83, 105, 108–9, 161, 178, 182, 191
Tiglath-Pileser I, 162, 167

Tikulti-Ninurta I, 124, 128
Tree of Life, 159
Tubal, 75, 89, 105, 163
Tyre, 134, 136–39, 141, 145–47, 150–51, 154, 156, 169

Urash, 192
Ur-nammu, 165
Urim and Thummim, 66-67

Victory Feast, 98-100, 109
Vision of the Dry Bones, 25, 176–80, 196

wheel, 119–20

Yamm, 51-52, 65, 103, 109, 119, 153, 161–62

Zadokite priesthood, 16, 18
Zaphon, 106–7, 112, 116, 150
Zechariah, 18
Zephaniah, 134
Zion (Sion), 18, 107, 116

The Catholic Biblical Quarterly
Monograph Series (CBQMS)

1. Patrick W. Skehan, *Studies in Israelite Poetry and Wisdom* (CBQMS 1) $9.00 ($7.20 for CBA members) ISBN 0-915170-00-0 (LC 77-153511)
2. Aloysius M. Ambrozic, *The Hidden Kingdom: A Redactional-Critical Study of the References to the Kingdom of God in Mark's Gospel* (CBQMS 2) $9.00 ($7.20 for CBA members) ISBN 0-915170-01-9 (LC 72-89100)
3. Joseph Jensen, O.S.B., *The Use of tôrâ by Isaiah: His Debate with the Wisdom Tradition* (CBQMS 3) $3.00 ($2.40 for CBA members) ISBN 0-915170-02-7 (LC 73-83134)
4. George W. Coats, *From Canaan to Egypt: Structural and Theological Context for the Joseph Story* (CBQMS 4) $4.00 ($3.20 for CBA members) ISBN 0-915170-03-5 (LC 75-11382)
5. O. Lamar Cope, *Matthew: A Scribe Trained for the Kingdom of Heaven* (CBQMS 5) $4.50 ($3.60 for CBA members) ISBN 0-915170-04-3 (LC 75-36778)
6. Madeleine Boucher, *The Mysterious Parable: A Literary Study* (CBQMS 6) $2.50 ($2.00 for CBA members) ISBN 0-915170-05-1 (LC 76-51260)
7. Jay Braverman, Jerome's Commentary on Daniel: A Study of Comparative Jewish and Christian Interpretations of the Hebrew Bible (CBQMS 7) $4.00 ($3.20 for CBA members) ISBN 0-915170-06-X (LC 78-55726)
8. Maurya P. Horgan, *Pesharim: Qumran Interpretations of Biblical Books* (CBQMS 8) $6.00 ($4.80 for CBA members) ISBN 0-915170-07-8 (LC 78-12910)
9. Harold W. Attridge and Robert A. Oden, Jr., *Philo of Byblos*, The Phoenician History (CBQMS 9) $3.50 ($2.80 for CBA members) ISBN 0-915170-08-6 (LC 80-25781)
10. Paul J. Kobelski, *Melchizedek and Melchireša'* (CBQMS 10) $4.50 ($3.60 for CBA members) ISBN 0-915170-09-4 (LC 80-28379)
11. Homer Heater, *A Septuagint Translation Technique in the Book of Job* (CBQMS 11) $4.00 ($3.20 for CBA members) ISBN 0-915170-10-8 (LC 81-10085)
12. Robert Doran, *Temple Propaganda: The Purpose and Character of 2 Maccabees* (CBQMS 12) $4.50 ($3.60 for CBA members) ISBN 0-915170-11-6 (LC 81-10084)
13. James Thompson, *The Beginnings of Christian Philosophy: The Epistle to the Hebrews* (CBQMS 13) $5.50 ($4.50 for CBA members) ISBN 0-915170-12-4 (LC 81-12295)

14. Thomas H. Tobin, S.J., *The Creation of Man: Philo and the History of Interpretation* (CBQMS 14) $6.00 ($4.80 for CBA members) ISBN 0-915170-13-2 (LC 82-19891)
15. Carolyn Osiek, *Rich and Poor in the Shepherd of Hermes* (CBQMS 15) $6.00 ($4.80 for CBA members) ISBN 0-915170--14-0 (LC 83-7385)
16. James C. VanderKam, *Enoch and the Growth of an Apocalyptic Tradition* (CBQMS 16) $6.50 ($5.20 for CBA members) ISBN 0-915170-15-9 (LC 83-10134)
17. Antony F. Campbell, S.J., *Of Prophets and Kings: A Late Ninth-Century Document (1 Samuel 1-2 Kings 10)* (CBQMS 17) $7.50 ($6.00 for CBA members) ISBN 0-915170-16-7 (LC 85-12791)
18. John C. Endres, S.J., *Biblical Interpretation in the Book of Jubilees* (CBQMS 18) $8.50 ($6.80 for CBA members) ISBN 0-915170-17-5 (LC 86-6845)
19. Sharon Pace Jeansonne, *The Old Greek Translation of Daniel 7-12* (CBQMS 19) $5.00 ($4.00 for CBA members) ISBN 0-915170-18-3 (LC 87-15865)
20. Lloyd M. Barré, *The Rhetoric of Political Persuasion: The Narrative Artistry and Political Intentions of 2 Kings 9 -11* (CBQMS 20) $5.00 ($4.00 for CBA members) ISBN 0-915170-19-1 (LC 87-15878)
21. John J. Clabeaux, *A Lost Edition of the Letters of Paul: A Reassessment of the Text of the Pauline Corpus Attested by Marcion* (CBQMS 21) $8.50 ($6.80 for CBA members) ISBN 0-915170-20-5 (LC 88-28511)
22. Craig Koester, *The Dwelling of God: The Tabernacle in the Old Testament, Intertestamental Jewish Literature, and the New Testament* (CBQMS 22) $9.00 ($7.20 for CBA members) ISBN 0-915170-21-3 (LC 89-9853)
23. William Michael Soll, *Psalm 119: Matrix, Form, and Setting* (CBQMS 23) $9.00 ($7.20 for CBA members) ISBN 0-915170-22-1 (LC 90-27610)
24. Richard J. Clifford and John J. Collins (eds.), *Creation in the Biblical Traditions* (CBQMS 24) $7.00 ($5.60 for CBA members) ISBN 0-915170-23-X (LC 92-20268)
25. John E. Course, *Speech and Response: A Rhetorical Analysis of the Introductions to the Speeches of the Book of Job, Chaps. 4 - 24* (CBQMS 25) $8.50 ($6.80 for CBA members) ISBN 0-915170-24-8 (LC 94-26566)
26. Richard J. Clifford, *Creation Accounts in the Ancient Near East and in the Bible* (CBQMS 26) $9.00 ($7.20 for CBA members) ISBN 0-915170-25-6 (LC 94-26565)
27. John Paul Heil, *Blood and Water: The Death and Resurrection of Jesus in John 18 – 21* (CBQMS 27) $9.00 ($7.20 for CBA members) ISBN 0-915170-26-4 (LC 95-10479)
28. John Kaltner, *The Use of Arabic in Biblical Hebrew Lexicography* (CBQMS 28) $7.50 ($6.00 for CBA members) ISBN 0-915170-27-2 (LC 95-45182)

29. Michael L. Barré, S.S., *Wisdom, You Are My Sister: Studies in Honor of Roland E. Murphy, O.Carm., on the Occasion of His Eightieth Birthday* (CBQMS 29) $13.00 ($10.40 for CBA members) ISBN 0-915170-28-0 (LC 97-16060)
30. Warren Carter and John Paul Heil, *Matthew's Parables: Audience-Oriented Perspectives* (CBQMS 30) $10.00 ($8.00 for CBA members) ISBN 0-915170-29-9 (LC 97-44677)
31. David S. Williams, *The Structure of 1 Maccabees* (CBQMS 31) $7.00 ($5.60 for CBA members) ISBN 0-915170-30-2
32. Lawrence Boadt and Mark S. Smith (eds.), *Imagery and Imagination in Biblical Literature: Essays in Honor of Aloysius Fitzgerald, F.S.C.* (CBQMS 32) $9.00 ($7.20 for CBA members) ISBN 0-915170-31-0 (LC 2001003305)
33. Stephan K. Davis, *The Antithesis of the Ages: Paul's Reconfiguration of Torah* (CBQMS 33) $11.00 ($8.80 for CBA members) ISBN 0-915170-32-9 (LC 2001007936)
34. Aloysius Fitzgerald, F.S.C., *The Lord of the East Wind* (CBQMS 34) $12.00 ($9.60 for CBA members) ISBN 0-915170-33-7 (LC 2002007068)
35. William L. Moran, *The Most Magic Word: Essays on Babylonian and Biblical Literature* (CBQMS 35) $11.50 ($9.20 for CBA members) ISBN 0-915170-34-5 (LC 2002010486)
36. Richard C. Steiner, *Stockmen from Tekoa, Sycomores from Sheba: A Study of Amos' Occupations* (CBQMS 36) $10.50 ($8.40 for CBA members) ISBN 0-915170-35-3 (LC 2003019378)
37. Paul E. Fitzpatrick, S.M., *The Disarmament of God: Ezekiel 38–39 in Its Mythic Context* (CBQMS 37) ISBN 0-915170-36-1 (LC 2004005524)

Order from:

The Catholic Biblical Association of America
The Catholic University of America
Washington, D.C. 20064